# CLASSICO e MODERNO

# CLASSICO e MODERNO

## Essential Italian Cooking



MICHAEL WHITE

AND ANDREW FRIEDMAN

Foreword by Thomas Keller

BALLANTINE BOOKS NEW YORK

As of press time, the URLs displayed in this book link or refer to existing websites on the Internet. Penguin Random House is not responsible for, and should not be deemed to endorse or recommend, any website or content available on the Internet (including without limitation at any website, blog page, information page) other than its own.



Published in the United States by Ballantine Books, an imprint of The Random House Publishing Group, a division of Random House LLC, a Penguin Random House Company, New York.

BALLANTINE and the HOUSE colophon are registered trademarks of Random House LLC.

ISBN: 978-0-345-53052-3
eBook ISBN: 978-0-345-54553-4

Printed in the United States of America on acid-free paper

www.ballantinebooks.com

2 4 6 8 9 7 5 3 1

First Edition

*Book design by Liz Cosgrove*

I dedicate this book to the memory of my mother, Mary Ann,
who taught me to appreciate the fine things in life;
to my father, Gerry, who showed me how to achieve them;
to my wife, Giovanna, who makes it all possible and shares every moment with me;
and to my daughter, Francesca, who makes it all worthwhile.

PARMIGIANO
REGGIANO
CONSORZIO
TUTELA
MAG 11
1050

# CONTENTS



## CLASSICO

## MODERNO

PARMIGIANO-REGGIANO
DOP
2009
2010
LUG 09
CONSORZIO
4
5

# FOREWORD

At its best, food is a journey.

For those of us who have made the kitchen our professional home, the journey is one of discovery, both of ourselves and of our vocation, and it's necessarily a slow and deliberate process. For all of the public attention chefs receive these days, cooking is essentially a lonely business, especially during one's formative years. Talent is a must, but a cook's fate is largely determined by his or her willingness to put in the hard yards required to master the craft, as well as additional years defining and honing a personal style.

Meeting those challenges requires physical and mental stamina, which is why I have such empathy for young cooks, and a special appreciation for the commitment Michael White made early in his career. As you'll learn in these pages, in his twenties, driven purely by instinct, he spent the better part of eight years away from family and friends, and from his native land and language, to immerse himself in the food and culture of Italy. It cannot have been easy for this extrovert to live and work in a foreign land where he couldn't communicate well, at least not initially; but he endured, with nothing but his own passion telling him it was the right thing to do and that it would pay off one day.

And pay off it has: I've followed Michael since he emerged as the chef of New York City's Fiamma restaurant in 2002. Since then, I've watched and tasted as he's matured into his current position as one of the preeminent stewards and pioneers of Italian culinary tradition in America. A few years ago, when asked by a magazine to name my favorite restaurant of the moment, I instead praised my favorite dish at the time: Michael's Fusilli with Red Wine-Braised Octopus. Eating it is a thrilling and highly pleasurable experience, a little journey all its own. At first glimpse, the dish looks like a Bolognese; but as you get into it, it reveals hidden treasures and complexities, chief among them exquisitely viscous bone marrow that constitutes a match made in heaven with the toothsome octopus, for a sublime and sophisticated variation on surf and turf.

Like many great dishes, that fusilli is simultaneously revelatory and inevitable; Our initial sense of wonder at its interplays of tastes and textures gives way to an appreciation for how utterly natural they seem. Michael's restaurant menus are replete with such delights. Another of my favorites is one of his contemporary crostini, topped with sea urchin roe that's hugged by luscious lardo and topped with sea salt. It's a small morsel, but a feast for the senses, delivering cool, warm, silken, and crunchy elements in each bite.

These dishes, served at his restaurant Marea, represent the cutting edge of Italian food in America today. But Michael doesn't just do cutting edge. On the contrary, he retains a reverence for the classics of Italian cuisine, such as the Tortellini in Cream Sauce and Pasta Ribbons with Mushroom Sauce that he came to love during his near-decade spent overseas. Today he serves them at his restaurant Osteria Morini, which pays loving and faithful homage to the food of the Emilia-Romagna region.

In cooking, as in life, timing is everything. While Michael was soaking up inspiration and knowledge in Italy, the rest of us were on our own journeys. Like many Americans, my earliest memories of Italian food aren't of high-end restaurants but rather of Chef Boyardee, frozen pizza, and casual eateries where meals began with garlic knots and ended with spumoni. We've come a long way in our culinary knowledge and sophistication since those days, and just as we arrived at the apex of our Italian-food learning curve, there was Michael, poised to meet the moment with a deeply personal cuisine commensurate with our ability to appreciate it.

I'm hesitant to dissect Michael's food too much, preferring simply to enjoy it. But when you consider the totality of his repertoire, it becomes clear that his respect for the classics isn't at odds with his contemporary cooking; rather, his mastery of the classics forms the backbone of his success with the contemporary. This book, divided into Classico and Moderno sections, shares Michael's recipes for both traditional and contemporary Italian dishes and explains the connection between them. Just as compellingly, it traces the story of his discovery of the classics and his own creative development. I wrote once that recipes have no soul, requiring the cook to bring an ineffable something to them. I still believe that, but I know, too, that Michael's soul, captured here in words and pictures, will help guide even novice cooks on *that* journey.

In his earlier days, Michael mingled classic and contemporary dishes on the same menu; today he devotes entire restaurants to one or the other, but the relationship between past and present always matters. Innovation is important, but we connect best with dishes grounded in tradition, to flavors and combinations that were first arrived at to satisfy something primal in those cooks—their names long since lost to the ages—who first thought to pair and eat them.

That link is always present in Michael's food, which explains why even his signature modern dishes are as relatable as the classics—and perhaps are destined to be deemed classics in their own right someday.

*—Thomas Keller*

# INTRODUCTION

## A BRIEF HISTORY

I still vividly remember the first time I ate Italian food. *Real* Italian food. Or maybe I should say that I remember the first time I *experienced* real Italian food, because my senses were reeling even before I took my first bite. It was a dish of potato and leek ravioli adorned with a creamy Parmigiano-Reggiano sauce and topped with a generous spoonful of deep-green pesto. To begin with, there was the stark beauty of the composition: a half dozen ravioli arranged neatly on the plate, the white sauce clinging to the pasta, the pesto popping against a pristine backdrop. The ravioli themselves were unlike any I'd ever seen. Rather than the typical squares, they were perfectly round, with a ruffled edge that added a flourish to their simple beauty.

I was smitten, swept up by the poetry on the plate, and eating them only reinforced my infatuation: When cut open, the ravioli unleashed an intense aroma of garlic and herbs. I put a forkful in my mouth, and flavors and textures followed one upon another in quick succession: the earthy, salty Parmigiano mingled with the pesto—a version of the classic Ligurian condiment with parsley, basil, walnuts, and pignoli (pine nuts)—and then gave way to the toothsome, house-made pasta and the oniony mix of potato and leek within.

There I sat, staring in wonder at the plate, where five ravioli remained. I could scarcely fathom how so much complexity could be contained in something that, although it featured two sauces, seemed so simple: There weren't more than a dozen or so ingredients on that plate, but like a great rock band that creates a signature sound with just three musicians, it felt perfect.

This significant moment didn't take place in Italy, but in Chicago, Illinois. It changed my life and set me on the course that I've been on ever since, one that I hope and expect to continue on for the rest of my days.

It was 1991, and I was a young cook who had moved to the Windy City from my hometown of Beloit, Wisconsin, to work at Spiaggia restaurant. Under the stewardship of chef Paul Bartolotta, Spiaggia had distinguished itself as one of the finest Italian restaurants in the United States.

In truth, I had lucked out. Seeking a kitchen job and a life in the "big city," I'd begun a search for an Italian restaurant in Chicago for no reason other than that Italian food, or my concept of it at the time, felt familiar and comfortable to me. When I learned that the chef was also from Wisconsin, Spiaggia went right to the top of my list. I knew nothing of its reputation, or of its potential to inspire.

Those ravioli were just the first of many Italian dishes I would come to taste, cook, and appreciate at Spiaggia. Things have changed a lot since those days: Ingredients such as burgundy-hued radicchio and dishes such as risotto were known to those who had traveled and eaten in Italy, or dined in the finest, most cutting-edge New American restaurants of the day, but not to the general public. They were unfamiliar to me, as were rapini (broccoli rabe), cavolo nero (black kale), and cheeses such as Gorgonzola, to name just a few of the building blocks of Italian food that I came to know and appreciate in my early weeks on the job.

Mostly, though, I was fascinated by how those ingredients came together in dishes like that ravioli. Another early favorite, which I was positively obsessed with in my first winter at the restaurant, was a very traditional zuppa di gran farro alla Lucchese, a pureed bean and grain soup from Tuscany, that I can still taste, with all its flavors and textures in perfect balance: the smoky richness of pancetta; the piney scent of rosemary, delivered via an infused olive oil; and the toothsome farro, which was both blended into the soup and used as a garnish, along with a generous grinding of black pepper. As with the ravioli, the miracle of the soup was that, on paper, it was unremarkable: it depended on neither luxury ingredients nor complicated cooking techniques. But when those ingredients came together, an alchemy took place and they added up to something greater than the sum of its parts, or so I thought. In reality, the parts themselves were great, and their coming together only served to underscore their respective attributes. But that's a lesson that it takes time to fully comprehend, and I had a long way to go.

## ITALY CALLING

When I was a kid, the last place I thought I'd end up was . . . well, there were a lot of last places I thought I'd end up. I was, and in many ways remain, a creature of the American Midwest. I grew up in a small town amid the vast green pastures of the American heartland. My father was the vice president of a bank and my mother was a homemaker. They raised me with values and manners that I guess you'd call old-fashioned today: my mother fostered a sense of curiosity in me, always encouraging me to ask questions and buying me *Tell Me Why* books that explained everything from what made it rain to how to calculate the distance from the Earth to the sun; my father taught me to look people in the eye when you shook their hands (with a shake as firm as a vise), to call my elders Mr. and Mrs., to never shy away from a challenge, and to work like a dog.

I didn't mind work. In fact, I loved it: As soon as I was old enough to have a job, I got one in the plumbing department of the local Ace Hardware store, which I supplemented by mowing lawns in the summer and shoveling snow in the winter. I also pumped gas for free at the local Mobil station so that I could have access to their garage and work on my car there whenever I needed to. I had good friends, and we had a good time, cruising chicks and chowing down at McDonald's after school and on weekends.

At six foot four, I was a big kid, and I loved competition, becoming an offensive tackle on my high school football team. As a sophomore, I got to travel a little with the varsity team, sitting on the sidelines to observe. The next year, when I was a junior, we made the Division 1 play-offs. We drove out to Oconomowoc, Wisconsin, and we got spanked. The drive home was the longest sixty miles I have ever traveled. I learned about much more than football playing for our school team, the Purple Knights: As a sophomore on the sidelines, I developed patience. And as a junior, getting to the play-offs and losing, I gleaned something about riding out the ups and downs of life.

For all of their careful rearing of me and my brother, Scott, the one thing my parents could never instill in me was a love of learning—or maybe I should say a love of school. I have to say that I hated academics. They bored me damn near to tears, and my educational future stretched out before me as a bleak and barren road to nowhere. I knew that I had the ability and drive to do something, but I had no idea what that might be. Though I lived in a decidedly landlocked region, I was rudderless.

I did have something of a hobby, however, although

I didn't think of it that way at the time. My father was and is a zealous home cook, and as I grew into my teens, I started helping him out in the kitchen and our backyard garden, cooking omelets, soups, and other simple dishes and growing vegetables. We'd often sit and watch cooking segments on the morning shows, like *Good Morning America*, where, in those days, celebrity chef Wolfgang Puck demonstrated recipes every Friday.

I was also a passionate eater who gravitated toward bold food. I loved big in-your-face flavors and textures, from a bag of Fritos to a bowl of chili. My favorite kind of food was Italian, which was popular in our town, as it was in small towns all across America. I looked forward to nothing more than spaghetti and meatballs, or pasta with cream sauce. Today I recognize that those dishes, or at least the versions we ate in Beloit, were Americanized renditions, but that didn't change the basics, such as the smell of garlic and oregano that hit you when you first set foot in an Italian restaurant, or the potent flavors of the most-often-called-on ingredients, such as tomatoes or Parmigiano cheese.

A lightbulb went off for me when Dad and I started tuning in regularly to a television series called *Great Chefs*, narrated by Mary Lou Conroy. The show profiled some of the biggest chefs in the United States and around the world, and—most important for me—depicted them *in a professional kitchen* as they worked. The more I watched, the more I was drawn to the idea of cooking for a living, and as soon as I graduated from high school, I took a job in a local restaurant called the Butterfly Club. As a line cook there, I learned how to pump out au gratin potatoes and fry fish during dinner service. I loved everything about it, not only the act of cooking, for which I had a natural aptitude, but also hanging out with the guys in the kitchen, both during work and after hours.

Cooking quickly became a calling, and a sanctuary. I decided to commit to this new direction, and after about six months at the Butterfly Club, I applied for that job at Spiaggia. By the time I moved to Chicago, I was so relieved to be on the right track that not only did I go to work, but I also, at last, became a passionate student, taking culinary classes at Kendall College in the suburb of Evanston. It was a grueling schedule: My first class was at eight-thirty in the morning, and I'd show up with everything I needed for the rest of the day and night, namely my chef's clothes and knife kit for the restaurant. After learning the basics of Western cuisines, such as braising and sauce work, all of it based on the French tradition, I'd sleep on the "L" into Chicago, then arrive at Spiaggia, change into my uniform, and cook my way through the dinner shift, not returning to my apartment until after midnight.

Whether standing in the French-focused kitchen classroom or cooking in the Italianate restaurant kitchen, I always had the exhilarating feeling that I was learning and moving toward something, and this helped me power through the long hours when my body, despite my youth and athletic training, would feel the burn of my schedule.

After completing the nine-month course at Kendall College, I continued to cook at Spiaggia, working my way around the kitchen, in time learning how to prepare an array of dishes including zuppa di pesce, lamb chops scottadito (glazed with balsamic vinegar), and osso buco. Though dressed up for their big-city restaurant environs, these and countless other dishes had much in common with the kind of food I had loved eating all my life, brimming with robust flavors and luscious textures that I responded to more than the fussier, restrained French classics I had learned in school.

I also began reading books and magazines about Italian food and culture and how the two are intertwined. My interest expanded beyond the food itself to the language used to describe it and to the stories about where dishes hailed from and how they came to be, such as carpaccio with arugula, Parmigiano-Reggiano, olive oil, and lemon, or stracci, a wide pasta, served with a mushroom ragù; and I felt a growing desire to try those and other classics in their native regions. The food began to paint a picture for me: eating sublimely salty anchovies, I would imagine the Amalfi Coast in the south of Italy, the sun peering over the docks during summer, even as I was immersed in a brutal Windy City winter; a spoonful of that farro and bean soup, and I'd see the rolling, manicured hills of Tuscany; and carne all'Albese, an Italian steak tartare showered with white truffles, brought to mind the fog-shrouded mountains of Piedmont, in the north.

Chef Bartolotta and his lieutenants at Spiaggia knew passion when they saw it, and they were only too happy to help me learn as much as I could, exposing me to as many new dishes as possible and patiently answering my endless questions. One of my favorite things to cook was risotto, because it required constant stirring and attention all the way through the cooking process, rather than simply popping something in the oven. One night, Billy Joel appeared at the kitchen window, asking who had made his risotto of Taleggio, Brussels sprouts, and borlotti beans. When I raised my hand and he told me, "That was great," it was a high point of my life.

But there was only so far I could go in Chicago, and after two years, I'd reached a point of diminishing returns. Though I'd never been to Italy, I felt that I had to take the logical next step and cook there for an extended period of time. I spoke to Bartolotta about it. He wasn't surprised, having had the same desire earlier in his career, and he did what any chef who wants the best for his cooks would do, arranging for me to *stage* (intern in a professional kitchen, often unpaid) for ten months at the same restaurant he had: San Domenico, a two-Michelin-star dining temple in the town of Imola in Emilia-Romagna. The region is renowned for its rich and lusty food, from locally produced gems such as balsamic vinegar and Parmigiano-Reggiano cheese to dishes such as tortellini in brodo (meat-filled pasta in broth) and cotechino (a lightly spiced pork sausage that's simmered and served with stewed lentils and fruity mostarda).

## SETTING SAIL

The next thing I knew, I had arrived at the airport in Bologna, a young American cook with a duffle bag at my feet. Lorenzo Boni, a former cook from San Domenico who was acting as an emissary for the restaurant, picked me up and drove me into town, where he and his father owned a restaurant on Via San Vitale. As it had for so many before me, the flesh-and-blood Italy proved just as enchanting and unspoiled as the Italy of my imagination. A light rain pelted the car's windshield. Outside, a nonstop symphony of Vespa engines ripped through the air. It was a Saturday afternoon, and as we slowed down in town, a picture of daily life came into focus: People walked to and fro carrying brown paper bags full of groceries, nodding at each other in recognition.

A sense of unreality passed over me: this seemed more like a romanticized film set than an actual town. I joined the staff at the Bonis' restaurant for their preservice, or "family," meal. There was baked branzino (sea bass); a small tomato salad dressed with extra virgin olive oil and sea salt; and ricotta tortelli sauced with brown butter and sage. The humble meal, more simple and elemental than the fancified restaurant food at Spiaggia but equally flavorful, was the first validation of my decision to come to Italy.

In my hotel room later, I pushed open windows that let the sounds of the town flood the room—those Vespas, the rain, the occasional impromptu conversation on the sidewalk. In the morning, I crossed the street and ordered my first true-blue cappuccino, impossibly frothy, and a brioche, which I was surprised to see, but which in time I'd learn was commonplace in parts of Italy that are relatively close to France. I felt conspicuous, a big, pasty, fair-haired American clumsily sipping my drink. Copying those around me, I dunked the brioche in the cappuccino for a little taste of heaven—cloud-on-cloud action, I joked to myself.

The next day I met the man who would become my mentor: Valentino Marcattilii, an accomplished and inexhaustible chef with caffeine and nicotine pumping through his veins and an irrepressible, impish sense of humor. Valentino had been at San Domenico on and off since he was sixteen years old and had *staged* in some of the great kitchens of France. Having helped open the New York outpost of San Domenico in the late 1980s, he also spoke better-than-broken English, which was extremely rare in the small town of Imola. He picked me up in his beat-up station wagon, which smelled vaguely of herbs from years of market visits, and delivered me to San Domenico, where he showed me to my living quarters. The restaurant operated in time-honored European fashion, employing a handful of *stages* who worked for nothing and putting them up in a row of dorm rooms over the restaurant, where a few of the more seasoned, salaried cooks lived as well. When I was there, it was a mix of Italians, Germans, and a Japanese kid with whom I shared my room. My Italian was limited to two words, ciao and cappuccino, and I wondered what I had gotten myself into. That night, my roommate and I, having nothing but food in common, sat and looked at cookbooks together, pointing to dishes we liked and nodding our approval.

On my first day on the job, Antonio di Cesare, a hardworking chef's chef, took me into the kitchen, introduced me to the other cooks, and assigned me to the meat station. Mercifully, having worked with Valentino at the New York San Domenico, Antonio spoke English and was able to show me the ropes. My first task was to break down a saddle of venison, removing the meat, roasting the bones to get a stock started, and then portioning the meat into individual servings that I marinated in rosemary, crushed juniper berries, garlic slivers, and olive oil.

This was all revelatory to me: In most American kitchens, the world is divided into prep and service. The prep guys do the butchering, slicing and blanching of vegetables, and other advance work, and then the line cooks come in, fire up the dishes, and get everything on the plate, piping hot, for the customers. But in Italy, if you work, say, the meat station, you are responsible for the entire process, from butchering in the morning to putting the finished plates up on the pass to be delivered by the waiters to the diners that evening. I gleaned much from my inaugural task with the venison, from the butchering itself to the stock making to the idea of adding juniper berries to the marinade to the cocoa powder in the sauce we made from the stock, which added body and offset the venison's gaminess.

Before I knew it, I was cooking a wide variety of meats and game for such classic dishes as roasted squab with spinach and porcini mushrooms, squab liver timbale, and venison with chestnuts, all the while learning how to break down the beast itself.

So began my great Italian adventure.

It's clichéd to rhapsodize about Italy's culture of warmth and friendliness, but only because it's what strikes so many visitors: The country's bigheartedness was first revealed to me behind the scenes in San Domenico's kitchen, which operated on a hair less testosterone than a typical French one. I'd heard enough about the Gallic hierarchy to know that the way things usually worked was that as soon as somebody got a little authority, he began verbally abusing those beneath him. In Italy, though, or at San Domenico at least, the senior cooks were more like big brothers than lords and masters: As long as you worked hard, and tried your best, they were patient and nurturing. I've adopted the same style in all my kitchens today; one of my favorite lessons to impart to other chefs is that screaming doesn't make the food come out better or faster.

The most profound takeaway from my first months at San Domenico was a heightened connection to raw ingredients, and to the earth and the seasons. In Chicago, most of the foodstuffs arrived at the restaurant from large food-service corporations, packed in corrugated cardboard boxes or shrink-wrapped in plastic. At San Domenico, everything came, or was procured, directly from the actual sources, almost all of which were located less than an hour's drive from the town center. If we needed to make chicken stock, one of the

1980
VILLERO. CASTIGLIONE FALLETTO
CUNEO

8
SAN DOMENICO
8
ristorante dal 1970

chefs would send me around the corner to the butcher to ask for some bones. The farms weren't far-off places where anonymous workers tended to the fields, but close enough that the farmers themselves would show up at the restaurant's back door with all kinds of riches, like the forager, with dirt still caked on his boots, who would reach into his pocket and pull out three white truffles as if they were a handful of change. Or the woman who periodically showed up with whatever she'd deemed most appealing and appropriate to Valentino's style at her farm that morning. She might arrive one day with, say, a faraona (guinea hen) and a case of eggs. Valentino would never refuse her: If she had rabbit, he'd buy it from her, then break it down and use every part, sautéing the livers, making a farce (stuffing) from the back legs, and wrapping the saddles with pancetta for dinner service that night.

As fascinating and rewarding as all of this was, the isolation in Imola could also be crushing at times. This was in the days before the Internet, so I wasn't able to e-mail back and forth with friends and family. I was always aware of the excruciating distance between Italy and Beloit, which felt as far away as a distant planet. My father had ordered me an AT&T calling card before I pushed off, and I can still remember the dialing code that I had to punch into pay phones to call home, where my mother would answer, her voice the ultimate salve for my homesickness.

Fortunately, I picked up Italian quickly. I had taken Spanish in high school, and enough of the roots were similar that I could make out and absorb much of what was thrown at me in the kitchen. I supplemented that crash course with another surprisingly effective one, watching hours of television at night and gradually developing a formidable vocabulary.

As I surmounted the language barrier, I found that Imola had much in common with Beloit: both were small, tight-knit communities that gave back whatever you gave to them. As I developed a routine and a daily itinerary, including my morning espresso bar, I began to recognize more and more faces as I pedaled my bicycle around town. I also developed a relationship with Gianluigi Morini, the founder of San Domenico, who was omnipresent at the restaurant and who knew something about everything, with a special passion for wine (the restaurant has a legendary cellar) that rubbed off on me.

Gianluigi Morini

In my free time, I explored the more casual restaurants and trattorias of Imola and the surrounding towns, discovering foods that I loved as much as, if not more than, the formal cuisine we served at San Domenico: affettati misti, a platter of Italian cold cuts that began many meals, with freshly baked bread and marinated olives alongside, and the little pizzettes, just four inches in diameter and topped with tomato and cheese, that you could order at a taverna, along with, say, a Campari and soda, to cap off an afternoon or begin an evening.

I was beginning to recognize the kind of chef I

hoped to become: I didn't know exactly when or where that might be, but I saw myself operating an elevated Italian restaurant along the lines of Spiaggia or San Domenico.

When my ten months were up, I just couldn't leave. Imola had begun to feel like a second home to me, and the cooking and eating I'd been doing made me hungry for more. I had learned a lot, but I also knew that I had only scratched the surface of Italian cuisine.

## DELVING DEEPER

I ended up staying in Italy, on and off, for the better part of eight years, although I did return to Spiaggia for long stretches to earn enough money to subsidize my time abroad. During my time in Italy, my education was twofold. In the professional kitchen, I took a turn at all of the various stations, including garde-manger (cold salads and preparations), fish, meat, pastry, bread, and pasta; and on my days off, I traveled around Italy with the express purpose of tasting and learning how to cook as many regional specialties as possible. I'd go on my own, or with coworkers who invited me to join them for family visits, where I'd eat with them in restaurants and visit their homes, watching as their mothers cooked traditional dishes for us and learning how to make everything from great Bolognese to salumi.

In some respects, my solo ventures were more intense and beneficial, because I focused on nothing but the food; for instance, I'd take the train to Venice and find myself suddenly dwarfed by the immensity of the Grand Canal. I had squirreled away enough money during my Spiaggia gigs to stay in a pensione instead of a youth hostel, and I'd explore the city, visiting outdoor markets and cafés and dining in famous restaurants such as the legendary Harry's Bar and newer standouts like Al Covo.

The trips were exhilarating. I remember sitting at an outdoor restaurant pondering a zupetta of blue lobster meat and cherry tomatoes in an intensely flavored broth and turning the dish over in my mind, divining the cooking process that had led to its creation and locking it in my taste memory so that I'd be able to draw on it later.

I also had an epiphany at Al Covo, where I met a young American woman who was there on hiatus from Zuni Cafe in San Francisco, working in the kitchen for a few weeks. Following her example, I decided that I needed to expand my horizons and actually cook in restaurants other than San Domenico, and I began calling or writing to restaurants such as Romano in Viareggio, Lorenzo in Forte dei Marmi, and countless others.

I'd work in these places for a few days, or a few weeks, and no matter where I went, whether alone or with fellow cooks, I'd visit local osterias and trattorias, street carts and hole-in-the-wall tavernas, the unassuming kinds of places that are the soul and heartbeat of Italy. The more people I got to know, the deeper my understanding of Italian food became, and the more friends I had. To a person, my growing network was only too willing to show me the most unvarnished culinary traditions; an especially memorable one was the street cart in Baronissi, a small community outside Salerno in the Campania region, where a man sliced meat from a boiled veal snout, selling it on torn sheets of white butcher paper with a wedge of aromatic local lemon for squeezing. Thanks to my growing personal network, I also discovered little towns that weren't prominently featured in American guidebooks, such as the southern fishing community of Cetara, where the anchovies are netted a few hundred yards from the restaurants where you might eat them with bread and butter or baked onto a pizza.

The more I traveled, the more I came to appreciate that there's really no such thing as "Italian food" per se. There had been a hint of this in restaurants back in the States that broke down along Northern and Southern Italian lines, but that didn't really get at the heart of the matter, which is that each of Italy's twenty regions has its own indigenous ingredients and specialties—

whether it's tagliatelle al ragù Bolognese (thin pasta with meat sauce) in Bologna; baccalà mantecato (pureed salt cod and potatoes) in the Veneto, caponata (an eggplant, pepper, and caper condiment) in Sicily, or brasato di manzo (braised beef ribs) in Piedmont. My goal became to understand each region's culinary profile: I put a map of Italy on the wall of my dorm room and kept track with pushpins of where I'd been, working my way through my own personal itinerary and curriculum. I've still not been to Sardinia. I used to insist that it was simply because I ran out of time, but I've come to believe that, subconsciously, it was to keep one last lesson on tap, a reminder that I'll always have more to learn and understand.

### FRENCH INTERLUDE

During my time in Europe, I also, despite years of it leaving me cold, came to love French cuisine, both its time-honored flavors and dishes and the techniques it calls on to create them. I made my first trip to France in 1996 and was intrigued by the formality of the food. In 1997, Valentino, who had worked with Alain Ducasse, Daniel Boulud, and David Bouley in the kitchen of Roger Vergé's Moulin de Mougins on the French Riviera, arranged for me to spend the summer *staging* there. In Vergé's kitchen, I began with typical grunt work, such as cleaning lobsters, then moved around the kitchen, learning everything from terrine-making to how to quenelle properly to making sauce américiane for a signature lobster dish. It was a whiplash-worthy shift: the formality of French cuisine wasn't entirely new to me, because San Domenico operated in a somewhat French mode, but it was a sharp contrast to the style of food I'd eaten during my travels throughout Italy, especially the reliance on butter and cream over olive oil.

In autumn 1997, I was paid the ultimate honor: Valentino asked me to become the chef de cuisine of San Domenico, a rare honor for a non-Italian. That was also the year I met my future wife, Giovanna Cornacchione, a native of the province of Campobasso in the southern region of Molise. At the time, she was living in Imola and working in the community affairs office at City Hall. Mutual friends arranged for us to connect over a coffee, and we quickly developed a close relationship. Among the things we had in common was a love of dining, and she began joining me on my expeditions, adding new layers to my understanding of various foods, sharing information and insights that only a native Italian could know. To this day, she remains my barometer for truly authentic Italian fare.

After almost two years as chef de cuisine of San Domenico, I felt that I'd earned my doctorate in Italian food, and I was ready to return to the United States for good, and I went back to Spiaggia in 1999, becoming chef de cuisine of the restaurant where it all began for me, bringing my journey full circle.

### MAKING ITALIAN FOOD MY OWN

Upon returning to the United States, I experienced a bit of culinary culture shock. Whereas Italy was still tradition-bound, American chefs were obsessed with taking liberties, interpreting everything from Pan-Asian to South American to European cuisines in their own ways. All of my contemporaries, it seemed, had staked out some part of the world that they were mining for personal expression: Spain, Portugal, China, Japan. You name it, somebody was making it their own.

It was an exciting time, and it wasn't long before I began to have ideas about how I might apply everything I'd learned in Italy in the United States. I decided that the key would be to follow the Italian way, letting seasonality and simplicity be my guides and adapting dishes and ideas to what was available and popular here.

I looked for a job where I could make that vision a reality, and I connected with Steve Hanson, an uber-successful hospitality mogul who was planning an

Italian restaurant in Manhattan's SoHo neighborhood. Following an interview in Chicago and a tasting I prepared for him and his team in New York City, he hired me to become the chef of the restaurant, which was eventually called Fiamma. There, all of the ideas I'd been gathering for the past several years were unleashed in dishes that combined new and old, Italian and American, such as pressed tuna carpaccio with bottarga (sun-dried gray mullet roe), snapper with Sicilian couscous, and braised short rib tortelli. Additionally, my food was informed by my stays in France, which were the glue, the bridge, between inspiration and execution: French techniques allowed me to bring my new ideas for Italian food to life. Sometimes this meant little more than using French methods to clarify and sharpen the flavors in a classic Italian preparation: for example, to make cappon magro (a Ligurian seafood salad), most Italian recipes would poach all the various types of shellfish together; instead, I poached them individually to achieve the ideal texture for each one and preserve their individual flavors. In my more interpretive, modern dishes, I used French templates to make sauces and other preparations that riffed on classic Italian flavors and recipes. For example, instead of making a simple pan sauce for squab, which would be the Italian way, I'd reinforce the sauce by roasting the bones, adding trim from the bird, and patiently skimming the sauce as it simmered, all things I picked up in France.

The restaurant succeeded beyond my wildest imagination. Here I was, a kid from the Midwest who had gone off the grid for close to a decade, and suddenly I was being reviewed in *The New York Times* and interviewed by journalists from the glossiest of glossy magazines.

After Fiamma, I joined restaurateur Chris Cannon when I became the chef at two existing midtown Manhattan restaurants: Alto, which focused on the cuisine of the Alto Adige, and L'Impero, in Tudor City, with a focus on Southern Italian cooking. I was immediately drawn to the idea of exploring regional Italian food in my own style, and I took over the kitchens of those restaurants, keeping Alto's theme but putting my own stamp on it, and transforming L'Impero into Convivio, with a more interpretive Southern Italian menu. Both received three stars from *The New York Times*; they also earned Michelin stars: one for Convivio and two for Alto.

After I left those restaurants, I founded the Altamarea Group with my partner, Ahmass Fakahany, a former top executive of Merrill Lynch & Co. In spring 2009, we opened Marea, a restaurant devoted to coastal Italian cuisine, from my take on the raw seafood preparations called crudo to unusual pastas such as fusilli with braised octopus and bone marrow. Like many chefs, I'm more drawn to fish and shellfish than to poultry and meat, because of the incredible variety these raw ingredients offer and the range of possibilities they provide. For the same reason, there are more seafood than meat recipes in this book.

Marea was followed by Ai Fiori in the Setai Hotel, the first of our restaurants where I combined my love of Italian food with the cuisine of the French Riviera that I knew from my days working for Vergé and traveling with Giovanna.

Then, in late 2009, I had an epiphany. I loved conceiving and sharing my own take on Italian food, but I had strayed from my adopted roots; it was time to get back to them, and to focus on the cuisine of one region, the region where I'd always found my greatest inspiration: Emilia-Romagna. Working with the Altamarea team, I located a space in SoHo and set about creating a replica of an Italian osteria there. For the name of this restaurant, I decided to pay tribute to the founder of San Domenico, Gianluigi Morini. Osteria Morini opened in 2010 and continues to offer as authentic an Italian dining experience as you'll find anywhere outside Italy.

Other restaurants have followed, including Al Molo (The Pier) in Hong Kong, where we offer an assortment of popular dishes from our other restaurants to a completely different audience, and Nicoletta, our pizzeria in Manhattan's East Village, where we serve our signature style of Wisconsin-meets-Italy pizzas.

Whatever the venue, whether I'm faithfully recreating a dining experience from Emilia-Romagna or serving my own ever-evolving repertoire of interpretive Italian cuisine, my goal today remains the same as it was when I first went to Italy more than twenty years ago: to be true to the food I fell in love with then, to remain curious and always try to deepen my understanding, and to base everything I do on the essential flavors and traditions that have made Italian food endure for centuries and will preserve its character for generations to come.

# COOKING FROM THIS BOOK

This book is divided into two main parts that capture the two sides of my culinary persona.

Classico is a collection of nearly 125 recipes for my favorite dishes from all over Italy. Like Osteria Morini, it is based on reverence for the old ways, the cooking you find in homes and casual restaurants. The recipes are my own, but I consider them authentically Italian because there's no one way of cooking any Italian dish; they all vary from restaurant to restaurant and house to house. In my case, in addition to bringing my own personal taste to the plate, I incorporate a touch of French technique here and there when I think it helps sharpen and improve a dish.

In the second half of the book, Moderno, you will find about the same number of recipes for many of the most popular dishes I serve in my restaurants, as well as others conceived in the same contemporary style.

Where it applies, a recurring feature called Ispirazione (Inspiration) in the Classico section will point you to dishes in Moderno that are based on them.

**Ingredients** To reflect the dishes they make, the recipes in the Classico section are presented as one would be apt to cook them in Italy, inviting adaptation, while the recipes in the Moderno section call for more specificity, offering fewer ways to adapt them.

There are notes on some of the most commonly used ingredients in the book beginning on page xxviii. Additionally, please note that ingredients are described differently in the two sections of the book: In Classico, in keeping with the casual nature of regional Italian cooking, I don't want you to fuss too much over the size of ingredients such as vegetables and how you slice or chop them. Unless otherwise specified, all vegetables should be medium-size. If you need to dice or mince them, for the most part, you are instructed to cut them into small dice, by which I mean about ¼-inch dice. "Minced" means cut as small as possible, and "large dice" means roughly ½-inch cubes.

But in Moderno, as befits the more formal restaurant-style recipes there, the specifications are more exact, and they should be followed as precisely as possible.

**Equipment** I urge home cooks not to be seduced by the wealth of products and gadgets available on the market today. My experience is that you can do most of your cooking with a modicum of equipment: a set of mixing bowls; heavy stainless-steel or copper sauté pans in various sizes; a Dutch oven or other large heavy pot for braises and stews; a wooden spoon, a rubber spatula, and a strainer; and a food processor, stand mixer, and blender. In other words, standard equipment that most home cooks will have all or most of on hand.

Rather than specify exact diameters and capacities, most of my recipes simply call for small, medium, or large cooking vessels or indicate that the ingredients should be able to fit in them in a single layer (or else recommend cooking them in batches).

**Shopping and Stocking** There's just no way around it: Because of its inherent simplicity, one of the prerequisites for cooking Italian food successfully, especially many of the dishes in the Classico section, which often showcase the natural characteristics of the ingredients with very little transformation, is to use the best ingredients available.

I therefore suggest that you act like an Italian when you shop, by which I mean that, as often as possible, you purchase food from purveyors or businesses that specialize in them: bread from a bakery; fish and shellfish from a fish store; poultry, meats, and game from a butcher shop; and produce from a farmers' market. (If you have access to a Whole Foods or similar all-purpose gourmet store, many of these high-quality ingredients can be found under one roof.) Of course, we all have limited time, so following this advice can be easier said than done, but if you can do so, your cooking will be greatly rewarded.

**Variations** Many recipes include variations, which will help guide you in adapting and adjusting them where possible for seasonality, availability of ingredients, and personal taste.

# NOTES ON AN ITALIAN PANTRY

Getting the most out of each and every ingredient is central to great Italian cooking, and to any good cooking, really. With that in mind, here are notes on shopping, storing, and working with some of the most frequently used ingredients in this book.

**Anchovies (canned or jarred)** Anchovies have been among the most important ingredients in the world since time immemorial: They were ground up and used as a seasoning agent back in the days of the Roman Empire. Today, anchovy fillets preserved in salt or oil have the unique ability to boost the flavor of just about anything with which they are cooked, including vegetables such as broccoli rabe and cauliflower and braising liquids for non-seafood dishes such as lamb shanks. (The same qualities are called on in the condiment colatura, which is made from the juices of pressed anchovies and used as a finishing agent.) A small amount of anchovy can be a potent addition to a recipe even when an anchovy flavor itself is not desired.

Fresh anchovies hold a revered place in Italian cuisine, but the fillets sold in small tins or jars, packed in oil or salt for preservation, are far more common. Stay away from the cheapest canned anchovies, which can taste overwhelmingly salty. Instead, seek out those from Italian producers such as IASA and Recca, or from Spanish producers such as Ortiz; a good, readily available supermarket standby is the Spanish brand Roland.

**Beans** Not long ago, most cookbooks insisted that you use dried beans and soak them overnight before cooking them. The recipes in this book adhere to that tradition, but there are many respectable brands of canned beans available that can save you this step. My favorite is Cirio, from Emilia-Romagna, which offers cannellini beans packed in glass jars that retain the essential texture of the bean.

When using dried beans, pick through them for any stones or debris, and soak them overnight in cold water or use the quick-soak method on page 30.

**Black Pepper** Black pepper should always be freshly ground from a mill. Many supermarkets now sell peppercorns in disposable plastic jars with grinding caps, some of which allow you to adjust the size of the grind. Use the finest grind for cooking and a coarser grind for finishing a dish with pepper, as I often do with salads, soups, and pastas.

**Bread Crumbs** Making your own bread crumbs (see page xxix) is a good and economical way to get a second life out of stale bread and loaf-ends, but there's nothing wrong with purchasing prepared unseasoned bread crumbs, even from mass producers such as Progresso. The en vogue Japanese panko bread crumbs, more and more commonly available in supermarkets, are also viable, but they are coarser than most so should be pulsed a few times in a food processor before using them.

### HOMEMADE BREAD CRUMBS

Bread crumbs are traditionally made from stale bread, but it's easy to make them from fresh loaves as well: Position a rack in the center of the oven and preheat the oven to 200°F. Cut the loaf in half to expose the mollica (soft white interior) and pull it away from the crust in large chunks; discard the crust or save it for another use. Put the bread on a baking sheet, put it in the oven, and turn the oven off. Leave the bread in the oven for at least 8 hours, or overnight. The next day, pulse the bread, a handful at a time, in the bowl of a food processor. Bread crumbs will keep in an airtight container at room temperature for several weeks; they can also be frozen in plastic bags and then thawed in a matter of minutes.

For darker bread crumbs with a toastier flavor that you might prefer in, say, autumn dishes, leave the crust on.

For finer bread crumbs, for use as a thickening or binding agent in meatballs and other preparations, pass them through a sifter and discard the coarser crumbs (or reserve for another dish).

### TOASTED BREAD CRUMBS

For a topping that adds even greater texture and flavor to preparations such as pasta dishes and roasted tomatoes, heat a tablespoon or so of olive oil in a wide sauté pan. Add a cup of bread crumbs and toss until golden brown and crispy. Drain on paper towels and use within an hour for the best flavor.

### SEASONED TOASTED BREAD CRUMBS

To make Seasoned Toasted Bread Crumbs, add 1 minced garlic clove and 1 tablespoon thinly sliced flat-leaf parsley leaves to the pan with the bread crumbs.

**Butter** All of my recipes call for unsalted butter, which allows you to control the amount of salt in your cooking. I also prefer it because many producers use better cream in their unsalted varieties, where inferior taste and impurities aren't masked by salinity.

## CHEESE

**Parmigiano-Reggiano** Parmigiano-Reggiano, a cow's-milk cheese produced in the Emilia-Romagna region, is the most popular cheese in Italian cooking, used in sauces and pastas, grated or shaved over salads and other cold dishes, and served in chunks as part of an antipasti offering. In many preparations where the cheese is stirred or whisked into cooked food, it brings a salty, lactic effect that thickens the preparation and pulls the flavors together. It also imparts a subtle umami-like quality.

Parmigiano-Reggiano is the gold standard, and the only Parmigiano I recommend if you're serving it in slices or chunks, as for an affettati misti (see page 13). But if it's going to be stirred into a sauce, or used in, say, a gnocchi dough, Grana Padano, a similar cheese produced north of the Po River, is less expensive and a perfectly suitable alternative. (There are many in Italy who actually prefer Grana Padano and other cousins, such as Piave.) You might also see Parmesans from everywhere from Wisconsin to Argentina in your market, and these, too, are acceptable for cooking.

Many markets have taken to stocking precut, plastic-wrapped wedges of Parmigiano in baskets. This has a charming Old-World feeling, but the plastic can cause the cheese to sweat or glisten, which causes salt deposits to form—a sign that it is beginning to break down. Rather than purchasing these pieces, have a wedge cut to order at the cheese counter, or seek out pieces in the refrigerator case. For most cooking, a two-year aged Parmigiano is ideal; if it's not dated, look for Parmigiano with a straw color, rather than a dark tan, which indicates a cheese that's been aged longer.

If your market sells freshly grated cheese in plastic containers, it's generally fine to use it in these recipes, but examine the cheese to be sure it's stringy, not curled; curls indicate that the cheese was grated down to the rind. On the other hand, at home, save Parmigiano-Reggiano rinds and add them to soups and other preparations to impart extra flavor.

**Pecorino Romano** Pecorino Romano, one of the four main types of Pecorino cheese, is as ubiquitous in the south of Italy as Parmigiano-Reggiano is in the north. Aged for about eight months, this sheep's-milk cheese has an intensely funky presence; it's less appealing on its own than it is grated into recipes such as meatballs or served over pastas with meat sauces, where it adds a tremendous flavor that is one of the defining characteristics of Southern Italian cooking.

**Ricotta** Ricotta (literally, "recooked") cheese is a creamy, lactic "whey cheese," meaning that it's made from the whey that remains after the curds of other cheeses have been drained. In Italy, ricotta is often set out in a small bowl to be spread on warm bread or spooned over pasta. It sometimes serves as the centerpiece of a quick meal, perhaps plated alongside sliced tomatoes and drizzled with extra virgin olive oil, and as a breakfast indulgence, topped with fig jam or drizzled with honey.

For the best flavor and texture, seek out an Italian market, specialty store, or cheese shop that sells high-quality freshly made ricotta, and buy only a full-fat, rather than a reduced-fat, version; the difference in taste is significant.

---

**Flour** For most cooking uses, such as dredging ingredients before frying them or thickening braises, all-purpose flour is a fine go-to choice. The exceptions are pizza dough, some bread doughs, and certain delicate pastas (especially filled pastas), for which I prefer Italian 00 flour. The most important characteristic of 00 flour is not its protein content, as some literature suggests, but rather that it has been double-milled, resulting in a very fine flour that gives especially tender results. (King Arthur Flour makes an "Italian-Style Flour" that mimics 00 flour; see Sources, page 379.) Most of the recipes in this book can be made with more than one type of flour, although you will get the best results with the first type listed; if using an alternative flour, such as all-purpose instead of Italian 00, you may need to use slightly less or more.

**Garlic** When shopping for garlic, look for heads that have abundant papery skin and a tight, uniform shape, which indicates that there will be lovely thick cloves inside. Don't refrigerate garlic; store it in an unglazed ceramic jar at room temperature, which will keep it from sweating. In most of my recipes, I slice garlic rather than mince it; having more garlic surface area in a preparation infuses it with a greater, truer garlic flavor. To make it easier to peel garlic, soak it in warm water for 10 to 15 minutes to loosen its skin, or purchase a peeler tube. Alternatively, if you don't need uniform slices of garlic, you can smash garlic cloves with the side of a chef's knife, then peel away the split skin.

## HERBS

I divide fresh herbs into two categories: sweet, leafy herbs such as basil, parsley, and mint, which I slice rather than chop to preserve their delicate flavor and texture; and sturdy, robust herbs such as oregano, rosemary, sage, and thyme, which must be chopped, bruised, or warmed to unlock their flavor.

**Basil** It's generally best to add basil to cold dishes or to hot ones only after cooking, because even a moment's exposure to heat will wilt the delicate leaves. I do occasionally add a sprig of basil to the base of a sauce or soup, then add sliced fresh basil leaves just before serving to reinforce the flavor. I don't subscribe to the school that says you have to tear basil rather than slice it for fear of bruising it. I tear or slice it depending on my mood, or what's dictated by tradition or a specific recipe. The best way to slice basil is into a chiffonade (ribbons), stacking about five leaves at a time, rolling them up like a cigar, and thinly slicing them crosswise with a very sharp knife.

**Bay Leaves** For stocks, soups, and braises, I prefer the pungent flavor of dried bay leaves. Fresh bay leaves can be a bit more difficult to find, but they are essential for dishes such as quick sautés, where brief cooking in butter or oil releases the leaf's oil and essence. For both dried and fresh, choose the widest leaves; the thinner ones can have an almost medicinal flavor.

**Mint** In certain Southern Italian regions where there are Greek influences, such as Sicily, Puglia, and Calabria, mint is sliced and incorporated into everything from salads to pastas to frying batters to simple fish dishes.

**Oregano** Other than bay leaves, oregano is the only herb I use in dried form, because fresh oregano has a very pungent flavor. It's also very finicky, turning black the moment it's sliced, no matter how sharp the knife. (Dried oregano, bagged on the stalk, is available in many Italian-American markets. It offers a happy middle ground between fresh and dried, because it has more flavor than jarred dried oregano but isn't overpowering.) Dried oregano is used in a great many Italian-American preparations, including meat sauces, meatballs, and salad dressings, but it is deployed much more sparingly in Italy, primarily in the southern regions as a summertime alternative to basil.

**Parsley** Parsley is popular here, but often for the wrong reasons, or for no real reason, considered a "default" herb without much consideration given to its flavor. That's not how it's used in Italy, where it's probably the most called-upon herb. (It's no accident that flat-leaf parsley, the only type called for in these pages, is also called "Italian" parsley by Americans.)

When using parsley in any cooking, don't mince it, but instead slice it just a few times with a very sharp knife so it maintains its flavor and character. (You know that green stain on your cutting board that remains after chopping parsley? The larger and darker that stain, the more flavor you've sacrificed through overchopping.) Also, be sure to slice your parsley as close to *à la minute* as possible; precut parsley can develop an aroma more like grass clippings than an herb.

**Rosemary** There are dozens of varieties of rosemary in Italy, from those with long, soft needles to rugged, sturdier ones. To me, rosemary ranks alongside olive oil, garlic, pepper flakes, and Parmigiano as among the most indispensable ingredients in Italian cooking. In fact, I frequently begin a dish with some combination of rosemary, garlic, and red pepper flakes. Those three elements, when presented in balance and harmony, sum up classic Italian cooking for me: Just as when you walk into a French kitchen you will immediately smell red wine and bay leaves, when you first set foot in an Italian kitchen, you will always smell rosemary and garlic.

**Sage** Before traveling to Italy, I only knew sage as one of the ingredients in Thanksgiving stuffing. But this herb has a central place in the cooking of Emilia-Romagna, where it turns up in many dishes, including the iconic butter and sage sauce for filled pastas. Whole sage leaves are also sometimes fried as a garnish for soups.

**Thyme** Like rosemary, thyme is an assertive, woodsy herb. I associate it more with French than with Italian cooking, but I do call on it sometimes for the homey feeling it evokes (think of a roasting chicken or simmering stock) and for its affinity with mushrooms. Other thyme varieties, such as lavender thyme and lemon thyme, aren't called for much in this book, but if you have access to them, or are able to grow your own, it's worth getting to know them. They have potent aromas that can bring a unique quality to stocks, sauces, soups, and other preparations.

### STORING FRESH HERBS

Roll fresh herbs up in a barely moistened paper towel and refrigerate in a resealable plastic bag. You will get more life out of them this way, especially basil.

**Liqueurs** Don't use your best aged brandy, cognac, or Marsala in recipes that call for these spirits; instead, much as when cooking with wine (see page xxxiii), select what the bartenders call "well" spirits: the most inexpensive (but decent) brands.

## OILS

**Canola Oil** For frying, cooking most meats and fish, and other preparations where the flavor of olive oil isn't desired, my neutral-flavored oil of choice is canola, but you can substitute vegetable oil or grapeseed oil.

**Olive Oil** In this book, olive oil is most often used for sautéing vegetables and marinating vegetables, fish, and shellfish.

**Extra Virgin Olive Oil** More nuanced (and expensive) than regular olive oil, extra virgin olive oils vary dramatically in flavor profile, from spicy to fruity. In this book, they are most often used as a finishing agent for soups, pastas, and other dishes, or to dress fresh vegetables and salads.

---

**Pasta** See pages 77–88.

**Polenta** When shopping for polenta, bear in mind that it's synonymous with cornmeal, so you can purchase products sold under either name. The most important consideration is to obtain the meal with the best flavor and texture; heirloom grains such as those from Anson Mills (see Sources, page 379) take longer to cook, but they result in polenta with an intense corn flavor and a suave, satiny texture that cannot be beat.

I'm not a fan of instant or quick-cooking polenta, because it's easy to make it from scratch and the precooked versions simply can't match the clear corn flavor. (For more on polenta and a basic recipe, see page 168.)

**Red Pepper Flakes** Many Americans associate red pepper flakes with pizzerias, but they are used throughout Italian cooking, where a pinch is added to everything from fry batters to vinaigrettes to sauces to deliver a subtle hint of heat and spice.

**Rice/Risotto** The most popular and well-known rices for risotto are arborio, carnaroli, and vialone nano, all of which are short-grain or superfino. Although some people believe that different varieties are better for different types of risotto—vialone nano, for instance, is preferred in Venice and closely associated with seafood risottos—I find that any one of them is suitable

### SALT

**Kosher Salt** For general cooking, I prefer kosher salt, both for its purity (i.e., no added iodine) and for its coarse texture, which makes it easy to pick up with your fingertips. I recommend Diamond Crystal kosher salt.

**Sea Salt** I use sea salt as a finishing agent, especially for seafood preparations, or in recipes where an exceptionally fine grind and subtle flavor are called for. Generally speaking, any fine sea salt will do, but for special cases, such as seasoning a superior cut of cooked meat, the exquisitely flaky Maldon sea salt brings noticeable texture and flavor to the plate.

---

**Stock** There are recipes for stocks in the Basic Recipes and Techniques section that begins on page 366, but for most of these recipes, it's fine to use store-bought stocks or broths, preferably low-sodium and organic. The exceptions are when the flavor of a stock is crucial, as in sauces, soups, and risottos.

**Tomatoes (canned)** Canned fruits and vegetables have a terrible reputation, and usually rightfully so, but canned tomatoes are an exception. San Marzano tomatoes from Italy are the best, with the brightest, sweetest flavor, but you can also use a high-quality, organic American brand, such as Muir Glen.

**Tomato Paste** Tomato paste in a tube is the most convenient option; you can pipe it easily into spoon measures, and then simply screw on its cap to save the unused paste, extending its lifespan several times over.

**Vinegars** There are three vinegars worth having on hand for cooking Italian: red wine, white wine, and balsamic. True balsamic vinegar goes by the designation Aceto Balsamico Tradizionale di Modena and is an expensive condiment meant to be used sparingly. For some of the dishes in Moderno, I call for sherry vinegar, an ingredient with strong French and Spanish associations that brings a pleasing, round, slightly sweet quality to certain salads.

**Wine** Except in cases where a particular varietal is called for, wine used for cooking can be inexpensive, just as long as you don't use so-called "cooking wine," which has a very unpleasant flavor. Unless otherwise specified, in my recipes, Sangiovese and Chianti are ideal for red, and Pinot Grigio for white. Stay away from oaky whites such as Chardonnay and overly perfumed ones such as Chablis and Sauvignon Blanc, which can bring a distracting flavor to recipes.

CLASSICO

There's something inherently antithetical about a traditional Italian cookbook, because so much about classic Italian cuisine and why it charms us has to do with an absence of structure, a free-flowing connection to the natural world, and, if we're honest with ourselves, a minimum of manipulation. In other words, exactly the opposite of what we expect between the covers of a cookbook.

Indeed, some of my most indelible taste memories from Italy are founded on simple pleasures that require no recipe: raw fava beans eaten out of the pod, alternated with slices of a young Pecorino Toscano cheese; affettati, assorted cured meats, presented with freshly baked bread and marinated olives alongside; or even the elemental delight of something as pure as Parmigiano-Reggiano or a drizzle of true balsamic vinegar.

Even where there are recipes, whether for soups or salads, pasta or risotto, fish or meat, they are there to be adapted. By now, the statement that recipes for any common dish vary from house to house throughout every region of Italy is a cliché, and I wouldn't repeat it except for the fact that it's so immutably true. Take ragù Bolognese, which offers a world of choices: whether or not to make it with chicken livers; to stir in milk at the end or not; to use red or white wine; to use skirt steak exclusively or to combine it with chuck and blade cuts; to add broth or not; and so on.

That is the main way in which this section of the book differs from Moderno. The recipes in this section can and should be freely adapted to suit any number of factors: what you have on hand (or don't), what's in season, and what looks good at the store or market that day.

On a more fundamental level, the dishes should be tweaked to suit your own personal taste: Use more or less garlic in sauces, add more acid to vinaigrettes, make soups thicker or thinner based on your preference, or vary the presentations as you like. These are all things that a cook would do without hesitation in Italy, and I encourage you to do the same with the recipes in this section.

# PER COMINCIARE

## TO START

Italians often mark the end of the day with a glass of wine, or an aperitivo, and something to nibble. What that "something" is called depends on where in Italy you find yourself: stuzzichini (in the north), sfizi (Campania), cicchetti (Venice). Many of these foods were expressly created to accompany, if not encourage, a drink, and so are often referred to simply by what they have in common as un po' di salatini, which means, roughly, "a little bit of salty things" and can refer to anything from nuts to breadsticks to the kind of prepared dishes found in this chapter.

While I love that Italian tradition, the devotion to quality of life, to transitioning from the workday to one's personal time, it could not be more different from the corresponding American ritual: There's no "happy hour" culture in Italy, no hordes of patrons raiding buffets and drinking themselves to intoxication as a blaring sound system rattles the bar. The after-work respite in Italy is more restrained in every way, from portion size to general disposition. The drink doesn't even have to necessarily be alcoholic; it might be, say, a Crodino (bitter aperitif), or a Chinotto (orange soft drink). And the bars themselves are a different animal from their American cousins; in addition to alcohol, you are apt to find a refrigerator proffering a small selection of beverages such as bottled water, lemon soda, and beer to go, and there's almost always an espresso machine against the back wall, right alongside the wines and spirits.

This custom falls under the umbrella of la dolce vita, the sweet life, and it's one of the things that tourists in Italy fall in love with and that, even after all these years, I become enamored all over again on each visit. When I'm in Italy, I can't wait for four or five o'clock to roll around so that I can step into a bar, take a seat at a marbled café table, and have a quick snack and a drink and—yes—an occasional cigarette. (Hey, when in Rome . . .) If you have a constant urge to check your smartphone or e-mail, nothing will help it melt away like this ritual.

In Italy, many of the dishes featured in this chapter and the one that follows it (Salads and First Courses) would be categorized as antipasti, which means "before the meal (*pasto*)." It's generally considered imperative to have a mix, or misto, of appetizers. Regarding numbers: Though rarely discussed, it's generally assumed that three is the minimum, and four or five is the maximum. A good rule of thumb is that whatever comfortably fits on the table alongside your drink or bottle of wine without crowding it is the right amount.

# ZUCCHINE ALLA SCAPECE

## MARINATED FRIED ZUCCHINI

SERVES 4

This is the Italian version of the more well-known Spanish preparation escabeche, in which fish is fried, then marinated in a puckery mixture. The marinade includes white wine vinegar, herbs (mint is the traditional choice in the dish's home region of Campania, but you needn't be bound by it), and garlic. Because the zucchini is hot when the marinade is introduced, it drinks in those flavors, which offer an acidic, zesty counterpoint to the crispy fried exterior, a contrast that softens into harmony as the zucchini is refrigerated for several hours. (If you like, to help ensure a crispy crust, toss the zucchini with a tablespoon of all-purpose flour before frying.)

Note the zucchini must marinate for at least 6 hours before serving.

- A few cups of canola oil or other neutral oil, for deep-frying
- 3 green zucchini, about 10 ounces each, sliced crosswise into ¼-inch rounds
- Kosher salt
- Freshly ground black pepper
- ⅓ cup white wine vinegar
- ¼ cup thinly sliced fresh herb leaves, such as mint or basil, or a combination
- 1 garlic clove, thinly sliced
- ¼ teaspoon red pepper flakes
- Extra virgin olive oil, for serving
- 4 lemon wedges, for serving

Set a large heavy saucepan over medium-high heat. Pour in enough oil to reach 1 inch up the sides of the pan, clip a deep-fry thermometer to the side of the pan, and heat over medium heat to 350°F (see below). Line a large plate with paper towels.

Add the zucchini to the oil, in batches, and fry, occasionally stirring them gently with a slotted spoon, until lightly golden, about 3 minutes. Use the slotted spoon to transfer the zucchini to the paper towels. Season immediately with salt and pepper and let drain. Be sure to allow the oil to return to 350°F between batches.

Transfer the zucchini slices to a heatproof vessel, such as a glass baking dish large enough to hold the slices in a thin layer. Immediately drizzle the vinegar over them, then scatter the herbs, garlic slices, and red pepper flakes over the zucchini. Let cool, then cover loosely with plastic wrap and marinate in the refrigerator for at least 6 hours, or overnight, but no longer than 24 hours, or the zucchini will begin to break down.

To serve, use a slotted spoon to transfer the zucchini to a small serving bowl. Drizzle with extra virgin olive oil and serve with the lemon wedges alongside for squeezing over individual portions.

**Variations** This is a versatile recipe. To approximate the sweet-and-sour Sicilian version, for example, dissolve a little sugar in the vinegar before drizzling it over the zucchini. In the summer, change things up by grilling rather than frying the zucchini; the contrast between the char of the grill and the marinade will be different but just as compelling. You can also make this with other summer vegetables, such as eggplant or yellow squash, or a combination. And it's equally at home as a side dish; it's especially good alongside grilled fish.

### No Thermometer?

If you don't have a deep-fry thermometer, you can check to see if the oil is hot enough for frying by flicking a scant drop of water into it. If it sizzles on contact, the oil is hot enough. You can also dip the handle of a wooden spoon into the oil; if the oil is hot enough, the moisture in the wood will cause the oil to sizzle around the handle.

## CAPONATA

### COLD EGGPLANT AND CAPER SALAD

MAKES ABOUT 2 CUPS

Caponata, the popular Sicilian condiment, is such a mainstay of Italian cooking that one might easily forget it was created out of necessity: In the days before refrigeration, eggplant was harvested and preserved at the height of freshness with a generous amount of vinegar. While it's made in other regions as well, to this day Sicilian caponata is regarded as superior, because Sicily's eggplant remains Italy's best—just as, say, pesto from Liguria reigns supreme because of the delicate basil grown there. (Although the predominant ingredient in caponata is eggplant, the dish is believed to have taken its name from the Italian word for caper, capero.)

A crucial decision must be made when preparing caponata: skin or no skin? Personally, I find skin distracting, but many enjoy the rusticity provided by its texture. You can leave the skin on your eggplant or, if conflicted, peel the skin off in strips, leaving about half of it intact.

Serve caponata on its own as an antipasto or part of a spread, with mozzarella, or as an accompaniment to fish or chicken. *Don't* toss it with hot pasta (hot vinegar doesn't taste good), although it can be a fine accompaniment to cold leftover pasta.

Like so many Italian vegetable dishes, caponata should really be made only at the peak of the vegetable's season, which for eggplant is late summer. While any eggplant will work fine, I prefer white to purple, because it is less porous and will soak up less oil, resulting in a more refined preparation.

5 tablespoons olive oil
2 large eggplants, about 1¼ pounds each, peeled and cut into ¾-inch cubes
3 large red bell peppers, cored, seeded, ribs removed, and cut into large dice
1 large onion, cut into small dice (about 1 cup)
1 large celery stalk, trimmed and cut into small dice (about ½ cup)
1 small garlic clove, minced
¼ cup granulated sugar
1 cup white wine vinegar
2 tablespoons capers, soaked in warm water for 5 minutes and drained
½ cup golden raisins, soaked in warm water for 10 minutes and drained
6 oil-packed anchovy fillets
Kosher salt
Freshly ground black pepper
½ cup fresh basil, cut into chiffonade (see page xxx)

Line a large plate with paper towels.

Heat a large heavy sauté pan over medium-high heat. Pour in 3 tablespoons of the oil and tilt and turn the pan to coat it, heating the oil until it is shimmering and almost smoking. Add the eggplant and bell peppers, turn the heat up to high, and cook, shaking the pan periodically to prevent scorching and ensure even cooking, until the eggplant is soft at the center but still retains its shape, 6 to 7 minutes. Use a slotted spoon to transfer the eggplant and peppers to the paper-towel-lined plate and let drain briefly, then transfer the vegetables to a large heatproof mixing bowl.

Carefully wipe out the pan with paper towels and return it to medium-high heat. Pour in the remaining 2 tablespoons oil and tilt and turn the pan to coat it, heating the oil until it is shimmering and almost smoking. Add the onions and celery and cook, stirring with a wooden spoon, until slightly softened but not browned, about 2 minutes. Add the garlic and cook, stirring, for 1 minute. Sprinkle the sugar over the vegetables and stir it in, then stir in the vinegar, capers, raisins, and anchovies. Bring the liquid to a boil over medium-high heat, then lower the heat and simmer, stirring occasionally to help the sugar dissolve, until the liquid is reduced by half, 10 to 12 minutes. Pour the mixture over the eggplant and peppers and stir just to mix. Season with salt and pepper, then stir in the basil and let cool.

The caponata can be used right away or refrigerated in an airtight container for up to 3 days. Let come to room temperature before serving.

**ISPIRAZIONE** In the fall, after eggplant's season has come and gone, I make a butternut squash caponata with currants, raisins, pine nuts, and pistachios; see page 215.

# SARDINE MARINATE

## MARINATED SARDINES

SERVES 4 TO 6

Along the Amalfi Coast, beside the pristine azure waters of the Tyrrhenian Sea, sardines are practically a way of life—the small, fatty, exquisitely salty fish are canned by area fisheries and exported around the world. They are also consumed by the local population just about any way you can imagine: Two of the most popular options are arranging them on pizzas like the spokes of a wheel and tossing them with spaghetti and bread crumbs in *pasta con le sarde*.

You can also, of course, eat marinated sardines on their own. However you enjoy them, they are made via a simple three-step process: salting the sardines to draw out their impurities, then marinating them twice, first in white wine vinegar to cut the fattiness of the fish, followed by a more complex olive oil marinade. As the fish absorb the oil, the intensely tangy vinegar is muted, and within minutes, the dish achieves a balance.

You might serve these alongside Caponata (page 5), another staple of Southern Italy.

Fresh sardines aren't as popular in the United States as they are in Italy, so they can be hard to come by; you might need to ask your fishmonger to special-order them for you. Note that the sardines must be salted for 1 hour, then marinated for at least 1 ½ hours.

12 to 16 fresh sardines, 2 to 3 ounces each and at least 3 inches long if possible, cleaned (see page 8)
Kosher salt
¾ cup white wine vinegar
½ cup extra virgin olive oil
3 large garlic cloves, thinly sliced
2 flat-leaf parsley sprigs, very thinly sliced (stems and all)
1 teaspoon red pepper flakes

Arrange the sardine fillets in a glass baking dish large enough to hold them in a single layer. Shower with a light dusting of salt, cover loosely with plastic wrap, and refrigerate for 1 hour to draw out the impurities.

One at a time, rinse the sardines under gently running cold water and pat them dry with paper towels.

Rinse and dry the baking dish and arrange the sardines in the dish in a single layer again. Drizzle the vinegar over the sardines. Cover loosely with plastic wrap and refrigerate for 1 hour.

Remove the baking dish from the refrigerator and carefully pour off and discard the vinegar. Gently blot the sardines dry with paper towels and drizzle the oil over them. Scatter the garlic, parsley, and red pepper flakes over the sardines, cover the dish with the plastic wrap, and return to the refrigerator for at least 30 minutes, or overnight, but no more than 24 hours, or the sardines will begin to break down.

To serve, arrange the sardines on a serving plate or small platter).

**Variation** To turn these sardines into the centerpiece of a quick salad: Stir a few drops of lemon juice into ½ cup sour cream and divide it among 4 salad plates. Top with greens such as arugula and dress them with a scant amount of extra virgin olive oil and lemon juice, then drape a few sardines atop the greens on each plate. For a special, though not necessarily Italian, touch, flick some osetra caviar or trout roe over each serving.

## SARDINES

Blue fish such as sardines, anchovies, and mackerel are among the most abundant fish in the Mediterranean. As Americans, we're more accustomed to these blue fish in their canned state, or to the bluefish that's popular on the East Coast and eaten just one way: grilled.

In Italy, Spain, and France, there is an entire culture based around these fish: They are consumed marinated and raw, used to top pizzas, tossed into pastas, grilled, and fried, to name just a few preparations. Their high oil content allows them to take on a considerable amount of acidity, one of the defining elements of Italian cooking.

Procuring fresh sardines might require some planning ahead in the United States. Most of what you can find here comes from Portugal, and you may need to ask your fishmonger to special-order them for you a day or two in advance.

Just about any recipe for sardines requires you to clean them. This is best done by your fish shop, but if you'd like to do it yourself, here's how: Fill a large bowl with cold water and add a pinch of salt. Use a boning knife or other small, sharp, thin-bladed knife to cut off the head and tail from each sardine. Starting at one end, use the point of the knife to fillet each sardine, working along the backbone to remove the flesh from each side in one piece, cutting off the first fillet and adding it to the bowl of water, then flipping the fish and removing the second one; change the water periodically as it takes on blood and other impurities. Once all of the sardines are filleted, remove them from the water, rinse under cold gently running water, and carefully blot dry with paper towels.

# BACCALÀ MANTECATO

## WHIPPED SALT COD

SERVES 4 TO 6

Salt cod is probably best known as the central ingredient in the Provençal dish brandade. This is the Italian version, meant to be spread over the grilled bread called fettunta (see page 11). (For a quick meal, top each baccalà-spread toast with a fried egg, and serve with simply dressed salad greens.)

You can find baccalà mantecato throughout Italy, but it's most popular in Venice, where it's a popular cicchetti (see page 3). The baccalà can be made with or without whipped potatoes, which are traditionally folded in after processing the salt cod mixture to thicken it; the desired texture can also be achieved with the patient addition of olive oil to emulsify the puree.

Note that the salt cod must soak for 36 to 48 hours.

1 pound salt cod (see Sources, page 379)
1 large russet or Idaho potato (about 8 ounces), cut into large dice
1 cup whole milk, or as needed
2 thyme sprigs
1 bay leaf
3 large garlic cloves, smashed with the side of a chef's knife and peeled
½ cup extra virgin olive oil
Kosher salt
Freshly ground black pepper
1 tablespoon sliced fresh flat-leaf parsley leaves
8 to 12 slices (2 per serving) fettunta (see page 11)

Put the salt cod in a medium bowl and cover by at least 1 inch with cold water. Cover loosely with plastic wrap and refrigerate for 36 to 48 hours, draining the water and replacing it with fresh cold water every 8 hours or so. The best way to know if you've soaked the fish long enough is to stick a clean index finger into the water and taste it; you want a hint of salt, but not an excessively salty taste.

Drain the salt cod and transfer to a large heavy saucepan. Add the potatoes, milk, thyme, bay leaf, and garlic cloves. The milk should cover the potatoes and cod; if it does not, add a little more. Set over medium heat, and heat just until the liquid begins to simmer, taking care not to let it boil, which could cause the fish to disintegrate. Lower the heat to maintain a gentle simmer and cook until the potatoes are tender to the tines of a fork, 25 to 30 minutes. Scoop about 1 cup of the cooking liquid into a heatproof measuring cup and reserve, then carefully drain the contents of the pan in a colander.

Use a slotted spoon to return the salt cod and potatoes to the saucepan, discarding the other ingredients. Cook over medium heat, stirring with a wooden spoon, so the cod and potatoes release their excess liquid, until steam is no longer produced, 8 to 10 minutes; take care to turn the ingredients constantly to prevent them from scorching.

While they are still hot, transfer the salt cod and potatoes to the bowl of a stand mixer fitted with the paddle attachment. Paddle on medium-low speed until the salt cod and potatoes begin to break up, then drizzle the olive oil into the bowl in a thin, steady stream, mixing until well incorporated. With the mixer running, season with salt and pepper, bearing in mind that the salt cod is naturally salty. Drizzle in a few tablespoons of the reserved cooking liquid, gradually raise the speed to medium-high, and mix until the mixture is slightly aerated and fluffy. Turn off the motor and gently fold in the parsley with a rubber spatula (don't beat in the parsley, or the mixture will turn green).

Transfer the baccalà to a serving bowl and serve with the fettunta alongside.

**ISPIRAZIONE** The sauce in the cod and artichoke dish on page 315 is based on the flavors of baccalà mantecato.

# PASTICCIO DI FEGATO D'ANATRA E POLLO

## CHICKEN AND DUCK LIVER PÂTÉ

SERVES 4

While I've always enjoyed chicken livers, I was unprepared for the richness that Italians achieve with them. Here they are sautéed and chopped for one of the most popular crostini toppings.

This recipe is a smoother, creamier variation on the version we made at San Domenico, which was fashioned in the style of Tuscany, featuring both chicken and duck livers. The livers are cooked with aromatics and anchovy, then the pan is deglazed with fortified wine, and the livers are processed with butter until smooth. The result is so rich that it could almost pass for foie gras.

Note that the livers must be soaked for 1 to 2 hours and then marinated for at least 6 hours.

8 ounces chicken livers
8 ounces duck livers (an additional 8 ounces chicken livers can be substituted)
1 cup whole milk
2 bay leaves, preferably fresh
1 small garlic clove, minced
About ½ cup brandy
½ cup dry Marsala
8 tablespoons (1 stick) cold unsalted butter, cut into small cubes, plus 2 tablespoons butter
2 tablespoons canola oil
2 oil-packed anchovy fillets, minced
1 small shallot, minced
2 tablespoons capers, soaked in warm water for 5 minutes and drained
3 large fresh sage leaves, minced
Kosher salt
3 tablespoons Chicken Stock (page 374) or store-bought low-sodium chicken broth
8 crostini, for serving (see page 11)

Use a paring knife to trim the fat, membranes, and bile ducts from the chicken and duck livers, then rinse them. Pour the milk into a small bowl, add the livers, and soak for 1 to 2 hours in the refrigerator to draw out impurities.

Drain the livers, rinse, and drain again, then pat dry with paper towels.

Transfer the livers to a glass dish. Add the bay leaves and garlic, then drizzle the brandy and Marsala over the livers. Toss briefly and gently, cover loosely with plastic wrap, and refrigerate at least 6 hours, or overnight.

Remove the livers from the marinade and pat them dry with paper towels. Set a fine-mesh strainer over a small bowl and strain the marinade; reserve the bay leaves and garlic separately.

Heat a medium heavy sauté pan over medium heat. Add the 2 tablespoons butter and the oil and heat until the butter is foaming. Add the anchovies, shallots, capers, sage, and reserved bay leaves and garlic to the pan and sauté for 1 minute.

Season the livers with salt and arrange them in the pan in a single layer. Cook, using tongs or a large kitchen spoon to turn the livers, until they are brown at the edges but still pink inside, 4 to 5 minutes, taking care to not overcook them. Pour in the reserved marinade and the stock and raise the heat to medium-high. Cook, shaking the pan occasionally, until the marinade reduces slightly and begins to glaze the livers, about 5 minutes. Remove the pan from the heat and use tongs or a slotted spoon to remove the bay leaf and discard it. Let the livers and liquid cool in the pan.

Transfer the contents of the pan to the bowl of a food processor and pulse to a coarse puree. Add the cold butter a few pieces at a time, pulsing after each addition to incorporate the butter and achieve a smooth consistency.

Fill a wide, deep bowl halfway with ice water. Using a rubber spatula, scrape the liver puree into a smaller stainless-steel bowl, and set in the ice water. Whisk the puree until fluffy; the ice water will keep it cold and maintain the emulsification. Transfer to a serving bowl and serve with the crostini, or refrigerate in an airtight container for up to 2 days.

**Variation** Make leftover pâté the base of a wonderful quick pasta sauce by heating it gently in a heavy sauté pan and slowly stirring in some cream.

**ISPIRAZIONE** For a contemporary version of this starter, see Chicken Liver Crostini with Marsala-Braised Onions (page 218).

## BRUSCHETTA, CROSTINI, AND FETTUNTA

Bruschetta and crostini are among the most popular starters in Italian cuisine. They are essentially the same thing—a slice of grilled or toasted bread topped with savory food—although, classically, crostini are the thinner of the two, and bruschetta are rubbed with garlic and olive oil after grilling or toasting, while the oil is optional for crostini. In Tuscany, garlic-and-oil-rubbed toast is called fettunta, which means "oily slice." It's easiest to cut the garlic clove in half crosswise and impale it on a fork, then use the fork to rub the cut side of the garlic over the bread.

Bruschetta and crostini may be served with a variety of toppings, from the ubiquitous tomatoes, garlic, and basil to chopped sautéed chicken livers to white bean puree, prosciutto and Fontina, sautéed mushrooms, or olive paste, to name just a few possibilities.

Bruschetta and crostini may be casual, but they should not be approached in a haphazard fashion: In particular, choosing and toasting or grilling the bread should be treated with the same consideration and attention as any other part of a dish. The desired result is for the toasts to be hard on the outside but still soft and ever-so-slightly chewy on the inside. To achieve this, I suggest purchasing a quality peasant bread and slicing it at least ½ inch thick for bruschetta, or buying a baguette and slicing it about ¼ inch thick for crostini; that thickness is key to the inside remaining soft while the outside toasts. You can bake the slices in an oven preheated to 400°F until nicely crisp on the bottom and slightly charred around the edges, then turn and bake on the other side, or cook on a grill. If you're not using a very fresh baguette, cook crostini only on one side to maintain the soft interior.

# AFFETTATI MISTI

## NOTES ON SELECTING AND SERVING CURED MEATS, CHEESES, AND BREAD

One of my favorite Italian dining rituals doesn't involve any cooking at all, but, rather, availing oneself of some of Italy's most sublime food products. I'm talking about salumi, the cured and aged meats that are used in Italian cooking but can also be an end in themselves.

Having been raised on American cold cuts, I found my introduction to the Italian equivalent a revelation. I still remember my inaugural affettati experience, which took place the day after I first arrived in Italy, on the Sunday when Valentino drove me to Imola to begin working at San Domenico. En route, he took me to a late lunch at a trattoria in the town of Rivabella, just south of Bologna in the foothills of the Apennines. Our meal began with small, griddled breads called tigelle (see page 15), which I spread with Rosemary-Lardo Pesto (see page 16). I thought that was all you were supposed to put on them, but then Valentino began putting some of the meats on the bread too. I followed suit and within minutes had revealed myself to be a typical American: I ate so much salumi that I couldn't eat the fresh handmade pastas that followed.

When selecting meats to serve as part of an affettati misti, I suggest picking at least one aged meat, one ground (as in sausage) or cured meat, and one cooked meat. The most traditional choices would be prosciutto for the aged, salami for the cured, and mortadella for the cooked.

To round out the plate, a cheese or two is desirable, the must-include being Parmigiano-Reggiano, although some regions have their own mandatory cheeses, such as squacquerone, a super-fresh cow's-milk cheese that's produced only in Emilia-Romagna. For a more widely available choice, a semisoft cheese such as a thirty-day Pecorino would be delicious.

The conventional wisdom is that most condiments only serve to distract from the meats and cheeses, although—in addition to lardo pesto—Marinated Olives (page 20), Pickled Vegetables (page 18), and Mostarda di Cremona (see page 149) have come to be accepted as worthy of inclusion.

Regardless of whether or not you serve condiments, you will want some small-form breads to provide a vehicle and offer some relief from the potent, salty flavors. My favorites are Gnocco Fritto (page 14) and Piadina e Tigelle (page 15). If you prefer to buy bread, sliced and lightly toasted ciabatta would be a fine accompaniment.

# GNOCCO FRITTO

## FRIED BREAD

MAKES ABOUT 18 PIECES

When I think of the English translation for gnocco fritto, the phrase "lost in translation" comes to mind, because while "fried bread" implies something leaden and greasy, gnocco fritto are, in reality, ethereally soft, pillowy kerchiefs of bread, little magic carpets created for the express purpose of floating cured and aged meats from the table to your mouth.

As with so much Italian food, gnocco fritto vary from region to region. From Bologna southeast toward the Adriatic Coast, they call the little breads crescentina, although the two are essentially the same thing. Directly south of Emilia-Romagna, they serve a large sandwich-appropriate version called ficattola, made with fresh yeast and reminiscent of pizza dough.

While you can usually substitute shortening for lard, there are some Italian recipes that are greatly diminished if not made with lard, and this is one of them. The distinctive flavor of lard is part of the essence of many Italian baked goods, and it also helps create thin, flaky layers. (Lard can be purchased at many supermarkets, especially in Italian-American neighborhoods, though you might need to ask the butcher for it.)

Gnocco fritto are fried in strips and then cut into rhombus-shaped bits with a jagged rolling cutter, which results in dramatic and ornate ruffled edges. (If you don't have such a cutter, a sharp chef's knife will work as well.) The main thing is to serve the bread warm, so it heats and releases the fat in the meats.

1 package (2¼ teaspoons) active dry yeast
¼ cup warm water, plus more if needed
2 cups all-purpose flour, plus more for dusting
1 teaspoon kosher salt
1 teaspoon baking soda
2 tablespoons lard or vegetable shortening, at room temperature
A few cups of canola oil or other neutral oil, for deep-frying
Fine sea salt

Put the yeast and water in a small bowl and stir together. Set aside, uncovered, until the mixture is frothy, 10 to 15 minutes.

Put the flour, salt, and baking soda in a medium bowl and whisk together.

Transfer the yeast mixture to the bowl of a stand mixer fitted with the dough hook. Start mixing at low speed, then gradually sift the flour mixture into the bowl, continuing to mix just until incorporated. Add the lard and mix until well incorporated. Remove the bowl from the mixer and cover with a damp kitchen towel. Set aside for 15 minutes; the dough will rise slightly during this time.

Generously dust your work surface with flour and turn the dough out onto it. Flour a rolling pin and roll the dough out to a 12- to 14-inch square about ⅛ inch thick. Use a fluted pastry wheel or a pizza cutter to cut the dough diagonally into 2-by-2-inch rhombus-shaped pieces.

Pour enough oil into a large heavy saucepan to reach 1½ inches up the sides of the pan. Clip a deep-fry thermometer to the side of the pan and heat the oil over medium heat to 350°F (see No Thermometer?, page 4).

Line a baking sheet with paper towels. Using a slotted spoon, add one third of the dough squares to the oil and fry until they are golden brown and floating at the top, about 1 minute. Use the slotted spoon to lift the pieces out of the pan, letting the excess oil drip back into the pan, and transfer them to the paper-towel-lined baking sheet. Sprinkle immediately with sea salt so that it dissolves onto the gnocco fritto.

Let the oil come back to 350°F and repeat with another batch of dough, then fry the remaining dough. Serve warm.

# PIADINA E TIGELLE

## GRIDDLED BREADS

MAKES 6 PIADINA OR ABOUT 16 TIGELLE

Piadina means "little plate," and these griddled breads, 7 to 8 inches in diameter, are the preferred accompaniment to an affettati misti (see page 13) in Emilia-Romagna. The dough made in and around Bologna uses a fair amount of lard, but the farther south one travels, the less lard is used and the more milk you find in the mix, resulting in the thinner, crispier bread known as riminese, meaning "in the style of Rimini," a city on the Adriatic Coast. (For ease of use, I call for butter in this recipe, but you can by all means replace it with lard or shortening.)

Made from the same dough, the smaller round breads called tigelle, no more than 2 to 2½ inches in diameter, are traditionally baked on heated terra-cotta tiles or in a special mold. Here I offer a way to make them as we do at Osteria Morini, cooking them in a cast-iron pan.

Piadina are also wonderful with butter and jam in the morning, or opened up like a pita and stuffed with a sandwich filling.

- 3½ cups all-purpose flour, plus more for dusting
- ½ teaspoon baking soda
- 1 teaspoon kosher salt
- 8 tablespoons (1 stick) cold unsalted butter, cut into ½-inch cubes
- About ¼ cup whole milk

Put the flour, baking soda, and salt in the bowl of a food processor and pulse to blend. Add the cold butter a few pieces at a time, pulsing until the mixture takes on a sandy consistency. With the processor running, pour in the milk in a thin, steady stream, mixing just until a ball of dough forms, taking care not to overmix; you may need slightly more or less than ¼ cup milk. Using a rubber spatula, scrape the dough onto a well-floured work surface.

Use dry clean hands to knead the dough gently until smooth and no longer tacky, and place on a floured baking sheet. Cover with a damp kitchen towel and place in the refrigerator for 15 minutes to keep it from rising.

When the dough has rested, remove it from the baking sheet and place on a floured work surface.

### TO MAKE PIADINA

Divide the dough into 6 equal pieces, using a pastry cutter or your hands. With a floured rolling pin, roll each piece into a 7- to 8-inch round about ¼ inch thick, rotating the dough as you work to ensure even rolling and to keep it from sticking.

Heat a large nonstick pan or griddle over medium heat. One at a time, add the dough rounds and cook until golden brown on the bottom and slightly puffed, about 3 minutes, then turn over with a spatula and cook on the other side until golden brown, about 3 more minutes. (The cooked rounds can be kept warm by wrapping them in a clean kitchen towel or linen napkin.) Serve warm.

### TO MAKE TIGELLE

Break off small balls of dough and pat them into circles 2 to 2½ inches in diameter and about ⅓ inch thick. (Alternatively, you can roll out the ball of dough to a thickness of ⅓ inch and use a cookie cutter to punch out circles; gather the dough scraps into a loose ball, refrigerate until chilled, and then roll out to make more circles.) You should have about 16 circles. Put the circles on a baking sheet or clean kitchen towel, dust lightly with flour, cover loosely with a clean kitchen towel, and let rest for 30 minutes so they rise slightly; this will prevent a doughy center from forming when they are cooked.

Heat a large cast-iron skillet over medium-high heat. Working in batches, cook the circles until lightly golden brown, about 2 minutes on each side. Serve from a linen-lined basket.

## ROSEMARY-LARDO PESTO

MAKES ABOUT 1½ CUPS

This condiment was once made from salted, cured fatback and otherwise unusable trim from cured pork products, then ground into a paste with rosemary, garlic, and black pepper. These days, we use already-cured pancetta and cured, salted lardo to produce it. Spread on piadina or tigelle, it's an ideal complement to an affettati misti. Or stir a little of the pesto into soups, pastas, or risottos, spread it on sandwiches, or melt it over grilled or roasted meats to instantly add a complex flavor.

8 ounces thick-sliced pancetta, cubed
8 ounces lardo (see Sources, page 379), cut into small dice
2 tablespoons olive oil
1 garlic clove, smashed with the side of a chef's knife and peeled
1 teaspoon minced fresh rosemary
1 teaspoon minced fresh sage
Kosher salt
½ teaspoon freshly ground black pepper

Chill the pancetta, lardo, and the bowl and blade of a food processor in the freezer for about 10 minutes; keeping everything cold when processing will help ensure a proper emulsification.

Meanwhile, warm the oil in a small heavy sauté pan over medium-low heat. Add the garlic, rosemary, and sage, give them a stir, and remove the pan from the heat. Set aside to allow the aromatics to infuse the oil as it cools to room temperature.

Set up the food processor, put the lardo and pancetta in the bowl, and pulse until they come together in a paste. Add the oil, garlic, rosemary, and sage, season with a pinch of salt and the pepper, and pulse until the ingredients are uniformly distributed.

Serve the pesto right away, or refrigerate it in an airtight container for up to 1 week.

# FOCACCIA

MAKES 12 LARGE SQUARES

This light and airy Ligurian bread is unique in that it is made with a tremendous amount of extra virgin olive oil incorporated into a very wet dough. The dough is worked for a long time in a mixer, then poured onto a generously oiled tray and allowed to rest until all the gluten that was developed begins to relax and a bubbly texture develops. Because of the odyssey the dough experiences, this is the one bread for which I use bread flour. Note that the poolish must be refrigerated overnight and the dough must proof for about 2 hours.

FOR THE POOLISH

1 cup water

1½ cups bread flour, preferably King Arthur

¾ teaspoon active dry yeast

FOR THE DOUGH

¼ cup water

¾ teaspoon active dry yeast

½ cup bread flour, preferably King Arthur

2¼ teaspoons kosher salt

⅙ cup olive oil, plus more for oiling the bowl and brushing the dough

Flaky sea salt, preferably Maldon

To make the poolish: Put the water, bread flour, and dry yeast in a mixing bowl and whisk together. Let proof at room temperature for 3 hours, then seal completely and securely with plastic wrap and refrigerate overnight.

To make the dough: Stir together the water and yeast in the bowl of a stand mixer fitted with the dough hook attachment until the yeast dissolves. With the mixer off, add the poolish, bread flour, and salt (in that order), then turn the mixer on, starting at a low speed to prevent the ingredients from flying out of the bowl and increasing to high speed. Continue to mix until the dough pulls away from the sides of the bowl, about 10 minutes. Lower the speed to medium and slowly add the olive oil and continue mixing until the dough again pulls away from the sides of the bowl, about 8 minutes.

Transfer the dough to a large, lightly oiled bowl. Cover with a damp towel and let proof at room temperature until doubled in size, about 1 hour.

Turn the dough out onto a lightly floured surface. Fold it over, first from left to right, then top to bottom, to form a square. Line a 13 x 18-inch baking sheet with parchment paper and brush the paper lightly with olive oil. Set the dough in the center of the baking sheet, brush the top of the dough very lightly with oil, cover loosely with plastic wrap, and let proof until the dough can be pulled without retracting, about 40 minutes.

Meanwhile, position a rack in the center of the oven and preheat the oven to 425°F.

Remove the plastic wrap and stretch the dough out so it fills the pan. Prick it with a fork and drizzle it lightly with additional oil. Let the dough rest for 15 minutes more. Gently massage the top of the dough, and drizzle it lightly with olive oil. Bake the focaccia for about 30 minutes or until the bottom is golden brown, almost fried (peer underneath by lifting a corner with a rubber spatula). Remove the sheet from the oven, brush the top of the focaccia with olive oil and season with the sea salt. Let rest for about 10 minutes. Transfer to a cutting board, slice into twelve 4-inch squares, and serve. The focaccia is best eaten right away but can be stored in an airtight container at room temperature for up to 2 days.

# VERDURE SOTTO ACETO

## PICKLED VEGETABLES

MAKES 2½ QUARTS

Pickled vegetables can be enjoyed on their own as a snack or antipasto, or served as an accompaniment to an affettati misti (see page 13), their acid and crunch providing a refreshing counterpoint, a similar effect to alternating bites of cornichon with bites of a terrine. They also pair well with braised meats. Sliced into smaller pieces and speared on toothpicks, they can be used to garnish cocktails such as vodka martinis and Bloody Marys.

- 4 cups white wine vinegar
- 1 cup water
- 2 tablespoons granulated sugar
- 12 large garlic cloves, smashed
- 2 bay leaves
- 2 tablespoons kosher salt
- 1 tablespoon whole black peppercorns
- 2 large carrots, cut into 4-by-¼-inch batons
- ½ head of cauliflower (about 8 ounces), cut into small florets
- 2 large celery stalks, trimmed and cut into 4-by-¼-inch batons
- 2 red bell peppers, cored, seeded, and cut into julienne strips
- 2 yellow bell peppers, cored, seeded, and cut into julienne strips
- 2 basil sprigs
- 1 small red chile, such as Fresno or jalapeño, seeds removed, sliced into rings
- About 1 quart extra virgin olive oil

Add the vinegar, water, sugar, 2 of the garlic cloves, the bay leaves, salt, and peppercorns to a large heavy pot and bring to a boil over high heat, then reduce the heat to low and simmer for 10 minutes. Meanwhile, line a baking sheet with paper towels.

Add the carrots, cauliflower, and celery to the pickling liquid and simmer until the vegetables are slightly tender, 6 to 8 minutes. Use a slotted spoon to transfer the vegetables to the paper-towel-lined baking sheet. Add the red and yellow peppers to the vinegar mixture and simmer until they are slightly tender, about 3 minutes. Transfer the peppers to the baking sheet and let the vegetables cool completely.

Transfer the cooled vegetables to a large mixing bowl and toss gently. Divide the vegetables evenly among 5 pint-size airtight containers. Divide the basil sprigs, chile, and the remaining garlic cloves among the jars. Pour enough oil into each container to cover the vegetables. Put the lids on the containers and refrigerate for at least 24 hours before serving; use within 2 weeks.

# OLIVE MARINATE

## MARINATED OLIVES

MAKES ABOUT 3 CUPS

There's nothing wrong with purchasing marinated olives, which are increasingly available at "olive bars" everywhere from corner groceries to large supermarket chains. But there's also nothing quite like making your own "house olives," which allows you to tweak the selection of olives and marinade ingredients until you arrive at your own ultimate version. You can vary this recipe by changing the mix and ratio of olive types, increasing or decreasing the amount of pepper flakes, and omitting or reducing the amount of citrus peel, to name just a few possibilities.

Note that the olives must marinate for at least 24 hours before serving.

- 1½ cups black olives with pits (such as oil-cured kalamata or taggiasca)
- 1½ cups green olives with pits (such as Castelvetrano or Cerignola)
- 1 cup extra virgin olive oil
- 2 large rosemary sprigs
- Zest of 1 orange, removed in strips with a vegetable peeler, with no white pith attached
- Zest of 1 lemon, removed in strips with a vegetable peeler, with no white pith attached
- ¼ teaspoon red pepper flakes
- 2 large garlic cloves, smashed with the side of a chef's knife and peeled

Put the olives, oil, rosemary sprigs, orange zest, lemon zest, red pepper flakes, and garlic cloves in a 1-quart glass jar. Cover tightly and let marinate at room temperature for 24 hours, then refrigerate for up 1 month.

**Variation** For a surprising change of pace, serve the olives warm: Heat a large skillet over medium-low heat and add 2 tablespoons of the marinating oil. Tip and tilt the pan to coat it and heat the oil, then add the olives and warm them, stirring frequently, until they are plump and warmed through, about 5 minutes. Transfer to a serving vessel and serve immediately, with toothpicks for spearing the olives or a serving spoon for transferring them to individual plates.

# FRITTELLE DI MELANZANE

## EGGPLANT FRITTERS

SERVES 6 TO 8

There is a seemingly endless number of ways to cook and serve eggplant in Italy, and this is one of the more popular options in the south. It's a simple recipe that requires little more than splitting the eggplants and roasting them, then scraping out the flesh and mixing it with mint and basil.

These are perfect for entertaining for two reasons: They are an ideal complement to a glass of white or sparkling wine, and they don't have to be served hot. Room temperature is a perfectly fine option, and that will keep you from deserting your guests to fry batch after batch.

A few cups of canola oil or other neutral oil, for brushing the baking sheet and deep-frying
2 large eggplants, about 1½ pounds each, split lengthwise
½ cup dried bread crumbs
¼ cup finely grated Pecorino Romano
2 large garlic cloves, minced
1 tablespoon basil, chiffonade (see page xxx)
1 tablespoon minced fresh mint
1 tablespoon thinly sliced fresh flat-leaf parsley leaves
2 teaspoons finely grated lemon zest
2 large eggs, lightly beaten
Kosher salt
Freshly ground black pepper
All-purpose flour, for dusting

Position a rack in the center of the oven and preheat the oven to 350°F.

Lightly grease a baking sheet and preheat in the oven for 5 minutes. Set the eggplant halves cut side down on the baking sheet and roast for almost 15 minutes, until the flesh is lightly charred. Turn the eggplant over, tent loosely with aluminum foil, and continue roasting until the flesh is soft, 20 to 25 more minutes. Remove from the oven and let the eggplant cool.

When the eggplant is cool enough to handle, use a tablespoon to scoop the flesh into a colander set in the sink. Discard the skin. Let the eggplant drain to release excess moisture, stirring it periodically with a wooden spoon.

When the eggplant has cooled to room temperature, transfer it to a cutting board and coarsely chop it, so that no large pieces remain. Transfer it to a large mixing bowl, add the bread crumbs, cheese, garlic, mint, parsley, lemon zest, and eggs, and season with salt and pepper. Use your hands to mix and gently squeeze the ingredients together into a uniform batter. Cover and let rest in the refrigerator for 1 to 2 hours so the dry ingredients can hydrate.

To fry the fritters, fill a heavy-bottomed pot to a depth of 2 inches with oil. Clip a deep-fry thermometer to the side of the pot and heat over medium heat to 350°F (see No Thermometer?, page 4). Line a large plate with paper towels.

Meanwhile, remove the batter from the refrigerator. Dust a baking sheet with flour. Use a small ice cream scoop or tablespoon to scoop up small portions of dough, roll them into 1-inch balls between the palms of your hands, and arrange them on the baking sheet; dust your hands with flour to prevent the balls from sticking. You should have about 25 balls. Gently roll the balls in the flour to dust them all over.

Fry the balls in small batches, carefully lowering them into the oil, until lightly golden brown and slightly puffy, 3 to 4 minutes. Use a slotted spoon to transfer the fritters to the paper-towel-lined plate and sprinkle at once with salt. Let the oil return to 350°F between batches.

Arrange the fritters on a serving platter or in a small bowl and serve warm or at room temperature.

# MOZZARELLA EN CARROZZA

## FRIED MOZZARELLA, ANCHOVY, AND BASIL SANDWICHES

SERVES 4

On bar menus all over America, mozzarella en carrozza has come to mean breaded, fried mozzarella served with marinara sauce alongside for dipping. There's nothing wrong with that, except that true mozzarella en carrozza, or "mozzarella in a carriage," is much more complex: mozzarella, anchovy, and basil sandwiched between slices of bread, dipped in egg, and fried until the filling melts together in a decadent ooze. (I use Pullman bread for its square shape and flat top, perfect for cutting out the desired circle.) This starter, popular in Campania, never fails to elicit oohs and aahs, and that's *before* people take their first bite. For larger gatherings, the recipe multiplies very well.

8 slices white Pullman (sandwich) bread, ideally ¼ inch thick
32 large fresh basil leaves
Eight ½-inch-thick slices fresh mozzarella (about 2½ inches in diameter), drained
About 4 teaspoons anchovy paste, preferably from tube
3 extra-large eggs
¼ cup water
1 to 2 cups canola oil or other neutral oil, for shallow-frying
Kosher salt

Lay 4 slices of the bread on a small baking sheet. Arrange 4 basil leaves on each slice of bread, slightly overlapping them in the center. Set 1 slice of mozzarella on each slice. Squeeze about 1 teaspoon anchovy paste over each slice of mozzarella. Top with another slice of mozzarella and another layer of basil. Lay the remaining slices of bread on top to make sandwiches.

Place another baking sheet on top of the sandwiches and weight down with a few heavy cans to press them tightly together. Refrigerate for at least 1 hour, or overnight. (If refrigerating for more than 1 hour, wrap each sandwich in plastic wrap to prevent the sandwiches from drying out.)

Lift off the baking sheet and weights, transfer the sandwiches to a cutting board, and use a 3-inch-round cutter (or a glass) to punch out the center of each sandwich. Discard the scraps and press down on the sandwiches to help them stay together.

Make an egg wash by cracking the eggs into a shallow bowl and whisking in the water.

Pour ½ inch of oil into a shallow heavy skillet and heat it over medium-high heat until hot. Line a large plate with paper towels.

Lower 1 sandwich into the egg wash, completely submerging it, then remove it and gently squeeze out any excess egg wash. Add it to the pan and cook until golden brown on the first side, 2 to 3 minutes, then turn with a spatula and cook on the other side until golden brown, another 2 to 3 minutes. As soon as you've added the first sandwich to the pan, dip and squeeze out another sandwich and add it to the pan. Continue to soak and add sandwiches to the pan, without crowding, and cook until all are done. As the sandwiches are cooked, transfer them to the paper-towel-lined plate and season immediately with salt.

Serve on a platter or in a linen- or napkin-lined basket.

**Variations** If you like, incorporate some tomato paste into the sandwiches. The easiest way to do this is by using tomato paste in a tube and squeezing a little into each sandwich along with the anchovy paste. You could do as they do in Naples and deep-fry these for a street-food-worthy indulgence. These can also be served plated, sauced with Tomato Sauce with Basil (page 74).

# FONDUTA PIEMONTESE CON CUBETTI DI PANE TOSTATO

## FONTINA FONDUE WITH TOASTED BREAD CUBES

SERVES 4 TO 6

Yes, the name of this dish, fonduta, is derived from the French word fondue, because its home region of Piedmont is near France, and because the dish is based on melted cheese. But the similarities end there: Rather than Emmentaler or another alpine cheese, this fonduta is made with Italian Fontina, a pungent, funky cheese from the neighboring region of Valle d'Aosta that has a caramelized-onion aroma. The cheese is melted with cream over a low flame, then enriched with egg yolks and butter. It's essential that you serve this as soon as it's cooked, before the fats congeal. (If they do, reheat for 10 seconds on low heat in a microwave, or in the top of a double boiler over simmering water.)

You can serve this with forks for dunking the bread cubes, or let everybody use their fingers.

1 large loaf ciabatta, cut into 1-inch cubes
¼ cup extra virgin olive oil
Kosher salt
1 pound Fontina cheese, preferably Italian, cut into large dice
⅔ cup heavy cream
3 large egg yolks
4 tablespoons unsalted butter, cut into ½-inch dice

Position a rack in the center of the oven and preheat the oven to 400°F.

Put the bread cubes in a large mixing bowl and drizzle with the olive oil, tossing to coat. Transfer the bread to a baking sheet, place in the oven, and bake until browned and crisp, 6 to 8 minutes, shaking the tray periodically to ensure even browning. Remove the bread from the oven, sprinkle with salt, and toss gently.

Meanwhile, put the Fontina and cream in a medium saucepan suitable for serving and heat over medium-low heat, whisking frequently, until all the cheese has melted, 5 to 7 minutes. Remove the pan from the heat and whisk in the egg yolks and butter. Return the pan to low heat and cook, whisking constantly, until the fonduta is smooth and creamy, 3 to 4 minutes. Season with salt.

Place the warm bread in a serving bowl or basket and serve with the fonduta right in its pan.

**Variation** The fonduta also makes a fine sauce for blanched asparagus, cauliflower, or broccoli.

## SPUMA DI MORTADELLA

### MORTADELLA MOUSSE

SERVES 6

The legendary resourcefulness of the Italian people is on full display in this mousse, which was initially created as a way to use up the unattractive end of a mortadella, although it can be made with any part. Spuma di mortadella is sometimes served by restaurants as a welcome to their guests, and it's also offered as a bar snack, especially in Emilia-Romagna. Most people make the mousse with a běchamel, but I prefer to use ricotta cheese, to attain a fluffier, more delicate result.

- 12 ounces mortadella, cut into large dice (about 1½ cups)
- ½ cup ricotta cheese
- 1 ounce Parmigiano-Reggiano, finely grated (about ½ cup)
- ¼ cup heavy cream
- Pinch of freshly grated nutmeg
- Kosher salt
- Freshly ground black pepper
- 1 medium loaf ciabatta, sliced into ½-inch-thick slices
- ¼ cup olive oil

Put the mortadella in the bowl of a food processor and pulse just until finely ground; do not grind to a paste. Add the ricotta, Parmigiano, and cream and process just until smooth. Scrape the mousse into a bowl and fold in the nutmeg. Season the mixture with salt and pepper to taste. (The spuma can be refrigerated in an airtight container for up to 2 days; it will be better even after just 1 hour, which gives the flavors a chance to develop.)

Position a rack in the center of the oven and preheat the oven to 400°F.

Arrange the ciabatta slices in a single layer on a baking sheet and drizzle with the oil. Sprinkle with salt and toast in the oven, turning once, until the ciabatta slices are golden brown on both sides, about 5 minutes per side. Remove the baking sheet from the oven.

Spread the mortadella mousse on the warm ciabatta slices, arrange on a platter, and serve immediately.

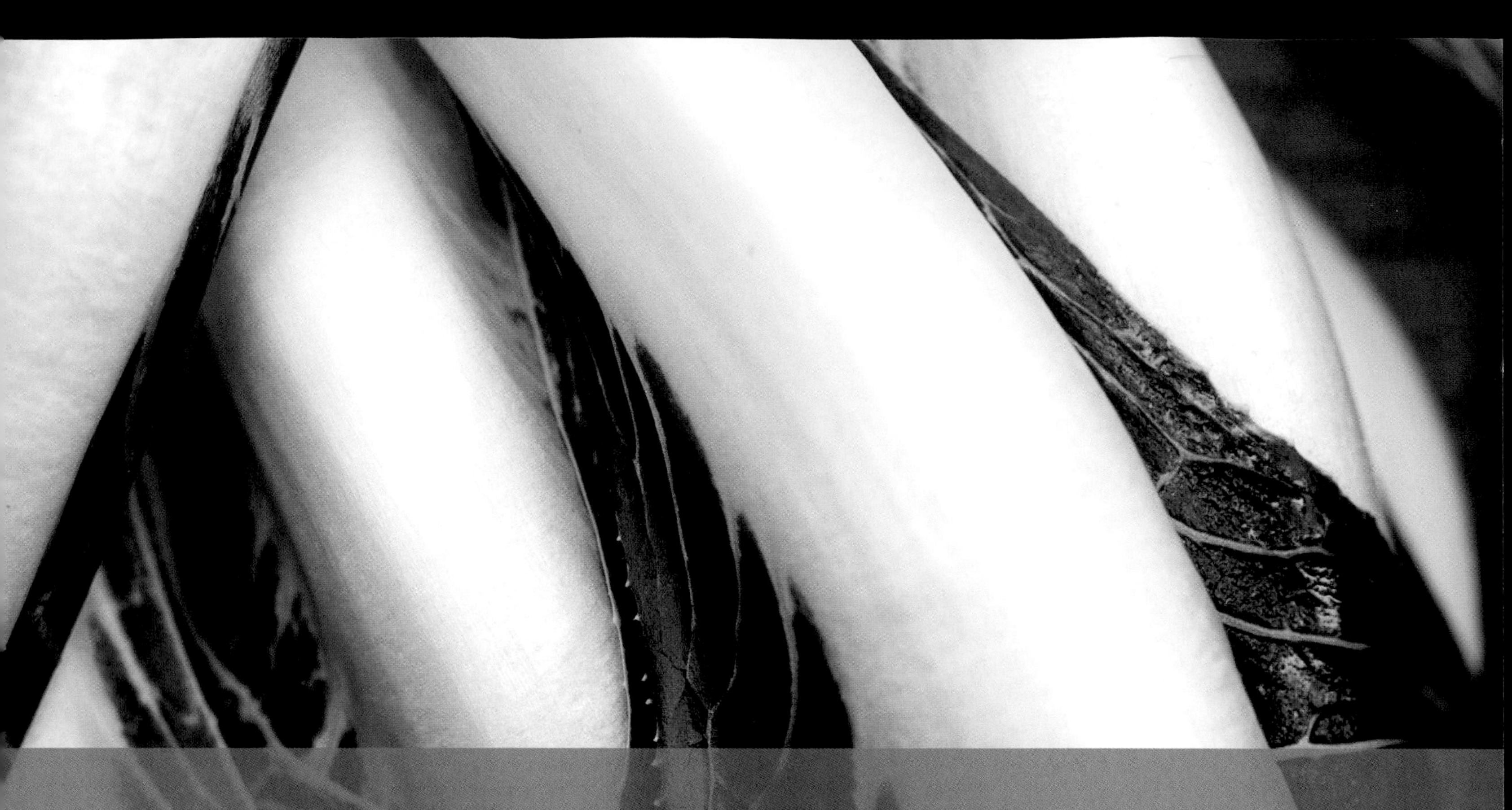

# ANTIPASTI E INSALATE

# SALADS AND FIRST COURSES

I've organized this chapter to reflect the way we eat in the United States, where, in contrast to Italy, the definitions of salads and first courses have become blurred over the past few decades to the point that they are inseparable.

A number of the dishes in this chapter would actually not be first courses in Italy but rather would be served alongside the main course as a contorno, or side dish. This is especially true of dishes featuring leafy greens. More often than not, in an Italian meal, a leafy green salad will be served as an accompaniment to fish or meat. For example, if eating a steak, you would very likely have, say, an arugula salad next to it, both because they complement each other beautifully and because the roughage and acid in the salad aid digestion.

The variety of salad greens and chicories called on in the canon of Italian salads is a more assertive, oftentimes bitter-tasting, selection than is common in the United States. Radicchio, Belgian endive, and mâche are all featured in the following recipes, each offering such distinct flavor that they render complex or creamy dressings unnecessary; more often than not, Italian salads are dressed simply with olive oil and an acid such as lemon juice or vinegar, and little or nothing more.

More in keeping with traditional Italian starters, or antipasti, are Sliced Chilled Veal with Tuna Sauce (page 34) and Alba-Style Steak Tartare (page 36), small and intensely flavored plates that wake up the palate and leave you hungry for more.

# INSALATA DI GIOVANNA

## GIOVANNA'S SALAD

SERVES 4

My standard insalata mista (mixed salad) is based on the one my wife, Giovanna, used to make back in Italy and still does today at our home in New York City. It's our go-to salad, and one I sometimes make for myself late at night when I get home from work: a mix of fennel, endive, Bibb lettuce, radicchio, and herbs, dressed with a lemony vinaigrette.

This will be good with run-of-the-mill supermarket vegetables and spectacular with fresh local vegetables procured from a farm stand, organic market, or your own garden. While you don't need to use the exact mix or ratios of lettuces and other leafy vegetables called for here, it's important to have a good balance of textures and flavors, from soft, neutral, juicy greens to sturdier bitter ones, with peppery arugula and radishes livening things up. When a salad is this simple, the tendency is to overdress it, but the savvy approach is to dress it just enough to perk up and unify the flavors of the vegetables and greens.

1 head of Bibb lettuce, trimmed, washed, dried, and torn into bite-size pieces
1 large Belgian endive, trimmed at the root end and separated into spears
1 fennel bulb, trimmed and very thinly sliced, ideally on a mandoline
1 small head of radicchio, cored, leaves separated, washed, dried, and torn into bite-sized pieces
1 seedless cucumber, thinly sliced into rounds
1 cup cherry tomatoes or grape tomatoes, halved
1 small bunch of radishes, washed, dried, and thinly sliced
1 cup (loosely packed) fresh herbs, such as basil leaves or 2-inch chive batons, or wild arugula
Kosher salt
Freshly ground black pepper
⅓ cup extra virgin olive oil
¼ cup freshly squeezed lemon juice

Put the lettuce, endive, fennel, radicchio, cucumber, tomatoes, radishes, and herbs in a large salad bowl and gently toss to combine. Season with salt and pepper.

In a small bowl, whisk together the olive oil and lemon juice and season with salt and pepper. Drizzle over the salad and toss. Divide the salad among 4 salad plates and serve.

**Variations** This is one of those dishes that in Italy wouldn't be a starter, but rather an accompaniment to grilled or roasted chicken or beef, and you can certainly serve it that way. You can also toss in slices of grilled or roasted meats, or even chunks of poached and chilled shellfish, to make it a summer main course.

To make this a more substantial dish, spread Robiola cheese on fettunta (see page 11) and drizzle with extra virgin olive oil. Serve the fettunta on a plate, or perch one or two on the side of each salad plate.

## TONNO E FAGIOLI

### PRESERVED TUNA, BORLOTTI BEAN, AND RED ONION SALAD

SERVES 4

Versions of this quick and nutritious salad are served all over Italy, especially in Bologna, where I first encountered it. It takes advantage of the convenience of preserved tuna, a supermarket product that's not to be confused with canned tuna as we know it here. Preserved tuna is a delicacy that captures the essence of fresh tuna by slow-cooking it in good-quality oil; it also boasts a generous flake.

You can make this dish with any good Italian or Spanish brand of preserved tuna. I also provide a recipe for preserved tuna, if you'd like to do as they do in Sicily, Calabria, and Liguria and make your own.

1 cup dried borlotti (cranberry) beans or white beans, such as cannellini
4 cups Vegetable Stock (page 371)
1 rosemary sprig
1 garlic clove, smashed with the side of a chef's knife and peeled
Kosher salt
Freshly ground black pepper
2 6-ounce cans preserved tuna packed in olive oil (see the headnote), drained and broken into chunks, or 12 ounces Preserved Tuna (page 33)
½ cup very thinly sliced red onion
1 cup thin diagonal slices peeled celery, plus ½ cup coarsely chopped celery hearts (pale yellow and green stalks and leaves from the center of the bunch)
3 tablespoons extra virgin olive oil
Finely grated zest of 1 lemon
2 tablespoons freshly squeezed lemon juice
2 tablespoons sliced fresh flat-leaf parsley leaves
2 tablespoons chopped fresh mint leaves (optional)
Red wine vinegar (optional)

Put the beans in a bowl, cover with cold water, and soak overnight. (Alternatively, you can quick-soak the beans; see below.) Drain.

Add the beans, vegetable stock, rosemary, and garlic to a large heavy saucepan, bring to a simmer, and simmer until the beans are tender, 1 to 1½ hours. Season with salt and pepper, remove the pan from the heat, discard the rosemary and garlic, and let the beans cool. (The beans can be cooked in advance, cooled, and refrigerated in an airtight container for up to 24 hours. Let come to room temperature before proceeding.)

Put the beans in a large mixing bowl or, if you plan to serve the salad family-style, a salad bowl. Add the tuna, onion, and sliced celery and set aside.

Put the oil, lemon zest, and lemon juice in a small bowl and whisk together. Season to taste with salt and pepper, then gently stir in the parsley and the mint, if using.

Drizzle the dressing over the salad and toss gently. Season with salt and a few grinds of black pepper and toss again. Scatter the celery hearts over the salad and, if desired, splash a little vinegar over the top to perk up the salad with its distinct acidity.

Divide the salad among 4 salad plates, or serve family-style.

**Variations** This is a salad to have in your repertoire in the summertime, when it can be served as a starter or a light meal. If you like, augment it with greens such as watercress, or with halved cherry tomatoes. Or increase the quantities to make it a main course.

### Quick-Soaking Dried Beans

To quick-soak beans, put them in a heavy pot and add enough water to cover by 3 inches. Bring to a simmer over medium-high heat and simmer for 2 minutes, then remove the pot from the heat and immediately cover it with a tight-fitting lid. Let the beans soak for 1 hour, then drain.

## PRESERVED TUNA

MAKES 12 OUNCES

While you can buy preserved tuna, making your own is easy and will yield a superior product; I suggest you try it at least once if for no other reason than to deepen your connection to the tradition that gave rise to this dish.

This is one of those recipes for which you want to visit a top-notch fish shop. Tell the fishmonger that you want tuna belly, the portion at the bottom (belly side) of the fillet, which is what Italians call ventresca. It's relatively stringy, but it has a high fat content that will keep it nicely moist when slow-cooked and then preserved in oil. For a change of pace, try the recipe with mackerel.

Kosher salt
2 rosemary sprigs
12 ounces tuna belly fillet (see the headnote)
6 large garlic cloves, unpeeled
1½ teaspoons finely grated lemon zest
About 2 cups extra virgin olive oil

Bring a small heavy pot of salted water to a boil over high heat. Holding the rosemary sprigs by the bottom, dip them into the water and blanch for 30 seconds to activate the herb's natural oils and release its flavor. Set the rosemary aside.

Drain and rinse out the pot and carefully wipe it dry. Put the tuna in the pot and scatter the rosemary, garlic, and lemon zest over and around it. Pour in enough oil to cover the tuna by 1 inch and clip a deep-frying thermometer to the side of the pot. Heat over medium heat until the oil reaches about 120°F. Cook, lowering or raising the temperature as necessary to keep it as close to 120°F as possible, until the tuna is cooked through (a sharp thin-bladed knife or metal skewer will pierce easily to the center), about 20 minutes. Remove from the heat and let the tuna cool in the oil.

Once both the tuna and oil are at room temperature, use a slotted spoon to remove the tuna and gently wipe off any solids. Use immediately, or transfer to an airtight container, strain the cooking oil over the tuna, and store in the refrigerator for up to 1 week.

# VITELLO TONNATO

## SLICED CHILLED VEAL WITH TUNA SAUCE

SERVES 4

Vitello tonnato, which has its origins in Piedmont, is one of the all-time-great Italian dishes, a classic that, despite its seemingly disparate parts—who would ever think to sauce veal with a mayonnaise thickened with preserved tuna?—offers perfect harmony.

There are two ways to prepare vitello tonnato. One is with the slices of chilled roasted veal alternated with the thick sauce. While this is an impressive presentation, it requires a bit of finesse and can also be heavier in the eating than I think this dish should be. The other, lighter and simpler, preparation involves draping the slices of veal over a salad and drizzling it with the sauce, which is what I do here. Note that the veal must be chilled for at least 4 hours.

- 1½ pounds veal eye-round, trimmed of any fat or silverskin
- Kosher salt
- Freshly ground black pepper
- ¼ cup plus 2 tablespoons canola oil or other neutral oil
- 1 Spanish onion, coarsely chopped
- 1 carrot, coarsely chopped
- 1 celery stalk, trimmed and coarsely chopped
- 2 large garlic cloves
- 4 oil-packed anchovy fillets
- 2 thyme sprigs
- 1 bay leaf, preferably fresh
- 1 cup dry white wine
- 1 cup Chicken Stock (page 374) or store-bought low-sodium chicken broth
- 3 cups (loosely packed) mixed greens, such as mesclun
- 2 tablespoons extra virgin olive oil
- Tuna Sauce (recipe follows)
- ¼ cup capers, soaked in warm water for 5 minutes and drained

Position a rack in the center of the oven and preheat the oven to 350°F.

Season the veal liberally with salt and pepper.

Heat a Dutch oven or other wide, heavy, ovenproof pot with a tight-fitting lid over medium-high heat. Add ¼ cup of the oil and heat until it is shimmering and almost smoking. Add the veal and sear, turning it with tongs, until nicely browned on all sides, about 4 minutes per side. Transfer the veal to a rack set over a baking sheet, tent loosely with foil, and let rest for 10 minutes.

Meanwhile, pour the remaining 2 tablespoons oil into the pot and heat it until hot. Add the onions, carrots, celery, garlic, anchovies, thyme, and bay leaf and sauté until the onions and garlic are golden brown, about 5 minutes. Pour in the wine and bring it to a boil, stirring with a wooden spoon to loosen any flavorful bits cooked onto the bottom of the pot.

Return the veal to the Dutch oven and pour the stock over it. Bring to a simmer, cover, and transfer to the oven. Cook until an instant-read thermometer plunged into the center of the eye-round reads 135°F, about 15 minutes. Remove the pot from the oven, return the veal to the rack, and let cool. Discard the braising liquid and solids.

When the veal is cool, wrap tightly in plastic wrap, twisting the ends of the plastic wrap to make a tight cylindrical package. Refrigerate for at least 4 hours, or up to 2 days.

When ready to serve, remove the veal from the refrigerator and let it come to room temperature.

Put the greens in a medium mixing bowl, drizzle with the extra virgin olive oil, and season with salt and pepper. Toss, then divide the greens evenly among 4 salad plates.

Unwrap the veal and, using a sharp chef's knife and a steady hand, slice it in smooth, continuous movements into rounds. Drape the veal slices over the greens. Drizzle with the tuna sauce, spooning the sauce up with a tablespoon. (If the sauce is too thick to drizzle elegantly, thin it slightly by whisking in a few drops of hot water.) Top with the capers and a few grinds of black pepper. Serve.

**ISPIRAZIONE** A thinner tuna sauce is drizzled over an appetizer of charred octopus and smoked potatoes for one of the most popular starters at my restaurant Marea; see page 204.

## TUNA SAUCE

MAKES ABOUT 2 CUPS

In addition to serving as the requisite sauce for Vitello Tonnato, this is delicious with boiled ham, as a dip for crudités, and as a sandwich spread.

1 6-ounce can preserved tuna packed in olive oil, preferably Italian or Spanish, or ½ recipe Preserved Tuna (page 33), with its oil
1 cup mayonnaise
2 tablespoons capers, soaked in warm water for 5 minutes and drained
2 oil-packed anchovy fillets
2 tablespoons freshly squeezed lemon juice

Put the tuna and its oil, the mayonnaise, capers, anchovies, and lemon juice in a food processor and pulse just until smooth. Use right away, or refrigerate in an airtight container for up to 3 days. Let come to cool room temperature and rewhisk before serving.

# CARNE ALL'ALBESE

## ALBA-STYLE STEAK TARTARE

SERVES 4

This dish has always been one of my favorite testaments to just how self-sufficient great ingredients can be in a simple combination.

This steak tartare from Alba is the go-to starter once white truffles arrive in the fall, providing the perfect earthy counterpoint to the natural sweetness of the beef, the fresh green flavor of oil and chives, and the potent accompaniment of Parmigiano-Reggiano. Here I pair it with a simple salad of mâche dressed with lemon juice and olive oil, but it's also wonderful on its own. Either way, grilled bread makes a fine accompaniment.

1 pound beef tenderloin or top sirloin, trimmed of fat and any silverskin
2 tablespoons plus 1 teaspoon extra virgin olive oil
1 tablespoon plus 1 teaspoon freshly squeezed lemon juice
2 tablespoons minced fresh chives
Kosher salt
Freshly ground black pepper
2 cups (lightly packed) mâche, washed and spun dry (other fresh greens, such as arugula or watercress, can be substituted)
4 ounces Parmigiano-Reggiano, shaved into shards with a vegetable peeler
4 lemon wedges, for serving

Wrap the beef in plastic wrap and freeze for 10 minutes to firm it up and make it easier to slice. Fill a large metal bowl halfway with ice water and set a smaller metal bowl inside it to chill.

Using a sharp knife, cut the beef into 1/8-inch slices. Stack the slices a few at a time and slice into 1/8-inch-wide strips, then cut into 1/8-inch dice, transferring the dice to the chilled bowl as you work to keep the beef cold.

Add 2 tablespoons of the olive oil, 1 tablespoon of the lemon juice, and the chives to the bowl and season with salt and pepper. Blend the mixture using the back of a fork, to avoid mashing the meat.

In a small bowl, lightly dress the mâche with the remaining 1 teaspoon olive oil and the remaining 1 teaspoon lemon juice. Season with salt and pepper.

Shape the meat into 4 equal patties and set one in the center of each of 4 chilled salad plates. Divide the greens among the plates, arranging them around the meat. Scatter some Parmigiano shards over each serving and serve with the lemon wedges alongside.

**Variations** In the fall, when they're in season, the ultimate finishing touch for this dish would be to shave white truffles (see page 37), the pride of Alba, over each serving. At other times of year, shaved raw white button mushrooms make a surprisingly satisfying addition.

Or, for a pleasing crunch, shave ribbons of celery with a vegetable peeler, put them in ice water for 5 minutes to make them curl, drain, and pat dry with paper towels. Garnish each portion with a few celery curls.

# PORCINI CON UOVO, RADICCHIO, E PARMIGIANO

## BAKED PORCINI MUSHROOMS WITH EGG, RADICCHIO, AND PARMESAN

SERVES 4

On one of my first trips to the Northern Italian region of Piedmont, I visited Ristorante da Cesare in Albaretto della Torre, where chef Cesare Giaconne, one of the masters of Piedmontese cooking, still plies his trade today. There I savored a version of this dish, which unites a number of the foods most closely associated with the region: porcini mushrooms, bagna cauda (see page 185), and white truffle (see below). Specifically, the stem is removed from a porcini mushroom, creating a well perfectly sized to hold an egg yolk, then the two are baked together and served atop a salad of radicchio and endive dressed with an anchovy-rich vinaigrette. The white truffle is optional, but if you are lucky enough to get one, the effect is truly sublime, as the truffle flavor has an incredible affinity with eggs.

4 large (4- to 6-inch) porcini mushroom caps (portobellos can be substituted; in either case, save the stems for another use or slice thin lengthwise and toss raw into the salad)
¼ cup olive oil
Kosher salt
Freshly ground black pepper
4 large egg yolks
1 cup (loosely packed) torn radicchio leaves
1 Belgian endive, trimmed at the root end and separated into spears
¼ cup 2-inch fresh chive batons
¼ cup Bagna Cauda Vinaigrette (page 185)
1 white truffle (1 to 1½ ounces; optional)
4 ounces Parmigiano-Reggiano, shaved into shards with a vegetable peeler

Position a rack in the center of the oven and preheat the oven to 400°F.

Use a pastry brush to brush the porcini caps all over with the oil, setting them top side down on a baking sheet as they are dressed. Season the caps with salt and pepper. Bake until the mushrooms are soft to the touch and very lightly browned, 6 to 8 minutes. (This can be done up to 4 hours ahead of time; cover the mushrooms loosely with foil and keep at room temperature until ready to proceed.)

Use a tablespoon to carefully set one egg yolk in the middle of each mushroom cap without breaking the yolk. Season with salt and pepper. Return the pan to the oven and bake until the yolks are warm but not set, 4 to 5 minutes; check after 2 minutes to prevent overcooking them.

While the mushrooms are baking, put the radicchio, endive spears, and chives in a large bowl. Drizzle with the vinaigrette, season with salt and a few grinds of pepper, and toss gently to coat. Divide the salad among 4 small plates.

When the mushrooms are ready, use a spatula to set one mushroom cap atop the salad in the center of each plate. If using it, shave the white truffle over the mushrooms and salad. Scatter some Parmigiano shards over each serving and serve immediately.

### Storing and Slicing Truffles

Truffles should be consumed as soon as possible after purchase. To prolong their freshness, store them in a clean napkin or paper towel in a glass jar in the refrigerator to keep them from drying out. They may keep for as long as 4 days, but with each passing day, they will lose some of their potency.

The only way to slice truffles is with a truffle slicer, an implement that's expressly designed to shave them paper-thin.

Truffles, especially white truffles, are famously expensive, but there are some alternatives: Spoon some truffle butter over hot dishes instead of shaving fresh truffles over them, or stir truffle paste into preparations in place of black truffles. There are also high-quality frozen black truffles available that are surprisingly reliable (see Sources, page 379).

# SFORMATI DI PARMIGIANO

## PARMESAN CUSTARDS

SERVES 6

Sformati, or custards, are a popular dish in Emilia-Romagna, where they are often made with spring vegetables such as peas or asparagus.

These Parmesan custards are one of my favorites, and they are extremely versatile: top them with sautéed mushrooms in the fall, or serve in place of a cheese course, perhaps drizzled with fig preserves or paired with Mostarda di Cremona (page 149). They can be served warm or cold and need little more than a drizzle of balsamic vinegar. They can also be plated alongside a simple salad or bruschetta for a light meal.

At my Emilia-Romagna–inspired restaurant Osteria Morini, we serve the custards right in the ramekins, showering them with sautéed mushrooms. (At home, this has the extra benefit of making the recipe more forgiving, as accidents can happen when unmolding a custard.)

Unsalted butter, for greasing the ramekins
4 large eggs
1 cup finely grated Parmigiano-Reggiano (about 2 ounces)
1 cup heavy cream
Pinch of freshly grated nutmeg
Kosher salt
Freshly ground black pepper

Position a rack in the center of the oven and preheat the oven to 325°F.

Lightly grease six 4-ounce ramekins or other ovenproof molds with butter. Set aside.

Whisk the eggs in a medium bowl. Add the cheese and whisk just until incorporated (the less you whisk, the more body the finished custards will have). Whisk in the cream and nutmeg and season with a pinch of salt and a few grinds of pepper.

Carefully pour the mixture into the prepared ramekins and use a toothpick or sharp thin-bladed knife to pop any bubbles that form on the surface. (Do not fill the ramekins to the very top; you may not use all of the batter.) Put the ramekins in a deep baking dish and pour enough hot water around the ramekins to come halfway up their sides, taking care not to let any water splash into them. Vent a piece of aluminum foil large enough to cover all of the ramekins by poking it with the toothpick or knife and loosely tent the ramekins. Place the baking pan in the oven and bake until the custards start to pull away from the sides of the ramekins and do not jiggle when gently shaken, 15 to 18 minutes.

Remove the roasting pan from the oven and use oven mitts to carefully lift the ramekins out of the water bath and onto a heatproof surface. Let rest for 5 minutes before serving (see the headnote).

## LUMACHE BRASATO CON POLENTA E FUNGHI

### BRAISED SNAILS WITH POLENTA AND WILD MUSHROOMS

SERVES 4 TO 6

If you find snails to be a surprising ingredient in an Italian cookbook, you're not alone: Most cooks and diners associate them with French cuisine, and with the more appealing French name escargot, than with Italy. But if you venture to the northern region of Piedmont, you will encounter a great deal of French influence, including the use of butter in many recipes.

In addition to being a celebration of autumnal ingredients, this dish offers a wonderful way to introduce the uninitiated to the pleasures of snails, braised here with an assortmentof wild mushrooms that almost serve to camouflage the mollusks because of their similar size and texture. The resulting stew is served over polenta, which drinks in the sauce.

3 tablespoons unsalted butter
2 tablespoons olive oil
1 small Spanish onion, cut into small dice
1 small celery stalk, trimmed and cut into small dice
1 small carrot, cut into small dice
1 shallot, minced
2 large garlic cloves, minced
Kosher salt
Freshly ground black pepper
12 ounces mixed wild mushrooms, such as cremini, hen-of-the-woods, and porcini, trimmed and quartered
1 28-ounce can poached snails, preferably from Burgundy (available at specialty stores, or see Sources, page 379)
8 fresh sage leaves, minced
Needles from 1 rosemary sprig, minced
1 bay leaf, preferably fresh
½ cup brandy
1 cup dry red wine
1½ cups Dark Chicken Stock (page 374)
Polenta (page 168)

Heat a medium heavy saucepan over medium-high heat. Add 2 tablespoons of the butter and the oil and heat until the butter is melted, tipping and tilting the pan to coat it. Add the onions, celery, carrots, shallots, and garlic, season with salt and pepper, and cook until the vegetables begin to soften but do not brown, 4 to 5 minutes. Add the mushrooms, snails, sage, rosemary, and bay leaf and stir to incorporate. Cook until the mushrooms begin to give off their liquid, about 5 minutes.

Pour in the brandy, bring to a simmer, stirring frequently, and simmer until the brandy has almost completely evaporated, about 4 minutes. Pour in the wine, bring to a simmer, and cook, stirring frequently, until the wine has almost completely evaporated, about 5 minutes. Stir in the stock and bring to a boil, then lower the heat so the liquid is simmering and cover with a lid. Braise until the vegetables are tender and the sauce is thick enough to coat the back of a wooden spoon, about 10 minutes. Stir in the remaining tablespoon of butter and season to taste with salt and pepper. Discard the bay leaf.

Spoon some polenta into the center of each plate and top with the snails, mushrooms, and sauce. Serve.

**ISPIRAZIONE** Snails are incorporated into a flavor-packed risotto in the recipe on page 287.

# PEPATA DI COZZE E CANNOLICCHI

## MUSSELS AND RAZOR CLAMS WITH WHITE WINE, GARLIC, AND CHILE

SERVES 4

A dish such as this, dependent on fresh seafood for its success, would be considered a coastal specialty in the United States, but Italy is such a narrow country that one might encounter variations of this dish anywhere, whether inland or along either coast.

3 tablespoons olive oil
2 garlic cloves, smashed with the side of a chef's knife and peeled
4 flat-leaf parsley sprigs, leaves removed and thinly sliced, stems minced
2 bay leaves, preferably fresh
Pinch of red pepper flakes
1 pound razor clams, scrubbed
1 pound mussels, preferably Prince Edward Island, scrubbed and debearded
1½ cups dry white wine
Kosher salt
Freshly ground black pepper
Extra virgin olive oil (optional)
Crusty bread, such as ciabatta, sliced and toasted

Heat a large heavy pot over medium heat. Pour in the olive oil and tip and tilt the pot to coat it, heating the oil until it is shimmering and almost smoking. Add the garlic, parsley stems, bay leaves, and red pepper flakes and cook, stirring frequently with a wooden spoon, until the mixture is fragrant and the garlic has softened but not browned, about 2 minutes. Add the clams and mussels and stir gently to coat them with the oil, without cracking their shells. Add the wine, bring it to a simmer, cover the pot, and let steam for about 5 minutes, gently shaking the pot a few times to help the mollusks open. Remove the lid and use tongs or a slotted spoon to divide the mussels and clams, in their shells, among 4 shallow bowls, discarding any clams or mussels that have not opened.

Raise the heat, bring the liquid to a boil, and boil until reduced by about half, about 6 minutes. Taste the broth and adjust the seasoning with salt and pepper if necessary. Discard the bay leaves.

Pour the broth over the shellfish and top with the sliced parsley leaves. Drizzle with extra virgin olive oil, if desired, finish with a few coarse grinds of pepper, and serve with the bread alongside and an empty bowl for collecting the shells.

**Variations** This dish is best with razor clams, named for their uniquely elongated shells, which resemble a straight razor. But since razor clams are really only available on the East Coast of the United States, you can substitute Manila clams, littlenecks, cockles, or even steamers if necessary.

For a wonderful shellfish risotto, make the Basic Risotto on page 106, using Fish Stock (page 373), and fold in the shellfish just before serving. You can leave the clams and mussels in their shells or shell them, or remove just some from their shells, stirring them into the risotto and garnishing it with those still in their shells.

# CALAMARI RIPIENI

## SQUID STUFFED WITH ZUCCHINI AND SHRIMP

SERVES 6 TO 8 AS AN APPETIZER OR 4 AS A MAIN COURSE

Over my years of visiting and working on the coast of Tuscany, I fell in love with this dish of calamari stuffed with the shrimp called mazzancolle, sautéed with a variety of vegetables that emphasize the shrimp's natural sweetness. In the United States, wild shrimp from the Gulf of Mexico are a suitable stand-in.

If you like, serve this alongside a salad of tomato and arugula dressed with extra virgin olive oil and lemon juice.

3 to 4 tablespoons olive oil, plus more for greasing the baking dish
1 small shallot, minced
1 cup coarsely grated peeled carrots
1 cup coarsely grated zucchini
1 small garlic clove, minced
Scant pinch of red pepper flakes
8 large shrimp (see the headnote), peeled, deveined, and finely diced
1 ¼ pounds cleaned calamari, tentacles and bodies separated, tentacles coarsely chopped
1 tablespoon tomato paste
½ cup dry white wine
10 large fresh basil leaves, thinly sliced lengthwise
½ cup dried bread crumbs
1 large egg, lightly beaten
Kosher salt
Freshly ground black pepper
¾ cup Seasoned Toasted Bread Crumbs (page xxix)

Heat a medium skillet over medium heat. Pour in 2 tablespoons of the oil and tip and tilt the pan to coat it, heating the oil until it is shimmering and almost smoking. Add the shallots, carrots, zucchini, garlic, and red pepper flakes and cook, stirring with a wooden spoon, until the vegetables are softened but not browned, about 5 minutes. Stir in the shrimp and chopped calamari tentacles and cook, stirring periodically, until they begin to firm up, about 2 minutes. Add the tomato paste, stirring to coat the other ingredients, and cook until it turns a shade darker, about 2 minutes.

Stir in ¼ cup of the wine, bring to a simmer, and simmer until it has almost completely evaporated, 3 to 4 minutes. Stir in the basil, transfer the shellfish mixture to a bowl, and set aside to cool.

Meanwhile, position a rack in the center of the oven and preheat the oven to 350°F. Grease a glass baking dish large and deep enough to hold the stuffed calamari in a single layer without crowding.

Add the dried bread crumbs and egg to the cooled shellfish mixture and season with salt and a few grinds of black pepper. Stir just to incorporate the ingredients; do not overmix.

Use a teaspoon to carefully fill the calamari bodies about two-thirds full with the shellfish mixture, arranging them in the baking dish. Drizzle them with a tablespoon or two of the remaining oil. Season with salt and pepper and top with the seasoned bread crumbs. Pour the remaining ¼ cup wine around the calamari. Bake until the calamari are lightly golden brown and the filling is hot to the touch, 10 to 12 minutes.

Divide the calamari among individual plates and serve hot.

**Variation** For a luxurious version of this dish, replace the shrimp with the meat from the claws and body of a poached 1½-pound lobster, preferably Maine lobster. If your grocery store or fish shop sells already steamed lobster, you can use the meat from one of those in this recipe.

# CAPPON MAGRO

## LIGURIAN SEAFOOD SALAD

SERVES 4

The essence of Italian cookery, this very loosely defined, interpretive salad, believed to have originated in Genoa, was first conceived as a way for frugal fishermen to make use of whatever they didn't sell dockside or at the market on a given day. Its name, which means "lean capon" or "lean chicken," is a playful nod to the fact that there's no actual meat in the dish. Feel free to incorporate other shellfish, or even pieces of poached finfish such as bluefish.

- 1 garlic clove
- 4 oil-packed anchovy fillets
- 2 hard-boiled eggs, halved, plus whites from 2 hard-boiled eggs, minced
- ½ cup extra virgin olive oil
- Juice of 1 lemon
- Kosher salt
- Freshly ground black pepper
- An herb sachet (3 thyme sprigs, 1 bay leaf, and 1 teaspoon whole black peppercorns, tied in a cheesecloth bundle)
- 8 ounces medium shrimp, peeled and deveined
- 8 ounces mussels, preferably Prince Edward Island, scrubbed and debearded
- 8 ounces cleaned calamari, tentacles and bodies separated
- 8 ounces Red Bliss potatoes
- 1 cup string beans (halved crosswise)
- 1 cup (about 4 ounces) grape tomatoes
- ¼ cup taggiasca or other Ligurian black olives, or Niçoise or kalamata olives
- 2 tablespoons capers, soaked in warm water for 5 minutes and drained
- 4 big cup-shaped butter lettuce leaves
- ½ cup (loosely packed) diced celery heart (pale yellow and green stalks and leaves from the center of a bunch of celery)
- 2 tablespoons thinly sliced fresh flat-leaf parsley leaves

To make the vinaigrette: Put the garlic, anchovies, and 2 hard-boiled eggs in the bowl of a food processor. With the processor running, slowly add the oil in a thin stream, processing until a thick, emulsified dressing is formed, then add the lemon juice. Season with salt and pepper. (The vinaigrette can be refrigerated in an airtight container for up to 1 week.)

Bring a large pot of salted water to a rolling boil. Fill a large bowl halfway with ice water. Add the herb sachet to the boiling water and let the herbs infuse the water for 5 minutes.

Using a fine-mesh strainer or pasta insert, cook the seafood, one type at a time, by lowering it into the boiling water, then transferring it to the ice water when done to cool it and stop the cooking. Cook the shrimp until firm and pink, 2 to 3 minutes; the mussels until they have opened, about 5 minutes (discard any that have not opened); and the calamari until firm and white, about 4 minutes. Drain again and transfer to a bowl.

Empty the pot, fill it halfway with fresh water, and bring to a boil over high heat. Refill the ice-water bowl with fresh ice water. Add the potatoes to the boiling water and boil until tender to the tines of a fork, about 12 minutes, adding the string beans to the water for the last 2 minutes of cooking. Use tongs or a slotted spoon to transfer the beans to the ice water to shock them and stop the cooking, then drain them. Drain the potatoes and, when cool enough to handle, quarter them. Set aside.

Put the poached seafood, potatoes, string beans, tomatoes, olives, and capers in a large bowl. Drizzle with the vinaigrette and gently toss to coat. Put 1 lettuce leaf on each of 4 chilled salad plates and fill with the seafood salad. Garnish with the hard-boiled egg whites, celery heart, and parsley. Serve.

## STRACCETTI DI MANZO CON RUCOLA

### SEARED STEAK AND ARUGULA SALAD

SERVES 4

This gloriously down-and-dirty all-in-one meal comes from Rome, where inexpensive cuts of beef—what we'd call the top round or sirloin—are seared hard in a cast-iron pan, then cut into strips, or *straccetti*. The pan is deglazed with balsamic vinegar to create a quick dressing, which is tossed with a salad of arugula and tomatoes right in the pan, then plated and topped with the sliced beef.

12 ounces top round, sirloin, or eye-round, trimmed of excess fat
Kosher salt
Freshly ground black pepper
2 tablespoons canola oil or other neutral oil
¼ cup balsamic vinegar
3 cups (loosely packed) arugula, rinsed and spun dry
¼ cup olive oil
2 cups grape or cherry tomatoes, halved
1 tablespoon minced fresh rosemary
4 ounces Parmigiano-Reggiano, shaved into shards with a vegetable peeler

Season the beef generously with salt and pepper and drizzle on both sides with the canola oil.

Heat a large cast-iron skillet over high heat until very hot. (If you have an exhaust fan over your stove, turn it on. If there's a smoke detector in or near your kitchen, turn it off; be sure to turn it back on after cooking the meat.) Add the beef to the pan and cook until it is nicely seared on the first side and no longer sticks to the pan, 4 to 5 minutes. Use tongs to turn the beef over and cook on the other side until medium-rare, another 4 to 5 minutes. Transfer to a rack and tent loosely with foil; let rest for 5 minutes.

Meanwhile, let the pan cool slightly then return to the stove top over medium heat; add the vinegar to the pan and stir with a wooden spoon to loosen any flavorful bits cooked onto the bottom of the pan. Remove the pan from the heat, add the arugula, and toss briefly to wilt it and coat it with the vinegar. Add the olive oil, tomatoes, and rosemary, season with salt and pepper, and toss quickly. Divide the salad among 4 plates.

Slice the meat into thin strips, drape the strips over the salad, and garnish with the cheese shards. Serve at once.

**ISPIRAZIONE** Skirt Steak Salad (page 225) is an updated, slightly fancified version of this dish.

# BRUCIATINI ALL'ACETO BALSAMICO

## WARM RADICCHIO AND PROSCIUTTO SALAD

SERVES 4

This Emilia-Romagna classic was first dreamed up as a way to use the ends and other odd cuts of prosciutto that would otherwise go to waste, employing them to flavor a warm balsamic dressing where their less-than-appealing appearance wouldn't be a liability. In this salad of un-shy flavors, the assertive dressing is matched by the sturdy greens, scallions, and red onions.

4 1-inch-thick slices peasant bread, crusts removed
1 garlic clove, halved
About 2 tablespoons olive oil
Kosher salt
1 small head of radicchio, cored and leaves separated
1 small head of baby romaine or romaine heart, coarsely chopped
½ cup thinly sliced scallions
½ small red onion, thinly sliced
Warm Balsamic Vinaigrette (recipe follows)
Freshly ground black pepper
4 ounces Parmigiano-Reggiano, shaved into shards with a vegetable peeler

Toast the bread slices. Rub one side of each slice with a cut side of the garlic clove. Drizzle with the olive oil and sprinkle with a pinch of salt. Cut each slice into 1-inch cubes.

Put the radicchio, romaine, scallions, and red onions in a large salad bowl. Pour the warm vinaigrette over the salad, season with salt and a few grinds of pepper, add the cubed bread, and toss gently.

Divide the salad among 4 small plates. Scatter some Parmigiano shards over each portion and serve.

**Variation** To add another layer of flavor to this salad, make it with the smoked prosciutto called speck (see Sources, page 379).

### *VINAIGRETTE ALL'ACETO BALSAMICO*

### WARM BALSAMIC VINAIGRETTE

MAKES ABOUT ⅔ CUP

This dressing is also delicious on spinach salad and salads made with other sturdy greens, such as frisée. Ask your butcher to set the slicer to the number 3 setting when slicing the prosciutto.

4 tablespoons unsalted butter
4 ounces sliced prosciutto (see the headnote), sliced into ½-inch-wide strips
¼ cup red wine vinegar
¼ cup balsamic vinegar
Kosher salt
Freshly ground black pepper

Heat a large heavy sauté pan over medium-low heat. Add 2 tablespoons of the butter and melt it, tipping and turning the pan to coat it. Add the prosciutto and cook, stirring frequently with a wooden spoon, until warmed through but not crispy or browned. Stir in the red wine vinegar and balsamic vinegar, bring to a simmer, and simmer until the vinegar is slightly reduced and its assertive acidic flavor has diminished, about 2 minutes. Add the remaining 2 tablespoons butter and melt it, stirring to incorporate. Season with salt and pepper and use immediately.

## POLPETTE ALLA BOLOGNESE

### MEATBALLS BRAISED IN TOMATO SAUCE

SERVES 4 TO 6

If you've had too many leaden meatballs, authentic Italian meatballs may be a revelation to you. These are fashioned in the style of Emilia-Romagna, and they are all about the meat—specifically pork, mortadella, and prosciutto—without the abundance of dried herbs such as oregano and garlic powder often added to American meatballs. Thanks to the inclusion of milk and eggs, they come out light as air. You can eat three or four of them and be satiated but not uncomfortably full. Here they are browned, then simmered in a classic tomato sauce. If your butcher or deli counter cannot grind the meats for you, cut them into small dice and pulse them in a food processor just until very finely chopped.

Note that the seasoned meat mixture must be refrigerated for 1 hour.

3 slices white bread, crust removed
1 cup whole milk
1 pound ground pork shoulder
4 ounces ground mortadella
4 ounces ground prosciutto
1 cup finely grated Parmigiano-Reggiano (about 2 ounces), plus more for serving
2 large eggs, lightly beaten
1/8 teaspoon freshly grated nutmeg
Kosher salt
Freshly ground black pepper
2 tablespoons canola oil
6 cups Tomato Sauce with Basil (page 74)
Seasoned Toasted Bread Crumbs (page xxix; optional)

Put the bread and milk in a small bowl and let soak for 10 minutes. Remove the bread (discard any milk that hasn't been absorbed by the bread), tear into 1/4-inch pieces, and transfer to a large mixing bowl.

Add the pork, mortadella, prosciutto, Parmigiano, and eggs to the bread; season with the nutmeg, salt, and a few grinds of pepper; and knead just until incorporated. Cover the bowl with plastic wrap and refrigerate for 1 hour.

Form the chilled pork mixture into golf-ball-size balls; you should have about 14 meatballs.

Heat a large wide nonstick sauté pan over medium-high heat. Pour in the oil and tip and tilt the pan to coat it with the oil, heating the oil until it is shimmering and almost smoking. Add the meatballs and cook, turning occasionally, until they are browned on all sides, about 10 minutes. Pour in the tomato sauce and bring to a simmer. Reduce the heat to medium-low, cover the pan, and simmer until the meatballs are cooked through (they will puff up), about 20 minutes.

Transfer to a serving platter, top with grated Parmigiano and with the bread crumbs, if using, and serve.

# PIZZE

## PIZZA

I grew up in the American heartland, and the pizza of my youth was thick and chewy, topped with "homegrown" cheese that was the subject of local pride, and loaded with enough toppings to constitute a meal in their own right. It was Americanized pizza, meant to be eaten after a long day's work or while watching the Sunday game, accompanied by a cold beer.

There are about twenty-five varieties of pizza in the United States, most of them named for cities or regions. Among others, there's that Midwestern-style thin-crust pizza; Chicago deep-dish pizza, which very much resembles a pie; and New York–style, which is a version of Neapolitan pizza, cooked in a large coal-fired oven.

I had my first taste of Italian pizza at Pizzeria Flo in Imola, in 1993, and I was struck by the exquisitely thin crust and the way they topped the pizza with prosciutto and arugula *after* it came out of the oven to preserve the character of those ingredients.

There are essentially three types of pizza in Italy: Roman-style, with a thin crust arrived at by rolling the dough out paper-thin with a wooden dowel and topped with very little condimento; the chewier Neapolitan-style, made with a more hydrated dough that cooks in 75 to 90 seconds in the 900-plus-degree furnace of a wood-fired oven; and the less well-known here but equally popular pizza al taglio (pizza by the slice), made with a long-fermented dough that is cut into squares and sold by weight. The dough is baked, usually on large blackened baking sheets in electric flatbread ovens, then finished with the toppings.

While you can make delicious pizza at home, the truth is that unless you own an outdoor pizza oven, you will not be able to replicate what is served in the finest restaurants, because your oven likely tops out at around 500 degrees. Accordingly, rather than attempt to match what is served in restaurants, in this chapter I offer a basic pizza dough that produces a crust somewhere between the Neapolitan and the Roman style and will yield good, consistent results in a home oven; in fact, it's modeled after the recipes I've seen made in home kitchens throughout Italy.

I do urge you to invest in a pizza stone, which will hold the heat and ensure even cooking and a crispy crust. Avoid small round stones and instead purchase a slab-style block that will essentially act as a shelf in the oven. Improvised techniques, such as using an inverted cookie sheet, will work, but these are clumsy and the results are spotty. I also suggest purchasing a pizza peel, the implement used to shuttle pizzas in and out of an oven, which will make it infinitely easier to accomplish that task at home.

# IMPASTO PER PIZZA

## PIZZA DOUGH

MAKES ENOUGH FOR TWO 12-INCH PIZZAS

This recipe produces a reliable all-purpose pizza dough for home baking. It's best made with 00 flour, but you can use all-purpose flour.

Each of the recipes in this chapter makes two pizzas, except for Sfincione (page 55), which makes one larger rectangular one. If you want to make more pizzas, simply multiply the ingredients accordingly.

2 tablespoons olive oil, plus more for oiling the bowl and the dough
1 1/3 cups lukewarm water
1 package (2 1/4 teaspoons) active dry yeast
1/2 teaspoon sugar
3 1/2 cups 00 flour or King Arthur Italian-Style flour (see Sources, page 379) or all-purpose flour plus more for dusting
1 tablespoon kosher salt

Lightly oil a large bowl with olive oil.

Put the water, yeast, and sugar in the bowl of a stand mixer fitted with the whisk attachment and whisk until well combined. Let rest until the mixture foams, about 5 minutes.

Replace the whisk with the dough hook and start the motor at low speed. Add 2 1/2 cups of the flour and the salt and mix just until incorporated, then gradually sprinkle in the remaining 1 cup flour, mixing until it is just incorporated.

With the mixer running, drizzle in the 2 tablespoons oil. Mix until a dough forms, then turn it out onto a floured surface and knead it until it is elastic and no longer tacky. Transfer the dough to the oiled bowl. Place a damp kitchen towel over the bowl and set aside in a warm place to rise until doubled in size, 1 1/2 to 2 hours.

Divide the dough into 2 equal pieces and shape each piece into a smooth ball. Use a pastry brush to brush the tops with olive oil to keep a skin from forming, then wrap each one in plastic wrap. Refrigerate for at least 12 hours, or up to 2 days.

### Tips for Successful Pizza Making

- Add the sauce before you bake the pizza, but do not add the cheese until halfway through the baking time, or it will likely overcook.
- Don't be afraid to cook pizza well; it might look done, but let it go until the dough is slightly charred and the cheese is bubbling.
- It can be tempting to load a pizza up with toppings, but too many will weigh it down and obscure the flavor of the cheese, sauce, and dough; use restraint.
- After removing the pizza from the oven, let it rest for 2 minutes to allow the molten cheese to set a bit and keep it from sliding off the pizza.

## POMODORO SEMPLICE

### BASIC PIZZA SAUCE

MAKES ABOUT 2 CUPS

If you're accustomed to slow-cooked pizzeria sauce redolent of garlic powder and oregano, you may be pleasantly surprised by the clean, vibrant flavor of this uncooked one, made with fresh garlic and just a pinch of dried oregano.

Note that the sauce must be refrigerated for at least 3 hours before using.

- 1 28-ounce can whole tomatoes, preferably Italian San Marzano or organic, crushed by hand or briefly blended with their juice
- ¼ cup extra virgin olive oil
- 2 garlic cloves, smashed with the side of a chef's knife and peeled
- 6 fresh basil leaves, torn into small pieces
- Pinch of dried oregano
- Kosher salt
- Freshly ground black pepper

Put the tomatoes, oil, garlic, basil, and oregano in a medium bowl. Season with salt and a few grinds of pepper. Stir, cover, and refrigerate for at least 3 hours, or up to 24 hours, to marry the flavors. Use a spoon to fish out and discard the garlic before spreading the sauce on the pizza dough.

# PIZZA MARGHERITA

## TOMATO AND BASIL PIZZA

MAKES TWO 12-INCH PIZZAS

This is the queen of all pizzas, the one that's known in some form around the world as the tomato-cheese original. If you've never made pizza, this basic pie is the perfect one to begin your education.

Note that the dough must be removed from the refrigerator about 2 hours before you bake the pizzas.

Pizza Dough (page 50)
All-purpose flour, 00 flour, or King Arthur Italian-Style flour, for dusting
Cornmeal, for dusting the pizza peel
2 cups Basic Pizza Sauce (page 51)
1 ball (about 1 pound) fresh mozzarella, drained and torn into 1-inch pieces
About ¼ cup extra virgin olive oil
5 large fresh basil leaves, torn into large pieces

Remove the dough from the refrigerator about 2 hours before you plan to make the pizzas; this will make it easier to roll.

Position a rack in the center of the oven, set a pizza stone on the rack, and preheat the oven to 500°F.

Generously flour a work surface and lightly roll out one piece of the dough with a floured rolling pin, rotating the dough as you roll, until it is about 12 inches in diameter and uniformly ¼ inch thick. In one smooth, deft movement, lift the pizza onto a cornmeal-dusted peel. (If you do not have a peel, use an inverted cookie sheet to transfer the pizza to and from the stone.)

Ladle half of the tomato sauce onto the dough, then use the bottom of the ladle to spread it evenly, leaving a ½-inch border all around. Slide the dough onto the pizza stone and bake for 3 to 4 minutes. Open the oven, slide out the rack, and quickly arrange half of the mozzarella over the pizza, then bake until the cheese is bubbly and the dough is golden brown around the edges, 3 to 4 more minutes.

Carefully slide the pizza back onto the peel, then transfer it to a cutting board. Drizzle with half the oil, scatter half of the basil over the pizza, and let the pizza rest for 2 minutes, then cut it into 6 or 8 slices, transfer to a serving plate or plates, and serve immediately.

Repeat with the remaining dough and toppings.

# PIZZA PROFUMATO AL ROSMARINO

## ROSEMARY AND OLIVE OIL PIZZA

MAKES TWO 12-INCH PIZZAS

If you're going to serve pizza as a starter rather than a meal, this variation on a pizza bianca, or white pizza, with no cheese or sauce, is lighter than most and gets along well with just about any cocktail or wine.

Note that the dough must be removed from the refrigerator about 2 hours before you bake the pizzas.

Pizza Dough (page 50)
All-purpose flour, 00 flour, or King Arthur Italian-Style flour for dusting
Cornmeal, for dusting the pizza peel
Needles from 4 large rosemary sprigs, chopped
¼ cup extra virgin olive oil
Kosher salt

Remove the dough from the refrigerator about 2 hours before you plan to make the pizzas; this will make it easier to roll.

Position a rack in the center of the oven, set a pizza stone on the rack, and preheat the oven to 500°F.

Generously flour a work surface and lightly roll out one piece of the dough with a floured rolling pin, rotating the dough as you roll, until it is about 12 inches in diameter and uniformly ¼ inch thick. In one smooth, deft movement, lift the pizza onto a cornmeal-dusted pizza peel. (If you do not have a peel, use an inverted cookie sheet to transfer the pizza to and from the stone.)

Sprinkle half the rosemary over the dough and drizzle with half the oil. Season with salt and slide the pizza onto the pizza stone. Bake until the pizza is golden brown and crispy, 5 to 6 minutes. Carefully slide the pizza back onto the peel, then transfer it to a cutting board and let it rest for 2 minutes.

Cut the pizza into 6 or 8 slices, transfer to a serving plate or plates, and serve immediately.

Repeat with the remaining dough and toppings.

# SFINCIONE

## CARAMELIZED ONION AND BREAD CRUMB PIZZA

MAKES 1 LARGE RECTANGULAR PIZZA

This specialty of the Sicilian town of Palermo is traditionally cooked in a large, deep rectangular pan. It is topped with tomato sauce, lightly caramelized onions, and bread crumbs. It is usually made with caciocavallo cheese, which has a firm mozzarella-like texture and is aged to yield a nutty flavor similar to that you'd find in an aged provolone.

Note that the dough must rest in the baking pan for about 2 hours before you add the toppings, and then it must rise for about 30 minutes before you bake the pizza.

About 3 tablespoons olive oil
Pizza Dough (page 50)
3 large Spanish onions, thinly sliced
2 cups Basic Pizza Sauce (page 51)
2 cups (about 8 ounces) shredded caciocavallo cheese (Provolone or fresh mozzarella can be substituted)
1 cup Seasoned Toasted Bread Crumbs (page xxix)

Use a pastry brush to brush a 9½ by 13-inch baking pan lightly with ½ tablespoon of the oil. Place the dough in the baking pan and brush the top of the dough with ½ tablespoon of the oil. Cover the dough with plastic wrap and let rise for 2 hours at room temperature.

Meanwhile, heat a large heavy skillet over medium-low heat. Add the remaining 2 tablespoons of oil and tip and tilt the pan to coat it, warming the oil. Add the onions and cook, stirring occasionally, until they are golden and tender and starting to caramelize, about 25 minutes. Remove from the heat and set aside to cool completely.

Remove the plastic wrap from the dough and stretch the dough so it fills the baking sheet and is uniformly about ¼ inch thick.

Spread the tomato sauce over the dough in an even layer, leaving a ½-inch border all around. Top with the caramelized onions. Loosely cover the pizza with plastic wrap and set aside at room temperature to rise, about 30 minutes.

Position a rack in the center of the oven, set a pizza stone on the rack, and preheat the oven to 450°F.

Place the baking sheet on the pizza stone and bake for 5 minutes. Open the oven, slide out the rack, and scatter the cheese over the pizza, then bake until it is golden brown and crispy, 5 to 7 minutes longer. Remove the pizza from the oven, sprinkle with the toasted bread crumbs, and let rest for 2 minutes, then slice and serve.

# PIZZA PROSCIUTTO E RUCOLA

## ARUGULA AND PROSCIUTTO PIZZA

MAKES TWO 12-INCH PIZZAS

Fashioned after the first genuine Italian pizza I ever had, this recipe adds the arugula and prosciutto after baking the crust, sauce, and cheese to keep them fresh and flavorful.

Note that the dough must be removed from the refrigerator about 2 hours before you bake the pizzas.

Pizza Dough (page 50)
All-purpose flour, 00 flour, or King Arthur Italian-Style flour for dusting
Cornmeal, for dusting the pizza peel
2 cups Basic Pizza Sauce (page 51)
1 ball (about 1 pound) fresh mozzarella, drained and torn into 1- to 2-inch pieces
6 ounces thinly sliced prosciutto, torn into large pieces
1 cup (loosely packed) arugula

Remove the dough from the refrigerator about 2 hours before you plan to make the pizzas; this will make it easier to roll.

Position a rack in the center of the oven, set a pizza stone on the rack, and preheat the oven to 500°F.

Generously flour a work surface and lightly roll out the dough with a floured rolling pin, rotating the dough as you roll, until it is about 12 inches in diameter and uniformly 1/4 inch thick. In one smooth, deft movement, lift the pizza onto a cornmeal-dusted pizza peel. (If you do not have a peel, use an inverted cookie sheet to transfer the pizza to and from the stone.)

Ladle half of the tomato sauce onto the dough, then use the bottom of the ladle to spread it evenly, leaving a 1/2-inch border all around. Slide the dough onto the pizza stone and bake for 3 to 4 minutes. Open the oven, slide out the rack, and quickly arrange half of the mozzarella over the pizza, then bake until the cheese is bubbly and the dough is golden brown around the edges, 3 to 4 more minutes.

Carefully slide the pizza back onto the peel, then transfer it to a cutting board. Scatter half of the prosciutto and arugula over the pizza and let rest for 2 minutes, then cut the pizza into 6 or 8 slices, transfer to a serving plate or plates, and serve immediately.

Repeat with the remaining dough and toppings.

# ZUPPE
# SOUPS

More than just about any other category of Italian food, soups have their roots in utility. The very nature of soup—combining vegetables with shellfish or fish, poultry, and/or meat in a base of water or stock—makes it the perfect destination for leftover or just-past-their-prime ingredients that are at the forefront of so many Italian dishes. Just consider ribollita, made with a long and flexible roster of vegetables; or pappa al pomodoro (Tomato and Bread Soup, page 65) made of stale bread and overripe tomatoes and not much else. Accordingly, many recipes for soups change with the seasons; for example, the eggplant that shows up in a minestrone in the summer might be replaced by potatoes in the fall.

Many Italian soups are finished with a spoonful of pesto, a drizzle of extra virgin olive oil, a scattering of grated Parmigiano-Reggiano, and/or a coarse grind of black pepper. To be honest, the original recipes can be somewhat "one-frequency," without a lot of peaks and valleys, and these finishing touches are a quick way to bring another dimension to the soup.

Of course, when we cook Italian food here in America, we are more likely to shop for the ingredients for soups than we are to call on them as a way to use leftovers. And soups are also often served as meals in their own right, as opposed to their place in the Italian meal, where they are an alternative to pasta or risotto. (Collectively, pasta, risotto, and soup are referred to as minestre, although I've given soup its own chapter here to reflect the way Americans eat.)

Because of their often improvisational origins, soups are especially amenable to interpretation and adjustment. Feel free to vary the vegetables, seafood, and meat in these recipes and to use water in place of stock when it's called for, as that's how many of them were originally prepared. You can also make the soups thicker, either by reducing the amount of liquid or by pureeing a portion of the soup and stirring it back into the pot; or thin them with additional stock or water.

# MINESTRONE

## VEGETABLE SOUP

SERVES 4 TO 6

Over the years, the availability of mass-produced canned soups in America has diluted the charms of minestrone, which many of us have come to associate with an anemic, nondescript vegetable soup. The irony is that while the word minestrone doesn't actually mean anything more than "vegetable soup," in Italy, it's a vehicle for using up an abundance of vegetables at the peak of their season, promising something quite special.

The versatility of minestrone allows for a wide range of options: It can be made with beef, chicken, or vegetable broth, or simply water; it may or may not include tomatoes; and it can be augmented with rice or pasta. My favorite minestrone is made with beans, with their cooking liquid employed to add flavor and texture to the soup, as in this recipe.

The better your vegetables, the better this soup will be, and like so many soups, it will be better still if you finish it with extra virgin olive oil and grated Parmigiano-Reggiano cheese.

1 cup dried cannellini beans
3 garlic cloves, 1 smashed and peeled, 2 minced
2 Spanish onions, 1 halved through the root end, 1 coarsely chopped
Kosher salt
Freshly ground black pepper
2 tablespoons olive oil
1 leek (white part only), well washed and coarsely chopped
1 carrot, coarsely chopped
1 celery stalk, trimmed and coarsely chopped
2 cups shredded cabbage, preferably savoy
1 14-ounce can chopped tomatoes, preferably Italian San Marzano or organic, with their juice
2 cups water
An herb sachet (2 thyme sprigs, 1 bay leaf, and 2 parsley stems, tied in a cheesecloth bundle)
3 cups chopped greens, such as Swiss chard or kale
Extra virgin olive oil, for serving (optional)
Basil Pesto (page 369; optional)
A wedge of Parmigiano-Reggiano, for grating (optional)

Put the beans in a bowl, cover with cold water, and soak overnight. (Alternatively, you can quick-soak the beans; see page 30.) Drain.

Put the soaked beans, smashed garlic clove, and onion halves in a medium heavy saucepan and cover by 1 inch with cold water. Bring to a boil over high heat, then lower the heat and simmer until the beans are tender, 1 to 1½ hours. Use a slotted spoon to remove and discard the onion and garlic. Season the broth to taste with salt and pepper.

Heat a medium heavy soup pot over medium heat. Pour in the olive oil, tilting and turning the pot to coat it and heating the oil until it is shimmering and almost smoking. Add the chopped onions, leeks, carrots, and celery and cook, stirring with a wooden spoon, until tender but not browned, about 5 minutes. Add the minced garlic and cabbage and cook, stirring, until the cabbage is wilted, about 4 minutes. Stir in the tomatoes, with their liquid, and cook until they begin to break down, about 7 minutes. Taste and adjust the seasoning with salt and pepper.

Stir in the beans, along with their cooking liquid, and add the water and herb sachet. Raise the heat to high and bring the liquid to a boil, then reduce the heat so the liquid is simmering, cover, and cook until the vegetables are nicely al dente and the broth has a robust vegetal flavor, about 30 minutes. Stir in the greens until wilted, then season with salt and pepper. Remove and discard the herb sachet.

To serve, divide the soup among 4 to 6 bowls. Drizzle with extra virgin olive oil and/or pesto, if using; grate some Parmigiano over each serving, if desired; and finish with a few grinds of black pepper.

**Variation** To make ribollita (meaning, literally, "twice-boiled"), a popular Tuscan bread soup, reheat leftover minestrone in a pot within 2 days of making it, then puree about one third of the soup with an immersion blender, or ladle it into a stand blender, puree, and stir it back into the pot. Meanwhile, arrange 4 to 6 bread slices (depending on how much soup you have) in a single layer on a baking sheet and drizzle with olive oil. Toast in a 400°F oven until golden brown, about 12 minutes. As soon as the slices are cool enough to handle, tear into pieces, add to the soup, and stir until the pieces begin to break down and thicken it, allowing several minutes for the bread to absorb the liquid. Ladle the soup into bowls, drizzle with extra virgin olive oil, grind a generous amount of pepper over the top, and finish with a grating of Parmigiano-Reggiano.

### Seasoning Bean Dishes

When seasoning soups and other preparations that feature beans, take care not to season too aggressively with salt, or the beans will become tough and shed their skins; you can correct the seasoning after the soup is finished.

# PASTA E FAGIOLI

## PASTA AND BEAN SOUP

SERVES 4 TO 6 GENEROUSLY

Pasta e fagioli is a thick soup of borlotti (cranberry) beans, herbs (I prefer rosemary and sage), and usually some kind of pork product. I like prosciutto skin, but you can use a number of common supermarket items to impart the desired porky saltiness; a smoked ham hock would also work well. Just before serving, a small tubular pasta such as tubetini or ditalini or a fresh pasta such as maltagliati is added, and then the soup is finished with olive oil, black pepper, sea salt, and parsley. This is the first soup I learned to make at Spiaggia, though there we actually made zuppa di gran farro alla Lucchese, meaning "in the style of Lucca," where pasta e fagioli is fortified with farro instead of pasta; see the variation below.

1½ cups dried borlotti (cranberry) beans
3 ounces smoky bacon, diced (slab bacon or salt pork can be substituted)
½ cup olive oil
1 Spanish onion, cut into small dice
1 large celery stalk, trimmed and cut into small dice
1 large carrot, cut into small dice
3 garlic cloves, thinly sliced
6 cups water
1 14-ounce can whole tomatoes, preferably San Marzano or organic, crushed by hand, with their juice
1 rosemary sprig
1 sage sprig
Kosher salt
1 cup ditalini, tubetini, or other small dried pasta
2 tablespoons thinly sliced fresh flat-leaf parsley leaves
Freshly ground black pepper
Extra virgin olive oil, for serving
A wedge of Parmigiano-Reggiano, for grating

Put the beans in a bowl, cover with cold water, and soak overnight. (Alternatively, you can quick-soak the beans; see page 30.) Drain.

Heat a large heavy pot over low heat. Add the bacon and cook, stirring, just until it is lightly browned, about 4 minutes. Pour in ¼ cup of the olive oil, raise the heat to medium-high, and heat it for a minute or two. Stir in the onions, celery, carrots, and garlic and cook, stirring occasionally, until the vegetables are softened but not browned, about 10 minutes. Add the beans, water, and tomatoes, with their juice, raise the heat to high, and bring to a boil. Lower the heat so the liquid is simmering, add the rosemary and sage, and cook until the beans are tender, 1 to 1½ hours.

While the soup is cooking, bring a medium pot of salted water to a boil. Add the pasta and cook until al dente, about 6 minutes. Drain and transfer to a mixing bowl. Add the remaining ¼ cup olive oil and the parsley and season with salt and pepper. Toss and set aside.

When the soup is ready, fish out the herbs with tongs and discard them. Season the soup to taste with salt and pepper.

The consistency of the soup is a matter of personal preference: I prefer a thicker soup in the winter and a brothier one in the summer. If you find it too thick, thin it with water. Or, for a thicker, heartier soup, ladle 1 to 2 cups of the solids into a food mill or food processor, pass through the mill or process, and stir back into the soup. Or use an immersion blender, tilting the pot to consolidate the solids, and blend some of them to attain your preferred consistency.

Stir the pasta into the soup and rewarm it.

Ladle the soup into large bowls, drizzle with extra-virgin olive oil, and grate some cheese over each serving. Finish with a few grinds of black pepper and serve immediately.

**Variations** This is a versatile recipe. To make zuppa di fagioli, or bean soup, such as the one pictured on page 63, simply omit the pasta.

For a richer flavor, replace the water with Chicken Stock (page 374) or add a bouillon cube.

For an even thicker, heartier soup, whisk a mashed peeled baked potato into the finished soup.

To make the soup with farro (see the headnote), replace the pasta with 1 cup farro (see page 167), cooked according to the package instructions. For a more Roman-style soup, substitute fresh maltagliati for the small pasta.

If you like, stir 1 pound kale (coarse stems and ribs removed), cut into thick ribbons (about 4 cups), into the soup along with the pasta.

# JOTA

## SAUERKRAUT AND POTATO SOUP

SERVES 4 TO 6

This soup hails from the northern region of Alto Adige, which was once a part of the Austro-Hungarian empire, a heritage that explains the distinctly non-Italian-seeming central combination. I add some cannellini beans, both for texture and to root it in people's expectations of an Italian soup. It's easy to prepare, and the earthy potatoes provide the perfect foil for the tang and crunch of the sauerkraut. The soup is delicious with a garnish of small croutons (see the variation), or with a last-second addition of about 2 tablespoons cooked pastina or other small pasta per bowl.

1 cup dried cannellini beans
¼ cup olive oil
2 ounces slab bacon, cut into small dice
1 large Spanish onion, cut into small dice
4 large garlic cloves, smashed with the side of a chef's knife and peeled
5 medium Idaho or russet potatoes, peeled and cut into large dice
2 cups packaged sauerkraut, with its liquid
8 cups Chicken Stock (page 374)
An herb sachet (10 juniper berries, smashed, 3 thyme sprigs, and 3 bay leaves, tied in a cheesecloth bundle)
Kosher salt
Freshly ground black pepper

Put the beans in a bowl, cover with cold water, and soak overnight. (Alternatively, you can quick-soak the beans; see page 30.) Drain.

Heat a wide, deep, heavy pot over medium-high heat. Pour in the oil and tip and tilt the pot to coat it, heating the oil until it is shimmering and almost smoking. Add the bacon and cook, stirring with a wooden spoon, until it renders some of its fat and becomes nicely crisp, about 6 minutes. Add the onions and garlic and cook, stirring, until softened but not browned, about 3 minutes. Add the beans and cook for 20 minutes, then add the potatoes and cook, stirring, until they are tender but still hold their shape, about 6 minutes.

Stir in the sauerkraut and its liquid and cook, stirring, for 2 minutes to coat it with the bacon fat. Pour in the stock and add the herb sachet. Raise the heat to high and bring to a boil, then lower the heat so the liquid is simmering and simmer until the beans are tender and the potatoes have broken down and thickened the soup, about 45 minutes.

Taste and adjust the seasoning with salt and pepper if necessary. Ladle the soup into 4 to 6 bowls and serve hot.

**Variation** To add croutons to the soup: Cut 4 to 6 slices of fettunta (page 11) into cubes. If desired, grate Fontina cheese over the warm croutons, so it melts. Garnish the soup with the croutons.

# PAPPA AL POMODORO

## TOMATO AND BREAD SOUP

SERVES 4

This Tuscan soup is one of the great examples of Italians' culinary resourcefulness. It's traditionally made with stale bread and tomatoes so ripe they have begun to crack and burst, turning those supposed liabilities into attributes: The juices of the tomatoes are soaked up by the bread, which is hard enough to maintain its texture. The soup is also a sort-of baby food; its name translates directly as "tomato pap," and my daughter, Francesca, has been a big fan since she first began eating solid foods.

The thickness of the soup is a matter of personal taste: I prefer it a bit on the porridgey side, but you can make it thinner by adding more stock or water.

2 tablespoons olive oil
1 Spanish onion, cut into small dice
3 large garlic cloves, thinly sliced
5 large super-ripe beefsteak tomatoes, crushed by hand, with their juice
10 large fresh basil leaves, 5 left whole, 5 thinly sliced
3 cups Vegetable Stock (page 371) or Chicken Stock (page 374)
2½ cups large cubes day-old rustic bread (crust removed)
Kosher salt
Freshly ground black pepper
¼ cup extra virgin olive oil, plus more for serving
Freshly grated Parmigiano-Reggiano, for serving

Heat a medium heavy soup pot over medium heat. Pour in the olive oil, tipping and tilting the pot to coat it and heating the oil until it is shimmering and almost smoking. Add the onions and garlic and cook, stirring occasionally with a wooden spoon, until the onions are softened but not browned, about 4 minutes. Stir in the tomatoes, whole basil leaves, and stock and bring to a simmer, then lower the heat and simmer for 30 minutes.

Stir in the bread and raise the heat to return the soup to a simmer. Season with salt and pepper, lower the heat, and simmer until the tomatoes are broken down and the soup is thick and porridge-like, about 20 minutes.

Stir in the extra virgin olive oil and sliced basil and ladle into soup bowls. Drizzle with more extra virgin olive oil, sprinkle some Parmigiano over the top, and grind some black pepper over each serving. Serve.

# ZUPPA DI BACCALÀ

## SALT COD SOUP

SERVES 6

A Roman soup of pureed salt cod and potatoes, this dish belongs to the fall and winter seasons when fresh fish is harder to come by and potatoes were traditionally one of the few available fresh vegetables. Versions of this soup are found in many cold-weather areas, including Norway and Finland, where it's made with "stockfish," which is dried but unsalted cod or other fish. The addition of a little lemon zest is actually quite important, because its oils lift the character of the soup, keeping it from being too heavy or murky; for a subtler lemon taste, blanch the zest for 10 seconds in boiling water. Note that the salt cod must be soaked for 36 to 48 hours; for more about salt cod, see page 9.

- 2 pounds salt cod
- 1 large Spanish onion, halved through the root end, 1 half left intact, the other coarsely chopped
- 2 celery stalks, trimmed, 1 halved crosswise, 1 coarsely chopped
- 2 bay leaves, preferably fresh
- ¼ cup olive oil
- 4 garlic cloves, smashed with the side of a chef's knife and peeled
- 2 cups thinly sliced leeks (white and light green parts only)
- Kosher salt
- Freshly ground black pepper
- 2 pounds Yukon Gold potatoes, peeled and cut into small dice
- Pinch of finely grated lemon zest

Put the salt cod in a medium bowl and cover by at least 1 inch with cold water. Cover loosely with plastic wrap and refrigerate for at least 36 hours, or up to 48 hours, draining the water and replacing it with fresh, cold water every 8 hours or so. The best way to know if you've soaked the fish long enough is to stick a clean index finger into the water and taste it; you want a hint of salt but not an excessively salty flavor.

Put the salt cod in a medium heavy pot and cover by 1 inch with cold water. Add the onion half, halved celery stalk, and bay leaves and bring to a simmer over medium-high heat. Lower the heat and simmer until the fish can be flaked, 4 to 5 minutes. Use tongs or a slotted spoon to transfer the salt cod to a plate. When it is cool enough to handle, remove any skin or bones and discard them. Set the salt cod aside.

Heat a wide, deep, heavy pot over medium-high heat. Pour in the oil and tilt to coat the pan; heat the oil until it is shimmering and almost smoking. Add the chopped onions, chopped celery, garlic, and leeks, season with salt and pepper, and cook, stirring with a wooden spoon, until the vegetables are softened but not at all browned, about 5 minutes.

Stir in the potatoes, season with salt and pepper, and pour in enough cold water just to cover them. Bring to a simmer and cook until the potatoes are tender to the tines of a fork, about 8 minutes. Remove from the heat.

Working in batches, transfer the contents of the pot and the salt cod to the bowl of a food processor and pulse just until uniformly smooth; transfer to a bowl. If the soup seems too thick, whisk in a few tablespoons of water.

Rinse out the pot, add the soup, and reheat over medium-high heat. Stir in the lemon zest. Taste and adjust the seasoning with salt and pepper.

Divide the soup among 6 bowls and serve.

**Variations** This soup lends itself to a number of personal adjustments: To enrich it, make it with fish or chicken stock in place of the water, or with a mixture of cream and water or stock.

For a more brothy soup, puree only half of it. For a more modern, elegant variation, don't puree any of the soup. Serve the broth, floating flakes of the salt cod on the surface.

Finish the soup with a drizzle of Salsa Verde (page 149) or colatura.

# TORTELLINI IN BRODO

## TORTELLINI IN BROTH

SERVES 4 TO 6

One of Emilia-Romagna's most famous soups, tortellini in brodo appears on just about every restaurant menu and is a mainstay of home cooking. It's sort of the chicken noodle soup of the region.

If you have any Parmigiano-Reggiano rinds on hand, this is the perfect place to use them: Drop a piece of rind into the broth to add flavor and a little body.

After making this soup, you could let it rest for 20 minutes, then gently reheat it. During that time, the essence of the meats in the tortellini will permeate the broth. The broth is instantly enriched and transformed into a sauce when it meets the butter that's put in the bottom of the bowls.

8 cups Chicken Stock (page 374)
Meat-Filled Tortellini (page 88)
4 to 6 tablespoons unsalted butter (1 tablespoon per serving)
A wedge of Parmigiano-Reggiano, for grating

Pour the stock into a large pot and bring to a simmer over medium-high heat. Reduce the heat so the broth simmers gently, add the tortellini, and cook until they float to the surface, about 2 minutes.

While the tortellini are cooking, put 1 tablespoon of butter in the bottom of each of 4 to 6 wide shallow bowls.

Ladle the tortellini and broth into the bowls; the hot broth will melt the butter. Grate some cheese over each serving and serve immediately.

# PASTA E RISOTTO
# PASTA AND RISOTTO

If a traditional Italian meal were a dramatic work, pasta would be the high point—where things turn the corner from opening nibbles and antipasti into the more substantial fare. I've always found this central placement symbolic of its larger place in Italian cuisine and life: Whatever region one hails from, pasta reigns above all else in the hearts and bellies of the people.

I'm not alone in my adoration of pasta, but I dare say that, having made a study of it for most of my adult life, I may appreciate it more than casual observers, many of whom believe that pasta is easy. It certainly looks that way, because most pasta dishes are composed of no more than a handful of ingredients, tossed together in a pan. But in reality, making great pasta requires first-class ingredients, starting with the pasta itself; proper technique, from mixing, rolling, and cutting the dough to cooking and saucing it correctly; and patience.

Pasta is what all Italian restaurants in America are judged by, and in my restaurants, there's a commitment to making authentic pasta that rivals any you might find in Italy. It's no exaggeration to say that within each of my kitchens there exists a boutique pasta shop where two or three experts spend their days kneading, rolling, and shaping the dough for the dishes we serve.

I love pasta, both in traditional dishes and as a medium for personal, contemporary expression. Because I love it, I respect it, and my respect begins by honoring the classics: At Osteria Morini, we make pasta in the style of Emilia-Romagna, using egg yolks or whole eggs and Italian 00 flour. But were I to open a restaurant serving the food of Southern Italy, where pasta is made with only water and a mixture of semolina and durum flour, I would make it that way. In this chapter, I share recipes for some of my favorite traditional pasta dishes, including some regional stuffed pastas.

Risotto satisfies in much the same way that pasta does, and once you've mastered the basic technique, you can cook pretty much any risotto you like. For that reason, along with some of my favorites, I've included a recipe here for a basic risotto that invites creativity and improvisation.

# LA SFOGLIA

## FRESH PASTA SHEETS

MAKES 1 POUND

I prefer fresh pasta to dried, a predilection I developed in Imola, while working at San Domenico. We didn't make all of our pasta in-house, but what we purchased was produced just around the corner, in a family-owned pasta shop where they patiently rolled and cut more than a dozen pasta shapes from scratch every day.

These days, there are so many world-class products on the market that it's possible to buy wonderful fresh or frozen handmade pasta from a gourmet shop, or to order it over the Internet. But I encourage you to make homemade pasta at least once; there's nothing like cooking and eating pasta that's just been made. (And if you purchase fresh pasta sheets, I recommend rolling them through a hand-crank machine set just thinner than the sheets to freshen the dough.)

In Italy, the method for producing pasta may vary depending on where you are: In the southern regions, only flour and water are used, no eggs. Farther north, eggs are a defining ingredient, providing a richness of flavor, and that's the style of pasta I make. The activation and interaction of proteins are essential to achieving the desired elasticity in fresh pasta, so beat the eggs well before adding them to the flour. And be sure to use a soft-wheat flour; the gold standard is Italian 00 flour.

There's a longstanding debate in the world of Italian cookery over whether or not fresh pasta can be cooked al dente. One school of thought believes that because the pasta is so soft and tender, it cannot be toothsome after it's cooked. I disagree. By following a few essential steps, it is possible to build enough structure into the dough that even when cooked, fresh pasta will offer a little resistance to the bite: First, be sure to have all the ingredients at room temperature prior to making the dough, which means taking the eggs out of the refrigerator about an hour before starting. Second, although it's important to flour the dough repeatedly while working, take care not to overflour it. Third, the step that occurs midway through the process, folding the pasta into thirds like a letter, is critical to achieving the proper texture. And finally, be sure to let the pasta rest for at least 30 minutes before rolling to allow the ingredients to amalgamate fully.

If possible, make the dough in a cool, somewhat humid location so it won't dry out too quickly as you work. And knead it on a wooden work surface, which will absorb the dough's moisture, as opposed to, say, a marble surface, which tends to make dough sweat.

It's best not to refrigerate or freeze fresh pasta, but if you do so, here's a trick: use rice flour to dust the finished pasta before wrapping and storing it. If you use flour or cornmeal, as many recipes instruct you to do, it will find its way into the pasta water, adding unwanted starch. Rice flour, on the other hand, practically melts away when the pasta is cooked.

3 large eggs, at room temperature
1 tablespoon extra virgin olive oil
Kosher salt
2¼ cups 00 flour or King Arthur Italian-Style flour (all-purpose flour can be substituted), plus more if needed
Rice flour (if storing the pasta)

Put the eggs, oil, and a pinch of salt in a small bowl and use a fork to beat them together thoroughly.

Lightly flour a work surface, preferably a wooden surface, and mound the flour in the center. Make a well in the center and pour the egg mixture into the well. Use the fork to gradually mix the flour into the egg mixture, working from the inside out, until the ingredients come together in a lumpy dough. Dust your hands with flour and knead the dough, flattening it out and folding it back into a ball, sprinkling a bit more flour over it if necessary, until it's no longer tacky. (Both the mixing and the kneading can also be done in a stand mixer fitted with the dough hook; start with the motor on the lowest setting and gradually increase the speed to medium.)

Reflour your work surface and continue kneading until the dough develops elasticity, about 4 minutes, then knead it for another 4 minutes. Use a bench scraper or chef's knife to cut the dough in half and shape each piece into a rectangle sized to fit through the rollers of a hand-crank pasta machine. Wrap in plastic wrap and set aside at room temperature for about 30 minutes.

Set up a hand-crank pasta machine and set the rollers to the widest setting. Feed one of the dough portions through the machine, catching it as it emerges by letting it drape over your other hand. Set the dough on your work surface and fold it in thirds, like a letter, then flour it lightly to prevent sticking and pass it through the machine two more times, reflouring it after each time. If the dough isn't smooth, with nice, even edges, pass it through the machine another time or two until it is.

Begin narrowing the setting on the machine and passing the dough through each one until you attain the desired thickness for the pasta you are making, which will almost always be the thinnest or second-to-thinnest setting. (You should not need to flour the dough again.) Use a wheel cutter to cut the dough into 18-inch lengths. Lay them out on a lightly floured surface and cover with a damp kitchen towel. Repeat with the remaining dough and let the dough rest for 30 minutes to 1 hour.

Roll each piece through the final setting on the machine two more times, then cut it into the desired shapes: Fettuccine and spaghetti are made by using the cutters on the machine. Dough for filled pastas should be cut by hand with a knife, roller, or metal cutters.

Cook the pasta immediately, or, if refrigerating or freezing it, spread it out on a baking sheet and dust with rice flour, then hang on a pasta drying rack or over the back of a kitchen chair to dry. When it is dry, roll the pasta around your hand into little nests, transfer to resealable plastic bags, and refrigerate for up to 2 days, or freeze for up to 2 weeks.

There is an almost endless variety of pasta lengths and widths. To make the pastas called for in this chapter, cut the dough as follows:

Tagliatelle: ¼ to ⅜ inch wide, 11 to 12 inches long
Tajarin: ⅛ inch wide, 11 to 12 inches long
Pappardelle: ¾ to 1 inch wide, 6 to 8 inches long
Stracci: ¾ to 1 inch wide, 4 inches long

### Pasta

Tools: Hand-crank pasta machine: An old-fashioned machine that clamps onto the work surface remains my favored device for rolling pasta, because it gives you the greatest control over and feel for the process.

Small wheel cutter and zigzag cutter: For cutting shapes from dough.

Ring cutter: For making round shapes such as ravioli and agnolotti.

Spray bottle: The best way to get sheets of pasta for ravioli and other filled pastas to adhere to one another is to apply water to the edges and then smooth them with a fork. And the best way to apply the water is to spray a gentle mist from a height of a few feet and let it float down over the pasta.

Cooking: All pasta should be cooked al dente (literally, "to the tooth"), meaning that it should have some bite to it, offering pleasing resistance to the chew. One way to achieve this is to shave a minute or two off the cooking time given on the package, especially with pastas produced in the United States, where people generally like their pasta softer. The best way to tell if pasta is properly cooked is to use a spoon, fork, or tongs to carefully remove a piece or strand of it from the pot, let it cool for a few seconds, and bite into it. The outermost part should be a straw-yellow color, indicating doneness, but the very center should still be an uncooked chalky white, and the pasta should be toothsome but not chewy or gummy.

Do not add olive oil to the cooking water, as many cooks do, to keep pasta from sticking together; this doesn't actually work. The oil also creates a coating that acts as a sort of culinary Teflon, preventing the sauce from adhering. The single best way to keep pasta from clumping together is to cook it in abundant water, enough to cover the pasta by at least 3 inches. And never rinse pasta after cooking it. There's just no good reason to do this and two good reasons not to: It washes away starch that helps bind pasta and sauce, and it cools the pasta down.

If the pasta will be sauced, then it should finish cooking in the sauce. Most of my recipes call for cooking pasta sauces in a wide sauté pan so that the drained pasta can be added to the pan and tossed with the sauce to integrate the two. In these cases, it's especially important to not overcook, or even fully cook, the pasta in the boiling water.

# BASIC TOMATO SAUCES

I use three types of tomato sauce for my pasta (and in other recipes as well): a simple everyday tomato-and-basil sauce with garlic and red pepper flakes; a sauce in the style of Emilia-Romagna, made with butter and salt pork; and a more vegetable-heavy sauce that moderates the tomato flavor.

## SALSA POMODORO

### TOMATO SAUCE WITH BASIL

MAKES ABOUT 3 CUPS

This is what most people imagine when they think of pasta sauce. From my Spiaggia chef, Paul Bartolotta, I learned the Neapolitan trick of including a small amount of red bell pepper to add some acidity and mellow out the tomatoes' sweetness.

- ¼ cup olive oil
- 2 large garlic cloves, smashed with the side of a chef's knife and peeled
- ¼ large red bell pepper, cored, seeded, and cut into small dice
- 1 28-ounce can whole tomatoes, preferably Italian San Marzano or organic, with their juice
- Leaves from 1 small bunch of basil (about 1½ cups loosely packed), cut into chiffonade (see page xxx)
- Kosher salt
- Freshly ground black pepper
- Pinch of red pepper flakes

Heat a medium heavy saucepan over medium heat. Pour in the oil and heat until it is shimmering and almost smoking. Add the garlic and cook, stirring with a wooden spoon, until it just begins to brown, 3 to 4 minutes. Add the red bell pepper and cook, stirring, for 1 minute. Add the tomatoes and their juices and about half the basil, season with salt and pepper, stir in the red pepper flakes, and bring to a simmer. Lower the heat and simmer until the sauce is nicely thickened and flavorful, about 1 hour.

Remove the pan from the heat, and stir in the remaining basil. Use right away, or let cool and refrigerate in an airtight container for up to 2 days.

# SALSA ALLA ROMAGNOLA

## TOMATO AND PORK SAUCE

MAKES ABOUT 3 CUPS

This is a rich Emilia-Romagna–style sauce with plenty of fat (butter and salt pork) and no garlic, basil, or pepper flakes. Sometimes called burro e oro (butter and gold) from the way the tomatoes and butter turn golden when combined, it is used primarily to sauce gnocchi, because the potato dumplings can stand up to its flavors and the sauce takes so well to gnocchi's traditional ridges. It is also wonderful for braising meats.

2 tablespoons unsalted butter
3 ounces salt pork (an additional 4 tablespoons butter can be substituted)
½ Spanish onion, minced
1 28-ounce can tomato sauce, preferably Italian San Marzano or organic, with their juice
Kosher salt

Heat a medium heavy pot over medium-low heat. Add the butter and salt pork and cook until the pork renders some of its fat, tipping and tilting the pot to coat it with the butter and pork fat. Add the onions and cook, stirring occasionally with a wooden spoon, until softened but not browned, about 4 minutes. Stir in the tomato sauce and bring to a simmer. Lower the heat and simmer, stirring occasionally, until thickened, about 1 hour. Season with salt.

Remove the pot from the heat and let cool slightly. Use an immersion blender to blend the sauce to a rough puree, or blend in batches in a stand blender (see Blender Safety below), leaving the sauce slightly chunky.

Use right away or let cool and refrigerate in an airtight container for up to 2 days.

### Blender Safety

When blending hot liquids, be sure to remove the central piece from the blender lid to allow steam to escape and keep the lid from popping off.

# RAGÙ FINTO

## TOMATO AND VEGETABLE SAUCE

MAKES ABOUT 3 CUPS

This vegetable-laden tomato sauce is common in parts of Southern Italy. Some cooks leave the vegetables in large chunks for a rustic effect, but I prefer them diced. (Unlike most recipes in the Classico section of this book, this one calls for specific amounts of diced vegetables to ensure balance.)

2 tablespoons olive oil
½ cup Spanish onion in small dice
½ cup carrots in small dice
½ cup celery in small dice
2 large garlic cloves, smashed with the side of a chef's knife and peeled
1 28-ounce can tomato puree, preferably Italian San Marzano or organic, with their juice
Kosher salt
Freshly ground black pepper
10 basil leaves, chiffonade (see page xxx)

Heat a wide, deep, heavy pot over medium-high heat. Add the oil, tipping and turning the pot to coat it and heating the oil until it is shimmering and almost smoking. Add the onions, carrots, celery, and garlic and cook, stirring with a wooden spoon, until softened but not browned, about 6 minutes.

Stir in the tomato puree and season with salt and pepper. Bring to a simmer, stir in the basil, then lower the heat and cook, partially covered, at a gentle simmer until the sauce is thickened and flavorful. It will be ready in about 1 hour, but the flavor will intensify if you cook it for 1½ hours.

Use right away, or let cool and refrigerate in an airtight container for up to 2 days.

# PASTA PUTTANESCA

## PASTA WITH ANCHOVIES, CAPERS, AND OLIVES

SERVES 6 AS AN APPETIZER OR 4 AS A MAIN COURSE

I've long considered this one of the essential pasta sauces, just below a classic tomato sauce in the pantheon of dishes integral to gaining an understanding of what makes the medium tick. There are few other pastas that feature as many of what I think of as the "impact" flavors of Italian cuisine: olive oil, garlic, tomato sauce, anchovies, olives, and oregano. They're all here, along with basil, an ingredient that isn't part of the traditional recipe but that I add to freshen up the deep-sea flavors from the anchovies.

Kosher salt
2 tablespoons olive oil
2 large garlic cloves, very thinly sliced
4 oil-packed anchovy fillets, minced
1 small red onion, cut into small dice
1 tablespoon capers, soaked in warm water for 5 minutes and drained
¼ cup dry white wine
1 15-ounce can tomato sauce, preferably Italian San Marzano or organic, with their juice
¼ cup chopped black olives, such as kalamata
1 pound spaghetti or other long dried pasta
Pinch of dried oregano
5 fresh basil leaves, chiffonade
1 tablespoon thinly sliced fresh flat-leaf parsley leaves
3 tablespoons extra virgin olive oil
Freshly ground black pepper

Fill a large pot about two-thirds full with water, salt it liberally, and bring to a boil over high heat.

Meanwhile, heat a wide, deep, heavy skillet over medium heat. Pour in the olive oil, tilting and turning the pan to coat it and heating the oil until it is shimmering and almost smoking. Add the garlic, anchovies, onions, and capers and cook, stirring with a wooden spoon, until the onions are softened but not browned, about 4 minutes. Pour in the wine and bring to a simmer, then lower the heat and simmer until the wine has almost completely evaporated, about 5 minutes.

Stir in the tomato sauce and cook, stirring frequently, until slightly thickened, 12 to 15 minutes. Stir in the olives and cook to warm them through, about 2 minutes.

Meanwhile, add the spaghetti to the boiling water and cook until al dente, about 8 minutes.

Stir the oregano, basil, parsley, and extra virgin olive oil into the sauce. Season to taste with salt and pepper, bearing in mind that many of the ingredients are salty.

Use a heatproof liquid measuring cup to scoop out and reserve about 1 cup of the pasta cooking liquid, then drain the pasta. Add the pasta to the sauce and toss well, adding a little pasta water if necessary to help the sauce nicely coat the pasta.

Transfer the pasta to serving plates and serve.

**Variation** This is one of the few pasta dishes I don't finish with Parmigiano-Reggiano or Pecorino Romano, neither of which gets along with the seafood in the sauce. If you like, you can use grated ricotta salata cheese, which is salty, dry, and creamy all at once and has a wonderful affinity with the other flavors here.

**ISPIRAZIONE** The defining ingredients of this pasta are relocated to a pizza in the recipe on page 230.

# CAPPELLACCI DI ZUCCA CON AMARETTI

## "LITTLE HATS" OF BUTTERNUT SQUASH WITH AMARETTI

SERVES 6 AS AN APPETIZER OR 4 AS A MAIN COURSE

Cappellaccci, a hat-shaped stuffed pasta, hails from the little province of Montova, a Lombardian community across the Po River from Emilia-Romagna. They are traditionally made with zucca, a gourd-shaped winter squash indigenous to the area. Here in the United States, the closest approximation of zucca's fiery orange color and understated sweetness is butternut squash, which makes a fine substitute.

The two strokes of genius in the origins of this pasta were the decision to mix crushed amaretti cookies and Mostarda di Cremona (page 149) into the filling, adding subtle spice, sweetness, and crunch. I leave out the mostarda in this version, because butternut squash is sweet enough that it doesn't need it. For a fun finishing touch, grate more amaretti over the pasta at the table using a Microplane.

Although this pasta is delicious on its own, it's a fine accompaniment to Mixed Boiled Meats (page 148), because the squash and other flavors are a perfect foil for the gaminess of some of the meats.

Note that the filling must be refrigerated for at least 2 hours.

- 2 tablespoons olive oil
- 1 medium butternut squash (about 1½ pounds), halved lengthwise, seeds removed
- Kosher salt
- Freshly ground black pepper
- Pinch or two of sugar
- 1 large egg, lightly beaten
- 1 cup finely grated Parmigiano-Reggiano (about 2 ounces), plus more for serving
- ½ cup crushed amaretti cookies (about 6 cookies)
- Pinch of freshly grated nutmeg
- Pinch of saffron threads
- Pinch of cayenne pepper
- Fresh Pasta Sheets (page 72) or 1 pound store-bought
- Rice flour, for dusting
- ½ cup water
- 4 tablespoons unsalted butter, cut into pieces

Position a rack in the center of the oven and preheat the oven to 375°F.

Drizzle the oil evenly over the cut sides of the squash and lay the halves cut side up on a rimmed baking sheet. Season with salt, pepper, and the sugar and roast until the flesh is tender to the tines of a fork, 45 minutes to 1 hour. Remove the squash from the oven and set aside to cool.

Once the squash is cool enough to handle, use a tablespoon to scoop the flesh out into a large mixing bowl. Discard the skin. Use a potato masher to mash the squash until uniformly smooth. Add the egg, ¾ cup of the Parmigiano, the amaretti, nutmeg, saffron, and cayenne and use a large rubber spatula to fold the ingredients together until uniformly incorporated. Season to taste with salt and pepper. Cover the bowl with plastic wrap and refrigerate until chilled, at least 2 hours, but no more than 8 hours.

Set your pasta machine to the thinnest setting and roll the pasta sheets through it.

Fill a spray bottle with water and set it so that it produces a fine mist when the trigger is pressed.

Line a baking sheet with parchment paper and lightly dust with rice flour.

Lay the pasta sheets on a floured work surface and use a wheel cutter or sharp chef's knife to cut the sheets into forty to forty-eight 3-inch squares (use a ruler or other straightedge to guide you). Working with one square at a time, and keeping the other squares under a damp kitchen towel, mound a teaspoon or so of filling in the center. Hold the spray bottle a foot or two above the pasta and press once to release a mist of water over the square, then fold the square in half to form a triangle and press the edges together to seal them. Hold the triangle with the center point facing down and bend it around, crossing the ends by about ¼ inch and pressing them together. Repeat until all of the squares and filling have been used, arranging the cappellacci on the rice-flour-dusted baking sheet. (The cappellacci can be refrigerated for up to 1 day or frozen for up to 2 months. Wrap the baking sheet in plastic wrap and refrigerate, or freeze the cappellacci on the sheet until frozen hard, then transfer to freezer bags.)

When ready to cook the cappellacci, fill a large pot about two-thirds full with water, salt it liberally, and bring to a boil over high heat.

Meanwhile, bring the ½ cup water to a boil in a wide sauté pan. Whisk in the butter, then whisk in the remaining ¼ cup Parmigiano. Cover the sauce to keep it warm.

When the water has come to a boil, lower the heat so the water is at a gentle boil and gingerly add the cappellacci a few at a time. Stir carefully once to keep them from sticking together, then cook until they float to the surface, 2 to 3 minutes for fresh, or 4 to 5 minutes for frozen. Remove with a slotted spoon, letting the excess water run off, and transfer to a bowl, or very gently drain in a colander.

Transfer the cappellacci to the butter sauce and toss gently to coat with the sauce. Divide among individual plates, grate some cheese and grind some pepper over each serving, and serve.

# TORTELLI DI RICOTTA

## RICOTTA TORTELLI WITH BUTTER AND SAGE

SERVES 6 AS AN APPETIZER OR 4 AS A MAIN COURSE

The secret of these little ravioli-like parcels is the back-and-forth between the creamy ricotta cheese and the sharp Parmigiano in the filling. Browned butter and sage is the most ubiquitous finishing sauce for pasta in Northern Italy, and deservedly so, because it's so good; it shows up on everything from these tortelli to ricotta ravioli to gnocchi and gnudi.

Note that the filling must be refrigerated for at least 1 hour.

1 pound ricotta cheese
1 large egg plus 1 large egg yolk, lightly beaten together
½ cup finely grated Parmigiano-Reggiano (about 1 ounce), plus more for serving
Pinch of freshly grated nutmeg
Kosher salt
Freshly ground black pepper
Rice flour, for dusting
Fresh Pasta Sheets (page 72) or 1 pound store-bought
8 tablespoons (1 stick) unsalted butter
10 fresh sage leaves

Put the ricotta, eggs, Parmigiano, and nutmeg in a medium bowl, season with salt and pepper, and fold together with a rubber spatula until just incorporated. Spoon the ricotta mixture into a piping bag fitted with a number 7 (⅜-inch) plain tip and refrigerate for at least 1 hour, but no more than 8 hours.

Line a baking sheet with parchment paper and lightly dust it with rice flour.

Set your pasta machine to the thinnest setting and roll the pasta sheets through it. Lay the pasta sheets on a floured surface and use a wheel cutter or sharp chef's knife to cut them into forty to forty-eight 3-inch squares (use a ruler or other straightedge to guide you). Lay half of the squares on the floured surface and keep the others under a damp kitchen towel. Pipe about 1½ tablespoons of filling into the center of half of the squares. Use a pastry brush or your finger to brush the edges of the squares with water, then place one of the remaining squares on top of each one, using your fingers to push out any air. (I don't use the spray bottle for this recipe, because the cheese filling is especially delicate and could become watery.) Tightly seal the edges, then trim the edges with the wheel cutter and arrange the tortelli on the rice-flour-dusted baking sheet. (The tortelli can be refrigerated for up to 1 day or frozen for up to 2 months. Wrap the baking sheet in plastic wrap and refrigerate, or freeze the tortelli on the sheet until frozen hard, then transfer to freezer bags.)

When ready to cook the tortelli, fill a large pot about two-thirds full with water, salt it liberally, and bring to a boil over high heat.

Meanwhile, melt the butter in a medium wide sauté pan over medium-high heat. Add the sage leaves and cook, stirring with a wooden spoon, until the butter is browned and fragrant, about 2 minutes. Remove from the heat and cover to keep warm.

When the water has come to a boil, lower the heat slightly so the water is at a gentle boil and gingerly add the tortelli a few at a time. Stir carefully once to keep them from sticking together, then cook until the tortelli float to the surface, 2 to 3 minutes for fresh, or 4 to 5 minutes for frozen. Remove with a slotted spoon, letting the excess water run off, and transfer to a bowl, or very gently drain in a colander.

Add the tortelli to the sage butter and toss briefly to coat. Divide among individual plates, sprinkle each serving with Parmigiano, and serve immediately.

# STRACCI CON RAGÙ DI FUNGHI

## PASTA RIBBONS WITH MUSHROOM SAUCE

SERVES 6 AS AN APPETIZER OR 4 AS A MAIN COURSE

This rustic pasta sauced with an aromatic mixture of mushrooms and herbs is one of the dishes that made me fall in love with Italy long before I ever crossed the Atlantic. I originally learned to make a version of it at Spiaggia in Chicago in 1991, and I was positively consumed by how intense and robust the flavors were. This was one of the first dishes to turn me on to what I consider the great triumvirate of Italian cooking: rosemary, garlic, and red pepper flakes.

In width, stracci are similar to the more well-known pappardelle, but they are far shorter, just about four inches. Layering the mushrooms and sauce with the pasta on the plates gives a free-form lasagna effect.

½ cup olive oil, or as needed
1 Spanish onion, cut into small dice
3 garlic cloves, thinly sliced
2 pounds mushrooms, ideally 8 ounces each white button, cremini, shiitake, and oyster, trimmed (discard shiitake stems) and thinly sliced
Kosher salt
Freshly ground black pepper
1 heaping tablespoon tomato paste
Needles from 2 rosemary sprigs, minced
4 fresh sage leaves, minced
Pinch of red pepper flakes
½ cup dry white wine
2 cups Dark Chicken Stock (page 374)
Fresh Pasta Sheets (page 72), cut into stracci or other wide pasta, such as pappardelle, or 1 pound fresh or dried store-bought stracci or other wide pasta (see Sources, page 379)
A wedge of Parmigiano-Reggiano, for grating

Pour the oil into a wide heavy sauté pan and heat over medium-high heat until the oil is shimmering and almost smoking. Add the onions and garlic and cook, stirring with a wooden spoon, until softened but not browned, about 4 minutes. Add the mushrooms, season with salt and a few grinds of black pepper, and cook, stirring, until they begin to give off their liquid, about 5 minutes, adding more oil if the pan becomes too dry.

Stir in the tomato paste, stirring to coat the mushrooms, and cook until it turns a shade darker, about 2 minutes. Stir in the rosemary, sage, and red pepper flakes.

Pour in the wine, bring to a simmer, and simmer until it has evaporated, about 5 minutes. Stir in the stock and bring it to a simmer, then lower the heat, partially cover the pan, and let simmer, stirring occasionally, until the sauce is thick enough to coat the back of a wooden spoon, about 1 hour. (The sauce can be cooled and refrigerated in an airtight container for up to 3 days; reheat gently before proceeding.)

Meanwhile, about 20 minutes before the sauce is ready, fill a large pot two-thirds full with water and salt it liberally. Bring to a boil over high heat. Add the pasta and cook until al dente, about 4 minutes for fresh, or 9 minutes for dried. Drain the pasta and add it to the sauce. Toss well.

Divide the pasta and sauce among 4 to 6 plates, using a kitchen spoon to layer the mushrooms and sauce between layers of pasta. Shave some cheese and grind some black pepper over each serving and serve.

**Variations** This dish is also good with thyme instead of rosemary. You can vary the mushrooms, using just about any variety. You can also use the mushroom sauce to top Parmesan Custards (page 38) or a grilled steak. It would be a somewhat modern touch, but adding some Tomato Confit (page 369) to the mushrooms just before tossing with the pasta, as pictured, bring welcome color and sweetness to the plate.

# STROZZAPRETI CON POMODORO, PECORINO, E BASILICO

## STROZZAPRETI WITH TOMATO, PECORINO, AND BASIL

SERVES 6 AS AN APPETIZER OR 4 AS A MAIN COURSE

Strozzapreti (the name means "priest stranglers") are three-inch-long twisted strands of fresh pasta, and they are one of the few pastas from Emilia-Romagna in which eggs are not used. The dough is made with 00 flour and a shot of olive oil that gives it the toothsome quality of a Southern Italian pasta. Here the strozzapreti are sauced with a simple tomato and basil sauce and finished with a shaving of Oro Antico (meaning "antique gold"), a semi-aged Pecorino Toscano that marries seamlessly with the sauce as it melts.

Kosher salt
¼ cup olive oil
2 large garlic cloves, thinly sliced
Pinch of red pepper flakes
2 cups Tomato Sauce with Basil (page 74)
1 pound fresh Strozzapreti, homemade (recipe follows) or store-bought (see Sources, page 379; cavatelli can be substituted)
½ cup (loosely packed) basil chiffonade (see page xxx)
4 ounces Oro Antico cheese, shaved into shards with a vegetable peeler (Pecorino Romano can be substituted)

Fill a large pot about two-thirds full with water, salt it liberally, and bring to a boil over high heat.

Meanwhile, heat a large heavy pot over medium heat. Add the olive oil, tipping and tilting the pot to coat it and heating the oil until it is shimmering and almost smoking. Add the garlic and red pepper flakes and cook, stirring with a wooden spoon, until the garlic is fragrant and lightly golden, about 3 minutes. Quickly pour in the tomato sauce to prevent the garlic from overcooking; bring to a simmer, and cook for 3 to 5 minutes.

When the water comes to a boil, add the pasta and cook until al dente, about 2 minutes for fresh, or 4 minutes for frozen. Use a heatproof liquid measuring cup to scoop out and reserve about ½ cup of the pasta cooking liquid, and drain the pasta.

Add the pasta and a little of the cooking liquid to the sauce and toss or stir to coat.

Divide the pasta among serving plates, scatter some sliced cheese shards and basil over each serving, and serve immediately.

### STROZZAPRETI

MAKES ABOUT 1 POUND

2¼ cups 00 flour or King Arthur Italian-Style flour, plus more for dusting
⅔ cup water
2 teaspoons olive oil
Pinch of kosher salt
Rice flour, for dusting

Put the flour, water, oil, and salt in the bowl of a stand mixer fitted with the dough hook. Mix, starting on low speed and gradually increasing to medium, until the ingredients come together and form a ball of dough. Remove the bowl from the machine, cover with a damp towel, and let the dough rest for 1 hour.

Lightly flour a work surface and rolling pin and roll the dough out into an even thickness of ⅛ inch. (This can also be done using a hand-crank pasta machine, but because the pieces will be twisted, it's not essential that the pasta be perfectly smooth here.)

Use a wheel cutter to cut the dough into ½-inch-wide strips. Working with one strip at a time, roll it between your fingers, twist the top 3 inches, tear it off, and transfer the strozzapreti to a rice-flour-dusted baking sheet. Continue to twist and tear, making about 8 strozzapreti from each strip. (The strozzapreti can be refrigerated for up to 1 day or frozen for up to 2 months. Wrap the baking sheet in plastic wrap and refrigerate, or freeze the strozzapreti on the sheet until frozen hard, then transfer to freezer bags.)

# TORTELLINI ALLA PANNA

## TORTELLINI IN CREAM SAUCE

SERVES 6 AS AN APPETIZER OR 4 AS A MAIN COURSE

Other than in brodo (see page 68), this is just about the only way that meat tortellini are served in Emilia-Romagna, usually from October through the cold winter months. Although undeniably rich, the cream sauce enhances rather than detracts from the meat filling.

Kosher salt
Meat-Filled Tortellini (page 88)
½ cup heavy cream
4 tablespoons cold unsalted butter, cut into 8 pieces
¼ cup finely grated Parmigiano-Reggiano, plus more for serving
Freshly ground black pepper

Fill a large pot about two-thirds full with water, salt it liberally, and bring to a boil over high heat. Add the tortellini and cook until they float to the surface, about 3 minutes for fresh, or 5 minutes for frozen.

Meanwhile, make the sauce: Heat the cream in a large heavy sauté pan over low heat until warm. Remove the pan from the heat and whisk in the butter one piece at a time until the butter is just melted and the sauce is emulsified. Whisk in the cheese a little at a time to thicken the sauce.

When the pasta is done, drain it thoroughly and add to the sauce. Toss or gently stir over medium heat until the sauce is reduced slightly and coats the pasta, about 2 minutes.

Divide the tortellini among plates or wide shallow bowls, finish with a grind of black pepper and some grated cheese, and serve.

# TORTELLINI ALLA BOLOGNESE

## MEAT-FILLED TORTELLINI

MAKES ABOUT 90 TORTELLINI, ENOUGH TO SERVE 6 TO 8 AS AN APPETIZER OR 4 AS A MAIN COURSE

Meat tortellini—handmade pasta filled with a mixture of prosciutto, Parmigiano-Reggiano, and mortadella, four of the most significant ingredients in all of Italy—sum up Emilia-Romagna in one bite. In addition to the dish, these may also be served in a sauce of cream with a tablespoon of ragū stirred into it (pasticciata) or in broth (in brodo, see page 68).

4 tablespoons unsalted butter
3 bay leaves, preferably fresh
8 ounces boneless pork shoulder, cut into 2-inch cubes (about 2 cups)
8 ounces sweet Italian pork sausage, removed from casings and crumbled
3 ounces prosciutto, coarsely chopped
3 ounces mortadella, preferably mortadella di Bologna, cubed
½ cup finely grated Parmigiano-Reggiano (about 1 ounce)
1 large egg, lightly beaten
Pinch of freshly grated nutmeg
Kosher salt
Freshly ground black pepper
Fresh Pasta Sheets (page 72) or 1 pound store-bought
Rice flour, for dusting

Heat a medium heavy sauté pan over medium heat. Add the butter and let it melt, tipping and turning the pan to coat it. Add the bay leaves and cook for 1 minute to infuse the butter with their flavor. Add the pork shoulder and sausage and cook, stirring frequently with a wooden spoon, until the meats are browned all over and cooked through, about 8 minutes. Remove the pan from the heat and set aside to cool; remove and discard the bay leaves.

Once they are cooled, transfer the meats to the bowl of a food processor, add the prosciutto and mortadella, and pulse until coarsely ground and amalgamated. Transfer the mixture to a large mixing bowl; add the cheese, egg, and nutmeg; and mix with a wooden spoon just until incorporated. Season with salt and a few grinds of pepper and mix again.

Fill a spray bottle with water and set it so that it produces a fine mist when the trigger is pressed.

Set your pasta machine to the thinnest setting and roll the pasta sheets through it. Line a baking sheet with parchment paper and lightly dust it with rice flour. Lay the pasta sheets on a floured surface and use a wheel cutter or sharp chef's knife to cut them into 1½-inch wide strips, then into about one hundred twenty-five 1½-inch squares (use a ruler or other straightedge to guide you). Working with 12 squares at a time, and keeping the other squares hydrated under a damp kitchen towel, use a teaspoon to spoon a scant amount of filling into the center of each square. Hold the spray bottle a foot or two above the pasta and press once to release a mist of water over the squares, then form the tortellini: Working with one square at a time, fold the square in half to form a triangle and press the edges together to seal them. Hold the triangle with the center point facing down and bend the two ends around, overlapping the ends by about ¼ inch and pressing them together. As they are done, arrange them point side up on the rice-flour-dusted baking sheet and repeat with the remaining dough and filling; there may be less than a dozen squares in the last batch.

(The tortellini can be refrigerated for up to 1 day or frozen for up to 2 months. Wrap the baking sheet in plastic wrap and refrigerate, or freeze on the sheet until hard, then transfer to freezer bags.)

# GNOCCHI CON GORGONZOLA E PESTO DI NOCI

## POTATO DUMPLINGS WITH GORGONZOLA AND WALNUT PESTO

SERVES 6 AS AN APPETIZER OR 4 AS A MAIN COURSE

This cold-weather classic comes from the Lombardy region, home of Italy's most famous blue cheese, Gorgonzola, which serves as the basis of the creamy sauce. The dish is finished with a walnut pesto that adds balance to the rich sauce with its earthy flavors and a welcome crunch.

Kosher salt
2 tablespoons unsalted butter
1 shallot, minced
4 large fresh sage leaves, thinly sliced
1 cup heavy cream
4 ounces Gorgonzola, crumbled
Pinch of freshly grated nutmeg
Gnocchi (page 90)
½ cup finely grated Parmigiano-Reggiano (about 1 ounce), plus a wedge for grating
Walnut Pesto (recipe follows)

Fill a large pot about two-thirds full with water, salt it liberally, and bring to a boil over high heat.

Meanwhile, heat a medium heavy skillet over low heat. Add the butter and let it melt, tipping and tilting the pan to coat it. Add the shallots and cook, stirring frequently with a wooden spoon, until softened but not browned, about 3 minutes. Add the sage and cook, stirring, for 2 minutes. Stir in the cream, then add the Gorgonzola and nutmeg and cook, stirring frequently, until the cheese is melted and a creamy sauce has formed.

When the water comes to a boil, add the gnocchi and cook until they float to the surface, about 2 minutes for fresh, or 4 minutes for frozen.

Drain the gnocchi thoroughly, add them to the sauce, and toss well to coat them. Cook, stirring, to integrate the gnocchi and sauce, about 2 minutes, then stir in the Parmigiano.

Transfer the gnocchi to wide shallow bowls. Spoon a heaping tablespoon of walnut pesto over each serving and serve with the wedge of Parmigiano alongside for grating.

### WALNUT PESTO

MAKES ABOUT ½ CUP

This pesto is also delicious tossed with hot pasta.

½ cup walnuts, toasted (see page 367)
⅓ cup extra virgin olive oil, or as needed
3 tablespoons fresh flat-leaf parsley leaves
1 large garlic clove, coarsely chopped
¼ cup finely grated Parmigiano-Reggiano
Kosher salt
Freshly ground black pepper

Put the nuts, olive oil, parsley, garlic, and Parmigiano in the bowl of a food processor, season with salt and a few grinds of pepper, and pulse until a coarse, slightly chunky mixture is formed, adding a little more oil or a few drops of water if it seems too thick.

The pesto can be refrigerated in an airtight container for up to 24 hours, but no longer, or the garlic will become overpowering.

# GNOCCHI

## POTATO DUMPLINGS

MAKES ABOUT 1 POUND, ENOUGH TO SERVE 6 AS AN APPETIZER OR 4 AS A MAIN COURSE

Among connoisseurs of Italian food, gnocchi serve as a perennial conversation piece, inspiring debate over whether or not they truly qualify as pasta. However you think of them, properly made gnocchi are light-as-air, melt-in-your-mouth potato dumplings that meld seamlessly with a variety of sauces; they are often sauced with a tomato and pork sauce (see page 75).

The keys to making great gnocchi are to use a minimal amount of flour, to work the dough as little as possible, and to mix the other ingredients into the potatoes while they are still warm, which makes a smooth integration easier. Above all else, when it comes to gnocchi making, all potatoes are not created equal: The waxy potatoes that are farmed on the outskirts of Bologna are ideal because they are so forgiving, not drying out as easily as, say, a russet or Idaho potato; the closest American option is Yukon Gold.

1 ¼ pounds Yukon Gold potatoes, preferably of uniform size
2 large eggs, lightly beaten
1 ½ cups all-purpose flour, plus more for dusting
½ cup finely grated Parmigiano-Reggiano (about 1 ounce)
Pinch of freshly grated nutmeg
Kosher salt
Freshly ground black pepper
Rice flour, for dusting

If they are not of uniform size, cut the larger potatoes into the size of the smaller ones so that all of the pieces cook at the same rate. Put the potatoes in a large heavy saucepan and cover by 1 inch with cold water. Bring to a boil over high heat and cook until the potatoes are tender to the tines of a fork, 15 to 20 minutes. Drain in a colander and let cool slightly.

When they are cool enough to handle, peel the potatoes and rice them or mash them with a potato masher, taking care not to leave any large pieces or chunks. Turn them out onto a lightly floured surface, shape into a mound, and let cool slightly so they are still warm but can be kneaded by hand.

Make a well in the center of the potatoes and pour in the eggs. Add the flour to the well, then add the cheese and season with the nutmeg, 2 teaspoons salt, and a few grinds of pepper. Knead the mixture first with a fork and then by hand, just until the ingredients are seamlessly integrated and come together in a dough.

Dust your hands with flour and, if necessary, reflour the work surface. Divide the dough into 6 equal pieces. Working with one piece at a time, roll it out into a rope about ½ inch in diameter. Use a sharp knife to cut each rope into 1-inch segments and transfer to a rice-flour-dusted baking sheet.

The gnocchi can be refrigerated for up to 1 day or frozen for up to 2 months. Wrap the baking sheet in plastic wrap and refrigerate, or freeze the gnocchi on the sheet until frozen hard, then transfer to freezer bags.

**ISPIRAZIONE** See page 337 for a macaroni-like treatment of gnocchi, paired with braised short ribs.

# SPAGHETTI ALLE VONGOLE, PREZZEMOLO, E BASILICO

## SPAGHETTI WITH CLAMS, PARSLEY, AND BASIL

SERVES 6 AS AN APPETIZER OR 4 AS A MAIN COURSE

Spaghetti with clams is one of the quintessential coastal dishes in the southern regions, and one of the combinations that sum up the charms of Italian cooking: a mere handful of ingredients that seem meant for one another. While red clam sauce is served in the United States, no such variation exists in Italy, where spaghetti alle vongole is always made with white wine, garlic, red pepper flakes, and herbs, all that's required to ensure that it tastes simple, salty, and utterly of its place.

Kosher salt
¼ cup olive oil
3 large garlic cloves, thinly sliced
1 teaspoon red pepper flakes
¾ cup dry white wine
2 pounds Manila or littleneck clams, scrubbed
1 pound dried spaghetti or linguine
¼ cup thinly sliced fresh flat-leaf parsley leaves
10 large fresh basil leaves, 5 torn into pieces, 5 cut into chiffonade (see page xxx)
Freshly ground black pepper
Extra virgin olive oil, for serving

Fill a large pot about two-thirds full with water, salt it liberally, and bring to a boil over high heat.

Meanwhile, heat a large, heavy, lidded sauté pan over medium-high heat. Pour in the olive oil and tip and tilt the pan to coat it, heating the oil until it is shimmering and almost smoking. Add the garlic and cook, stirring with a wooden spoon, until lightly toasted and fragrant, about 3 minutes. Add the red pepper flakes, wine, and clams, cover the pan, and cook, gently shaking the pan occasionally, until the clams just begin to open, 5 to 7 minutes. Remove the pan from the heat and use a slotted spoon to transfer the clams to a medium bowl, discarding any that have not opened. When the clams are cool enough to handle, remove half of them from their shells.

When the water comes to a boil, add the pasta and cook until al dente, about 8 minutes. Drain the pasta thoroughly and add it to the sauté pan over medium-high heat. Add half of the parsley, the torn basil leaves, and the shucked clams, toss, and season with salt and a few grinds of black pepper.

Transfer the pasta to a serving bowl and garnish with the clams that are still in their shells. Drizzle with extra virgin olive oil and finish with a scattering of the remaining parsley and the sliced basil. Serve.

**Variation** For a fresher chile flavor, replace the red pepper flakes with ½ Fresno chile or jalapeño, seeded and minced.

# GARGANELLI CON PROSCIUTTO, PANNA, E RUCOLA

## GARGANELLI WITH PROSCIUTTO, CREAM, AND ARUGULA

SERVES 6 AS AN APPETIZER OR 4 AS A MAIN COURSE

Garganelli are, in my estimation, the finest of the short fresh pastas, because of their textural complexity: Each one is formed by twisting a square piece of dough and then rolling it on a dowel, so that it is thin at the edges and thick in the center, with a narrow tunnel that catches sauces. When you eat them, they register almost as a hybrid of fresh and dried pasta.

Because of the intricacies involved (in addition to the dowel work, garganelli are finished on a reed comb that produces their characteristic ridges), I don't suggest making your own garganelli. But it's worth the effort to procure them from a local Italian market or specialty shop that makes them in-house.

Kosher salt
1 cup fresh or frozen peas (see below), optional
2 tablespoons unsalted butter or truffle butter (see Sources, page 379)
5 ounces thinly sliced prosciutto, sliced into ½-inch-wide strips
1½ cups heavy cream
1 pound fresh or dried garganelli (gemelli or penne can be substituted)
¾ cup finely grated Parmigiano-Reggiano (about 1 ounce)
Freshly ground black pepper
1½ cups (loosely packed) arugula, washed, spun dry, and torn or cut into strips

Fill a medium pot about two-thirds full with water and salt it liberally. Bring to a boil over high heat. Add the peas and cook just until they start to turn bright green, about 30 seconds, then immediately drain in a colander and rinse under gently running cold water to stop the cooking and preserve their green color. Set aside.

Fill a large pot about two-thirds full with water and salt it liberally. Bring to a boil over high heat.

Meanwhile, heat a large heavy sauté pan over medium-high heat. Add 1 tablespoon of the butter and let it melt, tipping and tilting the pan to coat it. Add the prosciutto and cook, stirring with a wooden spoon, just to warm it and infuse the butter with its flavor, about 1 minute. Stir in the cream and bring it to a simmer, then lower the heat and simmer gently until it reduces and thickens enough to coat the back of the spoon, about 5 minutes.

When the water comes to a boil, add the pasta and cook until al dente, about 2 minutes for fresh, or 7 minutes for dried.

Meanwhile, stir the peas and the remaining tablespoon of butter into the sauce, letting the butter melt.

Drain the pasta and add it to the sauté pan. Toss to coat the pasta with the sauce, then stir in ½ cup of the cheese to melt it and thicken the sauce.

Divide the pasta among individual plates, finish with a few grinds of black pepper, sprinkling of cheese, and arugula, and serve.

### Frozen Peas

Frozen vegetables are much maligned, but frozen peas are an exception: Freshly picked peas are ideal for cooking, but their sugars almost immediately begin to turn into starch, losing the sweetness we expect from them. For this reason, frozen peas are often a preferable option, especially delicate baby peas. I wouldn't serve frozen peas raw, but for sauces, soups, and purees, they are often the best possible choice.

ALBE
ALIA

# BUCATINI ALL'AMATRICIANA

## BUCATINI WITH GUANCIALE, CHILE, AND TOMATO

SERVES 6 AS AN APPETIZER OR 4 AS A MAIN COURSE

This Roman classic is founded on the interplay between the guanciale (cured pork jowl) and tomato and the perfect tubular pasta to stand up to the intense sauce they produce. As the guanciale and tomato come together, it reminds me of the early stages of making a veal stock, when the roasted bones are coated with tomato paste. That same foundational combination is at the heart of this dish. And the fat in the guanciale is crucial, because it flavors the entire sauce with the elements of its cure.

3 tablespoons olive oil
8 ounces sliced guanciale, cut into thin 2-inch-long strips (thick-cut bacon or blanched salt pork can be substituted)
1 Spanish onion, minced
4 large garlic cloves, thinly sliced
1 small red chile, such as Fresno, minced (about 1 tablespoon), or a pinch of red pepper flakes
1 28-ounce can crushed tomatoes, preferably Italian San Marzano or organic, with their juice
Kosher salt
Freshly ground black pepper
1 pound dried bucatini (perciatelli or spaghetti can be substituted)
A wedge of Pecorino Romano or ricotta salata cheese, for grating

Heat a large heavy sauté pan over medium-high heat. Pour in the olive oil and tip and tilt the pan to coat it, heating the oil until it is shimmering and almost smoking. Add the guanciale and cook, stirring with a wooden spoon, until slightly browned, 1 to 2 minutes. Stir in the onions, garlic, and chile and cook, stirring frequently, until the onions are softened but not browned, about 4 minutes. Stir in the tomatoes and bring to a simmer, then lower the heat and let the sauce simmer, uncovered, for 1½ hours. A slick of oil will form on the surface; periodically stir it back into the sauce. Season the sauce with salt and pepper.

Meanwhile, toward the end of the sauce's cooking time, fill a large pot about two-thirds full with water and salt it liberally. Bring to a boil over high heat, add the pasta, and cook until al dente.

Drain the pasta, add to the sauce, and toss to coat. Let cook for a minute or two to unite the pasta and sauce.

Divide the pasta among individual plates and grate some cheese over each serving, then finish with several grinds of black pepper. Serve immediately.

**ISPIRAZIONE** The recipe for a decadent ravioli stuffed with an amatriciana-like filling and sauced with cacio e pepe (cheese and black pepper) can be found on page 265.

### Soffritto

The term soffritto refers to a mixture of diced aromatic vegetables and herbs cooked in olive oil to create a foundation of flavor in many preparations. I regularly employ a soffritto of garlic and rosemary, oftentimes with a pinch of red pepper flakes. A soffritto may include diced bell peppers, onions, celery, and often pork products such as guanciale or pancetta.

# TAJARIN AL SUGO D'ARROSTO

## THIN RIBBON PASTA WITH PAN-DRIPPING SAUCE

SERVES 6 AS AN APPETIZER OR 4 AS A MAIN COURSE

Tajarin, the Piedmontese name for tagliolini, is a thin, ribbony pasta. If you eat it in Piedmont, you will find that it's exceptionally rich because it's traditionally made with more eggs relative to the amount of flour than just about any other pasta. The sauce here, made with veal, approximates a common way of serving it in Piedmont, where it's tossed with the drippings collected from just-roasted beef.

¼ cup canola oil
4 tablespoons unsalted butter
1 boneless veal breast, about 2 pounds, cut into 2-inch cubes
1 Spanish onion, coarsely chopped
1 carrot, coarsely chopped
1 celery stalk, trimmed and coarsely chopped
1 rosemary sprig
4 garlic cloves, smashed with the side of a chef's knife and peeled
2 bay leaves, preferably fresh
½ teaspoon cracked black pepper
1 tablespoon tomato paste
2 cups dry white wine
About 4 to 5 cups Chicken Stock (page 374)
Kosher salt
Freshly ground black pepper
Fresh Pasta Sheets (page 72), cut into tajarin (see page 73), or 1 pound store-bought fresh tajarin or other long thin pasta (see Sources, page 379)
A wedge of Parmigiano-Reggiano, for grating

Heat a Dutch oven or other heavy pot over high heat. Add the oil and 3 tablespoons of the butter and tip and tilt the pot to coat it with the oil and butter as it melts. Add the veal and brown it all over, about 8 minutes. Use a slotted spoon to transfer the veal to a large plate.

Add the onions, carrots, celery, rosemary, garlic, bay leaves, and cracked pepper to the Dutch oven and cook, stirring with a wooden spoon, until the vegetables are softened but not browned, about 4 minutes. Return the veal to the pot, then add the tomato paste, stirring to coat the other ingredients, and cook until it turns a shade darker, about 2 minutes. Pour in the wine and stir to loosen any flavorful bits cooked onto the bottom of the pot. Bring the wine to a simmer and simmer until reduced by half, about 8 minutes.

Add enough stock to cover the meat and vegetables and bring to a simmer, lower the heat, and cook at a gentle simmer until the sauce is slightly thickened and richly flavored, about 1½ hours. During that time, periodically use a spoon to skim off any impurities that rise to the surface.

Strain the sauce through a fine-mesh strainer into a bowl, pressing down on the solids to extract as much flavorful liquid as possible. Discard the solids. Swirl in the remaining tablespoon of butter and season with salt and pepper. Cover the sauce to keep warm.

Fill a large pot about two-thirds full with water, salt it liberally, and bring to a boil over high heat. Add the pasta and cook until al dente, about 2 minutes for fresh, or 3 minutes for frozen. Drain the pasta and return it to the pot, then add the sauce and toss to coat.

Divide the pasta among individual bowls, grate some cheese over each serving, and finish with several grinds of black pepper. Serve immediately.

# PAPPARDELLE CON RAGÙ DI CACCIAGIONE

## WIDE PASTA RIBBONS WITH HUNTER-STYLE SAUCE

SERVES 6 AS AN APPETIZER OR 4 AS A MAIN COURSE

When summer turns to fall in Tuscany, the palate turns as well, and when it comes to pasta, that means shifting the emphasis from beef to game and game birds. The combination of duck and pappardelle is classically Tuscan, as are the forward presence of sturdy herbs and the enriching addition of duck hearts to the sauce.

3 tablespoons olive oil
6 duck legs
Kosher salt
Freshly ground black pepper
1 Spanish onion, cut into small dice
½ carrot, cut into small dice
1 celery stalk, trimmed and cut into small dice
1 pound white button mushrooms, trimmed and quartered
4 ounces duck hearts, cleaned, trimmed of membranes, and coarsely chopped (chicken livers can be substituted)
2 tablespoons tomato paste
¼ cup brandy
2 cups dry red wine
An herb sachet (3 bay leaves, 1 thyme sprig, 1 rosemary sprig, 8 juniper berries, and 3 whole cloves, tied in a cheesecloth bundle)
Pinch of freshly grated nutmeg
4 cups Dark Chicken Stock (page 374) or store-bought low-sodium chicken broth
Fresh Pasta Sheets (page 72), cut into pappardelle (see page 73), or 1 pound store-bought fresh or dried pappardelle
2 tablespoons unsalted butter
A wedge of Pecorino Romano, for grating

Heat a large Dutch oven or other heavy pot over medium-high heat. Pour in the oil and tip and tilt the pot to coat it, heating the oil until it is shimmering and almost smoking. Season the duck with salt and pepper and add it to the pot. Cook, turning occasionally, until the skin has rendered its fat and the duck is browned on all sides, about 8 minutes. Use a slotted spoon to transfer the duck to a large plate. Pour off and discard all but ¼ cup of the fat from the pot.

Add the onions, carrots, celery, and mushrooms to the pot and cook, stirring occasionally with a wooden spoon, until softened and lightly browned, about 7 minutes. Add the duck hearts and cook for 1 minute, then add the tomato paste, stirring to coat the vegetables and duck hearts, and cook until it turns a shade darker, about 2 minutes.

Remove the pot from the heat and pour in the brandy, then return the pot to the heat, bring the brandy to a boil, and cook until it has almost completely evaporated, 2 to 3 minutes. Stir in the wine, bring to a simmer, and cook until the wine is reduced by about half, 8 to 10 minutes.

Add the herb sachet, nutmeg, and pour in the stock. Return the duck legs to the pot, and bring the liquid to a simmer, then lower the heat and simmer, stirring occasionally, until the sauce is reduced enough to thickly coat the back of a spoon, 1½ to 2 hours.

Use tongs or a slotted spoon to transfer the duck legs to a plate. Let the sauce continue to simmer.

Fill a large pot about two-thirds full with water and salt it liberally. Bring to a boil over high heat, add the pasta, and cook until al dente, 2 to 3 minutes for fresh, or 9 to 10 minutes for dried.

Meanwhile, as soon as the duck legs are cool enough to handle, pull the meat from the bones in pieces and stir them into the sauce. Discard the bones.

Drain the pasta and return it to its pot. Add the butter and stir until the butter has melted and coats the pasta. Add the ragù to the pot and stir to coat the pasta.

Divide the pasta and sauce among individual plates, grate some cheese over each portion, and serve.

# GRAMIGNA CON SALSICCIA

## "LITTLE WEEDS" WITH SWEET SAUSAGE, CREAM, AND PARMESAN

SERVES 6 AS AN APPETIZER OR 4 AS A MAIN COURSE

Befitting its name, "little weeds," gramigna is made in both yellow and green versions, the latter with a spinach dough, often served in combination. This pasta dish is perennially popular in Emilia-Romagna because the sausage adds so much flavor and the sauce is very simple and quick to make. The sauce changes character with the seasons: it's made with tomato paste in the fall and winter and without it in the warmer months, and, accordingly, it's optional in this recipe.

- Kosher salt
- 2 tablespoons canola oil
- 1 pound sweet Italian sausage, preferably without fennel, removed from casings and crumbled
- ¼ cup minced Spanish onion
- 1 to 2 tablespoons tomato paste (optional)
- 1 tablespoon unsalted butter
- 1 cup heavy cream
- 1 pound dried gramigna (see Sources, page 379; another small twisted pasta, such as casarecce or strozzapreti [page 84], can be substituted)
- ½ cup finely grated Parmigiano-Reggiano (about 1 ounce), plus a wedge for grating
- Freshly ground black pepper

Fill a large pot about two-thirds full with water, salt it liberally, and bring to a boil over high heat.

Meanwhile, heat a large heavy sauté pan over medium heat. Pour in the canola oil and tip and tilt the pan to coat it, heating the oil until it is shimmering and almost smoking. Add the sausage and cook, using a wooden spoon to break it into small pieces, until nicely browned, about 7 minutes. Add the onions and cook, stirring occasionally, until softened but not browned, about 4 minutes. Stir in the tomato paste, if using, stirring to coat the other ingredients, and cook until it turns a shade darker, about 2 minutes.

Stir in the butter and cream, bring to a simmer, and simmer until the cream is reduced by about three quarters and the sauce has thickened, about 7 minutes.

When the water comes to a boil, add the pasta and cook until al dente, about 9 minutes. Drain.

Add the pasta and cheese to the sauté pan and toss to melt the cheese and coat the pasta with the sauce. Season with salt and pepper and toss again.

Divide the pasta and sauce among 4 to 6 plates or wide shallow bowls. Finish with more grated cheese and a few grinds of black pepper.

PASQUA

# TAGLIATELLE ALLA BOLOGNESE

## TAGLIATELLE WITH MEAT SAUCE

SERVES 6 AS AN APPETIZER OR 4 AS A MAIN COURSE

Outside of Italy, Bolognese has come to mean just about any meat sauce, but the true-blue original is actually more meat than sauce, a beefy and unapologetically decadent concoction.

- 1 tablespoon canola oil
- 8 ounces salt pork or pancetta, cut into large dice
- 1 small Spanish onion, cut into small dice
- 1 carrot, cut into small dice
- 1 celery stalk, trimmed and cut into small dice
- 1 pound ground beef (skirt steak or chuck, ideally 80% lean)
- 3 tablespoons tomato paste
- ½ cup dry white wine
- 2 tablespoons all-purpose flour
- 2½ cups Chicken Stock (page 374) or store-bought low-sodium chicken broth, or as needed
- Kosher salt
- Freshly ground black pepper
- ½ cup whole milk
- ⅛ teaspoon freshly grated nutmeg
- Fresh Pasta Sheets (page 72), cut into tagliatelle (see page 73), or 1 pound store-bought tagliatelle, fettuccine, pappardelle, or garganelli, preferably fresh
- 1 tablespoon unsalted butter
- A wedge of Parmigiano-Reggiano, for grating

Heat a wide heavy sauté pan over medium-high heat. Add the oil, tipping and tilting the pan to coat it and heating the oil until it is shimmering and almost smoking. Add the salt pork and cook, stirring, until it is browned and crispy and has rendered much of its fat, about 6 minutes. Stir in the onions, carrots, and celery and cook, stirring with a wooden spoon, until softened but not browned, about 6 minutes. Add the ground beef and cook, using the spoon to break up the meat, until it is cooked through, about 6 minutes. Stir in the tomato paste, stirring to coat the other ingredients, and cook until it turns a shade darker, about 2 minutes.

Pour in the wine and bring to a boil, stirring to loosen any flavorful bits cooked onto the bottom of the pan. Boil until the wine has evaporated, 6 to 7 minutes. Scatter the flour over the contents of the pan, stir it in, and cook, stirring constantly, for 1 minute. Stir in the stock, season with salt and pepper, and bring to a simmer. Stir in the milk and nutmeg and bring to a simmer, then lower the heat and simmer, covered, until the Bolognese is thick and aromatic, about 2 hours, or a bit longer if you prefer a denser sauce. During that time, periodically remove the lid, skim any fat with a tablespoon, season with a modicum of salt and pepper, and stir; continue to season periodically just until the sauce is assertively seasoned but not overly salty or spicy.

Meanwhile, toward the end of the sauce's cooking time, fill a large pot about two-thirds full with water, salt it liberally, and bring to a boil over high heat. Add the pasta and cook until al dente, 2 to 3 minutes for fresh, or 3 to 4 minutes for frozen.

Drain the pasta and add it to the Bolognese. Add the butter and toss well, adding a little more stock if necessary, until the sauce thickly coats the pasta.

Divide the pasta among individual plates, grate some cheese over each serving, and serve.

# FUSILLI CON RAGÙ NAPOLITANO

## FUSILLI WITH NEAPOLITAN PORK SAUCE

SERVES 6 AS AN APPETIZER OR 4 AS A MAIN COURSE

The main elements of a Sunday dinner—meat, pasta, and sauce—in one bowl. I developed this recipe at Convivio and my customers still ask for it today. Whereas many cooks grind the pork, I dice it. The pancetta that starts the cooking infuses the entire dish with both the deep, rich flavor of pork fat and the spices with which it was cured.

1 tablespoon canola oil
2 ounces pancetta, cut into small dice
2 pounds boneless pork shoulder, cut into small dice
Kosher salt
Freshly ground black pepper
Pinch of red pepper flakes
1 large Spanish onion, cut into small dice
3 garlic cloves, smashed with the side of a chef's knife and peeled
1 6-ounce can tomato paste
1 cup dry red wine
1 28-ounce can diced tomatoes, preferably Italian San Marzano or organic, with their juices
4 cups Chicken Stock (page 374)
1 pound dried fusilli
¼ cup finely grated Pecorino Romano, plus a wedge for grating

Heat a Dutch oven or other large heavy pot over medium-high heat. Pour in the oil and tip and tilt the pot to coat it, then let the oil warm up. Add the pancetta and cook, stirring with a wooden spoon, until it turns lightly golden and has rendered much of its fat, about 6 minutes. Add the pork, season with salt and pepper, and cook, stirring, until browned all over, 8 to 10 minutes. Stir in the red pepper flakes, onions, and garlic, lower the heat to low, and cook, stirring periodically, until the onions are lightly caramelized, about 12 minutes. (If the pot becomes too dry or the onions or garlic begin to scorch, stir in a splash of water.)

Stir in the tomato paste, stirring to coat the other ingredients, and cook until it turns a shade darker, about 2 minutes. Pour in the wine and use the spoon to loosen any flavorful bits cooked onto the bottom of the pot. Bring to a simmer, lower the heat, and simmer until the wine is reduced by half, about 5 minutes. Stir in the tomatoes and stock and bring to a simmer, then lower the heat and simmer, uncovered, until the pork is tender and the sauce has thickened, about 1 hour.

Meanwhile, toward the end of the sauce's cooking time, fill a large pot about two-thirds full with water, salt it liberally, and bring to a boil over high heat. Add the pasta and cook until al dente, about 8 minutes.

Use a heatproof liquid measuring cup to scoop out and reserve about 1 cup of the pasta cooking liquid, then drain the pasta and add to the sauce. Toss and, if necessary, add a few tablespoons of the cooking liquid to help loosen the sauce. Remove the pot from the heat, add the cheese, and toss well.

Divide the pasta among 4 to 6 plates, top with additional grated Pecorino, and serve immediately.

## CAVATELLI CON RAGÙ DI AGNELLO E PEPERONI

### CAVATELLI WITH LAMB RAGÙ AND RED PEPPERS

SERVES 6 AS AN APPETIZER OR 4 AS A MAIN COURSE

Lamb neck ragù is sort of the Southern Italian equivalent of Bolognese sauce. It can be made with ground meat, but I prefer a more rustic version, braising the lamb neck, then pulling the meat from the bones and returning it to the sauce in which it was cooked. I also like to add red bell peppers, a plentiful crop in the south, to this dish, incorporating some in the soffritto and sautéed along with other vegetables in the sauce toward the end as well. Chewy cavatelli make a perfect foil for this lusty sauce, trapping it in its ridges and offering a pleasing textural counterpoint to the lamb.

2 to 2½ pounds lamb neck bones
Kosher salt
Freshly ground black pepper
¼ cup plus 2 tablespoons olive oil
2 large red bell peppers, cored, seeded, and cut into small dice
2 Spanish onions, cut into small dice
2 carrots, cut into small dice
1 celery stalk, trimmed and cut into small dice
6 large garlic cloves, minced
1 rosemary sprig
1 thyme sprig
2 bay leaves, preferably fresh
1 heaping tablespoon all-purpose flour
2 cups dry white wine
4 cups Chicken Stock (page 374) or store-bought low-sodium chicken broth
1 pound fresh or frozen cavatelli (see Sources, page 379)
A wedge of Pecorino Romano, for grating
Gremolata (recipe follows on page 102)

Position a rack in the center of the oven and preheat the oven to 350°F.

Season the lamb with salt and pepper. Heat a Dutch oven or other large heavy ovenproof pot over medium-high heat. Add ¼ cup of the oil and tip and tilt the pot to coat it, heating the oil until it is shimmering and almost smoking. Add the lamb neck bones and cook, using tongs or a slotted spoon to turn them, until they are browned all over, about 8 minutes. Transfer the lamb neck bones to a large plate. Pour off all but 2 tablespoons of the fat from the pot.

Add about half of the bell pepper and roughly three quarters of the onions, carrots, celery, and garlic, along with the rosemary, thyme, and bay leaves, to the pot and cook, stirring occasionally, until the vegetables are lightly browned and tender, about 6 minutes. Stir in the flour and cook, stirring constantly, for 1 minute to coat the vegetables with the flour. Return the lamb neck bones to the pot, pour in the wine, and stir to loosen any flavorful bits cooked onto the bottom of the pot. Bring the wine to a simmer and simmer until it has almost completely evaporated, about 10 minutes.

Stir in the stock and bring to a simmer. Cover the pot and place in the oven. Braise until the lamb is tender to the tines of a fork and almost falling off the bone, 2 to 2½ hours. During this time, check the liquid periodically to be sure that it is just barely simmering; you are looking for a slight, almost imperceptible bubbling on the surface. If it is not simmering, raise the heat to 375°F; if it's simmering too assertively, lower the heat to 325°F. Remove the pot from the oven, carefully remove the lamb to a plate, and let it cool. Set the pot aside.

Meanwhile, heat a medium sauté pan over medium-high heat. Add the remaining 2 tablespoons oil, tipping and tilting the pan to coat it and heating the oil until it is shimmering and almost smoking. Add the remaining bell peppers, onions, carrots, celery, and garlic and cook, stirring, until softened but not browned, about 5 minutes. Season with salt and pepper and remove from the heat.

By now, the lamb should be cool enough to handle. Use a sharp knife to remove any fat or cartilage, and pull the lamb meat into small pieces, transferring them to a plate. Discard the bones.

Return the pot of braising liquid to medium-high heat, bring to a simmer, and simmer until the liquid is reduced by about a third, 8 to 10 minutes.

Meanwhile, fill a large pot about two-thirds full with water, salt it liberally, and bring to a boil over high heat. Add the pasta and cook until al dente, about 2 minutes for fresh, or 3 to 4 minutes for frozen. Using a heatproof liquid measuring cup, scoop out and reserve 1 cup of the pasta cooking liquid, then drain the pasta.

*(continued)*

Add the lamb meat to the sauce, along with the sautéed vegetables, and stir to incorporate. Add the pasta and toss to coat it, adding a few tablespoons of the reserved cooking liquid if necessary to loosen it.

Divide the pasta and sauce among 4 to 6 plates or wide shallow bowls, top with grated cheese and gremolata, and serve.

## GREMOLATA

MAKES ABOUT ¼ CUP

Gremolata is a chopped herb garnish that's typically sprinkled over Osso Buco and other dishes, primarily braised meats. It's usually made with parsley, garlic, and lemon, but the mint here offers a more subtle flavor.

2 tablespoons thinly sliced fresh flat-leaf parsley leaves
2 tablespoons thinly sliced fresh mint leaves
Finely grated zest of 1 lemon

Put the parsley, mint, and zest in a small bowl and stir together just to combine.

# AGNOLOTTI DEL PLIN

## VEAL-STUFFED AGNOLOTTI

SERVES 6 AS AN APPETIZER OR 4 AS A MAIN COURSE

These stuffed pasta crescents are to Piedmont what tortellini are to Emilia-Romagna, a local institution. Plin means "pinched," referring to how they are made, shaped as rectangles, then pinched into their finished form. These agnolotti were once served on linen napkins, an aristocratic and regal touch. Today you're more apt to encounter them sauced with the drippings of a roast (see page 95), with a browned butter and sage sauce, or even just with melted butter. Here the cooking liquid from the filling is used as a glazing base. Note that the filling must be refrigerated for 1 hour before using it.

¼ cup canola oil
4 tablespoons unsalted butter
1½ pounds boneless veal breast or shoulder, cut into 1-inch cubes
1 small onion, cut into small dice
1 small carrot, cut into small dice
1 celery stalk, trimmed and cut into small dice
2 garlic cloves, smashed with the side of a chef's knife and peeled
¼ cup long-grain white rice
1 cup dry white wine
About 4 cups Chicken Stock (page 374)
An herb sachet (1 thyme sprig, 1 sage sprig, 1 rosemary sprig, and 1 bay leaf, tied in a cheesecloth bundle)
Kosher salt
Freshly ground black pepper
1 small bunch of escarole, trimmed and coarsely chopped
½ cup finely grated Parmigiano-Reggiano (about 1 ounce), plus a wedge for grating
2 large eggs, lightly beaten
All-purpose flour, for dusting
Fresh Pasta Sheets (page 72), rolled through the thinnest setting, or 1 pound store-bought fresh pasta sheets
Rice flour, for dusting
1 tablespoon thinly sliced fresh flat-leaf parsley leaves

Heat a large heavy skillet over medium-high heat. Add the oil and 2 tablespoons of the butter, tipping and tilting the pan to coat it with the oil and melting butter. Add the veal and cook, stirring occasionally with a wooden spoon, until browned on all sides, about 8 minutes. Add the onions, carrots, celery, and garlic and cook until the vegetables begin to brown and caramelize, about 7 minutes. Carefully drain the excess fat from the pan.

Scatter the rice over the vegetables and stir well, then add the wine and use the wooden spoon to scrape up any flavorful bits cooked onto the bottom of the pan. Bring to a simmer and simmer until the wine has almost completely evaporated. Add enough stock to cover the veal, then add the herb sachet, season with salt and pepper, and bring to a simmer. Cover and simmer until the veal is almost falling apart, about 1½ hours. Use a heatproof liquid measuring cup to scoop out and reserve 1 cup of the cooking liquid, then add the escarole to the pan, stirring it in until wilted.

Transfer the contents of the pan to the bowl of a food processor and pulse to a coarse puree.

Transfer the mixture to a bowl and season with salt and pepper. Let cool, then add the Parmigiano and eggs and stir together with a rubber spatula; the mixture should be moist. Cover the bowl with plastic wrap, and refrigerate for 1 hour to firm it.

Fill a spray bottle with water and set it so that it produces a fine mist when the trigger is pressed.

Lay the pasta sheets on a floured surface and use a sharp knife or pizza cutter to trim the pasta into forty to forty-eight 3-inch squares (use a ruler or other straightedge to guide you). You should have 12 squares.

Line a baking sheet with parchment paper and lightly dust it with rice flour. Spoon a heaping teaspoon of the filling into the center of the squares, keeping the other squares beneath a damp kitchen towel. Hold the spray bottle a foot or two above the pasta and spray once to release a mist of water over the squares, then place another square on top. Use your fingertips to press the edges of the pasta together, pressing out the air and sealing the edges. Trim the edges of each square with a zigzag pasta wheel and set on the prepared baking sheet. (The agnolotti can be refrigerated for up to 1 day or frozen for up to 2 months. Wrap the baking sheet in plastic wrap and refrigerate, or freeze the agnolotti on the sheet until frozen hard, then transfer to freezer bags.

*(continued)*

Refrigerate or freeze the reserved cooking liquid; if freezing it, thaw before reheating.

Fill a large pot two-thirds full with water, salt it liberally, and bring to a boil over high heat.

Meanwhile, melt the remaining 2 tablespoons butter in a medium heavy pot over medium heat. Remove the pot from the heat and let it cool slightly.

Add the agnolotti to the boiling water and cook until they rise to the surface, 2 to 3 minutes for fresh, 4 to 5 minute for frozen. Remove the agnolotti with a slotted spoon and transfer to the pot with the melted butter. Add the reserved cooking liquid, return the pot to low heat, and cook, stirring gently, until the sauce is reduced slightly and just glazes the agnolotti.

Divide the agnolotti among wide shallow bowls, top with grated Parmigiano and the parsley, and serve.

RISO
Gallo

# RISOTTO DI BASE

## BASIC RISOTTO

SERVES 6 AS AN APPETIZER OR 4 AS A MAIN COURSE

A few other essential risotto recipes follow this one, but because you can make risotto with just about anything, I offer this highly adaptable template that can be adapted to include vegetables, shellfish, or meat. (You also can use this recipe to produce a plain risotto bianca, or white risotto, topping it with grated Parmigiano-Reggiano. As a rule of thumb, use a stock that reflects the ingredients you will add to the risotto (i.e., vegetable stock for vegetables, shellfish for shellfish, and beef for meat). White wine is classic, but red wine is occasionally used; see page 110 for a red wine risotto.

8 cups homemade stock (pages 371–375)
4 tablespoons unsalted butter
2 tablespoons olive oil
1 small Spanish onion, minced
2½ cups risotto rice, such as arborio
½ cup dry white or red wine (see the headnote)
½ cup finely grated Parmigiano-Reggiano (about 1 ounce)
Kosher salt

Pour the stock into a large saucepan and bring it to a simmer over medium-high heat. Reduce the heat as necessary to keep the stock at a simmer.

Heat a large wide heavy pot over medium heat. Add 2 tablespoons of the butter and the olive oil and tip and tilt the pot to coat it with the oil and melting butter. Add the onions and cook, stirring frequently with a wooden spoon, until softened but not browned, about 4 minutes. Add the rice and cook, stirring to coat it with the fat, until the grains turn opaque at the center, about 3 minutes. Add the wine and cook, stirring, until it has evaporated, about 5 minutes.

Ladle in about 1 cup of the stock and cook, stirring constantly, in alternating wide and narrow circles, until the stock is absorbed by the rice. Then continue to add the stock in ½-cup increments, stirring constantly and adding the next addition only after the previous one has been completely absorbed; if the rice begins to scorch or stick to the bottom of the pot, lower the heat slightly. After about 15 minutes, when there is only about a cup of stock remaining in the saucepan, begin adding it more judiciously, just a few tablespoons at a time. Stop adding stock when the risotto is nicely moist and the grains are al dente. (Remove a few grains with a teaspoon and taste them; the rice should offer some resistance but not taste undercooked.)

Remove the pot from the heat and stir in the remaining 2 tablespoons butter and the cheese, then fold in any desired additions. Taste and, if necessary, adjust the seasoning with salt. Divide among wide plates and serve.

### Tips for Making Risotto

Next to the rice (see page xxxii), stock is the most important ingredient in a risotto. This is definitely one of those times that you want to use a homemade stock.

When it comes to the addition of liquid, the reason you add the stock a little at a time is so that the grains rub against each other as they cook, which helps release their starch and bind them together in the finished dish. Use a wooden spoon to keep from breaking the grains of rice during the long cooking process.

Some people prefer drier risottos, some soupier ones. I'm in the latter camp—I like my risotto a little wet, or all'onda (wavy). By all means, adapt risotto recipes to suit your own personal preference, adding more or less liquid accordingly. You can also add more Parmigiano at the end for a tighter result, or less for a wetter one.

To add a subtle baseline of flavor to your risottos, stir a fresh bay leaf into the rice just before adding the wine, then remove it at the end.

# RISOTTO AL LIMONE

## LEMON RISOTTO

SERVES 6 AS AN APPETIZER OR 4 AS A MAIN COURSE

The charm of risotto, to both cook and eat, is revealed in this dish, which adds just a few ingredients to the basic recipe but utterly transforms it. Lemon risotto can be eaten on its own or served as a side to other dishes, especially fish and shellfish. It benefits from the addition of sliced tender herbs, such as mint or basil, or blanched or sautéed spring vegetables, such as peas or sliced asparagus.

8 cups Chicken Stock (page 374) or Vegetable Stock (page 371)
4 tablespoons unsalted butter
2 tablespoons olive oil
1 small Spanish onion, minced
2½ cups risotto rice, such as arborio
½ cup dry white wine
1 large egg yolk, lightly beaten
Grated zest and juice of 1 large lemon
½ cup finely grated Parmigiano-Reggiano (about 1 ounce)
Kosher salt

Pour the stock into a large saucepan and bring it to a simmer over medium-high heat. Reduce the heat as necessary to keep the stock at a simmer.

Heat a large wide heavy pot over medium heat. Add 2 tablespoons of the butter and the olive oil and tip and tilt the pot to coat it with the oil and melting butter. Add the onions and cook, stirring frequently with a wooden spoon, until softened but not browned, about 4 minutes. Add the rice and cook, stirring to coat it with the fat, until the grains turn opaque at the center, about 3 minutes. Add the wine and cook, stirring constantly, until it has evaporated, about 5 minutes.

Ladle in about 1 cup of the stock and cook, stirring constantly, in alternating wide and narrow circles, until the stock is absorbed by the rice. Then continue to add the stock in ½-cup increments, stirring constantly and adding the next addition only after the previous one has been completely absorbed; if the rice begins to scorch or stick to the bottom of the pot, lower the heat slightly. After about 15 minutes, when there is only about a cup of stock remaining in the saucepan, begin adding it more judiciously, just a few tablespoons at a time. Stop adding stock when the risotto is nicely moist and the grains are al dente. (Remove a few grains with a teaspoon and taste them; the rice should offer some resistance but not taste undercooked.)

Remove the pot from the heat and stir in the remaining 2 tablespoons butter, the egg yolk, lemon zest, and half of the lemon juice. Taste the risotto: It should be unmistakably but not overwhelmingly lemony. If necessary, stir in a bit more of the juice. Stir in the Parmigiano and, if necessary, season with salt. Divide the risotto among wide plates and serve.

# RISOTTO CON PISELLI, PORRI, E FORMAGGIO DI CAPRA

## RISOTTO WITH PEAS, LEEKS, AND GOAT CHEESE

SERVES 6 AS AN APPETIZER OR 4 AS A MAIN COURSE

This springtime risotto puts the flavors of peas and leeks front and center, complementing them with the gentle tang of goat cheese. I especially recommend underscoring the fresh green flavors of the risotto with a fresh bay leaf; see Tips for Making Risotto, page 106.

8 cups Chicken Stock (page 374)
Kosher salt
½ cup fresh or frozen peas (see Frozen Peas, page 92)
½ cup minced leeks (white and light green parts only)
4 tablespoons unsalted butter
2 tablespoons olive oil
1 small Spanish onion, minced
2½ cups risotto rice, such as arborio
½ cup dry white wine
½ cup crumbled fresh goat cheese (about 2 ounces)
6 large fresh basil leaves, cut into chiffonade (see page xxx)
1 tablespoon minced fresh chives
2 tablespoons finely grated Parmigiano-Reggiano

Pour the stock into a large saucepan and bring it to a simmer over medium-high heat. Reduce the heat as necessary to keep the stock at a simmer.

Meanwhile, bring a small pot of salted water to a boil. Add the peas and cook just until al dente, about 3 minutes for frozen, or 5 minutes for fresh. Use a slotted spoon to transfer the peas to a colander, rinse under gently running cold water to stop the cooking and preserve the color, drain again, and transfer to a medium bowl. Add the leeks to the boiling water and cook for 2 minutes, then drain, rinse, cool, drain again, and add to the bowl.

Heat a large wide heavy pot over medium heat. Add 2 tablespoons of the butter and the olive oil and tip and tilt the pot to coat it with the oil and melting butter. Add the onions and cook, stirring frequently with a wooden spoon, until softened but not browned, about 4 minutes. Add the rice and cook, stirring to coat it with the fat, until the grains turn opaque at the center, about 3 minutes. Add the wine and cook, stirring constantly, until it has evaporated, about 5 minutes.

Ladle in about 1 cup of the stock and cook, stirring constantly, until the stock is absorbed by the rice. Then continue to add the stock in ½-cup increments, stirring constantly in alternating wide and narrow circles, and adding the next addition only after the previous one has been completely absorbed; if the rice begins to scorch or stick to the bottom of the pot, lower the heat slightly. After about 15 minutes, when there is only about a cup of stock remaining in the saucepan, add the peas and leeks to the pot and then begin adding the stock more judiciously, just a few tablespoons at a time. Stop adding stock when the risotto is nicely moist and the grains are al dente. (Remove a few grains with a teaspoon and taste them; the rice should offer some resistance but not taste undercooked.)

Stir in the goat cheese, basil, chives, and Parmigiano and season with salt. Divide among wide plates and serve.

# RISOTTO AI FUNGHI

## MUSHROOM RISOTTO

SERVES 6 AS AN APPETIZER OR 4 AS A MAIN COURSE

The key to this risotto is coaxing as much flavor out of the mushrooms as possible, sautéing them just enough to release their liquid, and punching up their flavor with the addition of brandy. This is a dish that I make frequently at home, because it can be a satisfying meal in its own right, a starter, or even an accompaniment to roasted meats. I never make it the same way twice and suggest you do the same, experimenting with different combinations of mushrooms or focusing on one mushroom and letting it shine.

- 8 cups Chicken Stock (page 374) or Mushroom Stock (page 371)
- 5 tablespoons unsalted butter
- 3 tablespoons olive oil
- 1 pound mixed mushrooms, such as white button, shiitake, and porcini, trimmed (if using shiitake, discard the stems)
- Kosher salt
- Freshly ground black pepper
- 2 tablespoons brandy
- 2 tablespoons chopped fresh thyme or sage
- 1 small Spanish onion, minced
- 2½ cups risotto rice, such as arborio
- ½ cup dry white wine
- ½ cup finely grated Parmigiano-Reggiano (about 1 ounce)
- Freshly ground black pepper

Pour the stock into a large saucepan and bring it to a simmer over medium-high heat. Reduce the heat as necessary to keep the stock at a simmer.

Meanwhile, heat a wide, deep, heavy skillet over medium heat. Add 1 tablespoon of the butter and 1 tablespoon of the olive oil and tip and tilt the pan to coat it with the fat. Add the mushrooms, season with salt and pepper, and cook until they have given off their liquid and are tender, about 8 minutes. Pour in the brandy and cook, stirring occasionally, until it has almost completely evaporated, 2 to 3 minutes. Stir in 1 tablespoon of the thyme and cook for another minute or two, then remove the pan from the heat and set aside.

Heat a large wide heavy pot over medium heat. Add 2 tablespoons of the butter and the remaining 2 tablespoons olive oil and tip and tilt the pot to coat it with the oil and melting butter. Add the onions and cook, stirring frequently with a wooden spoon, until softened but not browned, about 4 minutes. Add the rice and cook, stirring to coat it with the fat, until the grains turn opaque at the center, about 3 minutes. Add the wine and cook, stirring constantly, until it has evaporated, about 5 minutes.

Ladle in about 1 cup of the stock and cook, stirring constantly, in alternating wide and narrow circles, until the stock is absorbed by the rice. Then continue to add the stock in ½-cup increments, stirring constantly and adding the next addition only after the previous one has been completely absorbed; if the rice begins to scorch or stick to the bottom of the pot, lower the heat slightly. After about 15 minutes, when there is only about a cup of stock remaining in the saucepan, stir the remaining tablespoon of thyme into the risotto and then begin adding the stock more judiciously, just a few tablespoons at a time. Stop adding stock when the risotto is nicely moist and the grains are al dente. (Remove a few grains with a teaspoon and taste them; the rice should offer some resistance but not taste undercooked.)

Fold in the mushrooms, along with the remaining 2 tablespoons butter and the cheese. Taste and, if necessary, add salt and pepper. Divide the risotto among wide plates and serve.

# RISOTTO AL VINO ROSSO

## RED WINE RISOTTO

SERVES 6 AS AN APPETIZER OR 4 AS A MAIN COURSE

Since most risotto recipes are made with white wine, a red wine risotto, with the rice dyed a deep burgundy, can be a pleasant surprise at the table. Don't use a full-bodied red like a Cabernet Sauvignon; instead select a smooth-drinking wine such as Pinot Noir or Shiraz. This can be served on its own, but it also makes a wonderful accompaniment to roasted or grilled beef, especially steaks.

8 cups Chicken Stock (page 374)
4 tablespoons unsalted butter
2 tablespoons olive oil
1 small Spanish onion, minced
2½ cups risotto rice, such as arborio
½ cup dry red wine (see the headnote)
¾ cup finely grated Parmigiano-Reggiano (about 1 ounce)
Kosher salt

Pour the stock into a large saucepan and bring it to a simmer over medium-high heat. Reduce the heat as necessary to keep it at a simmer.

Heat a large wide heavy pot over medium heat. Add 2 tablespoons of the butter and the olive oil and tip and tilt the pot to coat it with the oil and melting butter. Add the onions and cook, stirring frequently with a wooden spoon, until softened but not browned, about 4 minutes. Add the rice and cook, stirring to coat it with the fat, until the grains turn opaque at the center, about 3 minutes. Add the wine and cook, stirring constantly, until it has evaporated, 8 to 10 minutes.

Ladle in about 1 cup of the stock and cook, stirring constantly in alternating wide and narrow circles, until the stock is absorbed by the rice. Then continue to add the stock in ½-cup increments, stirring constantly and adding the next addition only after the previous one has been completely absorbed; if the rice begins to scorch or stick to the bottom of the pot, lower the heat slightly. After about 15 minutes, when there is only about a cup of stock remaining in the saucepan, begin adding it more judiciously, just a few tablespoons at a time. Stop adding stock when the risotto is nicely moist and the grains are al dente. (Remove a few grains with a teaspoon and taste them; the rice should offer some resistance but not taste undercooked.)

Remove the pot from the heat and stir in the remaining 2 tablespoons butter and ½ cup of the Parmigiano. Taste and, if necessary, add salt. Divide among wide plates, garnish with the remaining cheese, and serve.

**Variation** To make this risotto in the style of Treviso, render a few tablespoons of diced pancetta in the oil and butter at the beginning of the recipe, and fold some sautéed chopped radicchio into the risotto during the final minutes of cooking.

# PESCE E FRUTTI DI MARE
# FISH AND SHELLFISH

The best, most memorable fish dishes I've eaten in Italy have been the simplest. While writing this book, I joked that this chapter could have included one recipe that went something like this: *Get a piece of sublimely fresh fish, grill it over an open fire, put it on a plate, season with salt and pepper, drizzle with extra virgin olive oil, and finish with a squeeze of lemon.*

Because Italy is a relatively narrow country that is surrounded on three sides by water—the Ligurian, Tyrrhenian, Mediterranean, and Adriatic seas—one is never very far from just-caught seafood: crustaceans, eels, blue fish, John Dory, wild sea bass, turbot, and other specimens are all readily available. Even chain supermarkets offer pristine fish, displayed on ice, that would rival that available at the ritziest of American gourmet shops.

Moreover, fish and shellfish exemplify the rewards of cooking with Italy's culinary materia prima, or raw materials. Everybody there is a hotshot when it comes to fish, because you don't need to be a professional to grill a fresh tuna steak to perfection, or poach a lobster and set it atop a vegetable salad, or crust a sea bass in salt and bake it.

Accordingly, more so than in almost any other place in the book, I encourage you to seek out the best and freshest ingredients available; for all the talk of how much Italian food was inspired by necessity, this is one area where the opposite is true. Italy's repertoire of seafood staples was created to take advantage of an embarrassment of riches, and starting with comparable raw ingredients will set you on your way to reproducing the essential character of these dishes in any setting.

# BRODETTO DI PESCE

## ADRIATIC-STYLE SEAFOOD STEW

SERVES 10 TO 12

This seafood stew combines a hodgepodge of finfish and shellfish in what might be considered Italy's bouillabaisse. (The word brodetto means "short broth," a reference to the quick stock traditionally made from the shrimp shells and fish bones, but this recipe calls for an already-prepared stock instead.) You can by all means vary the selection and proportions of seafood, but including a mix is essential to producing a complex broth that results in an alluring effect that I think of as a "symphony of the sea."

2 tablespoons olive oil
2 large garlic cloves, minced
1 bay leaf, preferably fresh
1 Spanish onion, thinly sliced
2 large beefsteak tomatoes, cut into small dice, or 1 28-ounce can whole tomatoes, preferably Italian San Marzano or organic, crushed by hand, with their juice
5 basil sprigs, 1 left whole, leaves removed from the remaining 4 and cut into chiffonade (see page xxx)
Pinch of red pepper flakes
1 cup dry white wine
Seafood Stock (page 372)
2 pounds firm white-fleshed fish fillets, such as monkfish, sea bass, or snapper, cut into 1½-inch cubes
Kosher salt
Freshly ground black pepper
All-purpose flour, for dusting
2 tablespoons canola oil
1 pound sea scallops
1 pound large shrimp
1 pound mussels, preferably Prince Edward Island, scrubbed and debearded
1 pound clams, such as Manila or cherrystone, scrubbed
¼ cup plus 2 tablespoons thinly sliced fresh flat-leaf parsley leaves
Extra virgin olive oil, for drizzling
10 to 12 slices fettunta (see page 11; 1 slice per serving)

Heat a large heavy pot over medium heat. Add the olive oil and tip and tilt the pot to coat it, heating the oil until it is shimmering and almost smoking. Add the garlic, bay leaf, and onions and cook, stirring frequently with a wooden spoon, until softened but not browned, about 4 minutes.

Stir in the tomatoes and sprig of basil and cook, stirring, until the tomatoes begin to break down, about 6 minutes. Add the pepper flakes, pour in the wine, and bring to a simmer. Cook, stirring to loosen any flavorful bits cooked onto the bottom of the pot, until the liquid has almost completely evaporated, 6 to 7 minutes. Pour in the seafood stock, bring to a simmer, and simmer until the mixture is slightly thickened and intensely flavored, but not murky, 5 to 8 minutes.

Meanwhile, season the fish with salt and pepper. Put the flour in a shallow bowl and add the fish, tossing to coat lightly. Remove the fish from the flour, shaking off any excess, and set on a plate. Heat a large skillet over medium heat, then add the canola oil, tipping and tilting the pan to coat it and heating the oil. Add the fish, in batches, and cook, stirring and turning frequently, until lightly golden brown all over and just cooked through, about 5 minutes per batch.

Add the fish to the pot, along with the scallops, shrimp, mussels, and clams; cover the pot and cook until the scallops and shrimp are opaque and the mussels and clams have opened; use a slotted spoon to fish out and discard any mussels and clams that have not opened. Stir in about half of the sliced basil and half the parsley and season to taste with salt and pepper.

Ladle the brodetto into wide shallow bowls, including a good mix of fish and shellfish in each serving. Drizzle with extra virgin olive oil, scatter the remaining basil and parsley over the stew, and serve with the fettunta alongside.

# INSALATA ALLA CATALANA

## POACHED LOBSTER AND VEGETABLE SALAD

SERVES 4

Taste memory, or the ability to recall the specific flavors of individual dishes, is one of the most powerful tools a chef can possess, because it imbues our cooking with both passion and precision as we try to re-create meaningful moments from our dining past and to conjure up the same emotions we experienced for those who eat our food. This recipe sprang from such a memory.

In the mid-1990s, my then-girlfriend Giovanna (today my wife) and I enjoyed one of the first seafood meals we'd ever shared, at the restaurant Al Caminetto (the Little Fireplace) in Milano-Marittima, a coastal resort town to which the denizens of Milan flock in the summer. The food there and in other communities along the Italian Riviera reflects the mind-set of the vacationers: Just as you want to kick back and let the setting wash over you in open-air bars and on the beach, when dining in restaurants, there's a desire to enjoy the local produce and seafood as simply as possible. A prime example is this poached lobster and vegetable salad, dressed with a lemony, garlicky vinaigrette. Make it with the freshest ingredients you can put your hands on, changing up the vegetables if necessary to use what's at the peak of season and, if possible, grown locally.

Kosher salt
4 lobsters, 1½ pounds each
⅓ cup olive oil
1 tablespoon red wine vinegar
1 tablespoon freshly squeezed lemon juice
2 tablespoons dried oregano
1 large garlic clove, minced
¼ cup minced fresh chives
Freshly ground black pepper
1 large red bell pepper, cored, seeded, and cut into thin strips
1 large yellow bell pepper, cored, seeded, and cut into thin strips
1 small bunch of radishes, thinly sliced
1 red onion, thinly sliced
1 fennel bulb, trimmed and thinly sliced
1 pint cherry tomatoes, halved, or quartered if large
1 medium Belgian endive, trimmed at the root end and separated into spears
2 romaine hearts, tough core removed and discarded, coarsely chopped
1 bunch of scallions (white and light green parts only), thinly sliced
4 thick slices ciabatta or other rustic bread, toasted or grilled

Fill a large deep pot about two-thirds full with water and salt it liberally. Bring to a boil over high heat. Gently lower the lobsters into the water and boil, uncovered, until the shells are bright red, about 8 minutes. Turn off the heat and let stand for 4 to 5 minutes to allow the lobsters to finish cooking gently in the hot water. Transfer the lobsters to a large platter to cool slightly.

When the lobsters are cool enough to handle, use a sharp heavy knife to cut them lengthwise in half. Use the knife tip or a tablespoon to remove the tomalley (the soft green matter) from the heads of the lobsters and transfer it to a medium bowl.

Add the olive oil, vinegar, lemon juice, oregano, and garlic to the tomalley and whisk to incorporate them into a vinaigrette. Fold in the chives and season with a pinch of salt and a few grinds of black pepper.

Put the bell peppers, radishes, red onion, fennel, tomatoes, endive, romaine, and scallions in a large bowl. Drizzle with about half of the vinaigrette and toss. Season with salt and pepper and toss again.

Set the halves of one lobster on each of 4 dinner plates. Drizzle with the remaining vinaigrette and top with the salad. Serve with the ciabatta alongside.

# SEPPIA CON SCAROLA

## CUTTLEFISH WITH ESCAROLE

SERVES 4

Seppia, or cuttlefish, is a relative of calamari, or squid (both are cephalopods, as is octopus) but it is less well known in the United States than in Italy, where it is particularly popular along the Adriatic Coast. Much as I like calamari, I actually prefer the more toothsome, stronger-flavored cuttlefish, largely because it can stand up to big flavors. Here it is paired with a piquant stew of escarole, tomato puree, anchovies, and capers.

I usually prefer my cuttlefish grilled, the way I came to know it along the beaches of Italy, but it's impractical to fire up a grill for the sole purpose of cooking cuttlefish for about 6 minutes. So this recipe cooks it alla piastra, or on a griddle—or, in this case, in a cast-iron skillet, which will produce the desired char. If you do happen to have your grill heated for other cooking, by all means grill the cuttlefish instead. Then cook the sauce in a sauté pan set on the grill. Note that the cuttlefish must marinate for 2 hours.

- 2 pounds cuttlefish, cleaned and separated into tubes and tentacles (by your fish shop)
- ¼ cup plus 3 tablespoons olive oil
- 6 large garlic cloves, 3 smashed with the side of a chef's knife and peeled, 3 sliced
- Finely grated zest and juice of 1 large lemon
- 2 mint sprigs
- 1 Spanish onion, minced
- 4 oil-packed anchovy fillets
- 2 tablespoons capers, soaked in warm water for 5 minutes and drained
- Kosher salt
- Freshly ground black pepper
- 2 small bunches of escarole, washed, dried, and coarsely chopped
- 1 14-ounce can tomato puree, preferably Italian San Marzano or organic
- 1 teaspoon dried oregano
- 1 large basil sprig, leaves only
- ¼ cup coarsely chopped black olives, such as kalamata or gaeta
- Extra virgin olive oil, for serving

Put the cuttlefish, 3 tablespoons of the olive oil, the smashed garlic, lemon zest, lemon juice, and mint in a large bowl and toss to coat the cuttlefish. Cover the bowl with plastic wrap and refrigerate for 2 hours.

When ready to proceed, remove the cuttlefish from the refrigerator and let it come to room temperature.

Heat a large heavy sauté pan over medium heat. Add the remaining ¼ cup oil and tip and tilt the pan to coat it, heating the oil until it is shimmering and almost smoking. Add the sliced garlic, onions, anchovies, and capers, season with salt and pepper, and cook, stirring, until the onions are softened but not browned, about 4 minutes. Add the escarole, toss to coat, and cook until wilted, about 5 minutes. Stir in the tomato puree, bring to a simmer, and cook until the sauce is slightly thickened, about 15 minutes.

Meanwhile, during the last few minutes of the sauce's cooking time, heat a large cast-iron skillet over medium-high heat. Remove the cuttlefish from the marinade, brush off the solids, and season with salt and pepper. Arrange the cuttlefish in the skillet in a single layer and sear until lightly charred, opaque, and cooked through, about 3 minutes per side, turning the pieces with tongs or a wooden spoon.

Stir the oregano, basil, and olives into the sauce. Spoon the sauce into the center of 4 wide shallow bowls and top with the cuttlefish. Drizzle with extra virgin olive oil and serve.

# IPPOGLOSSO CON SALSA DI BROCCOLI DI RAPE

## HALIBUT WITH BROCCOLI RABE SAUCE

SERVES 4

Usually served as a contorno, or side dish, broccoli rabe can also be the basis of a quick sauce, as it is here. Leaving the rabe a little damp after blanching helps it steam and nicely wilt when added to the hot pan. Serve this dish with roasted potatoes (as pictured) or buttered string beans.

2 tablespoons olive oil
3 large garlic cloves, thinly sliced
Red pepper flakes
4 oil-packed anchovy fillets
1 large bunch of broccoli rabe (about 1 pound), stalks trimmed, leaves cut into 2-inch pieces, blanched, shocked, and drained but left a little damp (see page 367)
Kosher salt
Freshly ground black pepper
1 cup Vegetable Stock (page 371)
½ cup finely grated Pecorino Romano (about 1 ounce)
½ cup extra virgin olive oil
2 tablespoons canola oil
4 skinless halibut fillets

Heat a large wide heavy sauté pan over medium heat. Add the olive oil and tip and tilt the pan to coat it, heating the oil until it is shimmering and almost smoking. Add the garlic, a pinch of red pepper flakes, and anchovies and cook, stirring with a wooden spoon, until the garlic and red pepper flakes are lightly golden and fragrant, about 2 minutes. Add the broccoli rabe and carefully toss the ingredients together. Season with salt and pepper and remove from the heat.

Add half of the broccoli rabe mixture to a blender or food processor. Pour in the vegetable stock and puree just until smooth. Coarsely chop the remaining broccoli rabe and place in a medium mixing bowl. Add the broccoli rabe puree, cheese, and extra virgin olive oil and stir until incorporated.

Heat a large heavy skillet over medium-high heat. Pour in the canola oil and tip and tilt the pan to coat it, heating the oil until it is shimmering and almost smoking. Season the halibut fillets with salt and pepper and add them to the skillet, skinned side up. Cook until the fillets are golden brown on the bottom, about 5 minutes. Gently turn the fillets over with tongs or a spatula and cook until the flesh is white and flaky and just cooked through, about 5 more minutes.

Transfer the fillets to dinner plates, spoon the broccoli rabe sauce over them, and serve.

**Variation** To serve the broccoli rabe as a side dish, season the sautéed broccoli with salt and pepper, stir in a few drops of lemon juice, and transfer to a serving bowl, then drizzle with olive oil and top with grated Parmigiano-Reggiano.

## BRANZINO AL SALE

### SALT-CRUSTED SEA BASS

SERVES 4

A whole sea bass baked in salt makes for a dramatic presentation at the table, where the crust is cracked, revealing the succulent fish within. While that ceremony is irresistible, it happens to be just a happy by-product of the cooking method, a variation on the age-old technique of cooking in a hermetically sealed environment, whether a pit or a crust. This technique lends itself particularly well to fish, trapping all of its juices inside, along with the flavor of any aromatics.

Some traditional recipes call for coating fish in just salt, or a mixture of salt and water, but mixing the salt with egg whites binds the salt together and provides the added benefit of browning the crust as it cooks, which tends to reflect the doneness of the fish within.

Do not skip the step of letting the fish rest after baking; it's essential to achieving the silky texture the cooking technique imparts.

Note that the salt mixture must rest for 30 minutes before baking the fish.

- 20 flat-leaf parsley stems
- 2 tablespoons fennel seeds
- 4 cups kosher salt
- 5 large egg whites
- 1 sea bass, about 2 pounds, cleaned and gills removed but scales left intact (red snapper can be substituted)
- 1 large lemon, sliced thin, plus the juice of 1 lemon, for serving
- 2 large garlic cloves, smashed with the side of a chef's knife and peeled
- 1 rosemary sprig
- Extra virgin olive oil, for serving

Put half of the parsley stems, the fennel seeds, and the salt in the bowl of a food processor and pulse until the parsley is chopped. Transfer the mixture to a large bowl and add the egg whites, stirring with a wooden spoon. Set aside for 30 minutes to allow the salt to dissolve into the whites.

Position a rack in the center of the oven and preheat the oven to 400°F. Line a baking sheet with parchment paper or aluminum foil.

Put the fish on a large platter and fill the cavity with the lemon slices, the remaining parsley stems, the garlic cloves, and the rosemary. Spread half of the salt mixture on the bottom of the lined baking sheet and top with the fish. Mound the rest of the salt mixture over the top of the fish, leaving the head free of salt, and use your hands to pack the salt around the fish.

Bake the fish until the salt is browned, 13 to 15 minutes. Remove the fish from the oven and set aside to rest for 10 minutes.

To serve, use a tablespoon to crack the salt crust, and remove the crust (along with the fish skin, which will have fused to the crust during cooking). Use 2 spoons to lift the top fillet off the bone structure and transfer to a serving platter. Use your index finger and thumb to remove the bone structure (it will come right off), tease away the rib bones with the back of one of the spoons, and use the spoons to transfer the other fillet to the serving platter. Drizzle the fish with extra virgin olive oil and lemon juice and serve immediately.

# COUSCOUS SICILIANA

## COUSCOUS WITH SHRIMP, TOMATO SAUCE, AND HERBS

SERVES 4

Every year, the Sicilian city of Trapani hosts a couscous festival, a sort of cook-off by the sea. It was during that event one year that I fell in love with a version of this dish, which marries a traditional couscous, enlivened with almonds, raisins, and parsley, with a tangy shrimp ragù. Cinnamon might seem an unusual ingredient in an Italian recipe, but it shows the influence of Moroccan cuisine on the region.

3 tablespoons olive oil
2 large garlic cloves, thinly sliced
1 large Spanish onion, minced
2 celery stalks, trimmed and minced
2 cinnamon sticks
Pinch of red pepper flakes
Splash of dry white wine
1 14-ounce can tomato puree, preferably Italian San Marzano or organic
2½ cups Seafood Stock (page 372, made with the shells from the shrimp rather than fish bones or lobster bodies)
1½ pounds large shrimp, peeled (shells reserved for the stock) and deveined
Kosher salt
Freshly ground black pepper
1 cup couscous
2 tablespoons extra virgin olive oil, plus more for serving
½ cup slivered almonds, toasted (see page 367)
½ cup raisins, soaked in hot water for 10 minutes and drained
¼ cup thinly sliced fresh flat-leaf parsley leaves
10 large fresh basil leaves, torn into pieces

Heat a large sauté pan over medium-high heat. Pour in the olive oil and tip and tilt the pan to coat it, heating the oil until it is shimmering and almost smoking. Add the garlic, onions, and celery and cook, stirring occasionally with a wooden spoon, until the vegetables are softened but not browned, about 4 minutes. Add 1 cinnamon stick, the red pepper flakes, and wine and bring to a simmer, then lower the heat and simmer until the wine has almost completely evaporated, about 10 minutes.

Stir in the tomato puree and 1 cup of the stock, bring the liquid to a simmer, and simmer until the sauce thickens slightly, 20 to 25 minutes.

Season the shrimp with salt and pepper, add them to the pan, using a wooden spoon to submerge them, and cook until firm and pink, 2 to 3 minutes. Remove the pan from the heat and cover to keep warm.

Meanwhile, make the couscous: Bring the remaining 1½ cups stock to a boil in a medium saucepan over high heat. Put the couscous and the remaining cinnamon stick in a medium heatproof bowl, drizzle with the extra virgin olive oil, and season with a pinch of salt and a few grinds of black pepper.

When the stock comes to a boil, pour it over the couscous and stir to incorporate. Cover the bowl with plastic wrap and a clean kitchen towel and let stand until the couscous has absorbed the stock, about 7 minutes. Remove the towel and plastic wrap and fluff the couscous with a fork. Stir in the almonds, raisins, and parsley.

Stir the basil into the sauce. Spoon some couscous into the center of each of 4 dinner plates and top with the shrimp and tomato sauce. Drizzle with extra virgin olive oil and serve.

# DENTICE IN ACQUA PAZZA

## SNAPPER IN "CRAZY WATER"

SERVES 4

Originally acqua pazza, or "crazy water," referred to cooking fish in seawater, as Neapolitan fishermen used to do it. Here instead it is poached in a quick stock enhanced with garlic and tomato. This is wonderful with baked or roasted potatoes (see page 170) alongside; for a more substantial dish, stir some mashed baked potato (without the skin) into the broth to thicken it.

- ¼ cup olive oil
- 6 large garlic cloves, 4 smashed with the side of a chef's knife and peeled, 2 thinly sliced
- 1 Spanish onion, cut into small dice
- 12 large shrimp, peeled (shells reserved) and deveined
- 2 tablespoons tomato paste
- Red pepper flakes
- 4 large beefsteak tomatoes, peeled (see page 367), seeded, and cut into small dice
- 2 basil sprigs, plus 8 large leaves, thinly sliced
- Kosher salt
- Freshly ground black pepper
- 4 red snapper fillets, 8 ounces each, with skin
- Extra virgin olive oil, for serving
- 4 slices fettunta (see page 11), optional

To make the shrimp stock: Heat a medium heavy pot over medium heat. Pour in 2 tablespoons of the olive oil and tip and tilt the pot to coat it, heating the oil until it is shimmering and almost smoking. Add the smashed garlic cloves, onions, and shrimp shells and cook, stirring frequently, until the onions are softened but not browned, about 4 minutes. Add the tomato paste, stirring to coat the other ingredients with the paste, and cook until it turns a shade darker, about 2 minutes. Stir in a pinch of red pepper flakes, half of the diced tomatoes, and 1 basil sprig. Pour in enough water to cover the ingredients and bring to a boil over high heat, then lower the heat so the liquid is simmering and simmer for 45 minutes. Strain the stock through a fine-mesh strainer set over a large bowl, pressing down on the solids with a wooden spoon or a ladle to extract as much flavorful liquid as possible. Discard the solids and season the stock with salt and pepper.

Carefully wipe out the pot and heat it over medium-high heat. Add the remaining 2 tablespoons olive oil and tip and tilt the pot to coat it, heating the oil until it is shimmering and almost smoking. Add the sliced garlic, a pinch of red pepper flakes, and the remaining basil sprig, stir in the remaining tomatoes and the shrimp stock, and bring the mixture to a simmer.

Meanwhile, season the snapper fillets with salt and pepper. When the liquid begins to simmer, carefully add the snapper to the pot, using a wooden spoon to gently submerge it, and cook until the fish is opaque and firm, 5 to 6 minutes. Add the shrimp to the poaching liquid, and cook until firm, 2 to 3 minutes.

To serve, use a slotted spoon to set 1 snapper fillet and 3 shrimp in each of 4 bowls, then spoon or ladle the acqua pazza over the fish. Drizzle each serving with extra virgin olive oil and finish with a scattering of the sliced basil. Serve with the fettunta, if desired.

## TONNO ALLA GRIGLIA CON SALSA PALERMITANA

### GRILLED TUNA WITH FRESH TOMATO SAUCE

SERVES 4

The sauce in this dish is based on a traditional table relish from Palermo, but this recipe departs from classic Italian cooking in one significant way: In Italy, tuna is often preserved (see page 33) or grilled to well-doneness, but it's not usually served rare.

Note that the tuna must marinate for 30 minutes before grilling.

- 4 yellowfin tuna steaks, 7 to 8 ounces each, ideally 1 inch thick
- 2 tablespoons olive oil
- Kosher salt
- Freshly ground black pepper
- 1 pint cherry tomatoes or small heirloom tomatoes, halved
- 1 large garlic clove, minced
- ½ cup sliced green and black olives, such as kalamata
- ½ small red onion, thinly sliced
- 2 tablespoons capers, soaked in warm water for 5 minutes and drained
- ¼ cup extra virgin olive oil
- 1 tablespoon red wine vinegar
- 10 fresh basil leaves, torn into pieces
- ½ teaspoon dried oregano
- Grated zest of 1 lemon
- 1 tablespoon seeded, sliced Fresno pepper or red jalapeño

About 30 minutes before you plan to grill the tuna, remove the steaks from the refrigerator and arrange them in a single layer on a large plate. Drizzle the olive oil over them and season on both sides with salt and pepper. Let marinate while you make the sauce and heat the grill.

Preheat an outdoor grill to high; if using a charcoal grill, let the coals burn until covered with white ash.

To make the sauce: Put the tomatoes, garlic, olives, onion, and capers in a medium bowl. Drizzle the extra virgin olive oil and vinegar over the top and toss gently. Sprinkle with the basil and oregano, season with salt and a few grinds of black pepper, and toss again. Set aside to marinate while you grill the tuna.

Set the tuna steaks on the grill and grill for 3 to 4 minutes on each side for medium-rare, using tongs to turn them over when nice grill marks have formed. Transfer the steaks to a large plate and let rest for 5 minutes.

Set 1 tuna steak in the center of each of 4 dinner plates. Use a slotted spoon to spoon some sauce over each one, garnish with the lemon zest and red pepper, and serve.

# POLLAME E CARNE
# POULTRY AND MEATS

Although we tend to think of poultry and meat as two distinct categories, in Italy they are both considered meats and you would only see one or the other served during a traditional multicourse meal; for the same reason, I've gathered them together in this chapter.

When Italian traditions are applied to the bounty of superior ingredients available in the United States today, something wonderful happens. Thanks to readily available organic chickens, heritage pigs, and dry-aged beef—to name just a few foodstuffs sold even in many supermarkets—dishes that were originally born of necessity and paired with accompaniments to mask imperfections now sing with layers of flavors and textures. In this chapter, you'll encounter game bird recipes that originally called on fruit and honey to offset their strong taste, and beef dishes that became the stuff of legend, even though they were produced with average specimens. (It's worth noting that, generally speaking, Italians don't like dry-aged beef, preferring to butcher and cook their meat relatively quickly. It's one of the few areas in which I prefer the product of another country to that of my adopted spiritual home.)

I've included three chicken recipes in this chapter as a nod to its popularity in America, but urge you to try the quail and squab dishes. Each of these birds has a distinctive, assertive character that is well worth becoming acquainted with and, while they may be unfamiliar, cooking them doesn't require any more skill than cooking a chicken. They are especially worth having in your repertoire for entertaining, where they will be both unexpected and appreciated.

# POLLO ALLA DIAVOLA

## DEVIL-STYLE CHICKEN

SERVES 4

A slightly spicy favorite from Emilia-Romagna, pollo alla diavola approximates the juiciness of a spit-roasted chicken by splitting the bird and cooking it on the grill, where the skin and bones keep the chicken from drying out, and the marinade ingredients—red pepper flakes, garlic, lemon, and herbs—come alive in the heat of the fire.

For a cooling companion to the chicken, serve the Shaved Fennel Salad on page 158.

Note that the chicken must marinate for at least 4 hours.

2 chickens, 3 pounds each
6 large garlic cloves, smashed with the side of a chef's knife and peeled
4 rosemary sprigs, bruised with the back of a chef's knife
1 tablespoon red pepper flakes
2 large lemons, juiced and cut into quarters, plus freshly squeezed lemon juice for serving
½ cup olive oil
Kosher salt
Freshly ground black pepper
Extra virgin olive oil, for serving

Working with 1 chicken at a time, use a pair of kitchen shears to cut along both sides of the backbone to remove it, then discard the backbone. Flatten the chicken by pressing down on it and flatten each chicken in its own large resealable plastic bag. Divide the garlic, rosemary, red pepper flakes, lemon juice, lemon quarters, and olive oil between the bags, then seal the bags and turn a few times to distribute the marinade. Place the bags on a plate and marinate the chicken in the refrigerator for at least 4 hours, or overnight, turning the bags occasionally.

When ready to grill the chicken, remove from the refrigerator and let come to room temperature.

Preheat a grill to high; if using charcoal, let the coals burn until covered with white ash.

Remove the chicken halves from the bags, brush off the solids, pat dry with paper towels, and season on both sides with salt and pepper. Put the chicken halves on the grill, skin side down, and grill, turning the chicken every 10 to 12 minutes with tongs and brushing the halves with a rosemary brush, if desired (see Herb Brushes, below), until the chicken is cooked through and the juices run clear when pierced to the bone, 35 to 40 minutes. Transfer the chicken halves to a platter, tent loosely with aluminum foil, and let rest for 10 to 15 minutes.

Drizzle the chicken with lemon juice and extra virgin olive oil and serve warm.

### Herb Brushes

An old Tuscan trick for imparting additional flavor to grilled fish and meats is to make an herb brush. Use kitchen twine to tie a few sprigs of sturdy herbs such as rosemary, sage, and thyme to the end of the handle of a wooden spoon and periodically brush the food on the grill with the herbs.

# POLLO AL LAMBRUSCO

## CHICKEN LAMBRUSCO

SERVES 4

Lambrusco is one of the signature wines of Emilia-Romagna, and it is considered the perfect accompaniment to many of the classic dishes of the region, both because it complements their flavors and because it cuts the richness of the foods. This is especially true of frizzante, the gently sparkling version of Lambrusco.

For this recipe, a cousin to coq au vin, the chicken is marinated in a Lambrusco-based mixture, which tenderizes and flavors it and also provides the base for a quick sauce. A year-round dish, the chicken can be served with almost any vegetable contorni.

Note that the chicken must marinate for at least 4 hours.

1 chicken, about 4 pounds, cut into 8 pieces by your butcher
1 cup Lambrusco
½ cup balsamic vinegar
2 tablespoons Dijon mustard
3 tablespoons olive oil
1 thyme sprig
1 rosemary sprig
2 bay leaves, preferably fresh
3 garlic cloves, smashed with the side of a chef's knife and peeled
Kosher salt
Freshly ground black pepper
All-purpose flour, for dusting
¼ cup canola oil or other neutral oil
About ¾ cup Chicken Stock (page 374) or store-bought low-sodium chicken broth

Put the chicken pieces in a large resealable plastic bag. Put the Lambrusco, vinegar, mustard, and olive oil in a large measuring cup or a small bowl and whisk together. Pour the mixture into the bag with the chicken, then add the thyme, rosemary, bay leaves, and garlic. Seal the bag, turn to coat the chicken, set it on a large plate, and refrigerate for at least 4 hours or, preferably, overnight.

Line a plate with paper towels. Remove the chicken from the marinade, discard the bay leaves and herbs, reserving the marinade, and put on the lined plate; blot dry with additional paper towels. Season the chicken pieces liberally all over with salt and pepper.

Put the flour on a wide plate and lightly coat the chicken pieces in flour, turning them, then gently shaking off any excess, and transfer to another plate.

Set a Dutch oven or other large heavy pot over medium-high heat and add the canola oil. Tip and tilt the pot to coat it with the oil and heat until the oil is shimmering and almost smoking. Add the chicken and cook, using tongs or a kitchen spoon to turn the pieces as they brown, until browned on all sides, about 10 minutes. Remove chicken, when browned, to a plate. (This may need to be done in batches; if so, transfer the first batch to the plate and cook the second batch, then return all the pieces to the Dutch oven.)

Carefully spoon out and discard any excess oil from the pot (this can also be done with a baster). Add the reserved marinade and bring to a boil, then lower the heat so the liquid is simmering and simmer until nicely thickened, about 5 minutes. Add the chicken back to the liquid and pour in ½ cup of the stock and bring to a simmer, then cover the pot, lower the heat, and cook until the chicken is cooked through, 10 to 12 minutes, basting occasionally with a pastry brush, tablespoon, or baster; if the sauce thickens too much, stir in a few tablespoons more stock. (To test for doneness, gently pry one piece of chicken open with a paring knife and check that the meat is cooked through at the center.)

Transfer the chicken pieces to a serving platter or individual plates. Spoon the sauce over the chicken and serve.

# QUAGLIA AVVOLTA IN PANCETTA CON FRIGGONE BOLOGNESE

## PANCETTA-WRAPPED QUAIL WITH STEWED BELL PEPPERS, TOMATOES, AND ONIONS

SERVES 4

Quail has a strong and distinct flavor, but it is also a lean bird that has a tendency to dry out when cooked. This version of a popular Tuscan recipe protects the breast by covering it with a layer of pancetta, which also adds delicious fat and a pleasing saltiness to the finished dish.

Note that the quail must marinate for at least 4 hours.

8 semiboneless quail
¼ cup olive oil
Needles from 1 rosemary sprig
1 sage sprig, coarsely chopped
2 bay leaves, preferably fresh
Leaves from 1 thyme sprig
2 garlic cloves, smashed with the side of a chef's knife and peeled
8 slices pancetta (about 2 ounces)
¼ cup canola oil
Kosher salt
Freshly ground black pepper
1 tablespoon unsalted butter
¼ cup dry white wine
1 cup Chicken Stock (page 374)
Stewed Bell Peppers, Tomatoes, and Onions (page 161)

Put the quail in a baking dish and add the olive oil, rosemary, sage, bay, thyme, and garlic. Turn the quail over to coat in the marinade, cover, and marinate in the refrigerator for at least 4 hours, or overnight.

When ready to cook the quail, position a rack in the center of the oven and preheat the oven to 400°F. Soak 4 bamboo skewers in water.

Remove the quail from the dish, reserving the herbs and garlic. Lay 2 pieces of pancetta over the breast of each quail, overlapping them, and secure them with a skewer, pinning them to the quail.

Heat a large ovenproof sauté pan over medium-high heat. Add the canola oil and tip and tilt the pan to coat it, heating the oil until it is shimmering and almost smoking. Season the quail with salt and pepper and add to the pan, breast side down. Cook until lightly golden, 3 to 4 minutes, then turn and cook for another 3 minutes.

Transfer the quail to the oven and roast until the juices run clear when a thigh is pierced with a knife, 5 to 7 minutes. Remove the pan from the oven, transfer the quail to a platter, and tent with foil.

Return the pan to medium-high heat, add the butter and the reserved herbs and garlic, and cook, stirring with a wooden spoon, for 2 minutes. Add the wine, stirring to loosen any flavorful bits cooked onto the bottom of the pan, bring to a simmer, and simmer until the wine has almost completely evaporated, about 2 minutes. Add the stock, bring to a simmer, and simmer until reduced by half, 6 to 8 minutes.

To serve, spoon the stewed vegetables onto 4 plates. Top with the quail and spoon the sauce over the quail.

# FARAONA CON CILIEGIE E MARSALA

## GUINEA FOWL WITH CHERRIES AND MARSALA

SERVES 4

Various combinations of meat and fruit turn up in Italian cooking. For the most part, the convention arose out of necessary creativity, the sweetness of the fruit providing a foil for the richness of the meats. Along the way, however, some extraordinary pairings were hit upon, such as guinea fowl and cherries, which have a meaty texture in their own right and tint the meat an alluring deep purple.

This is a useful one-pot meal to have in your repertoire: It is equally suited to an everyday family dinner and a special occasion.

2 guinea hens, about 2½ pounds each, rinsed and patted dry with a paper towel
Kosher salt
Freshly ground black pepper
3 rosemary sprigs
2 bay leaves, preferably fresh
3 sage sprigs
4 garlic cloves, smashed with the side of a chef's knife and peeled, plus 1 head of garlic, halved horizontally
¼ cup plus 1 tablespoon canola oil or other neutral oil
3 large celery stalks, trimmed and cut into 3-inch segments
1 large Spanish onion, cut into 6 wedges
3 large carrots, cut into 3 pieces each
1½ cups dry white wine
½ cup dry Marsala
1 cup Dark Chicken Stock (page 374)
1 pint Bing cherries, halved and pitted

Position a rack in the center of the oven and preheat the oven to 375°F.

Season the guinea hens inside and out with salt and pepper. Stuff the cavity of each hen with 1 rosemary sprig, 1 bay leaf, 1 sage sprig, and 2 smashed garlic cloves. Use a piece of butcher's twine to truss each bird: Start by crossing the legs and tying them together with a double knot. Tuck the wings under themselves and wrap the twine around each bird to secure it, tying it with another double knot and snipping away the excess string.

Pour ¼ cup of the oil into a roasting pan large enough to hold the hens comfortably, set it over two burners, and heat over medium heat. Add the hens, breast side down, and brown for 5 to 6 minutes, then turn over and brown for another 5 to 6 minutes. Transfer the hens to a large plate or platter.

Add the celery, onions, carrots, the halved head of garlic, and the remaining rosemary and sage sprigs. Cook, stirring with a wooden spoon, until the vegetables are softened but not browned, about 4 minutes. Pour in the wine, bring to a simmer, and cook, stirring, until slightly reduced, about 2 minutes. Return the hens to the pan, breast side up, drizzle with the remaining tablespoon of oil, and season with salt and pepper.

Roast the hens, basting periodically with the pan drippings, until cooked through, about 70 minutes; an instant-read thermometer inserted between the breast and the leg will read 160°F. Remove the roasting pan from the oven and transfer the hens to a large plate. Loosely cover the hens with aluminum foil and set aside to rest.

Meanwhile, set the roasting pan over two burners and turn the heat on to medium. Pour the Marsala into the roasting pan and stir with a wooden spoon to loosen any flavorful bits cooked onto the bottom of the pan. Bring to a simmer and cook until the Marsala has almost completely evaporated, about 6 minutes. Pour in the stock and bring to a simmer, then lower the heat and simmer for 10 minutes. Strain the sauce through a fine-mesh strainer into a bowl, pressing down on the solids with a wooden spoon or a ladle to extract as much flavorful liquid as possible. Discard the solids, return the sauce to the pan, and simmer until reduced by half, about 5 minutes. Add half of the cherries, crushing them with a wooden spoon to release their juices, then season with salt and pepper, lower the heat, and cook for 5 minutes to infuse the sauce with the cherries' flavor. Strain the sauce through a fine-mesh strainer into a bowl or serving vessel and stir in the remaining cherries.

Transfer the hens to a cutting board and carve them, reserving their juices. Pour the reserved juices into the sauce, stirring to incorporate. Divide the hens among 4 plates and drizzle with the sauce, or pass it alongside.

# PETTO DI PICCIONE AI PORCINI

## PAN-SEARED SQUAB WITH PORCINI MUSHROOMS, SPINACH, AND ROASTED GARLIC

SERVES 4

In a traditional Italian meal, squab would be served as a meat course. But in my restaurants, I've noticed that many American diners—for whom game birds are a rarity, if not a novelty—are more comfortable eating squab as an appetizer or first course. The beauty of this dish is that it's vegetable-heavy enough to be served as either a starter or a main course.

¼ cup canola oil
2 squab, about 1 pound each, split in half by your butcher
Kosher salt
Freshly ground black pepper
1 small head of garlic, halved horizontally, plus 1 garlic clove, thinly sliced
2 rosemary sprigs
1 sage sprig
1½ teaspoons juniper berries
3 tablespoons unsalted butter
½ cup dry white wine
1 cup Dark Chicken Stock (page 374)
Juice of ½ lemon, or to taste
3 tablespoons olive oil
8 medium porcini mushrooms, trimmed and thickly sliced
2 shallots, minced
2 cups (loosely packed) spinach leaves

Position a rack in the center of the oven and preheat the oven to 400°F.

Heat a cast-iron skillet large enough to hold the 4 squab halves over medium-high heat. Add 2 tablespoons of the canola oil, tilting and turning the pan to coat it, and heat the oil. Season the squab all over with salt and pepper. Add the squab to the pan, skin side down, and brown, pressing down with a spatula to ensure even cooking and a crispy brown skin, 3 to 4 minutes, then turn and brown on the second side, another 3 to 4 minutes. Carefully pour off and discard the oil from the pan, then add the remaining 2 tablespoons canola oil.

Transfer the pan to the oven and roast the squab for 6 to 7 minutes.

Return the pan to the stovetop over medium-high heat, add the head of garlic, rosemary, sage, juniper berries, and 2 tablespoons of the butter, and cook, basting the squab with the butter, for 2 to 3 minutes, taking care not to burn the butter. Transfer the squab halves to a rack set over a baking sheet and loosely tent with foil. Drain the fat from the pan into a heatproof liquid measuring cup, then discard all but 2 tablespoons of it, along with the garlic and herbs. Set the reserved fat aside.

Add the wine to the pan, stirring to loosen any flavorful bits cooked onto the bottom, bring to a simmer, and simmer until almost completely evaporated, 4 to 5 minutes. Add the stock, bring to a simmer, and reduce by three quarters, 6 to 8 minutes. Add a few drops of lemon juice and season with salt and pepper.

Meanwhile, heat 2 tablespoons of the olive oil in a large heavy sauté pan over medium-high heat. Add the porcini (in batches if necessary), season with salt and pepper, and sauté until lightly browned, 3 to 4 minutes. Transfer to a plate. Add the remaining 1 tablespoon of olive oil to the pan and heat it. Add the shallots and sliced garlic and cook, stirring with a wooden spoon, until softened but not browned, about 2 minutes. Add the remaining 1 tablespoon butter and melt it, then add the spinach and cook, stirring, until wilted, about 2 minutes. Add a few drops of lemon juice and season with salt and pepper.

Spoon some sauce onto each of 4 plates. Top with a squab half and drizzle with some of the reserved fat (when the fat meets the sauce, it will "break" it). Arrange the spinach and porcini alongside the squab and serve.

**Variation** *In the fall, finish the sauce by shaving some black truffle into it just before serving.*

# ZUCCHINE RIPIENE AL POMODORO

## STUFFED ZUCCHINI BRAISED IN TOMATO SAUCE

SERVES 4

This is a wonderful summertime dish that uses a vegetable of the season, zucchini, as a surprising vehicle for a pork and mortadella filling. The stuffed zucchini are as suitable as a starter as they are as a light main course and they don't have to be served piping hot, which lends them to casual, spontaneous entertaining.

8 zucchini, 1½ inches in diameter, 6 to 8 inches long
½ cup plus 2 tablespoons olive oil
2 Spanish onions, cut into small dice
Kosher salt
Freshly ground black pepper
1¼ cups fine fresh bread crumbs (see page xxviii)
⅓ cup whole milk
8 ounces ground pork
4 ounces mortadella, minced (boiled ham can be substituted)
2 tablespoons tomato paste
2 tablespoons thinly sliced fresh flat-leaf parsley leaves
1 large egg, lightly beaten
¾ cup finely grated Parmigiano-Reggiano (about 1½ ounces), plus more for serving
Pinch of freshly grated nutmeg
2 cups Tomato Sauce with Basil (page 74)
½ cup Seasoned Toasted Bread Crumbs (page xxix)

Trim the ends off each zucchini. Use an apple corer to cut straight down the center from each end, twisting to remove the insides. Use a paring knife to trim most of the residual interior flesh, leaving a ½-inch shell. Reserve the flesh (and seeds) for the filling.

Heat a large heavy skillet over medium-high heat. Pour in 6 tablespoons of the oil and heat the oil until it is shimmering and almost smoking. Add the onions and the reserved zucchini flesh and seeds, season with salt and pepper, and cook, stirring with a wooden spoon, until the vegetables are softened and lightly browned, about 4 minutes. Remove the pan from the heat and set aside to cool slightly.

Scrape the onion-zucchini mixture onto a cutting board and finely chop it. Spread the mixture out on a large plate or baking sheet and set aside to cool completely.

Put the fresh bread crumbs and milk in a small mixing bowl and stir them together. Let soak for 10 to 12 minutes.

Put the pork and mortadella in a large mixing bowl. Squeeze the bread crumbs free of excess milk and add them to the bowl, then stir in the cooled onion mixture and the tomato paste. Gently stir in the parsley, 2 tablespoons olive oil, the egg, ½ cup of the Parmigiano, and the nutmeg, taking care not to overmix. Season with salt and pepper. Spoon the mixture into a pastry bag fitted with a number 7 (⅜-inch) plain tip. (If you do not have a pastry bag, transfer the filling to a large resealable plastic bag, squeeze the air out of the bag, seal, and snip off a bottom corner to mimic a pastry bag.)

Pipe the filling into the hollowed-out zucchini, putting the filled zucchini on a large plate.

Position a rack in the center of the oven and preheat the oven to 325°F.

Coat a square or rectangular baking dish large enough to hold the zucchini in a single layer with 1 tablespoon olive oil. Add the tomato sauce and use a spoon to spread it evenly over the bottom of the dish. Arrange the stuffed zucchini on the sauce and drizzle the remaining 1 tablespoon oil over them, using a clean finger to spread the oil over the zucchini. Top with ¼ cup of the toasted bread crumbs.

Cover the pan with aluminum foil and bake until the zucchini are tender to the tines of a fork and the filling is cooked through, about 15 minutes. Remove the foil, scatter the remaining ¼ cup Parmigiano and ¼ cup toasted bread crumbs over the zucchini, and bake until the cheese is melted and the tomato sauce is bubbling, about 6 more minutes.

Remove the dish from the oven and let rest for 5 minutes, then divide the stuffed zucchini and sauce among 4 plates. Serve.

# COSCIA DI MAIALE

## ROASTED PORK LEG WITH ROSEMARY AND BLACK PEPPER

SERVES 10 TO 12

For the peerless, primal flavor of freshly roasted pork, my favorite cut is the hind leg, sometimes called "fresh ham." You may need to special-order this from your butcher, but it's worth planning for, because it's so easy to produce exceptional results with it. My preferred method for cooking it is to coat it with an herb-and-garlic paste before roasting it, for a crispy, insanely flavorful dish that you can serve to a large group. Or make it for a smaller group, perhaps for Sunday dinner, then enjoy the leftovers all week long, on their own, atop salads, in sandwiches, or chopped and incorporated into a ravioli filling, to name just a few possibilities.

2 tablespoons fennel seeds, toasted (see page 367)
Leaves from 4 rosemary sprigs, coarsely chopped
4 large fresh sage leaves, coarsely chopped
3 large garlic cloves, coarsely chopped
Finely grated zest of 2 lemons
1 cup kosher salt
1 tablespoon freshly ground black pepper
1 fresh ham (pork leg), 8 to 10 pounds
½ cup canola oil or other neutral oil

Position a rack in the center of the oven and preheat the oven to 325°F.

Put the fennel seeds, rosemary, sage, garlic, lemon zest, salt, and 1 tablespoon pepper in the bowl of a food processor and pulse until the ingredients come together in a coarse paste.

Score the ham's skin in a crosshatch pattern with a sharp thin-bladed knife. Drizzle the ham with the oil and rub the oil evenly over the ham to coat it. Use clean hands or a rubber spatula to apply the herb paste to the ham, rubbing it evenly over the entire surface. (You may not use all of the paste; refrigerate any extra in an airtight container for up to 2 weeks.) Position a rack in a roasting pan and set the ham on the rack, taking care not to dislodge any of the paste. Pour enough water around the ham to come to a depth of about 1 inch to keep the pan from drying out during roasting.

Roast the ham until the skin is a crispy, burnished brown and an instant-read thermometer inserted into the center of the ham reads 160°F, 2½ to 3 hours. Remove the roasting pan from the oven, tent the ham loosely with foil, and let rest for 20 minutes.

Transfer the ham to a cutting board, carve, and arrange the slices on a large serving platter. Serve.

**ISPIRAZIONE** A butter crust based on an herb crust like this one is applied to the beef filet in the recipe on page 344.

# COSTOLETTE D'AGNELLO ALLA SCOTTADITO

## GRILLED MARINATED LAMB CHOPS

SERVES 4

You can eat these lamb chops with a knife and fork, but they're more fun to eat with your fingers—hence their name, scottadito, which means "burnt finger." A grill pan is usually to be avoided, because it merely creates grill marks without replicating the other benefits of grilling; but because of the short cooking time, this is one of the rare times that it will produce effective results. So, if you are not grilling anything other than the chops, by all means cook these indoors.

Note that the chops must marinate overnight.

½ cup olive oil
2 rosemary sprigs, coarsely chopped
6 large fresh sage leaves, coarsely chopped
4 garlic cloves, smashed with the side of a chef's knife and peeled
12 lamb rib chops, 3 to 4 ounces each
Kosher salt
Freshly ground black pepper

Put the oil, rosemary, sage, and garlic in a small bowl and stir them together. Pour some of the marinade over the bottom of a shallow vessel, such as a baking dish. Arrange the lamb chops in a single layer in the dish and pour the remaining marinade over them. Cover with plastic wrap and refrigerate overnight, turning the lamb over periodically to ensure even marinating.

When ready to cook the lamb, remove it from the refrigerator and let come to room temperature.

Meanwhile, preheat an outdoor grill to high heat; if using charcoal, let the coals burn until covered with white ash.

Lift the lamb chops from their marinade, brushing off the solids; season generously with salt and pepper, and set on the grill. Grill for about 3 minutes on each side for medium-rare, turning the chops with tongs and basting with a rosemary brush (see Herb Brushes, page 128), if desired.

Remove the lamb from the grill and divide among 4 dinner plates, or serve family-style from a platter.

# STINCO DI AGNELLO CON FAGIOLI ALL'UCCELLETTO

## BRAISED LAMB SHANKS WITH STEWED WHITE BEANS

SERVES 4

Braised lamb shanks might be the ultimate example of the transformative power of the braising method, which begins with something forbiddingly tough and produces meltingly tender meat and a cooking liquid that becomes the basis for a complex sauce. One of the most popular accompaniments to lamb shanks in Italy is white beans, which offer a pleasing textural counterpoint to the lamb and get along beautifully with the sauce.

4 lamb shanks, about 1 pound each, trimmed of excess fat
Kosher salt
Freshly ground black pepper
½ cup canola oil or other neutral oil
2 tablespoons unsalted butter
1 small Spanish onion, coarsely chopped
1 small carrot, coarsely chopped
1 small celery stalk, trimmed and coarsely chopped
1 head of garlic, halved horizontally
3 rosemary sprigs
2 sage sprigs
2 bay leaves, preferably fresh
1½ teaspoons whole black peppercorns
2 cups dry red wine
3 cups Veal Stock (page 375), Dark Chicken Stock (page 374), or store-bought low-sodium beef broth
Cannellini Beans with Tomato and Sage (page 169)

Position a rack in the center of the oven and preheat the oven to 325°F.

Season the shanks all over with salt and pepper and set them aside.

Heat a Dutch oven or other large heavy pot over medium-high heat. Pour in ¼ cup of the oil and heat it until hot. Add the shanks and sear on all sides, 4 to 5 minutes per side, turning them with tongs as they brown. When they are browned all over, transfer the shanks to a large plate and set aside.

Pour off and discard the oil from the pot. Add the remaining ¼ cup oil and 2 tablespoons of the butter and heat until the butter melts. Add the onions, carrots, celery, and garlic and cook, stirring with a wooden spoon, until the vegetables are softened but not browned, about 4 minutes. Stir in 2 of the rosemary sprigs, the sage, bay leaves, and peppercorns and cook for 1 minute. Pour in the wine, bring to a simmer, and simmer until reduced by half, 8 to 10 minutes.

Pour in the stock and bring to a simmer, then return the shanks to the Dutch oven and let the liquid return to a simmer. Cover and braise in the oven until the meat is tender and falling off the bone, about 1½ hours, basting occasionally with the braising liquid. Check the liquid periodically to be sure that it is just barely simmering: You are looking for a slight, almost imperceptible bubbling on the surface. If it is not simmering at all, raise the heat to 350°F; if it's simmering too assertively, lower the heat to 300°F.

When the shanks are done, remove the Dutch oven from the oven and use tongs to transfer the shanks to a large plate.

Strain the braising liquid through a fine-mesh strainer into a medium heavy pot, pressing down on the solids with a spoon or a ladle to extract as much flavorful liquid as possible. Discard the solids. Add the remaining sprig of rosemary to the pot, bring the liquid to a simmer over high heat, and simmer until reduced and slightly thickened to a sauce consistency, 6 to 8 minutes, skimming any impurities and fat that rise to the surface.

To serve, put 1 shank on each of 4 dinner plates, spoon some sauce over and around the shank, and spoon some beans alongside.

FIRENZE
GALLERIA
i giglioli dei castagni
fortezza
medioevale
museo storico
piazza Garibaldi
OSTERIA PIZ
RISTORAN

## FILETTO ALL'ACETO BALSAMICO

### FILET MIGNON WITH BALSAMIC VINEGAR PAN SAUCE

SERVES 4

Filet mignon, which is tender but not especially flavorful, might not get the same respect from chefs as other cuts, but with the right treatment, it can be the centerpiece of a delicious and speedy meal. Here I make a quick balsamic vinegar and butter sauce that would be too rich for a fattier cut but elevates the filet mignon with luxurious and intense flavor. There's no need to use an aged balsamic vinegar (see page xxxiii) here; instead, choose an inexpensive young balsamico. This is also delicious with the steaks grilled and served with Giovanna's Salad (page 29), as pictured.

4 beef filet steaks, 6 ounces each, ideally 1½ inches thick
Kosher salt
Freshly ground black pepper
3 tablespoons canola oil or other neutral oil
1 garlic clove, smashed with the side of a chef's knife and peeled
1 rosemary sprig
½ cup balsamic vinegar (see the headnote)
2 tablespoons red wine vinegar
3 tablespoons unsalted butter

Position a rack in the center of the oven and preheat the oven to 400°F.

Generously season the steaks on both sides with salt and pepper.

Heat a wide heavy ovenproof sauté pan over high heat. Add 2 tablespoons of the oil, tipping and tilting the pan to coat it, and heat the oil until it is shimmering and almost smoking. Add the steaks and sear well on both sides, 3 to 4 minutes per side. Turn the meat over, transfer the pan to the oven, and cook for 3 minutes for medium-rare. Transfer the meat to a plate, tent loosely with foil, and set aside to rest.

Pour the oil out of the pan and discard it. Add the remaining tablespoon of oil to the pan, along with the smashed garlic and rosemary, and cook until fragrant, about 1 minute. Pour in the balsamic and red wine vinegars, bring to a boil, stirring with a wooden spoon to loosen any flavorful bits cooked onto the bottom of the pan, and reduce the vinegar by half, about 4 minutes. Remove the pan from the heat and swirl in the butter. Season to taste with salt and pepper.

Put 1 steak on each of 4 plates. Pour any juices that have accumulated on the plate into the sauce and swirl it in. Spoon some sauce over each steak, leaving the garlic and rosemary in the pan, and serve.

# BISTECCA ALLA FIORENTINA

## PORTERHOUSE STEAK FLORENTINE

SERVES 6 TO 8

Italy isn't a nation of beef lovers, with one significant exception: bistecca alla Fiorentina, a Tuscan institution unto itself.

On paper, this iconic dish seems like nothing more than a porterhouse or T-bone steak that's seasoned with salt and pepper, grilled over an open flame, drizzled with olive oil (an optional step), and served with lemon wedges (also optional). But when premium beef is used and properly grilled, this classic lives up to its reputation, and then some. (In Tuscany, the dish is usually made with beef from the Chianina or Maremmana breeds, which makes a big difference.) As porterhouse fans know, the cut appeals because it's actually two cuts in one, with some meat from the filet, a buttery, tender muscle, and some from the more developed and full-flavored strip, also known as shell steak or sirloin.

One of the keys to grilling bistecca alla Fiorentina properly is to stand the beef on the bone side for a portion of the cooking time to ensure even cooking throughout the enormous piece of meat. Also, even if you usually oil steaks before grilling them, do not do that here, because the size of the cut, with its greater-than-average surface area and fat content, increases the possibility of flare-ups and the presence of oil on the steak can result in an almost gasoline-like aroma that will ruin it. I also do not recommend using a gas grill; wood or charcoal is essential to getting the authentic Fiorentina char and flavor.

I punch up this version of this dish by seasoning it with rosemary salt, although you can by all means season as most cooks do, with salt and pepper. For an added flourish, grill the lemon halves you'll be serving alongside the steak. The white beans on page 169 are a traditional Tuscan accompaniment.

2 porterhouse steaks, 36 to 42 ounces each
Rosemary Salt (page 146)
Extra virgin olive oil, for serving
Kosher salt
Freshly ground black pepper
2 lemons, halved

Prepare a charcoal grill for grilling, banking the coals on one side and let them burn until covered with white ash.

Season the beef all over with the rosemary salt (or with kosher salt and pepper).

For rare beef, set the steaks over direct heat and grill, turning once with tongs, until nice grill marks form and the meat is charred, about 10 minutes per side. Then use the tongs to stand the steaks up over the cooler side of the grill (the bones will help them stand on their own) and grill for another 5 minutes. For medium-rare, add 3 to 5 minutes to the cooking time for each of the three sides, or cook a bit more for more well done. Transfer the steaks to a cutting board, tent loosely with foil, and let rest for 10 minutes.

Slice the meat and divide among 6 to 8 dinner plates. Drizzle the slices with oil and finish with a sprinkling of salt and a few grinds of black pepper. Set a lemon half alongside each portion and serve.

## ROSEMARY SALT

MAKES ABOUT ¾ CUP

Long before there was such a thing as seasoned salt and other seasoning salts, Italians used rosemary salt, salamoia Bolognese, on meats bound for the grill. I think of it as a secret weapon. Garlic can scorch over high heat, but it's ground so finely here that it doesn't. The salt extracts liquid from the beef, intensifying its flavor, and the lemon zest gives the meat an acidic lift.

½ cup kosher salt
½ tablespoon coarsely ground black pepper
3 large garlic cloves
10 fresh sage leaves
Needles from 2 rosemary sprigs
Grated zest of ½ lemon

Put 2 tablespoons of the salt in a food processor, add the pepper, garlic, sage, rosemary, and lemon zest, and pulse a few times to finely chop the herbs and integrate the ingredients into a green, almost pesto-like paste.

Using a rubber spatula, scrape the mixture into an airtight container. Stir in the remaining salt. (Adding the rest of the salt after processing allows the mixture to retain the properties of the coarse salt, preventing it from becoming too powdery or wet, which is essential to achieving the desired effect on the grill.)

Cover and refrigerate for at least 24 hours before using. The salt can be refrigerated for up to 1 month.

# BOLLITO MISTO

## MIXED BOILED MEATS

SERVES 8 TO 10

Just about every European country has in its canon of home cooking a large-scale offering of mixed boiled meats, cooked together and served with condiments such as mustard and horseradish. The French pot-au-feu and the Italian bollito misto are probably the most well known of these. Classic bollito misto recipes, which hail from the northern regions of Piedmont and Lombardy, with economy top of mind, feature tongue, calf's head, and other cuts that are off-putting to all but the most adventuresome American eaters. I've opted for a more conservative selection of beef short ribs, veal breast, sausage, and chicken here.

Kosher salt
1 teaspoon whole black peppercorns
2 bay leaves, preferably fresh
10 juniper berries, gently bruised with the side of a chef's knife
3 large celery stalks, trimmed and cut into large dice
2 large yellow onions, cut into large dice
4 large carrots, cut into large dice
2 pounds beef short ribs
1 boneless veal breast, about 2 pounds
1 chicken, 2½ to 3 pounds, cut into 8 pieces by your butcher
1 cotechino or veal sausage (see Sources, page 379), 12 to 16 ounces, pricked with the tines of a fork (Lyonnaise sausage can be substituted)
Sea salt
Salsa Verde (recipe follows)
Mostarda di Cremona (recipe follows)

Fill a large pot about two-thirds full with water and salt it liberally. Add the peppercorns, bay leaves, and juniper berries and bring to a boil over high heat. Add the celery, onions, carrots, short ribs, and veal breast, lower the heat so the liquid is simmering, and simmer for 30 minutes, periodically using a spoon to skim off any fat and scum that rise to the surface.

Add the chicken and sausage to the pot, let the liquid return to a gentle simmer, and simmer until the meats are tender and the chicken is cooked through, about 1½ hours longer.

Remove the pot from the heat and use tongs or a slotted spoon to transfer the meats to a cutting board. Cut between the short ribs to separate them. Slice the veal breast into 8 to 10 pieces. Slice the sausage into 8 to 10 pieces. Arrange the meats on a large serving platter. Strain the cooking liquid, discard the solids, and spoon a little liquid over all of the meats.

Serve, passing small bowls of sea salt, the salsa verde, and the mostarda alongside.

## SALSA VERDE

MAKES 1 CUP

This versatile sauce is used as a condiment for everything from fish to poultry to meats.

1 cup fresh flat-leaf parsley leaves
¼ teaspoon finely grated lemon zest
2 tablespoons capers, soaked in warm water for 5 minutes and drained
2 oil-packed anchovy fillets
½ garlic clove, minced
½ teaspoon fresh thyme leaves
1 tablespoon Dijon mustard
½ cup olive oil

Put the parsley, lemon zest, capers, anchovies, garlic, and thyme on a cutting board and coarsely chop them together. Transfer to a bowl and stir in the mustard. Slowly drizzle in the oil, stirring to incorporate it.

**Variation** For a modern salsa verde, refrigerate the oil in a measuring cup for 30 minutes (chilling the oil will prevent the herbs from heating up in the blender and turning brown). Add the remaining ingredients to a blender and pulse until the herbs, capers, and anchovies are finely chopped. With the motor running, slowly add the oil in a thin stream, blending just until smooth.

## MOSTARDA DI CREMONA

MAKES 2 CUPS

This Northern Italian condiment is traditionally served with boiled meats and sometimes with an affettati misti (see page 13).

¼ cup sugar
½ cup dry white wine
½ cup water
1 bay leaf, preferably fresh
1 tablespoon finely grated peeled fresh ginger
1 quince, cored and cut into small dice
1 unripe pear, peeled, cored, and cut into small dice
½ cup finely diced dried apricots (about 8 apricots)
2 teaspoons mustard powder, such as Colman's

Heat a small heavy pot over medium heat. Add the sugar, wine, water, and bay leaf and bring to a simmer, stirring until the sugar dissolves. Stir in the ginger and cook for 1 minute to infuse the mixture with its flavor.

Add the quince, pear, and apricot, let the liquid return to a simmer, and cook at a gentle simmer, adjusting the heat if necessary and stirring periodically with a wooden spoon, until the fruit is tender to the tines of a fork and the cooking liquid is slightly thickened, 20 to 30 minutes. Stir in the mustard powder, remove from the heat, and let cool completely.

The mostarda can be used right away or refrigerated in an airtight container for up to 3 days.

# GRIGLIATA MISTA

## MIXED GRILLED MEATS

SERVES 4

One of my most cherished memories of my time in Imola is of weekend get-togethers with friends, when we'd gather in somebody's backyard, grill a selection of meats, and pig out on the bounty. This assortment, featuring pork, lamb, and beef, is my combination of choice, but you can by all means vary the selection to include your favorite grilled foods; chicken wings would be a delicious addition.

To my mind, the only way to serve this is with Salsa Verde (page 149) and a few simple side dishes, such as roasted potatoes (see page 170) and grilled vegetables.

1½ pounds fresh pancetta (pork belly)
1 pound skirt steak
4 lamb shoulder chops, about 6 ounces each
About 3 tablespoons Rosemary Salt (page 146)
4 sweet Italian sausages, about 4 ounces each, pricked with the tines of a fork
Salsa Verde (page 149)

Preheat one side of a gas grill to high and the other to low; or, if using a charcoal grill, bank the coals on one side and let them burn until covered with white ash.

Season the pancetta, skirt steak, and lamb chops all over with the rosemary salt.

Put the pancetta over the cooler side of the grill and patiently grill it until its fat begins to render and it turns nicely golden brown, about 8 minutes. Turn the pancetta over and put the steak, lamb chops, and sausage over direct (high) heat. Grill, turning the pieces as they brown, until nicely charred on both sides (or, in the case of the sausage, all over), 8 to 10 minutes. As the meats are done, move them to the cooler part of the grill to keep them warm.

When all of the meats are cooked, transfer them to a cutting board, tent loosely with foil, and let rest for 10 minutes.

Slice the pancetta and skirt steak into 4 pieces each. Arrange the meats on a platter and serve with the salsa verde.

# BRASATO DI MANZO

## BRAISED SHORT RIBS OF BEEF

SERVES 4

A two-step process ensures a succulent result in this dish. The short ribs are first marinated in red wine and aromatics to break down their connective tissues, then braised in some of that same marinade.

The word manzo in the name of this dish simply means "beef," not any particular cut. This can be made with other cuts; it would be especially good with beef shank. These ribs are traditionally served with a soft starch such as Polenta (page 168) to soak up the sauce.

Note that the ribs must marinate for 24 hours.

4 large beef short ribs, about 10 ounces each and 2½ inches thick by 5 inches long (ask your butcher to cut them from the plate)
1 Spanish onion, cut into small dice
1 large carrot, cut into small dice
1 large celery stalk, trimmed and cut into small dice
3 bay leaves
2 rosemary sprigs
About 1 bottle (750 ml) dry red wine
Kosher salt
Freshly ground black pepper
¼ cup canola oil or other neutral oil, or more as needed
1 28-ounce can diced tomatoes, preferably Italian San Marzano or organic, with their juice
About 2 cups Veal Stock (page 375) or store-bought low-sodium beef broth
Freshly grated horseradish, for serving

Pat the short ribs dry. Put them in a baking dish and scatter the onions, carrots, celery, bay leaves, and rosemary over them. Pour in enough wine to cover, cover loosely with plastic wrap, and refrigerate for 24 hours.

When ready to proceed, line a baking sheet with paper towels. Remove the ribs from the marinade, brushing any solids back into the marinade. Season the ribs with salt and pepper. Strain the marinade through a fine-mesh strainer into a bowl; reserve the liquid and solids separately.

Heat a Dutch oven or other large heavy pot over high heat. Pour in the oil and heat until it is shimmering and almost smoking. Working in batches, add the short ribs to the pot, each piece of meat touching the oil, and brown on the first side for 5 to 7 minutes, then use tongs to turn the short ribs over and brown on the other side for 5 to 7 minutes. Transfer the ribs to the paper-towel-lined baking sheet to drain, then transfer them to a large mixing bowl. (If necessary, add more oil to the pot between batches.) Pour off and discard all but 2 tablespoons of the oil from the pot.

Add the marinade solids to the pot and cook, stirring occasionally, until the vegetables are softened but not browned, 6 to 7 minutes. Pour in 1 cup of the reserved marinade liquid, bring to a simmer, stirring to loosen any flavorful bits cooked onto the bottom of the pot, and simmer until almost completely evaporated, about 6 minutes. Stir in the tomatoes, with their liquid, and cook, stirring occasionally, until the liquid has evaporated, 3 to 4 minutes.

Return the short ribs to the pot and pour in enough stock to cover them completely. Raise the heat to high and bring the liquid to a boil, then lower the heat so the liquid is simmering and simmer until the meat is tender and falling off the bone, 2½ to 3 hours. Check the liquid periodically; you are looking for a slight, almost imperceptible bubbling on the surface. If it is not simmering at all, raise the heat slightly; if it's simmering too assertively, lower the heat slightly. Transfer the short ribs to a large plate and cover with aluminum foil. Remove the pot from the heat and set aside to cool.

Once the cooking liquid has cooled, use a spoon to skim the fat that has risen to the surface and discard it. Strain the liquid through a fine-mesh strainer into a bowl and discard the vegetables, then return the liquid to the pot. Bring to a boil over high heat and boil until reduced to about 2 cups, about 10 minutes. Lower the heat, return the short ribs to the pot, and rewarm them in the sauce.

Divide the short ribs among 4 large plates and spoon some sauce over each serving, or serve family-style from a platter, passing the sauce in a serving bowl. Serve with freshly grated horseradish.

# NODINO DI VITELLO ALLA BERGESE

## VEAL WITH SMOKED PANCETTA CREAM SAUCE

SERVES 4

This dish was created by Nino Bergese, the first chef at San Domenico, starting in 1970. It's something like a cross between an au poivre sauce and the French veal stew blanquette de veau, but made with veal chops, and with smoked pancetta in the sauce. This recipe is a bit more contemporary than the others in this part of the book, but I wanted to include it because it's simply delicious.

4 veal chops, 12 ounces each, ideally 1½ inches thick, trimmed and frenched (by your butcher)
Kosher salt
Freshly ground black pepper
3 tablespoons canola oil or other neutral oil
2 tablespoons unsalted butter
2 large garlic cloves, smashed with the side of a chef's knife and peeled
1 thyme sprig
2 bay leaves, preferably fresh
Smoked Pancetta Cream Sauce (recipe follows)

Position a rack in the center of the oven and preheat the oven to 400°F.

Season the veal chops with salt and pepper.

Heat a large cast-iron or other heavy ovenproof skillet over medium-high heat. Add the canola oil and tip and tilt the pan to coat it, heating the oil until it is shimmering and almost smoking. Add the veal chops, in batches if necessary (or work in 2 pans), and sear on both sides until golden brown, about 5 minutes per side.

Transfer the pan to the oven and roast until the veal is cooked to your preference, 6 to 8 minutes for medium-rare, a bit longer for more well done.

Remove the skillet from the oven and carefully pour off the oil. Set the pan over medium heat, add the butter, garlic, thyme, and bay leaves, and cook, using a pastry brush or tablespoon to baste the veal with the butter and herbs, until the butter begins to coat the veal, about 5 minutes. Transfer the chops to a serving platter. Drizzle with the basting butter, loosely tent the plate with aluminum foil, and let rest for 5 minutes.

Remove the foil, spoon the sauce over the veal, and serve.

### *SALSA BERGESE*

### SMOKED PANCETTA CREAM SAUCE

MAKES ABOUT 1½ CUPS

Most pancetta is simply cured, but smoked pancetta, a rarity even in Italy, is something else altogether, delivering a real punch of pork fat and smoke to this sauce. This is also delicious over steaks.

2 tablespoons unsalted butter
4 ounces smoked pancetta (see Sources, page 379) cut into small dice (smoky bacon can be substituted)
1 tablespoon whole black peppercorns, crushed under a heavy skillet
1 large shallot, minced
1/3 cup vodka
1 cup heavy cream

Heat a medium heavy saucepan over medium heat. Add the butter and melt it, tipping and tilting the pan to coat it with the butter. Add the pancetta and cook, stirring with a wooden spoon, until the pancetta has rendered some of its fat and browned, about 5 minutes. Stir in the peppercorns and shallots and cook until the shallots are softened but not browned, about 3 minutes. Pour in the vodka and use a wooden spoon to loosen any flavorful bits cooked onto the bottom of the pan. Bring the vodka to a simmer and simmer until it has evaporated, about 5 minutes.

Stir in the cream, bring to a simmer, and simmer until the sauce is thick enough to coat the back of the spoon, about 5 minutes.

The sauce can be made ahead and kept warm in a double boiler for up to 1 hour. Or let cool and refrigerate in an airtight container for up to 24 hours. Reheat gently in a small heavy saucepan, whisking to reincorporate any liquid that has separated.

# SALTIMBOCCA DI VITELLO

## VEAL PARCELS WITH PROSCIUTTO AND SAGE

SERVES 4

This classic favorite with an unforgettable name (saltimbocca means "jump in the mouth") relies on the neat trick of pinning prosciutto to veal scallops, allowing the former to impart its fat and flavor to the latter when they are cooked together. Though most closely associated with Rome, saltimbocca turns up throughout Italy. While the stuffed baby peppers are not absolutely essential, they provide complementary sweetness and crunch.

8 slices veal top round, 3 ounces each
Kosher salt
Freshly ground black pepper
2 tablespoons minced fresh sage, plus 8 large leaves
8 very thin slices prosciutto (about 2 ounces total)
All-purpose flour, for dredging
2 tablespoons unsalted butter, plus 2 tablespoons cold butter, cut into 6 pieces
1 tablespoon olive oil
1 large garlic clove, thinly sliced
½ cup dry white wine
1 cup Dark Chicken Stock (page 374)
½ lemon
Stuffed Baby Peppers (page 160; optional)

Working with one piece of veal at a time, lay the slices between pieces of plastic wrap and use a meat mallet or the bottom of a heavy pan to pound them to about ⅛ inch thick, taking care not to tear the meat.

Line up the veal scallops on your work surface. Season with salt and pepper and sprinkle with the minced sage. Top each piece of veal with a slice of prosciutto. Fold each veal scallop in half so the ends meet and the prosciutto encases the veal, then fold in half again to make a small parcel, set a sage leaf on top, and use a toothpick to seal the packet and secure the sage leaf.

Spread the flour on a large plate. Lightly dredge the veal parcels in the flour, pressing gently to help the flour adhere. Shake off any excess flour and set the parcels on another plate.

Heat a wide heavy skillet large enough to hold the parcels in a single layer over medium-high heat. Add the 2 tablespoons butter and heat until melted, tipping and tilting the pan to coat it. Add the veal parcels, sage side up, and cook until the parcels are golden brown on the first side, 5 to 7 minutes. Use tongs to turn them and brown on the other side, another 5 to 7 minutes. Transfer the veal to a large plate. Loosely tent the plate with aluminum foil and set aside.

Pour out and discard the butter from the skillet. Pour in the oil and tip and turn the pan to coat it, heating the oil until it is shimmering and almost smoking. Add the garlic and cook, stirring frequently, until softened but not browned, about 2 minutes. Pour in the wine and stir with a wooden spoon to loosen any flavorful bits cooked onto the bottom of the pan, then bring to a simmer and simmer until the wine has evaporated, 7 to 8 minutes. Stir in the stock, bring it to a simmer, and simmer until reduced by half, about 5 minutes.

Strain the contents of the skillet through a fine-mesh strainer into a clean skillet. Discard the solids. Off the heat, whisk in the 2 tablespoons cold butter, a piece or two at a time, to emulsify the sauce. Taste and season with a few drops of lemon juice; the desired effect is a balanced sauce with a pleasing acidity but without a distinctly lemony flavor.

Add the veal to the sauce and warm through over medium heat, using the wooden spoon or a tablespoon to baste the packages with the sauce, about 5 minutes.

Set 2 veal parcels on each of 4 dinner plates, arrange a few stuffed peppers alongside, if using, and serve.

# CONTORNI

# SIDE DISHES

When the steakhouse craze hit the United States in the mid-2000s and restaurant menus everywhere suddenly began offering side dishes à la carte, I couldn't help but laugh at the new "trend," because that's the way Italians have always eaten, and it's the way most Americans eat at home on an everyday basis as well. The flexibility to mix and match different proteins with different vegetable and starch accompaniments not only leaves one open to what seems appealing from day to day, it also allows a home cook to cook and use what's on hand at any given time.

This chapter contains a range of versatile side dishes. Many of them are as suitable alongside fish as they are next to pork or beef. I've offered some guidance in the headnotes, but you needn't be bound by my suggestions.

Many of these dishes would also be appropriate as part of an antipasti spread. And although they wouldn't be served as stand-alone starters in Italy, dishes such as the fennel salad on page 158, or the Sicilian-style cauliflower with anchovy paste, capers, and raisins on page 166, could also be served as first courses.

Leftovers from most of these recipes can be served at another meal, rewarmed or at room temperature, just one more example of how Italian cuisine's inherent flexibility pays off on a daily basis.

# INSALATA DI FINOCCHIO

## SHAVED FENNEL SALAD

SERVES 4 TO 6

Though unfamiliar to many Americans, fennel is hugely popular in Italy, where it is called on for a variety of purposes, from braising to use as the basis of a simple salad as it is here. If you'd like the fennel especially cold and crunchy, refrigerate the sliced fennel for 15 to 30 minutes before dressing and serving it. Fennel has a particular affinity for fish, but it can be served with just about any protein. Because fennel seeds are often included in sausage, I like pairing this dish in the same way with grilled or roasted pork.

2 large fennel bulbs (about 12 ounces each)
¼ cup extra virgin olive oil
2 to 3 tablespoons freshly squeezed lemon juice
Kosher salt
Freshly ground black pepper

Cut the fronds off the fennel stalks, finely chop them, and set them aside. Cut off and discard the stalks. Cut the fennel bulbs lengthwise into quarters and cut out and discard the cores.

Shave the fennel crosswise as thinly as possible on a mandoline, or use a sharp heavy knife and steady hands.

Put the fennel slices in a large mixing bowl. Pour in the olive oil and 2 tablespoons of the lemon juice and season with salt and pepper. Taste and add more lemon juice, if desired. Toss to coat, then transfer the fennel to a serving bowl or plate, top with the fennel fronds, and serve.

## PEPERONI RIPIENI

### STUFFED BABY PEPPERS

SERVES 4

This easy side dish shows up all over Italy and has almost universal application, but I think it gets along best with fish and white meats, such as pork and veal. Baby bell peppers are available at farmers' markets, gourmet shops, and some supermarkets.

¼ cup olive oil
Kosher salt
8 baby bell peppers (about 2 inches long and 1 inch in diameter at the top), ideally 4 red and 4 yellow, cored, seeded, and halved lengthwise
About 1 cup Seasoned Toasted Bread Crumbs (page xxix)
½ cup finely grated Parmigiano-Reggiano (about 1 ounce)
Freshly ground black pepper

Position a rack in the center of the oven and preheat the oven to 375°F.

Pour 2 tablespoons of the oil into the bottom of a glass baking dish, spread it evenly over the surface, and sprinkle with salt.

Fill each pepper half with a tablespoon or so of the bread crumbs and set it in the baking dish. Sprinkle the peppers with the Parmigiano and drizzle with the remaining 2 tablespoons oil.

Bake the peppers until they are slightly softened and the cheese is melted, 10 to 12 minutes; use a tablespoon to periodically baste the peppers with the juices that accumulate in the bottom of the baking dish.

Remove the dish from the oven, season the peppers with a few grinds of black pepper, divide among individual plates or arrange on a serving platter, and serve.

# FRIGGONE BOLOGNESE

## STEWED BELL PEPPERS, TOMATOES, AND ONIONS

SERVES 4 TO 6

These stewed peppers, a common Bolognese condiment, are served with everything from Mixed Boiled Meats (page 148) to roasted lamb to sliced cured meats.

½ cup olive oil
3 large Spanish onions, cut into small dice
3 large garlic cloves, smashed with the side of a chef's knife and peeled
1 large red bell pepper, cored, seeded, and cut into small dice
1 large yellow pepper, cored, seeded, and cut into small dice
1 teaspoon sugar
1 28-ounce can whole tomatoes, preferably Italian San Marzano or organic, crushed by hand, with their juice
2 bay leaves, preferably fresh
Kosher salt
Freshly ground black pepper

Pour the oil into a medium heavy pot. Set over medium-high heat, and let the oil heat until it is shimmering and almost smoking. Add the onions, garlic, and red and yellow peppers and cook, stirring with a wooden spoon, until the vegetables are softened but not browned, about 4 minutes. Sprinkle with the sugar and cook, stirring, for 1 minute.

Stir in the tomatoes and bay leaves, season with salt and pepper, and bring to a simmer. Lower the heat and let simmer until reduced to a compote-like consistency, about 2 hours.

Use tongs or a spoon to fish out and discard the bay leaves. Taste and adjust the seasoning with salt and pepper.

Serve the stewed peppers warm or at room temperature in a serving bowl.

# POMODORI GRATINATI CON PANE ALLE ERBE

## BAKED TOMATOES WITH HERBED BREAD CRUMBS

SERVES 6

In August and September, when tomatoes are plentiful, it takes little more than a drizzle of olive oil, a pinch of salt, a few grinds of black pepper, and a quick turn in the oven to amplify their peak-of-season juiciness and flavor. These get along great with grilled fish and beef, with which they essentially act as both contorno and sauce.

- 6 ripe-but-firm tomatoes, preferably vine-ripened
- ¼ cup plus 1 tablespoon olive oil
- Kosher salt
- Freshly ground black pepper
- ¾ cup Seasoned Toasted Bread Crumbs (page xxix)
- 1½ tablespoons finely grated lemon zest
- 6 large fresh basil leaves, cut into chiffonade (see page xxx)

Position a rack in the center of the oven and preheat the oven to 350°F.

Use a sharp heavy knife to neatly slice off the top ½ inch of each tomato, revealing the pulpy interior.

Stand the tomatoes cut side up in a baking dish large enough to hold them without crowding. Drizzle with ¼ cup of the oil and season with salt and pepper.

Put the bread crumbs in a small bowl and add the lemon zest, basil, and remaining tablespoon of oil. Toss well, then scatter the mixture over the tomatoes. Season with salt and pepper.

Bake the tomatoes just until the bread crumbs are golden brown, about 20 minutes. Remove the baking dish from the oven and let the tomatoes rest for 5 minutes before serving.

# CIPOLLINI AGRO DOLCE

## SWEET-AND-SOUR BABY ONIONS

SERVES 4 TO 6

Here the natural sweetness of baby onions is augmented with sugar, then contrasted with a reduction of red wine vinegar and balsamic vinegar to achieve a potent but balanced flavor. This is one of those rare times when calling on an inexpensive balsamico makes more sense than using the real thing.

2 tablespoons olive oil
2 tablespoons unsalted butter
3 large bay leaves, preferably fresh
1 pound cipollini onions or pearl onions, peeled and trimmed
Kosher salt
Freshly ground black pepper
2 tablespoons sugar
¼ cup balsamic vinegar (see the headnote)
¼ cup red wine vinegar
1½ cups Chicken Stock (page 374) or store-bought low-sodium chicken broth

Heat a medium heavy sauté pan over medium heat. Add the olive oil and butter and heat, melting the butter and tipping and tilting the pan to coat it, until the mixture is foaming. Add the bay leaves and cook for 1 minute to infuse the butter and oil with their flavor. Add the onions and cook, stirring frequently with a wooden spoon, until lightly browned on all sides, about 10 minutes.

Season the onions with a pinch of salt and a few grinds of pepper and stir, then sprinkle with the sugar, stir, and cook for 1 minute to melt the sugar. Pour in the vinegars and stir with a wooden spoon to loosen any flavorful bits cooked onto the bottom of the pan. Cook, stirring frequently, until the liquid is reduced to a glaze and coats the onions, about 5 minutes.

Pour in the stock and bring it to a simmer. Cover the pan and simmer, shaking the pan occasionally to ensure even cooking, until the onions are tender to the tines of a fork and nicely glazed, 8 to 10 minutes; use a pastry brush or a spoon to baste the onions occasionally. Transfer the onions to a serving plate and serve warm.

# CIME DI RAPE CON OLIVE E CIPOLLA

## BROCCOLI RABE WITH OLIVES AND ONIONS

SERVES 4 TO 6

The exquisitely bitter quality of broccoli rabe means it can stand on its own with a simple sautéing, often with just slivered garlic and a pinch of red pepper flakes added. But broccoli rabe makes such a sublime foil for other high-impact ingredients that adding one or two to the pan produces complex results with very little extra work. Here black olives and onions contribute sweetness and salinity that make this an all-purpose accompaniment for everything from game birds and beef to fish and pork.

The broccoli rabe yields equally versatile leftovers: Eat them cold, chop and toss with a pasta, or use as a sandwich relish, perhaps with slices of the pork on page 138.

2 large bunches of broccoli rabe, trimmed
3 tablespoons olive oil
1 small Spanish onion, halved through the root end and thinly sliced
2 large garlic cloves, thinly sliced
Pinch of red pepper flakes
¼ cup black olives, such as kalamata, halved and pitted
Kosher salt
Freshly ground black pepper

Fill a large pot two-thirds full with water and salt it liberally. Bring to a boil over high heat. Fill a large bowl halfway with ice water.

Add the broccoli rabe to the boiling water and blanch until bright green and just tender, 3 to 4 minutes. Drain and transfer to the ice water to stop the cooking and preserve the color. Drain again and pat dry with paper towels.

Heat a wide heavy skillet over medium heat. Add the olive oil and tip and tilt the pan to coat it, heating the oil until it is shimmering and almost smoking. Add the onions, garlic, and red pepper flakes and cook, stirring with a wooden spoon, until the onions are softened but not browned, about 4 minutes. Add the broccoli rabe and olives and cook, tossing or stirring, until the broccoli rabe is cooked through but still al dente, about 4 minutes. Season to taste with salt and pepper.

Transfer the broccoli rabe, onions, and olives to a serving bowl or plate and serve.

# CAVOLFIORI FRITTI

## FRIED SICILIAN CAULIFLOWER

SERVES 4 TO 6

One of cauliflower's greatest values is as backdrop for, and receiver of, other flavors. This Sicilian preparation fries cauliflower to crisp it, then pairs it with salty, sweet, acidic, and herbaceous ingredients to create a versatile side dish. The lemon and capers make this especially good with white-fleshed fish. It can also be served as an antipasto.

A few cups of olive oil, for deep-frying
1 large head of cauliflower (about 2 pounds), cored and cut into 3-inch florets
Kosher salt
Freshly ground black pepper
1 tablespoon freshly squeezed lemon juice
1 teaspoon anchovy paste (optional)
1/3 cup golden raisins, soaked in warm water for 10 minutes and drained
2 tablespoons fried capers (see page 368)
2 tablespoons thinly sliced fresh flat-leaf parsley leaves
1/4 cup freshly grated Pecorino Romano
1/4 cup Seasoned Toasted Bread Crumbs (page xxix) or dried bread crumbs

Line a large plate or platter with paper towels. Pour enough oil into a medium sauté pan to come about 1 1/4 inches up the sides of the pan and heat over medium-high heat until the oil reaches 360°F on a deep-fry thermometer.

Add the cauliflower florets to the hot oil, in batches, and fry until golden brown, about 2 minutes. Use a slotted spoon to remove the florets from the pan and transfer them to the paper-towel-lined plate to drain, seasoning them immediately with salt. Return the oil to 360°F between batches.

Transfer the fried cauliflower to a large serving bowl, season with salt, pepper, lemon juice, and the anchovy paste, if using, and toss to incorporate. Add the raisins, capers, parsley, and Pecorino and toss. Top with the bread crumbs and serve at once.

## FARROTTO CON VERDURE DI STAGIONE

### FARRO WITH SEASONAL VEGETABLES

SERVES 4 TO 6

Farro, a spelt-like grain, is less well known outside Italy, where it's often prepared as farrotto, in the style of risotto. This recipe incorporates autumnal ingredients, most prominently butternut squash, but it can be adapted to use the vegetables of other seasons. In the spring, replace the squash with blanched peas, favas, or sliced leeks.

Kosher salt
1 cup farro
7 tablespoons unsalted butter
½ cup butternut squash in large dice
Freshly ground black pepper
1 tablespoon olive oil
1 Spanish onion, minced
1 garlic clove, minced
Needles from 1 rosemary sprig, minced
Leaves from 1 thyme sprig, minced
¼ cup dry white wine
1 quart Chicken Stock (page 374) or Vegetable Stock (page 371)
1 cup blanched and chopped kale or Swiss chard (see page 367)
1 cup finely grated Parmigiano-Reggiano (about 2 ounces)

Fill a medium pot two-thirds full with water, salt it liberally, and bring to a boil over high heat. Add the farro and boil for 20 minutes, then drain and set aside.

Heat a wide heavy sauté pan over medium heat. Add 2 tablespoons of the butter and let it melt, tipping and tilting the pan to coat it. Add the squash, season with salt and pepper, and cook, stirring periodically with a wooden spoon, until the cubes are lightly caramelized and softened but still holding their shape, about 4 minutes. Set the pan aside.

Heat a large heavy pot over medium heat. Add 1 tablespoon of the butter and the olive oil and heat until the butter is melted. Add the onions, garlic, rosemary, and thyme and cook, stirring, until the onions are softened but not browned, about 4 minutes. Stir in the farro and cook, stirring constantly, for 2 minutes. Stir in the wine, bring to a simmer, and cook until the wine has evaporated, about 3 minutes. Stir in the stock, bring to a simmer, and simmer, stirring occasionally, until the farro is al dente, about 45 minutes.

Fold in the squash and kale, then stir in the remaining 4 tablespoons butter and the Parmigiano. Serve.

**Variations** In the spring, omit the squash and kale and finish the farrotto with ½ cup blanched peas and ½ cup blanched, peeled baby onions sautéed in butter. In the winter, use red wine instead of white, omit the squash and kale, and fold some shredded radicchio and sautéed mushrooms into the finished farrotto.

# POLENTA

SERVES 4 TO 6

Polenta can be made with water, stock, and/or milk or cream. I prefer to use water so the defining corn flavor shines through. That said, I do sometimes stir in a few tablespoons of milk or cream as a finishing agent, with just a little butter and grated Parmigiano added at the end to enrich it and smooth out the texture. Polenta is an especially apt accompaniment to generously sauced dishes such as stews and braised meats. The amount of water may seem excessive at first, but the cornmeal will take it on during the long cooking process. (For more on polenta, see page xxxii.)

4 cups water
Kosher salt
2/3 cup yellow cornmeal
3 tablespoons unsalted butter
½ cup finely grated Parmigiano-Reggiano (about 1 ounce)

Pour the water into a large heavy saucepan and salt it. Bring to a simmer over medium-high heat. Add the polenta in a slow, steady stream, whisking all the while, and continue whisking until the polenta begins to thicken, about 3 minutes. Switch to a wooden spoon and cook, stirring periodically, until the polenta is nicely thickened, smooth, and fully cooked (it will taste of corn), about 1 hour. (The polenta can be kept warm in a double boiler over simmering water for up to 1 hour.)

Whisk in the butter and cheese just before serving.

# FAGIOLI ALL'UCCELLETTO

## CANNELLINI BEANS WITH TOMATO AND SAGE

SERVES 4 TO 6

This classic Tuscan side dish stews white beans with tomatoes and sage. Pair it with braised or grilled meats or with game birds. Its name refers to the fact that it is cooked with the flavors often used with small game birds.

1½ cups dried cannellini beans
¼ cup olive oil
1 small Spanish onion, cut into small dice
3 garlic cloves, minced
6 fresh sage leaves, minced
Pinch of red pepper flakes
1 14-ounce can chopped tomatoes, preferably Italian San Marzano or organic, with their juice
About 4 cups Chicken Stock (page 374) or Vegetable Stock (page 371)
Kosher salt
Freshly ground black pepper
Extra virgin olive oil, for serving

Put the beans in a bowl, cover with cold water, and soak overnight. (Alternatively, you can quick-soak the beans; see page 30.) Drain.

Heat a wide sauté pan over medium-high heat. Add the olive oil and let the oil heat until it is shimmering and almost smoking. Add the onions and garlic and cook, stirring with a wooden spoon, until softened but not browned, about 4 minutes. Stir in the sage and red pepper flakes, then stir in the tomatoes and beans and cook, stirring, for 2 minutes. Pour in just enough stock to cover by 1 inch and bring to a simmer. Lower the heat and simmer until the beans are tender and the mixture has thickened to a stew-like consistency, 1 to 1½ hours. Season with salt and pepper.

Drizzle extra virgin olive oil over the beans and serve.

# PATATE AL FORNO

## OVEN-ROASTED POTATOES

SERVES 4 TO 6

This all-purpose roasted potato recipe can be served with just about anything.

- ¼ cup olive oil
- 1½ pounds Yukon Gold potatoes, peeled, cut into small wedges, and patted dry
- 2 tablespoons fresh rosemary needles, coarsely chopped
- Kosher salt
- Freshly ground black pepper

Position a rack in the center of the oven and preheat the oven to 400°F.

Put a medium baking dish in the oven and preheat it for 5 to 10 minutes. Working quickly, slide out the oven rack, and add the oil to the baking dish, then add the potatoes and use a wooden spoon to toss with the oil. Slide the rack back into the oven and roast the potatoes, stirring every 10 minutes to ensure even cooking, until nicely golden brown, 25 to 30 minutes.

Remove the baking dish from the oven and scatter the rosemary over the potatoes. Season with salt and pepper. Toss well and serve.

# DOLCI
# DESSERTS

As with the other courses in a traditional Italian meal, desserts are kept in perspective: One is just as apt to conclude lunch or dinner with cheese or fruit as with something baked or frozen. Of course, as an American, I had developed a formidable sweet tooth during my childhood, so I usually choose the latter, although Italian desserts are on the whole less sugary than their American counterparts.

The recipes in this chapter represent a handful of the "greatest hits" of Italian desserts, such as affogato, an espresso and gelato "float"; a fruit-topped ricotta tart; a semifreddo, the creamy, semi-frozen classic; an Olive Oil Cake (page 177) with poached pears; and Panna Cotta (page 175), the eggless custard.

They are the desserts that I enjoy in restaurants in Italy and serve at home in the United States. What I love most about them is how straightforward they are: Each is based on one central component or flavor, or the interplay of two primary contrasting elements. They don't demand tremendous pastry-making acumen, and most can be made in advance and simply sliced or scooped and served when the time comes.

# AFFOGATO

## ESPRESSO-TOPPED GELATO

SERVES 4

If you have an espresso machine, there are few more simply perfect desserts than affogato, which tops a scoop of vanilla gelato with a freshly pulled shot of espresso. (The name of the dessert means "drowned.") While the basic recipe is satisfying, I also enjoy topping the gelato with some amaro, a slightly bitter Italian digestif.

1 pint vanilla gelato or excellent-quality vanilla ice cream
¼ cup amaro, preferably Ramazzotti
4 shots freshly pulled espresso
Freshly whipped cream

Put a scoop of gelato in each of 4 serving dishes, coffee cups, or dessert glasses. Top each with 1 tablespoon of amaro, then 1 shot of espresso. Finish each one with a dollop of whipped cream and serve immediately.

# PANNA COTTA

MAKES ONE 10-INCH TART

This creamy, eggless custard is one of Italy's most popular desserts. When properly made, an unmolded panna cotta should just barely hold its shape, then almost collapse after the first bite is taken. These are slightly more tart than the classic panna cotta, thanks to the addition of crème fraîche by my pastry chef, Bob Truitt.

FOR THE FRUTTI DI BOSCO

1 cup fresh strawberries, hulled, larger ones cut in half
1 cup fresh raspberries
1 cup fresh blueberries
1 ¼ cups sugar
½ cup freshly squeezed lemon juice plus finely grated zest of 1 ½ lemons
1 teaspoon apple pectin (available in supermarkets)

FOR THE PANNA COTTA

1 ¾ cups heavy cream
1 ¾ cups whole milk, plus ½ cup very well-chilled milk
¾ cup sugar
1 vanilla bean, split in half lengthwise, seeds removed, seeds and pods reserved
1 teaspoon finely grated lemon zest
1 ½ teaspoons powdered gelatin
Pinch of coarse salt
3 cups crème fraîche

To make the frutti di bosco: Put the strawberries, raspberries, blueberries, sugar, and lemon juice in a large mixing bowl and toss to incorporate. Cover loosely with plastic wrap and refrigerate for 12 hours.

When ready to proceed, heat a large pot over low heat and add the fruit mixture. Heat just until the fruits are warmed through, 3 to 4 minutes, making sure the liquids do not boil. Strain the mixture through a fine-mesh sieve, reserving the berries in a large bowl, and return the liquid to the pot. Set over medium heat. Stir in the lemon zest and the pectin and cook, stirring frequently, until the mixture thickens, 6 to 8 minutes. Pour the thickened liquid over the reserved berries and toss to coat. Cover with plastic wrap and refrigerate until the mixture is set, about 6 hours.

To make the panna cotta: Combine the heavy cream, 1¾ cups milk, sugar, vanilla pods and seeds, and lemon zest in a medium pot and heat, stirring occasionally, until a digital thermometer reads 160°F. Remove the pot from the heat, cover, and set aside to steep for 10 minutes.

Meanwhile, put the ½ cup well-chilled milk in a small bowl. Add the gelatin and set aside to soften for 5 minutes.

Uncover the pot and return it to medium heat. Add the salt and milk-gelatin mixture and stir to dissolve the gelatin. Strain the mixture through a fine-mesh sieve into a bowl. Whisk in the crème fraîche and transfer the panna cotta to 6 cups or molds. Refrigerate until completely set, at least 6 hours, or overnight.

To serve, run a paring knife around the edge of the panna cottas to loosen them, then unmold the panna cottas onto 6 dessert plates. Top each panna cotta with some frutti di bosco and serve.

# SEMIFREDDO ALL NOCCIÒLO

## CHOCOLATE-HAZELNUT SEMIFREDDO

SERVES 6

This version of a semifreddo (the name means "semi-frozen") is especially nuanced and balanced. Rather than the standard combination of gelato and whipped cream, this is made with a combination of meringue, cooled hot chocolate, and whipped cream. Once frozen, it can be scooped or sliced (depending on what type of vessel you freeze it in), and is topped with chocolate sauce, hazelnuts, and grapes.

FOR THE SEMIFREDDO

½ cup large egg whites (about 3 whites), at room temperature
1½ cups sugar
1½ teaspoons powdered gelatin
2 cups chopped 70% Valrhona guanaja chocolate (from about 5¼ ounces; see Sources, page 379)
2 cups heavy cream

FOR THE DARK CHOCOLATE SAUCE

2 cups chopped 70% Valrhona guanaja chocolate, melted (from about 5¼ ounces; see Sources, page 379)
2 cups heavy cream
1 teaspoon coarse salt

TO SERVE

¼ cup hazelnuts, toasted and lightly crushed (see page 367)
¾ cup halved seedless red grapes

To make the semifreddo, start by making a meringue: Put the egg whites in the bowl of a stand mixer fitted with the whisk attachment and mix the whites on low to medium speed while you cook the sugar. Combine the sugar and just enough water to moisten the sugar thoroughly (the mixture should be the consistency of wet sand) in a medium heavy saucepan and heat over medium heat, stirring, until the sugar dissolves, then cook until the syrup reaches 250°F on a digital thermometer. Immediately remove from the heat.

Turn the stand mixer to high speed and carefully stream in the hot syrup, being careful to avoid the spinning whisk. Then continue whipping until the meringue is shiny and has cooled to just a bit warmer than room temperature. Set aside.

Put ½ cup cold water in a small bowl. Add the gelatin and set aside to soften for 5 minutes. Set a heatproof bowl over a medium pot of simmering water, or set up a double boiler over simmering water. Add the chocolate to the double boiler. Whisk until the chocolate is melted, then remove the bowl from the heat.

Heat a small pot over medium-high heat and add 1 cup of the heavy cream. Bring the cream to a boil then add the gelatin and stir to dissolve. Pour the hot cream mixture over the melted chocolate and use a rubber spatula or a small hand blender to mix together the chocolate and cream.

Add the remaining 1 cup of heavy cream to a medium mixing bowl and whisk until stiff peaks form. Use a large rubber spatula to gently fold 1 cup of the prepared meringue into the chocolate mixture (you may not use all of the meringue) until just incorporated, then fold in the whipped cream. Transfer the semifreddo into a mold or a large bowl suitable for freezing, and cover with plastic wrap. Freeze until the semifreddo is set, about 4 hours.

Shortly before serving, make the dark chocolate sauce: Set a heatproof bowl over a medium pot of simmering water, or set up a double boiler over simmering water. Add chocolate to the double boiler. Whisk until the chocolate is melted. Heat a medium pot over medium heat and add the heavy cream and the salt. Bring to a boil, then pour the cream mixture over the chocolate and use a rubber spatula or a small hand blender to mix together the chocolate and cream. Remove the bowl from the heat and let the sauce rest at room temperature until ready to serve.

Remove the semifreddo from the freezer 5 to 10 minutes before serving. To serve, slice or scoop the semifreddo and divide among 6 dessert plates or wide, shallow bowls. Drizzle with the chocolate sauce, garnish with hazelnuts and red grapes, and serve.

# TORTA ALL' OLIO DI OLIVA

## OLIVE OIL CAKE

MAKES ONE 8-INCH CAKE

Made with eggs, butter, and, of course, olive oil, this dense cake pairs well with fruits that match its richness with a sweet counterpoint. It's served here with poached pears, but it can be paired with fresh fruit and/or whipped cream instead.

FOR THE OLIVE OIL CAKE

- 8 tablespoons (1 stick) unsalted butter, at room temperature, plus more for greasing the pan
- 1½ cups all-purpose flour, plus more for the pan
- 1½ cups granulated sugar
- 2 large eggs
- ½ cup extra virgin olive oil, preferably Monini
- ½ teaspoon baking powder
- ½ teaspoon kosher salt
- 1 cup whole milk

FOR THE PORT-POACHED PEARS

- 3 Seckel pears, peeled, cored, and halved
- 1 375ml bottle port
- 1 cup granulated sugar
- 10 juniper berries
- Zest of 1 orange, removed in strips with a vegetable peeler, with no white pith
- 5 star anise pods
- 1 vanilla bean, split in half lengthwise, seeds removed, seeds and pods reserved

TO SERVE

- Confectioners' sugar, for dusting

To make the cake: Position a rack in the center of the oven and preheat the oven to 300°F. Butter and flour an 8-inch round cake pan.

Put the butter and granulated sugar in the bowl of a stand mixer fitted with the whisk attachment and cream until light and fluffy, 7 to 10 minutes. Add the eggs one at a time, mixing until just incorporated. With the mixer running, add the olive oil in a steady stream, and mix for 10 minutes on medium speed.

Sift together the flour, baking powder, and salt into a medium bowl. Add one third of the flour mixture to the egg mixture and mix to incorporate. Add one third of the milk and mix to incorporate. Repeat, alternating the dry and wet ingredients, until incorporated into the batter, then mix for another 10 minutes on medium speed.

Pour the batter into the prepared cake pan and place in the oven. Bake until the top of the cake is browned and the cake begins to pull away from the sides of the pan, 30 to 40 minutes. Transfer the cake to a rack and let cool.

To make the poached pears: Combine the pears, port, granulated sugar, juniper berries, orange zest, star anise, and vanilla and seeds in a large pot, bring to a simmer over medium heat, and cook until the pears are tender but still holding their shape and easily pierced with a knife, 15 to 20 minutes. Remove the pot from the heat and let cool.

To serve, unmold the cake (ideally while it is still slightly warm), dust it with confectioners' sugar, and cut into slices. Serve with the poached pears.

# CROSTATA DI RICOTTA

## RICOTTA TART

MAKES ONE 10-INCH TART

If you're accustomed to creamy New York–style cheesecakes, this relatively dry ricotta tart might be a surprise, but it has a subtlety that I love. It goes perfectly with a post-meal shot of espresso or an after-dinner drink such as anisette or limoncello.

FOR THE DOUGH

6 tablespoons unsalted butter, at room temperature
½ cup sugar
3 large egg yolks
1 ¾ cups all-purpose flour

FOR THE RICOTTA FILLING

2 cups whole-milk ricotta cheese
½ cup heavy cream
⅓ cup honey
½ teaspoon kosher salt
1 vanilla bean, split in half lengthwise, seeds removed, pod reserved for another use
1 large egg plus 2 large egg yolks
4 large egg yolks
Finely grated zest of 1 lemon

FOR THE FRUIT TOPPING

4 Seckel pears, 3 of them peeled, cored, and halved
1 375ml bottle port
1 cup sugar
10 juniper berries
Zest of 1 orange, removed in strips with a vegetable peeler, with no pith
5 star anise pods
1 vanilla bean, split in half lengthwise, seeds removed, seeds and pods reserved
3 fresh figs, quartered
¼ cup diced dried figs
3 clusters seedless red grapes
6 mint leaves

To make the dough: Put the butter and sugar in the bowl of a stand mixer fitted with the paddle attachment and cream until the mixture lightens in color and becomes fluffy. Add the egg yolks one at a time, mixing until all the yolks are incorporated. Add the flour and mix just until incorporated, taking care not to overmix.

Transfer the dough to a sheet of parchment paper. Top with another sheet of parchment paper and roll the dough out to a 12-inch circle. Transfer the parchment-wrapped dough to a baking sheet and refrigerate for at least 30 minutes or preferably overnight.

When ready to bake the tart, position a rack in the center of the oven and preheat the oven to 325°F.

Remove the dough from the refrigerator and peel away the top sheet of parchment paper. Cut the dough into a 12-inch round and lay the dough in a 10-inch tart mold, allowing the excess dough to hang over the edges. Gently fit the dough into the mold and use a paring knife to trim the edges of the dough.

Line the dough with foil, fill the center with pie weights (dried beans or uncooked rice can also be used), transfer the tart pan to the oven, and bake until the tart shell is golden brown, 12 to 15 minutes. Remove the tart shell from the oven, carefully remove the foil and weights, and cool completely. (Leave the oven on.)

To make the ricotta filling: Put the ricotta, heavy cream, honey, salt, vanilla bean seeds, eggs, egg yolks, and lemon zest in the bowl of a stand mixer fitted with the paddle attachment and mix for 2 minutes. Pour the mixture into the tart shell and cover with aluminum foil. Return the tart to the oven and bake until the center is set, 30 to 45 minutes. Transfer to a rack to cool completely.

Meanwhile to make the fruit topping: Combine the halved pears, port, sugar, juniper berries, orange zest, star anise, and vanilla bean and seeds in a large pot, bring to a simmer over medium heat, and cook until the pears are tender but still holding their shape and easily pierced with a knife, 15 to 20 minutes. Remove the pan from the heat and strain the pears through a fine-mesh strainer set over a heatproof bowl. Return the poaching liquid to the same pot, set over high heat, bring the liquid to a boil, and continue to boil until thickened, 5 to 7 minutes. Let the reduced syrup cool slightly. Meanwhile, peel the remaining pear and scoop small balls out of it with a small melon baller or other small scoop.

Unmold the tart and brush with the reduced poached-pear syrup. Decorate the tart with the poached and fresh pears, fresh and dried figs, grapes, and mint leaves.

# MODERNO

I sometimes joke that I suffer from a *culinary* identity crisis, torn between the American and the Italian in me.

Of course, the truth is that it's not a crisis at all—it's a joy. Being able to express myself by drawing on the Italian culinary canon is the ultimate outlet for my passion for Italy's cuisine. I still discover something new every time I visit Italy and dine in its restaurants, and it always provides inspiration for what I'll cook next in my restaurants.

Many of the recipes in this section originated in those restaurants, as well as in those where I cooked earlier in my career; others were developed in my current professional homes, including Marea and Ai Fiori. Where possible, I've adapted particularly difficult restaurant kitchen techniques and procedures with more home-friendly methods (and easier-to-find ingredients), but the results will be comparable to what you've experienced at my restaurants.

While I refer to these dishes as "modern," they are not "modernist cuisine." That is, they do not rely on the techniques, additives, and equipment associated with that style of cooking, sometimes called "molecular gastronomy." It may surprise you, though, to learn that we do call on those elements on occasion, but in a subtle way that isn't necessarily apparent to the guest.

Most of the chapters in this section mirror those in the preceding one, with two notable exceptions: Because they do not figure prominently in contemporary dining, there is no chapter of finger foods and snacks, as in the Per Cominciare chapter in Classico, and, befitting the more restaurant-style dishes here, with an emphasis on composed plates, there's no chapter of contorni, or side dishes. Rather, accompaniments and garnishes appear alongside the dishes in which they are used.

Also, with the exception of the pastas and pizzas, many of the dishes in this section don't look like what you might commonly think of as "Italian food." They replace the rusticity and artful casualness of the classics with specificity and even a touch of formality in the presentation, much of it influenced by French technique. But all of them have their origins in authentic Italian food, either a popular preparation or a distinctly Italian ingredient or combination.

# SALADS AND FIRST COURSES

The structure of the Classico half of this book tracks the components of a traditional Italian meal, which moves from antipasti through a procession of courses before arriving at dessert. This section is more American in construct, with the opening salvo of the meal drawn from a grab bag of possibilities that can include almost anything, from contemporary crostini to salads to small plates centered around a fish or meat—almost anything but pasta, soup, or pizza, although there is a caviar-and-cream pasta dish included here because it's *only* intended to be served first. Most of the dishes here are more substantial than their counterparts in the Classico section, and because many of them feature seafood, poultry, or meat of some kind, they can also be served as lunches or small meals in their own right.

A frequent conundrum for home cooks is how best to pair starters and main courses, especially with contemporary dishes that often draw from myriad international influences. It's a good question. Generally speaking, I suggest a few strategies: Select all dishes in a meal to be in harmony with the current season; turn to different types of proteins in each course: For example, start with a seafood-based appetizer, serve a poultry- or meat-based dish for the main course, and, if including a pasta or pizza, perhaps choose one with no protein. Or go the other way and create a themed menu of all seafood or all meat dishes.

# SALAD OF RAW MUSHROOMS, CHARRED RADICCHIO, AND PISTACHIOS

SERVES 4

This is a very quick and simple salad built around warm, just-charred radicchio. Although it has a quintessentially Italian feeling thanks to the presence of garlic, pistachios, and Parmigiano-Reggiano, as well as the radicchio, the combination of seared, toasted, and uncooked ingredients is a break from Italian tradition, as is the sherry vinaigrette, a distinctly French touch, used here for its relatively low acidity.

1 garlic clove, one end cut off
1 head of radicchio, core removed and separated into leaves
¾ cup plus 2 tablespoons olive oil
Kosher salt
Freshly ground black pepper
1 pound mixed mushrooms, including at least three of the following: cremini, porcini, enoki, and white button, trimmed and thinly sliced or, in the case of enoki, separated
2 tablespoons sherry vinegar
2 teaspoons Dijon mustard
¼ cup pistachios, toasted (see page 367) and crushed with the bottom of a heavy pan
¼ cup fresh chive batons (½ inch long)
A wedge of Parmigiano-Reggiano, shaved into shards with a vegetable peeler

Rub the inside of a large bowl with the cut end of the garlic, then discard the garlic.

Put the radicchio leaves in another bowl, drizzle with 2 tablespoons of the olive oil, and season with salt and pepper.

Heat a wide cast-iron pan over high heat. Add the radicchio leaves and quickly sear them, turning them with tongs or a wooden spoon, until lightly charred all over. Transfer the leaves to the garlic-rubbed bowl. Add the mushrooms, give the salad a quick toss, and immediately seal the bowl with plastic wrap. Let the mushrooms and radicchio steam for 5 minutes.

Meanwhile, make the sherry vinaigrette: Put the vinegar and mustard in a small mixing bowl and whisk together. Whisk in the remaining ¾ cup olive oil, a few drops at a time at first and then in a thin, steady stream, until an emulsified vinaigrette is formed. Remove the plastic and dress the radicchio and mushrooms with some of the vinaigrette.

Divide the salad among 4 plates. Drizzle the remaining vinaigrette around the salads and finish with a scattering of the pistachios, chives, and Parmigiano shards. Grind some black pepper over each salad and serve.

**Note:** Rubbing a bowl with garlic before preparing a salad or other dish in it imparts a gentle hint of flavor that's much subtler than that of minced or sliced garlic.

# ESCAROLE AND CRISP VEGETABLE SALAD WITH BAGNA CAUDA VINAIGRETTE

SERVES 4

Bagna cauda (literally, "hot bath") is a warm Piedmontese preparation of garlic, anchovy, and oil that's used as a vegetable dip. Here the signature components of bagna cauda are brought together in a vinaigrette and tossed with a salad, turning the tradition into a plated affair.

1 head of escarole, core removed, separated into leaves, tough stems removed, washed, dried, and cut into bite-size pieces
1 medium fennel bulb, trimmed and very thinly sliced, ideally on a mandoline
1 cup cherry, grape, or teardrop tomatoes, halved lengthwise
4 small radishes, very thinly sliced
1 seedless cucumber, ends trimmed and thinly sliced into rounds
½ cup minced mixed fresh herbs, such as basil, tarragon, and flat-leaf parsley
⅓ cup Bagna Cauda Vinaigrette (recipe follows)
Kosher salt
Freshly ground black pepper

Put the escarole, fennel, tomatoes, radishes, cucumber, and herbs in a large mixing bowl. Drizzle with the vinaigrette, season with salt and pepper, and toss well.

Divide the salad among 4 salad plates and serve.

## BAGNA CAUDA VINAIGRETTE

MAKES ABOUT 1¼ CUPS

This recipe substitutes roasted garlic for the fresh found in a traditional bagna cauda, resulting in a sweeter garlic presence, while a touch of cream adds body and smooths out the flavors. It is suitable for any number of salads or as a sandwich condiment, as well as a dip, just like the original.

8 oil-packed anchovy fillets, minced and mashed to a paste
3 tablespoons pureed roasted garlic (see page 367)
2 tablespoons freshly squeezed lemon juice
2 tablespoons red wine vinegar
½ cup extra virgin olive oil
3 tablespoons heavy cream
Kosher salt
Freshly ground black pepper

Put the anchovy paste, garlic, lemon juice, and vinegar in a medium mixing bowl and whisk together. Whisk in the oil, a few drops at a time at first and then in a thin, steady stream, until the vinaigrette comes together in a thick emulsion. Whisk in the heavy cream and season with salt and pepper.

Use the vinaigrette immediately, or refrigerate in an airtight container for up to 24 hours; let come to room temperature before serving.

# CRUDO

Many American restaurant-goers take crudo, the Italian raw fish preparation, for a relatively new creation, when it is in fact an old Italian culinary tradition. True to form, Italians eat it largely unadorned, letting the character of the fish shine through: Most crudo consists of little more than fish dressed with olive oil and lemon juice. The oil is usually added first, providing a barrier to protect the flesh from the acid, which would otherwise begin to "cook" it, as in a ceviche. Many cooks do not even season crudo with salt, believing that it distracts from the flavor of the fish.

At Marea, my coastal-Italian seafood restaurant, crudo makes up a significant portion of the menu, with more than a dozen options available at any time. Truth be told, though, the crudo are largely inspired by sushi, with its diverse selection of fish and shellfish, intricate rolls, and array of condiments. I don't use any overtly Japanese ingredients, but the Japanese palate influences many of the offerings, such as the oyster cream that tops the tuna dish, with a brininess that recalls soy sauce.

Following are a variety of crudo recipes.

## SNAPPER WITH PROSCIUTTO DI PARMA AND PANZANELLA

SERVES 4

- 1 small slice baguette or country bread
- 1/4 cup peeled, minced seedless cucumber
- 1/4 cup peeled (see page 367), minced plum tomatoes, drained of juice
- 2 tablespoons extra virgin olive oil, plus more for brushing the fish
- 1 tablespoon freshly squeezed lemon juice
- Kosher salt
- 1 pound sushi-grade skinless snapper fillet, pin bones removed with tweezers
- 2 slices prosciutto di Parma

Toast the bread in a toaster oven, let it cool, remove and discard the crusts, and cut it into small dice. Reserve 1/4 cup of the dice and discard the rest.

Put the diced bread in a medium bowl. Add the cucumbers, tomatoes, olive oil, and lemon juice, and season with salt. Toss and let marinate for 20 minutes to develop the flavors and moisten the bread.

Use a sharp knife to slice the snapper diagonally against the grain into sixteen to twenty 1/4-inch-thick slices. Cut the prosciutto into sixteen to twenty (same number as the snapper) 1/2-inch by 1 1/2-inch rectangles.

To serve, divide the snapper among 4 chilled plates, slightly overlapping the slices. Brush lightly with olive oil, top with a prosciutto slice, and spoon some panzanella over the prosciutto-topped fish. Serve immediately.

# FLUKE, LEMON THYME, AND EXTRA VIRGIN OLIVE OIL

SERVES 4

1 pound sushi-grade fluke fillet
Extra virgin olive oil
½ lemon
Fine sea salt
About 1 tablespoon fresh lemon thyme leaves (regular thyme can be substituted)

Use a sharp knife to slice the fluke diagonally against the grain into sixteen or twenty ¼-inch-thick slices.

Arrange one quarter of the slices side by side on each of 4 chilled small plates. Brush the slices with extra virgin olive oil, then squeeze a few drops of lemon juice over the slices and season with sea salt. Top each slice with a few thyme leaves and serve.

## Working with Raw Fish

When serving raw fish, it's essential that you purchase it from a reliable purveyor, either a market that specializes in seafood or a larger store that has a dedicated seafood department, and make sure that it is of the best, freshest quality. Ask the fishmonger if the fish is sushi-grade, and tell him or her that you are planning to serve it raw. Prepare and serve raw fish the day you purchase it, keep it refrigerated until just before working with it, and be sure to start with a clean work surface and to clean it immediately after working on it. Finally, plan ahead and chill the plates for the crudo, which will help keep the fish cold right up to the moment it is eaten.

When making crudo at home, use a sharp slicing knife, and for the most elegant cuts, slide it forward and back like the blade of a slicing machine rather than employing a more severe up-and-down chopping motion.

# TUNA WITH OYSTER CREAM AND CRISPY SUNCHOKES

SERVES 4

Kosher salt

1 romaine lettuce heart, leaves separated, tough center ribs removed, and torn into large pieces

1 cup (loosely packed) spinach leaves

½ cup (loosely packed) fresh flat-leaf parsley leaves

¼ cup plus 2 tablespoons olive oil

1 large shallot, thinly sliced

3 large garlic cloves, thinly sliced

6 oysters, such as Blue Point, shucked (see below), juices strained and reserved

2 tablespoons cold water

¼ cup canola oil

½ lemon

1 pound sushi-grade tuna loin, preferably yellowtail or bigeye, cut into 1-inch cubes

1 tablespoon extra virgin olive oil

Fine sea salt

4 Crispy Sunchokes (recipe follows)

Fill a large pot two-thirds full with water, salt it liberally, and bring it to a boil over high heat. Fill a large bowl halfway with ice water. Add the romaine, spinach, and parsley to the boiling water and blanch for 1 minute, then drain and transfer to the ice water to stop the cooking and preserve the color. Drain the greens again and pat dry with paper towels. Transfer to a cutting board, coarsely chop, and set aside.

Heat a wide heavy sauté pan over medium-high heat. Add 2 tablespoons of the olive oil and tip and tilt the pan to coat it, heating the oil until it is shimmering and almost smoking. Add the shallots and garlic and cook, stirring occasionally with a wooden spoon, until softened but not browned, about 2 minutes. Remove the pan from the heat and let cool slightly, then add the chopped greens and toss just to mix. Season with kosher salt and set aside.

Fill a bowl halfway with ice water. Put the oysters and strained oyster juice in a blender and blend to a smooth puree, then add the greens mixture and water and blend until a very smooth puree forms. Slowly add the remaining ¼ cup olive oil in a steady stream, then add the canola oil, blending until the mixture is the consistency of a slightly loose mayonnaise. Immediately strain the cream through a fine-mesh strainer into a small stainless-steel bowl and set over the ice water. (The cream can be made up to 24 hours in advance and refrigerated in an airtight container. Let come to room temperature before proceeding.)

Transfer ¼ cup of the cream to a small bowl, season with kosher salt, and stir in a few drops of lemon juice. (Discard the extra cream, as it does not keep well.)

Put the tuna cubes in a bowl and drizzle the extra virgin olive oil over them. Toss gently to coat, then squeeze a few drops of lemon juice over the cubes, season with a pinch of sea salt, and toss again.

To serve, spoon about 1 tablespoon cream onto each of 4 small chilled plates. Arrange the tuna cubes over the cream and top each serving with a sunchoke chip. Serve immediately.

## CRISPY SUNCHOKES

MAKE ABOUT 50 CHIPS

*These chips are also a quick, convenient way to add crunch to salads, soups, and risottos.*

A few cups of canola oil or other neutral oil, for deep-frying

1 large lemon, halved

4 sunchokes, the more uniform and round the better

Kosher salt

Line a large plate with paper towels. Pour the oil into a medium heavy pot to a depth of 2 inches, set the pot over medium heat, and heat the oil to 325°F.

Meanwhile, fill a medium bowl with cold water and add the lemon juice. Peel the sunchokes, adding them to the acidulated water as you go to prevent them from oxidizing and turning brown. One by one, thinly slice the sunchokes on a mandoline, or use a very sharp knife and steady hands.

Pat the slices dry with paper towels. Add them to the oil, in batches, and fry until lightly golden brown and crispy, 1 to 2 minutes. Use a slotted spoon to transfer the slices to the paper-towel-lined plate and season immediately with salt.

The chips can be stored for up to 1 week in an airtight container at room temperature. Put a folded paper towel in the bottom of the container to absorb any moisture.

## YELLOWTAIL WITH OLIVES, GARLIC, AND SCALLIONS

SERVES 4

- 2 tablespoons capers, soaked in warm water for 5 minutes, drained, and minced
- 3 tablespoons extra virgin olive oil, plus more for brushing
- ¼ cup minced kalamata olives
- ¼ cup finely chopped Castelvetrano olives (Niçoise olives can be substituted)
- 4 sun-dried tomatoes (not oil-packed), soaked in warm water for 15 minutes, drained, and minced
- 1 garlic clove, finely grated on a Microplane or minced
- ½ small shallot, minced
- Finely grated zest and juice of ½ lemon
- Finely grated zest of ½ orange
- Kosher salt
- 1 pound sushi-grade yellowtail tuna loin
- Fine sea salt
- Greens from 1 scallion, thinly sliced diagonally

To make the olivada (see below): Put the capers, the olive oil, the olives, sun-dried tomatoes, garlic, shallots, lemon zest, and orange zest in a medium bowl and stir together with a rubber spatula. Season with kosher salt and set aside.

Use a sharp knife to slice the yellowtail diagonally against the grain into sixteen or twenty ¼-inch-thick slices. Divide the slices among 4 small chilled plates. Brush the slices with olive oil, then drizzle some lemon juice over them and season with sea salt. Top each slice with a small dollop of olivada, garnish with the scallion greens, and serve.

### Olivada

The garnish here is based on olivada, a tapenade-like mixture of olives, oil, garlic, herbs, and spices from Liguria that's traditionally used as a topping for chicken or salmon. It can also be folded into ricotta, mascarpone, or even cream cheese to make a vegetable dip or tossed with hot pasta for a quick sauce (add a few tablespoons of the pasta's cooking liquid to bind it).

# NANTUCKET BAY SCALLOPS, FENNEL POLLEN, AND ORANGE

SERVES 4

1 orange, cut into suprêmes (see below)
1 pound Nantucket Bay scallops, side muscles removed
Juice of 1 lemon
3 tablespoons extra virgin olive oil
Fine sea salt
1 tablespoon fennel pollen (see Sources, page 379; a scant pinch of toasted ground fennel seeds [see page 367] per serving can be substituted)

Use a sharp knife to slice the orange suprêmes crosswise into 1/4-inch-wide pieces.

Put the scallops in a medium mixing bowl and add the lemon juice and olive oil. Season with sea salt and gently toss to coat the scallops.

Divide the scallops among 4 chilled small plates. Top with the oranges, scatter some fennel pollen over each portion, and serve immediately.

**Variation** Bay scallops make for an elegant presentation, but you can also make this with diver scallops cut into small dice.

## Citrus Suprêmes

To cut suprêmes from a citrus fruit, cut off the top and bottom of the fruit with a large heavy knife. Stand it upright on the cutting board and, working from top to bottom and following the curve of the fruit, cut away the skin in strips, taking care to remove the bitter white pith as well. Separate the sections. Working with one section at a time, hold it over a bowl and use the tip of a sharp thin-bladed knife to make a slit in the membrane and remove it from the fruit, then drop the fruit into the bowl. (You may find it easier to cut the suprêmes away from the membranes rather than sectioning the fruit first and then removing the membranes.)

## WILD STRIPED BASS, STURGEON CAVIAR, AND MUSSEL CREAM

SERVES 4

2 tablespoons olive oil
1 large shallot, thinly sliced
2 large garlic cloves, thinly sliced
2 pounds mussels, preferably Prince Edward Island, scrubbed and debearded
5 thyme sprigs
2 bay leaves, preferably fresh
½ cup dry white wine
1 large egg yolk
½ cup canola oil
2 tablespoons extra virgin olive oil, plus more for brushing
Kosher salt
1 pound sushi-grade wild striped bass fillet
½ lemon
Fine sea salt
1 ounce American sturgeon (hackleback) caviar

Pour the olive oil into a wide heavy pot and set over medium-high heat, tipping and tilting the pot to coat it and heating the oil until it is shimmering and almost smoking. Add the shallots and garlic and cook until softened but not browned, about 2 minutes. Add the mussels, thyme, bay leaves, and wine and stir with a wooden spoon to coat the mussels. Cover the pot and cook, gently shaking the pot occasionally, until the mussels have opened, about 5 minutes. Use a slotted spoon to fish out and discard any unopened mussels, then transfer the remaining mussels to a bowl.

Strain the cooking liquid through a fine-mesh strainer into a bowl, pressing down on the solids with a wooden spoon or a ladle to extract as much flavorful liquid as possible. Discard the solids.

Carefully wipe out the pot and pour in the mussel stock. Bring the stock to a simmer over high heat, then lower the heat and simmer until reduced by half, about 8 minutes. Pour the mussel stock into a small stainless-steel bowl. Fill a slightly larger bowl halfway with ice water and set the bowl in the ice water to chill it.

Pour the chilled mussel stock into a blender. Add the egg yolk. With the motor running on low speed, pour in the canola oil, a few drops at a time at first and then in a thin, steady stream, and then the extra virgin olive oil, blending until the mixture emulsifies and is the consistency of a thick mayonnaise. Season with kosher salt.

Use a sharp slicing knife to slice the fish diagonally against the grain into sixteen or twenty ¼-inch-thick slices. Divide the slices among 4 chilled small plates, arranging them side by side. Brush with extra virgin olive oil, then squeeze a few drops of lemon juice over the slices and season with sea salt. Top each slice with a bit of the mussel cream and a small quenelle of caviar and serve.

# GARGANELLI WITH CAVIAR CREAM

SERVES 4

I created this small starter expressly as a vehicle for caviar. It's a rich and creamy way to kick off a celebratory meal.

Kosher salt
5 tablespoons cold unsalted butter
2 shallots, cut into ¼-inch dice
1 bay leaf, preferably fresh
1 thyme sprig
½ cup dry white wine
1 cup Fish Stock (page 373)
1 cup heavy cream
8 ounces fresh garganelli or other short pasta
1 tablespoon freshly squeezed lemon juice
2 ounces high-quality caviar, such as osetra
1 tablespoon minced fresh chives

Fill a large pot about two-thirds full with water, salt it liberally, and bring to a boil over high heat.

Meanwhile, heat a large heavy saucepan over medium heat. Add 2 tablespoons of the butter, tipping and tilting the pan to coat it with the butter as it melts. Add the shallots, bay leaf, and thyme and cook, stirring frequently with a wooden spoon, until the shallots are translucent. Pour in the wine, bring to a simmer, and simmer until the wine has almost completely evaporated, about 6 minutes.

Pour in the fish stock, bring to a simmer, and simmer until reduced by half, about 6 minutes. Stir in the cream, bring to a simmer, and simmer until the sauce is nicely thickened, 8 to 10 minutes. Strain the sauce through a fine-mesh strainer into a bowl, then carefully wipe out the pan and return the sauce to the pan. Season with salt. Cover it to keep warm.

Add the garganelli to the boiling water and cook until al dente, about 2 minutes. Drain the pasta and add it to the sauce. Toss with the remaining 3 tablespoons butter and the lemon juice. (The heat of the pasta should be sufficient to melt the butter, but return the pan briefly to medium heat if necessary.)

Divide the garganelli among 4 small bowls and top each with ½ ounce of caviar and a scattering of chives. Serve immediately.

# PAN-ROASTED RAZOR CLAMS WITH CHARRED CORN AND SOPPRESSATA

SERVES 4

As much as we anticipate fresh corn every summer in the United States, in Italy it's mostly milled into polenta or fed to livestock and rarely eaten fresh. The other distinctly non-Italian ingredient in this dish is piquillo peppers, which are associated with Spanish cuisine (although the combination of corn and peppers makes the dish vaguely reminiscent of the American Southwest).

The cooking method here, using a very hot cast-iron pan, is based on the Italian technique of cooking alla piastra ("on a hot griddle"; see page 41), which gives the essential charred flavor to the corn.

For a more traditional treatment of razor clams, see the recipe on page 41.

¼ cup olive oil
½ small Spanish onion, thinly sliced
2 garlic cloves, 1 sliced, 1 minced
Pinch of red pepper flakes
8 jarred or canned roasted piquillo peppers (see Sources, page 379), seeds discarded, 4 coarsely chopped, 4 thinly sliced
1 teaspoon sherry vinegar
2 ounces hot soppressata, cut into ¼-inch dice (about ½ cup)
5 shallots, thinly sliced
1 teaspoon coriander seeds, toasted and ground (see page 367)
1 teaspoon fennel seeds, toasted and ground (see page 367)
1 teaspoon whole black peppercorns, toasted and ground (see page 367)
2 bay leaves, preferably fresh
4 thyme sprigs
Finely grated zest and juice of 1 lemon
Kosher salt
Cayenne pepper
4 ears corn, shucked and kernels removed (about 2 cups kernels)
16 razor clams (about 2½ pounds), scrubbed
¼ cup dry white wine
¼ cup coarsely chopped fresh flat-leaf parsley

To make the sauce: Heat a small heavy saucepan over medium-high heat. Add 1 tablespoon of the olive oil and heat it until it is shimmering and almost smoking. Add the onions, sliced garlic, and red pepper flakes and cook, stirring with a wooden spoon, until the onions are softened but not browned, about 2 minutes. Add the chopped piquillo peppers and cook, stirring, until warmed, about 2 minutes. Stir in the vinegar. Transfer the mixture to the bowl of a food processor and puree until smooth. Return to the pan, cover, and keep warm over very low heat.

To make the soffritto: Heat a medium heavy pot over medium heat. Pour in 1 tablespoon of the olive oil and tip and tilt the pot to coat it, warming the oil. Add the soppressata and cook, stirring, until it renders some of its fat, about 5 minutes. Add the shallots and minced garlic and cook until softened but not browned, about 2 minutes. Stir in the ground spices, bay leaves, thyme, and the sliced piquillo peppers and cook, stirring occasionally, until the peppers are hot and the flavors have integrated, about 3 minutes. Add the lemon zest and lemon juice, season with salt and cayenne, and set aside. (The soffritto can be refrigerated in an airtight container for up to 2 days; let come to room temperature before using it.)

Heat a large deep cast-iron skillet over medium-high heat and add the remaining 2 tablespoons olive oil, tipping and tilting the pan to coat it and letting the oil heat up. Add the corn kernels and cook, stirring, until lightly charred, about 8 minutes. Stir in the soffritto. Add the razor clams and pour in the wine, using a wooden spoon to loosen any flavorful bits cooked onto the bottom of the pan. Cover and cook until the clams open, about 5 minutes, shaking the pan gently to help them open. Use a slotted spoon to remove and discard any clams that have not opened.

Divide the clams and corn among 4 plates and garnish with the parsley. Spoon some of the sauce around the clams on each plate and serve.

**Note:** The coriander seeds, fennel seeds, and black peppercorns can be toasted and ground together.

## BREAKING BOUNDARIES

Combining ingredients and recipes from different Italian regions can lead to dishes that feel new and exciting yet are firmly rooted in tradition.

This advice isn't offered lightly, because the well-defined cuisine of Italy's twenty regions is the backbone of the country's cultural and culinary identity. But when I began cooking my own food in the United States, I was heavily influenced by one of the founding practices of New American Cuisine: the commingling of foods from different regions and countries. In many ways, the freedom to mix and match influences from disparate places has been one of the defining characteristics of modern American restaurant food. That sensibility opened the creative floodgates for me when I applied it to the wealth of taste memories from my eight years of cooking and eating throughout Italy.

For instance, the mussel and barley soup on page 245 is based on a dish from Maremma, with the addition of broccoli rabe from the south; tajarin, a delicate Piedmontese pasta, is paired with black truffles, an Umbrian staple, on page 257, and Emilia-Romagna's strozzapretti are united with squid and pistachios, Southern Italian ingredients both, in the recipe on page 263.

In addition to mingling specialties from its different regions, Italian food can also be successfully combined with influences from other countries, as in the razor clam and corn dish, with its American and Spanish ingredients, on page 195. Similarly, there's an undercurrent of Japanese sushi in the crudo recipes (pages 186 to 192), and classic American liver and onions inspired the modern crostini of chicken livers and Marsala-braised onions on page 218. More broadly, the structuralized, formal nature of my modern recipes owes a great deal to French technique, from basic principles such as cooking key ingredients separately rather than together (see the caponata on page 215 for an example of this), to the prevalence of purees and wine-based sauces in the main courses, to the plating style.

# PANFRIED SOFT-SHELL CRAB WITH PROSCIUTTO AND MELON

SERVES 4

Prosciutto and cantaloupe are a timeless Italian combination, the sweet flesh of the melon a perfect foil for the salty cured meat. This distinctly American variation adds soft-shell crabs, which are captured shortly after molting, or shedding, their tough outer shells, in the spring and throughout the summer. It may seem a creative leap, but I got the idea for this dish from the very mainstream American hors d'oeuvre of bacon-wrapped shrimp.

Soft-shell crabs are rare in Italy, smaller and sweeter than what we're used to here, and harvested only from the Venice lagoon, where they are known as molleche. Here they are panfried, as they would also be in Venice, but there is a distinctly American trick in the coating, mixing all-purpose flour and Wondra flour, a mix of white and barley flour that helps ensure crispiness. The crabs are also soaked in buttermilk before cooking, which makes them creamy, almost custardy, on the inside.

1 cup buttermilk
4 soft-shell crabs, about 3½ ounces each, cleaned and cut into 4 pieces each (have the fishmonger "dress the crabs")
1 cup Greek yogurt
1 tablespoon finely grated lemon zest
Kosher salt
½ cantaloupe, seeded and peeled
1 cup white verjus (see Sources, page 379; white balsamic vinegar can be substituted)
1 tablespoon sugar
¼ cup (loosely packed) arugula
1 teaspoon extra virgin olive oil
½ lemon
A few cups of canola oil or other neutral oil, for panfrying
1 cup all-purpose flour
1 cup Wondra flour
Pinch of Espelette pepper
4 thin slices prosciutto (about 2 ounces total)

Pour the buttermilk into a large mixing bowl. Add the crab pieces and set the bowl aside.

Put the yogurt, lemon zest, and 1 teaspoon salt in a small mixing bowl and whisk together.

Slice the cantaloupe into ⅛-inch-thick slices. Use a 1½-inch ring mold or cookie cutter to punch out 16 circles. (You may not use all of the cantaloupe.) Place them in a medium mixing bowl.

Combine the verjus and sugar in a medium heavy saucepan and heat over medium heat, whisking, until the sugar is dissolved. Remove the pan from the heat and let cool to room temperature, then pour over the cantaloupe disks. Set aside.

Put the arugula in a small bowl. Drizzle with the olive oil and a squeeze of lemon juice and toss.

Pour oil to a depth of 1 inch into a large heavy pot and heat over medium-high heat to 350°F.

Combine the all-purpose flour and Wondra flour in a shallow bowl and season with 1 teaspoon salt. Remove the crab pieces from the buttermilk and shake off the excess liquid, then dredge the pieces in the flour and carefully add to the hot oil, taking care, as the crabs tend to pop in hot oil (see Note). Fry until the crab pieces float, 3 to 4 minutes.

To serve, spoon some of the yogurt mixture into the center of each of 4 salad plates. Top the yogurt on each plate with 4 pieces of fried crab. Season with the Espelette pepper and a squeeze of lemon. Place a disk of cantaloupe against each crab piece. Garnish the dish with the arugula and prosciutto and serve.

**Note:** Soft-shell crabs have a tendency to explode when cooked over hot oil because heat gathers in their legs. To prevent this, use a clean needle or safety pin before frying to puncture each leg in a few places, which will allow the steam to escape.

## SHRIMP TARTARE WITH CRUSHED ALMONDS AND LEMON

SERVES 4

This dish is an Italian answer to a shellfish tartare, with a cocktail sauce based on the piquant salsa rosa, a mayonnaisey sauce perked up with cognac that's been a go-to dip for chilled shellfish since the 1950s. Crushed almonds are scattered over the finished tartare for additional texture.

- 8 ounces large shrimp
- 1 teaspoon finely grated lemon zest
- 1 tablespoon freshly squeezed lemon juice
- 2 tablespoons extra virgin olive oil, plus more for serving
- Pinch of cayenne pepper
- Kosher salt
- ½ Shrimp Mayonnaise (recipe follows)
- ¼ cup lightly crushed Marcona almonds (crush with the bottom of a heavy pan)
- 1 tablespoon minced fresh chives

Fill a large stainless-steel mixing bowl with ice. Top with a smaller stainless-steel bowl. Peel and devein the shrimp, rinse them under gently running cold water, and pat dry with paper towels. Cut into ¼-inch dice, collecting the pieces in the chilled bowl as you work.

Fold the lemon zest, lemon juice, olive oil, and the cayenne into the diced shrimp and season with salt.

Spread some shrimp mayonnaise in the center of each of 4 chilled salad plates. Top with the shrimp tartare (for a formal presentation, shape the tartare into quenelles). Drizzle with olive oil, sprinkle the crushed almonds and chives over the top, and serve.

### SHRIMP MAYONNAISE

MAKES 1 CUP

This mayonnaise's intense flavor comes from the addition of shrimp stock. It is also delicious in shrimp sandwiches, of course, and as an unexpected alternative to cocktail sauce.

- 1 cup Shrimp Stock (page 372)
- 1 large egg yolk
- ½ teaspoon Dijon mustard
- ½ cup canola oil
- ¼ cup olive oil
- ½ teaspoon finely grated lemon zest
- Juice of ½ lemon, or to taste
- 1 teaspoon cognac
- Kosher salt
- Freshly ground black pepper

Pour the stock into a small heavy saucepan, bring to a boil over high heat, and boil until reduced to 2 tablespoons, about 7 minutes. Transfer the reduction to a small mixing bowl and let cool.

Add the yolk and mustard to the reduced shrimp stock and whisk together. Whisk in the canola oil, a few drops at a time at first and then in a thin, steady stream, then whisk in the olive oil until the mayonnaise comes together in a thick emulsion. Whisk in the lemon zest. Add the juice a little at a time, tasting as you go; you want to just barely register the bright acidity of lemon, allowing the shrimp flavor to dominate. Stir in the cognac and season to taste with salt and pepper.

# LOBSTER, BURRATA, AND TOMATOES

SERVES 4

There's a myth that's been propagated for generations that Italians do not combine fish or shellfish with cheese, and so when I first introduced this dish at Marea, it seemed revolutionary to some. But fish and shellfish are regularly paired with cheese up and down the Amalfi Coast, especially in the area affectionately nicknamed La Via Lattea (The Milky Way), where buffalo mozzarella is produced. This composed salad of lobster and burrata, a semiliquid fresh cow's-milk cheese produced from curds and sweet cream, was inspired by a dish a friend of mine used to serve at his restaurant in Cava de' Tirreni, where he layered red mullet fillets with mozzarella and basil and baked them. One might also look at this as an oceanic expansion of the classic Caprese salad of tomatoes, mozzarella, and basil. Whatever it reminds you of, it offers proof that the tang of burrata gets along sensationally with shellfish and firm white-fleshed fish, no matter what the legend may say. While the dish is pictured here with two subtle elements I love, basil seed and coral powder, they can be difficult to procure and make. The dish proves to be excellent without them.

1 eggplant (about 1½ pounds), peeled and cut into 1-by-¼-inch batons (avoid the seedy center if possible)
Kosher salt
1 cup white balsamic vinegar
1 cup rice wine vinegar
½ cup water
1 teaspoon sugar
¼ cup extra virgin olive oil, plus more for serving
2 lobsters, preferably Maine or Nova Scotia, 1 to 1¼ pounds each
12 grape tomatoes, peeled (see page 367) and halved
6 ounces burrata cheese (see Sources, page 379)
Freshly squeezed lemon juice, for serving
Basil Oil (page 306), for serving
12 large fresh basil leaves
1 bunch of mâche
Flaky sea salt, such as Maldon

Put the eggplant in a colander and sprinkle with 2 teaspoons kosher salt. Toss the eggplant and set the colander in the sink to drain for 10 minutes. (The salt will draw out excess moisture and bitterness.)

Meanwhile, combine the vinegars, water, sugar, and ½ teaspoon kosher salt in a medium heavy pot and bring the mixture to a boil over high heat. Carefully add the salted eggplant (the eggplant should be completely submerged in liquid; if it is not, add enough water to cover) and cook for 1 minute, then remove the pot from the heat and set aside for 30 minutes to lightly pickle the eggplant.

Drain the eggplant pieces and transfer to a medium bowl. Drizzle with 2 tablespoons of the olive oil and toss to coat.

Fill a large pot about two-thirds full with water and bring to a boil over high heat. Fill a large bowl halfway with ice water. Add the lobsters to the boiling water and cook for 7 minutes, then use tongs to transfer them to the ice bath. Once the lobsters are cool, remove the meat from the shells and cut into ¾-inch dice.

Put the tomatoes in a medium bowl and toss with the remaining 2 tablespoons olive oil.

To serve, place the burrata in the center of a serving plate. Put the lobster meat in a bowl, drizzle with olive oil and a scant bit of lemon juice, season with a pinch of kosher salt, and toss. Artfully arrange the lobster, eggplant, and tomatoes around the burrata. Drizzle the basil oil over the plate and garnish with the basil leaves and mâche. Drizzle with extra virgin olive oil and sprinkle with sea salt. Serve immediately.

# OCTOPUS WITH SMOKED POTATOES, GRILLED FRISÉE, AND TUNA SAUCE

SERVES 4

This streamlined version of one of Marea's most popular starters focuses on the components that have endeared it to so many of our guests: an unexpected touch of the grill (charred octopus, smoked potatoes, and grilled frisée), evoking casual summertime dining in a formal context, and an unconventional use of tuna sauce, the sauce classically served with Vitello Tonnato (page 34), which turns out to have a natural affinity with octopus. Saba vinegar, made with unfermented wine must, adds a sweet, almost prune-like flavor that is a sharp and welcome contrast to the smoky elements of this dish. If you do not own a smoker, you can skip the step of smoking the potatoes.

1 octopus, about 3 pounds
1 Spanish onion, cut into ½-inch dice
1 large carrot, cut into large dice
2 large celery stalks, trimmed and cut into large dice
2 heads of garlic, halved horizontally, plus 2 large garlic cloves, finely grated on a Microplane or very finely minced
1 cup dry red wine
An herb sachet (½ bunch of thyme, 2 bay leaves, preferably fresh, and 1 tablespoon whole black peppercorns, tied in a cheesecloth bundle)
1 pound fingerling potatoes, preferably assorted colors
3 thyme sprigs
1 rosemary sprig
2 bay leaves, preferably fresh
1 cup sweet wood chips, such as pecan or cherry (optional)
1 cup thinly sliced fresh flat-leaf parsley leaves
Finely grated zest of 1 lemon, plus half the lemon
Finely grated zest of 1 lime
Finely grated zest of ½ orange
1 cup extra virgin olive oil, plus more for serving
Kosher salt
Pinch of cayenne pepper
¼ cup olive oil
5 French breakfast radishes, thinly sliced
½ cup Pickled Red Onions (page 225)
Freshly ground black pepper
2 small heads of frisée, core removed and separated into leaves
Tuna Sauce (page 35), thinned with 2 to 3 tablespoons warm water, until pourable
Saba vinegar, for serving (balsamic vinegar can be substituted)

To cook the octopus: Position a rack in the center of the oven and preheat the oven to 350°F.

Place the octopus in a roasting pan and add the onions, carrots, celery, 1 halved garlic head, the wine, and the herb sachet. Cover the roasting pan with aluminum foil and roast until the octopus is tender to the tines of a fork, 1 to 1½ hours. Remove the pan from the oven, uncover, and set aside to cool.

When it is cool, remove the octopus from the pan and use a sharp knife to carefully cut the tentacles from the head, avoiding the beak. Set the tentacles aside and discard the head.

Put the potatoes, thyme, rosemary, bay leaves, and the remaining halved garlic head in a medium saucepan and add enough cold water to cover by 1 inch. Bring to a boil over high heat, then lower the heat and simmer until the potatoes are tender, about 15 minutes. Drain, discard the herbs and garlic, and set the potatoes aside to cool.

If smoking the potatoes: Once the potatoes have cooled, transfer to a smoker filled with the wood chips and smoke for 10 to 15 minutes, depending on the desired smokiness. Remove the potatoes from the smoker and let cool.

Halve the potatoes lengthwise and set aside.

To make the gremolata dressing: Put ½ cup of the parsley, the lemon zest, lime zest, orange zest, and grated garlic in a bowl. Pour in the extra virgin olive oil and whisk together. Season with salt and the cayenne. Set aide.

Heat a grill pan or a large cast-iron skillet over high heat. Once the pan is very hot, drizzle with 2 tablespoons of the olive oil and tip and tilt the pan to coat it. Add the octopus tentacles and cook on one side for 3 minutes. Use tongs to turn the tentacles over and cook for another 2 minutes. Remove the octopus from the pan and drizzle or brush with some of the gremolata dressing, then return the tentacles to the pan for another minute. Transfer the octopus to a plate and drizzle with a squeeze of lemon juice and 1 tablespoon of gremolata dressing. Cover to keep warm. Set the pan aside.

Heat a large heavy sauté pan over high heat. Add 1 tablespoon of the olive oil, tipping and tilting the pan to coat it, and heat until the oil is shimmering and almost smoking. Add the potatoes, season with salt, and cook until lightly browned, about 4 minutes. Add the radishes, pickled onions, and the remaining gremolata dressing and toss to coat. Season with salt and pepper and stir in the remaining ½ cup parsley.

Use a silicone spatula to scrape the grill pan clean. Drizzle with the remaining tablespoon of olive oil and heat over medium-high heat until hot. Add the frisée, season with salt, place a large skillet or heavy baking pan on top of the frisée, and cook until the lettuce chars slightly and wilts, about 2 to 3 minutes.

Spread some tuna sauce onto the center of each of 4 plates. Top with some of the potato and pickled onion mixture. Add some frisée to each plate and drizzle with Saba vinegar. Top with the octopus and serve.

# SEA URCHIN AND LARDO CROSTINI

SERVES 4

Sea urchins have become a trendy restaurant ingredient in recent years, largely because chefs have immense appreciation for the innate intensity and exquisitely soft texture of their roe. (Put another way, we chefs love nothing so much as a raw ingredient that does all the work for us!) Sea urchin roe is best appreciated with a textural foil, something crispy and crunchy that complements its exquisitely briny quality and brings it into high relief. Accordingly, the roe is often melted into pasta dishes that are topped with bread crumbs, such as the recipe on page 258.

Here sea urchin roe is the focal point of a contemporary crostini, with a thin slice of seasoned lardo gently melted over the top. Lardo, also known as prosciutto bianco ("white prosciutto"), is a Tuscan product made by curing pork fatback in a spice mixture featuring rosemary and crushed black pepper. It's used in parts of Italy the way Americans use salt pork. Two especially impressive applications are whipping a julienne of the lardo into finished risotto just before serving and wrapping warm grilled large shrimp or prawns in slices of lardo. A first-rate American brand is produced by La Quercia (see Sources, page 379).

This dish came about one night when one of my best chefs, Gordon Finn, and I were preparing an elaborate tasting menu for some special guests. Although it is a crostini, there's really no counterpart for this dish in classic Italian cuisine, because there's no "surf and turf" in that culture.

The recipe calls for more lardo than you will need; extra lardo is necessary to enable you to hold on to and slice the piece. Use any extra for flavoring soups, or slice it and whip it into risotto, as described above. If you have extra sea urchin, make extra crostini should you have enough bread and lardo.

1 8-ounce piece lardo (see Sources, page 379)
1 baguette, sliced on the bias into six 2-inch-long, 1½-inch-wide, and ½-inch-thick slices
Extra virgin olive oil, for drizzling
1 tray (4 ounces; 20 to 30 pieces) sea urchin roe (see Sources, page 379)
Fine sea salt
1 tablespoon minced fresh chives

Put the lardo in the freezer for 10 minutes to firm it up and make it easy to slice.

Position a rack in the center of the oven and preheat the oven to 350°F.

Remove the lardo from the freezer and use a sharp knife to slice it crosswise into 12 paper-thin sheets.

Put the bread slices on a rimmed baking sheet and drizzle with olive oil. Toast in the oven until the slices are lightly browned but not dried out, about 7 minutes. Remove the bread from the oven, turn off the oven, and let the bread cool for 3 to 4 minutes, then work quickly through the following steps so that the turned-off oven is still warm when you are ready for it.

Carefully arrange 3 sea urchin roe on a piece of the toasted bread. Return the toasts to the baking sheet as you go. Put the baking sheet in the oven just until the roe is warmed through, about 1 minute. Drape 2 overlapping slices of lardo over the sea urchin roe on each crostini, covering the tops. Return the baking sheet to the oven and heat just until the lardo begins to soften, about 1 minute.

Remove the sheet from the oven and sprinkle the crostini with sea salt. Drizzle with olive oil and sea salt, sprinkle with the chives, and serve immediately.

# CHICORY SALAD WITH ANCHOVY CROUTONS AND BLACK TRUFFLE

SERVES 4

When something is as unadorned as pane burro e acciughe, or bread topped with butter and anchovy, it doesn't require much to turn it into something modern. This take dresses up the combination by topping slices of fettunta with a salad of puntarelle, a crunchy Italian chicory, and radicchio and finishing the dish with anchovies and black truffle. (Black truffles, a central component in Umbrian cooking, are primarily available in December and January.)

This can be turned into a more substantial starter, or even a light lunch, by doubling the amount of greens (and lemon juice and olive oil) and serving the fettunta alongside the salad.

2 cups thinly sliced puntarelle or frisée, soaked in ice water for 10 minutes and drained
½ head of radicchio, core removed and separated into leaves
1 tablespoon freshly squeezed lemon juice
3 tablespoons extra virgin olive oil, plus more for serving
Kosher salt
Freshly ground black pepper
4 slices fettunta (see page 11), still warm
4 tablespoons unsalted butter, at room temperature
16 oil-packed anchovy fillets
1 ounce black truffle

Put the puntarelle and radicchio in a medium mixing bowl. Drizzle with the lemon juice and 3 tablespoons of the extra virgin olive oil and season with salt and pepper. Toss to coat the greens with the dressing.

Spread the fettunta with the butter and set one slice in the center of each of 4 salad plates. Top with the salad and nestle 4 anchovy fillets in the salad on each plate. Finish each serving with a shaving of black truffle and a drizzle of extra virgin olive oil. Serve while the toasts are still warm.

# RAW TUNA WITH RADICCHIO AND GRAPEFRUIT

SERVES 4

Northern and Southern Italian influences meet in this starter. The raw tuna is based on the crudo tradition of the south, while the radicchio, a northern crop, represents the other end of the geographic spectrum. The dish was inspired by a raw beef and grapefruit appetizer I prepared when I was cooking at a restaurant early in my career. While I never felt that those two got along, I was intrigued by the use of grapefruit on a carpaccio, and years later I hit on the combination of tuna and grapefruit. The parsley in this dish is a prime illustration of my belief that no herb should ever be taken for granted, as parsley often is; here it adds a crucial lift to the other ingredients.

½ cup extra virgin olive oil
2 tablespoons freshly squeezed lemon juice
2 tablespoons freshly squeezed orange juice
1 shallot, minced
Kosher salt
Freshly ground black pepper
12 ounces sushi-grade tuna loin
1 large grapefruit, peeled and cut into suprêmes (see page 191)
1 head of radicchio, core removed, halved, and thinly sliced, preferably on a mandoline
1 tablespoon thinly sliced fresh flat-leaf parsley leaves

Put the olive oil, lemon juice, orange juice, and shallots in a small bowl and season with salt and pepper. Whisk to blend and set aside.

Use a very sharp knife to slice the tuna across the grain into 28 paper-thin slices. Arrange the slices on 4 chilled salad plates, overlapping them. Arrange the grapefruit segments over the tuna and scatter the radicchio over them. Drizzle with the vinaigrette, top with a scattering of parsley, and serve.

## ACIDITY

Acidity serves a number of crucial roles in cooking. Its central place in classic Italian food is well known, from the prevalence of red and white wine vinegar in salad dressings and marinades to the iconic status accorded balsamic vinegar to the omnipresence of lemons, so great that we have a saying in my kitchens: "No lemon, no Italian."

But these and other acidic ingredients are more than just a piece in a dish's flavor makeup. Acidity is the thing that keeps dishes, especially rich ones, from becoming monotonous, that freshens the palate after each bite and keeps you coming back for more. Lemons, vinegars, wines, spirits, and other acidic elements (including particularly lactic cheeses such as ricotta and some goat cheeses) all have one thing in common: They bring an indispensable brightness to the plate.

The simplest example of acidity's power is how much effect a squeeze of lemon or a drizzle of balsamic vinegar over a finished dish can have. In the modern recipes in this section, the acidity is often more nuanced and carefully calibrated than in the classic dishes: Some salad dressings use specialty items such as white balsamic vinegar or verjus, each producing a very specific effect, and many of the soups, sauces, and braises are made with a succession of acidic ingredients that are reduced before the next one is added, such as the red wine vinegar followed by vin santo in the Duck with Peaches and Vin Santo (page 327).

# OVEN-BAKED RED MULLET WITH EGGPLANT, PEPPERS, AND CALAMARI

SERVES 4

Thanks to the presence of bell peppers, the accompaniment to the mullet here is a cross between caponata (see page 5) and ratatouille, cooked the French way: sautéing the ingredients separately rather than together to preserve their distinct characters. If you're unfamiliar with red mullet, known in France by the more appealing name rouget, it's well worth exploring: It has a stronger flavor than most white, flaky fish and can be served with just a drizzle of extra virgin olive oil.

- 6 tablespoons olive oil, plus more for drizzling
- 1 large red bell pepper, cored, seeded, and cut into small dice
- 1½ cups eggplant cut into small dice (about ½ eggplant)
- 1 cup white wine vinegar
- ½ cup sugar
- 1 Spanish onion, cut into small dice
- 1 large celery stalk, trimmed and cut into small dice
- ½ cup golden raisins, plumped in warm water for 10 minutes and drained
- 3 oil-packed anchovy fillets, rinsed, blotted dry with paper towels, and coarsely chopped
- Kosher salt
- Freshly ground black pepper
- 8 skin-on red mullet fillets, 3 ounces each (red snapper can be substituted)
- 1 garlic clove, minced
- 8 ounces cleaned calamari bodies, sliced into ¼-inch-wide rings
- ½ cup (loosely packed) thinly sliced fresh basil leaves, plus 8 large leaves for garnish
- ½ cup Basil Pesto (page 369)
- Extra virgin olive oil, for serving
- Balsamic vinegar, for serving

Heat a large heavy sauté pan over high heat. Add 2 tablespoons of the olive oil and tip and tilt the pan to coat it, heating the oil until it is shimmering and almost smoking. Add the bell peppers and cook, stirring occasionally with a wooden spoon, until al dente, about 5 minutes. Transfer the peppers to a medium heatproof bowl, add another 2 tablespoons of oil to the pan, and heat it. Add the eggplant and cook, tossing, until al dente, about 8 minutes. Transfer to the bowl with the peppers.

Heat a medium heavy pot over medium heat. Add the vinegar, sugar, onions, celery, raisins, and anchovies and bring the liquid to a boil, then lower the heat and simmer, stirring occasionally, until the sugar is dissolved and the liquid is reduced by half, about 10 minutes. Season with salt and pepper and set aside to cool. (The vegetables and the vinegar mixture can be refrigerated separately in airtight containers for up to 6 hours. Let come to room temperature before proceeding.)

Heat the oven to 375°F.

Place the fillets on a nonstick baking tray, skin side up. Drizzle with olive oil and sea salt, and cook until the fish looks about three quarters of the way done when viewed from the side and the skin is golden brown, about 6 minutes. Use a fish spatula to gently turn the fillets over and cook until the fish is flaky and cooked through, about 2 more minutes. Transfer the fillets to a plate and set aside to rest.

Heat a large nonstick skillet over high heat. Add the remaining 2 tablespoons olive oil, and tip and tilt the pan to coat it, heating the oil until it is shimmering and almost smoking. Add the garlic and cook, stirring with a wooden spoon, until it is fragrant but not browned, about 1 minute. Add the calamari and cook, stirring, until it is opaque and just cooked through, 2 to 3 minutes. Remove the pan from the heat.

By now, the vinegar mixture should be cool; finish the caponata by stirring in the peppers, eggplant, calamari, and sliced basil.

To serve, spoon the pesto onto the center of 4 salad plates and top with 2 of the fillets. Spoon some caponata alongside the mullet on each plate. Drizzle with extra virgin olive oil and balsamic vinegar, garnish each plate with 2 basil leaves, and serve.

# SAUTÉED ASPARAGUS WITH POACHED EGGS AND PARMIGIANO CREAM

SERVES 4

Asparagus alla Milanese is a Northern Italian ritual in the spring, when asparagus first come into season, pairing them with eggs, another ingredient with a strong seasonal association. This contemporary version cuts the asparagus into bite-size pieces, rather than serving it whole; poaches the egg rather than frying it, for a cleaner effect on the plate and the palate; and finishes them with a crown of bread crumbs and Parmigiano. Finally the dish is topped off with a Parmigiano cream, the most distinctly modern touch of all.

Kosher salt
1 pound large asparagus, ends trimmed, stalks peeled
1 tablespoon distilled white vinegar or white wine vinegar
4 large eggs
About 3 tablespoons olive oil
¼ cup finely grated Parmigiano-Reggiano
¼ cup fresh bread crumbs
2 tablespoons unsalted butter
Parmigiano Cream (recipe follows)
Freshly ground black pepper

Bring a large pot of salted water to a boil over high heat. Fill a large bowl halfway with ice water. Add the asparagus to the boiling water and blanch for 2 to 3 minutes. Use tongs to transfer the asparagus to the ice water to stop the cooking and preserve their brilliant green color. Drain the asparagus in a colander and pat them dry with paper towels.

Transfer the asparagus to a cutting board. Slice off the tips, then slice the stalks diagonally into pieces about the same size as the tips. Set aside in a bowl.

Fill a medium pot two-thirds full with water, salt it, and stir in the vinegar. Bring the water to a gentle simmer over medium heat; do not allow the water to boil. One at a time, crack the eggs into a cup and carefully add them to the water. Poach just until the whites are firm, about 4 minutes, then use a slotted spoon to transfer the eggs to a plate.

Position a rack in the center of the oven and preheat the broiler.

Brush the bottom of a small baking dish with olive oil. Carefully transfer the eggs to the dish and top each egg with a drizzle of oil, then scatter the Parmigiano and bread crumbs over them. Set under the broiler until the bread crumbs are golden brown and the cheese is melted, 2 to 3 minutes.

Meanwhile, working quickly, melt the butter in a heavy skillet and add the asparagus. Toss to coat the asparagus with butter and season with a pinch of salt.

To serve, divide the asparagus among 4 salad plates. Top the asparagus on each plate with an egg, transferring it from the baking dish to the plate with a spatula, then drizzle some Parmigiano cream over each serving and finish with a generous grinding of black pepper.

**Variations** You could also serve this for breakfast. For a richer effect, make it with guinea hen or duck eggs.

## PARMIGIANO CREAM

MAKES ABOUT ½ CUP

You can spoon this frothy cream over pastas, soups, and other dishes as a contemporary alternative to a grating of cheese.

½ cup heavy cream
⅓ cup finely grated Parmigiano-Reggiano

Put the cream in a small heavy saucepan, bring to a simmer over low heat, and reduce by half, about 4 minutes. Whisk in the cheese and remove the pan from the heat. Use right away or cover to keep warm for up to 20 minutes.

## ROASTED SQUAB WITH BUTTERNUT SQUASH CAPONATA

SERVES 4

Two autumnal ingredients come together in this dish that pairs roasted squab with a sweet counterpoint of butternut squash.

½ Spanish onion, coarsely chopped
1 medium carrot, coarsely chopped
1 medium celery stalk, trimmed and coarsely chopped
1 head of garlic, separated into cloves, skins left on
2 rosemary sprigs
1 sage sprig
4 squab, 1 pound each, rinsed and patted dry with paper towels
Kosher salt
Freshly ground black pepper
3 tablespoons olive oil
1 cup dry white wine
2 cups Chicken Stock (page 374)
Butternut Squash Caponata (recipe follows)

Position a rack in the center of the oven and preheat the oven to 400°F.

Put the onions, carrots, celery, garlic, rosemary, and sage in a roasting pan. Season the squab with salt and pepper and drizzle with the olive oil. Lay the squab breast-side up on top of the vegetables and roast until they are browned and the legs move easily when tugged, about 25 minutes; use a tablespoon to baste the squab with the pan juices two or three times as they roast. Remove the squab from the oven.

Move the squab aside and transfer the vegetables from the roasting pan to a medium heavy saucepan. Tent the squab with foil. Pour the wine into the saucepan and bring to a boil over high heat. Reduce the heat to a simmer and cook, stirring frequently with a wooden spoon, until almost all of the wine has evaporated, about 8 minutes. Pour in the stock, bring to a simmer, and simmer until slightly reduced, about 10 minutes.

Strain the sauce through a fine-mesh strainer into a medium saucepan; discard the solids. Use a spoon to skim the fat off the top of the sauce, bring to a simmer, and simmer until thick enough to coat the back of the spoon, about 10 minutes. Season with salt and pepper and remove from the heat.

Meanwhile, remove the foil from the squab and briefly reheat them in the oven.

To serve, mound some caponata on each of 4 dinner plates. Set a squab on top and spoon the sauce over and around the squab and caponata.

### BUTTERNUT SQUASH CAPONATA

SERVES 4

In the spring, substitute 8 artichoke hearts, thickly sliced, for the squash.

¼ cup plus 1 tablespoon olive oil
1 Spanish onion, cut into ¼-inch dice
3 large garlic cloves, thinly sliced
½ butternut squash (about 1 pound), peeled, seeds removed, and cut into ¾-inch dice
4 large celery stalks, trimmed and cut into ¼-inch dice
½ cup dry white wine
¼ cup white wine vinegar
3 to 4 tablespoons sugar
¼ cup pine nuts
2 tablespoons capers, soaked in warm water for 5 minutes and drained
Kosher salt
Freshly ground black pepper
1 tablespoon minced fresh chives

Heat a large skillet over medium-high heat. Add ¼ cup of the olive oil and heat until almost smoking. Add the onions and garlic and cook, stirring with a wooden spoon, until the onions are softened but not browned, about 4 minutes.

Add the butternut squash and celery and cook, stirring frequently, until the squash is lightly browned, about 6 minutes. Pour in the wine and vinegar, add 3 tablespoons sugar, the pine nuts, and the capers, and season with salt and pepper. Lower the heat to medium and cook, stirring, until the squash is tender, about 8 minutes. Remove the pan from the heat, stir in the chives, taste, and adjust the seasoning with salt, pepper, and more sugar if necessary.

Serve the caponata right away, warm, or at room temperature. It can be refrigerated in an airtight container for up to 2 days.

## DUCK BREAST SALAD WITH HAZELNUTS AND LA TUR CHEESE

SERVES 4

This elegant autumn salad is based on the combination of mesclun and frisée lettuces, thin slivers of roasted duck breast, and hazelnuts. It has an unmistakable French influence but is anchored by the flavors of Piedmont, namely a modern-day riff on mostarda (see page 149) and a crostini topped with La Tur, a luscious Piedmontese cheese made from cow's, goat's, and sheep's milk.

2 duck breasts, about 10 ounces each
Kosher salt
¾ cup plus 2 tablespoons olive oil
1 baguette
¼ cup balsamic vinegar
Freshly ground black pepper
2 tablespoons hazelnut oil
4 cups (loosely packed) mesclun greens
2 heads of frisée, core removed and separated into leaves
1 cup salted hazelnuts, toasted (see page 367), lightly crushed with the side of a chef's knife
Dried Fruit Marmalata (page 217)
1 round (8 ounces) La Tur cheese, sliced into 8 wedges, at room temperature (see Sources, page 379; a triple-crème cheese such as L'Explorateur can be substituted)

Position a rack in the center of the oven and preheat the oven to 400°F.

Heat a medium ovenproof skillet over medium heat. Season both sides of each duck breast liberally with salt. Pour 2 tablespoons of the olive oil into the pan, tipping and tilting the pan to coat it and heating the oil until it is shimmering and almost smoking. Add the duck breasts, skin side down, and cook until the fat starts to render, about 3 minutes. Lower the heat to medium-low and cook the duck until more fat renders and the skin becomes crispy, about 5 minutes; periodically drain the excess fat from the pan and discard it, leaving just enough in the pan to baste the flesh, using a pastry brush or tablespoon.

Transfer the pan to the oven and roast until the meat is medium-rare, 4 to 5 minutes. Remove the pan from the oven, transfer the duck breasts to a large plate, and set aside to cool to room temperature. Once the breasts are cooled, cover them with plastic wrap and refrigerate to cool them while you finish preparing the salad. (The duck can be refrigerated overnight.) Lower the oven temperature to 350°F.

Use a serrated knife to slice the baguette on a sharp angle into 8 long diagonal slices, about ¼ inch thick and 8 inches long. Arrange the slices on a rimmed baking sheet and drizzle with olive oil, using about ¼ cup. Season the slices with salt and toast in the oven until lightly golden brown and crisp, about 6 minutes. Remove the crostini from the oven and set aside.

To make the dressing: Put the vinegar in a small bowl and season with salt and pepper. Whisk in the remaining ½ cup olive oil, then the hazelnut oil.

Transfer the duck breasts to a cutting board. Use a sharp knife to thinly slice them diagonally.

Put the mesclun and frisée in a large bowl, drizzle about half the dressing over the greens, season with salt and pepper, and toss to coat. Taste a leaf or two and add more dressing to taste, if desired.

Divide the salad among 4 plates and top with the sliced duck. Scatter some hazelnuts over and around each serving and finish with a grinding of black pepper. Spoon some marmalata alongside each salad. Finally, perch a wedge of La Tur on each crostini and set the crostini on the rim of the plate. Serve.

## DRIED FRUIT MARMALATA

MAKES ABOUT 2 CUPS

You can also serve this autumnal marmalade as an accompaniment to other birds and game, such as venison.

1 cup water
½ cup sugar
A small piece of fresh ginger, peeled and cut into 4 slices
1 cinnamon stick
1 bay leaf, preferably fresh
1 teaspoon freshly ground black pepper
1 teaspoon ground juniper berries
½ cup dried apricots in large dice
½ cup dried figs in large dice
½ cup dried apples in large dice
½ cup dried cherries
Finely grated zest and juice of 1 orange

Combine the water, sugar, ginger slices, cinnamon, bay leaf, pepper, and juniper berries in a medium heavy saucepan, stir with a wooden spoon, and bring the mixture to a boil over medium-high heat. Boil for 2 minutes.

Line a fine-mesh strainer with cheesecloth and strain the liquid into a bowl. Discard the solids and return the liquid to the pan. Add the apricots, figs, apples, cherries, and orange juice, set over medium heat, and bring to a simmer. Cook, stirring frequently, until the fruit is nicely softened and the mixture has come together into a marmalade-like condiment, about 20 minutes. Remove from the heat and stir in the orange zest.

The marmalata can be refrigerated in an airtight container for up to 24 hours; let come to room temperature or reheat gently in a small saucepan over low heat before serving.

## CHICKEN LIVER CROSTINI WITH MARSALA-BRAISED ONIONS

SERVES 4

One of the most ubiquitous crostini meets the American tradition of liver and onions: The onions are slowly cooked with Marsala, veal stock, and rosemary for a garnish as flavorful as the livers themselves. For the classic version of this dish, see page 10.

Note that the chicken livers must be soaked for 1 to 2 hours before making the dish.

1 pound chicken livers
1½ cups whole milk
1 tablespoon unsalted butter
3 tablespoons olive oil
2 large Spanish onions, thinly sliced
Kosher salt
3 garlic cloves, 2 smashed with the side of a chef's knife and peeled, 1 minced
1 cup dry Marsala
½ cup Veal Stock (page 375) or store-bought low-sodium beef broth
1 rosemary sprig
Freshly ground black pepper
2 to 3 oil-packed anchovy fillets, coarsely chopped
2 tablespoons capers, soaked in warm water for 5 minutes and drained
1 cup dry white wine
Extra virgin olive oil
16 crostini (see page 11)
1 tablespoon minced fresh chives

Trim the fat, membranes, and bile ducts from the chicken livers and rinse them. Pour the milk into a small bowl, add the livers, and soak for 1 to 2 hours to draw out any impurities. Drain, rinse, and drain again, then pat the livers dry with paper towels.

Heat a medium skillet over medium-low heat. Add the butter and 1 tablespoon of the olive oil, tipping and tilting the pan to coat it with the butter and oil. Add the onions and cook, stirring occasionally with a wooden spoon, until very soft and golden brown, about 20 minutes. Season with salt, stir in the minced garlic, and cook until the garlic is fragrant, about 30 seconds. Pour in the Marsala and stir, using the wooden spoon to loosen any flavorful bits cooked onto the bottom of the pan. Bring to a simmer and simmer until the liquid is reduced by half, 5 to 6 minutes.

Pour in the stock and add the rosemary sprig, bring to a simmer, and simmer until the sauce is thickened into a syrupy glaze, 6 to 7 minutes. Season with salt and pepper and set aside.

To make the chicken liver mousse: Heat a large heavy skillet over medium heat. Add the remaining 2 tablespoons olive oil, tipping and tilting the pan to coat it and heating the oil until it is shimmering and almost smoking. Add the anchovies, capers, and smashed garlic and cook, stirring, until the anchovies dissolve, about 5 minutes. Add the chicken livers and cook, stirring occasionally, until the livers are golden brown but still pink inside, about 4 minutes. Pour in the wine and stir to loosen any flavorful bits cooked onto the bottom of the pan. Bring to a simmer and cook until the wine is reduced by half, 5 to 6 minutes.

Scrape the mixture into the bowl of a food processor and process until smooth. Season the mousse with salt, finish with a drizzle of extra virgin olive oil, and process to blend.

Spread the chicken liver mousse over the crostini, top with the onions and then the chives, and serve from a platter.

# BEEF CARPACCIO WITH ANCHOVY AND MUSHROOMS

SERVES 4

This dish takes pounded slices of raw beef, the foundation of a classic carpaccio, and rolls them around the other ingredients, using a sheet of plastic wrap in the manner of a sushi mat to make a roll. The inclusion of anchovy underscores the mingling of Eastern and Western influences.

1 8-ounce piece center-cut beef tenderloin, sliced into 8 pieces
4 oil-packed anchovy fillets, minced and mashed to a paste
4 tablespoons unsalted butter, at room temperature
Kosher salt
Freshly ground black pepper
2 cups (loosely packed) arugula, coarsely chopped
¼ cup Parmigiano-Reggiano shards (shaved with a vegetable peeler)
½ cup thinly sliced white mushrooms (ideally sliced on a truffle slicer or mandoline)
3 tablespoons extra virgin olive oil, plus more for serving
1 tablespoon freshly squeezed lemon juice
Balsamic vinegar, for serving
Pickled Mushrooms (recipe follows; optional)
4 Parmigiano Tuiles (page 222)

Place a 12-inch square of plastic wrap on a flat surface. Lay 2 pieces of the beef on the plastic wrap, overlapping them slightly. Place another piece of plastic on top of the beef and pound lightly with a meat mallet or the bottom of a heavy pan until it is flattened to a rough square and uniformly ⅛ inch thick. Leave the meat in the plastic and repeat with the remaining pieces of beef.

Stack the sheets on a baking tray, set them in the freezer, and chill for 30 minutes, or refrigerate for up to 24 hours.

When ready to serve, put the anchovy paste in a medium bowl, add the butter, and stir with a rubber spatula until completely integrated. Season with salt and pepper.

Remove the plastic wrap from the top of each square of beef. Evenly divide the butter among the beef squares and spread it over them with a rubber spatula.

Put the arugula, Parmigiano, mushrooms, 3 tablespoons olive oil, and lemon juice in a medium mixing bowl, season with salt and pepper, and toss to combine. Divide the salad among the 4 squares of beef. Pull up one end of the plastic wrap under one beef square and gently roll the beef up over on itself, as you would a sushi roll; make sure that the arugula salad is tightly rolled inside the meat, and take care not to roll the plastic wrap inside the meat. Discard the plastic wrap. Repeat with the remaining squares of beef.

Cut each roll crosswise into 3 equal slices. Arrange the slices of 1 roll on each of 4 chilled plates and drizzle with vinegar and a little extra virgin olive oil. Garnish each serving with some pickled mushrooms, if using, and a Parmigiano tuile and serve. (For a more dramatic presentation, arrange the mushrooms atop the tuiles, as pictured.)

## PICKLED MUSHROOMS

MAKES 1 CUP

You can also strew these over salads and other dishes, or add them to sauces just before serving for a touch of acidity.

1 tablespoon olive oil
1 garlic clove, smashed with the side of a chef's knife and peeled
1 cup baby (acorn-size) chanterelle mushrooms (enoki mushrooms can be substituted)
Kosher salt
Freshly ground black pepper
2 tablespoons red wine vinegar

Heat a large heavy sauté pan over medium-high heat. Add the olive oil and tip and tilt the pan to coat it, heating the oil until it is shimmering and almost smoking. Add the garlic and cook, stirring with a wooden spoon, until softened but not browned, about 2 minutes. Add the mushrooms, season with salt and pepper, and cook, stirring, just until the mushrooms begin to give off their liquid, without letting them brown, about 3 minutes.

Remove and discard the garlic and transfer the mushrooms to a heatproof bowl. Add the vinegar and toss. Let cool to room temperature.

Serve the mushrooms with a slotted spoon, leaving the vinegar in the bowl. The mushrooms can be refrigerated in an airtight container for up to 2 days; let come to room temperature before serving.

## PARMIGIANO TUILES

MAKES ENOUGH TO GARNISH 4 DISHES

There are very few impressive garnishes that are easier to make than these cheese crisps, which require nothing more than grating cheese, baking it, and cutting or shaping tuiles. Add them to just about any dish featuring Parmigiano-Reggiano cheese. For an especially artful flourish, punch circles out of the baked tuile, or cut the still-soft tuile into 4 strips and bend them over a rolling pin to create curled tuiles that can stand on their own.

1 cup finely grated Parmigiano-Reggiano (about 2 ounces)

Position a rack in the center of the oven and preheat the oven to 350°F.

Sprinkle the cheese in an even layer on a nonstick baking sheet or Silpat-lined baking sheet. Bake until the cheese melts into a lace-like pattern, without letting it brown, about 4 minutes.

Remove the pan from the oven and let the cheese cool and set slightly, 1 to 2 minutes, then use a spatula to remove it from the pan. Cut and form into shapes (it will bend easily until it fully sets) or simply let cool and break into shards.

The tuiles can be refrigerated in an airtight container for up to 24 hours.

# CRISPY RABBIT LOIN WITH MINT, SAGE, AND ARTICHOKES

SERVES 4

Based on a Florentine recipe in which rabbit is dusted in flour, then coated with an egg batter that includes herbs and Parmigiano, this dish boasts rabbit loins with a compellingly wrinkled exterior and depth of flavor. Although the rabbit is normally a main course, here it is part of a salad with the decadent inclusion of double-fried artichoke quarters (if you've ever made French fries, you'll recognize the inspiration), resulting in an exceedingly crispy, crunchy vegetable. Both the rabbit and artichokes are cut into bite-size pieces to encourage alternating bites of each.

Finely grated zest and juice of 1 lemon, plus 1 tablespoon lemon juice
Kosher salt
Freshly ground black pepper
4 boneless rabbit legs, cut crosswise into 1-inch pieces
1 to 2 cups canola oil or other neutral oil, for panfrying
4 baby artichokes, trimmed and cut into 4 wedges each
2 large eggs
2 teaspoons minced fresh rosemary
1 tablespoon minced fresh sage
1 tablespoon thinly sliced fresh mint leaves
2 tablespoons finely grated Parmigiano-Reggiano
1 garlic clove, minced
About 2 cups all-purpose flour, for dredging
2 bunches of mâche
2 heads of frisée, core removed and separated into leaves
3 tablespoons extra virgin olive oil
A wedge of Pecorino Romano or Oro Antico cheese, for grating

Put the zest and juice of the 1 lemon in a large bowl and season with salt and pepper. Add the rabbit pieces and toss to coat. Cover the bowl loosely with plastic wrap and let marinate for 15 to 30 minutes, but no longer.

Meanwhile, pour the oil into a wide, deep, heavy skillet to a depth of ¼ inch and heat to 260°F. Line a large plate or platter with paper towels.

Add the artichoke quarters to the oil and fry, turning them with a slotted spoon, until golden brown all over and easily pierced with a sharp thin-bladed knife. Use the slotted spoon to transfer the quarters to the paper-towel-lined plate to drain.

Meanwhile, heat the oil to 350°F.

Put the eggs in a wide shallow bowl. Add the rosemary, sage, mint, Parmigiano, and garlic, season with salt and pepper, and whisk together. Spread the flour out on a plate.

Blot the rabbit dry with paper towels. Dredge the pieces in the flour, shaking off any excess, then dip in the egg mixture. Add the rabbit pieces to the pan and panfry, turning the pieces as they brown, until golden brown all over and cooked through, about 6 minutes. Use a slotted spoon to transfer the pieces to the paper-towel-lined plate.

Let the oil return to 350°F. Add the artichoke quarters to the pan and cook, turning them with the slotted spoon, until very crispy all over, about 2 minutes. Use the slotted spoon to transfer the artichoke quarters to the paper-towel-lined plate and season immediately with salt.

Put the mâche and frisée in a large bowl. Drizzle the remaining tablespoon of lemon juice and the extra virgin olive oil over the greens, season with salt and pepper, and toss. Add the artichoke quarters and toss again.

Divide the artichokes and greens among 4 salad plates. Nestle the rabbit pieces in the greens and shave the cheese over the top. Finish with a grinding of black pepper and serve.

# SKIRT STEAK SALAD

SERVES 4

This salad, a modern version of the one on page 44, is intended as a late-summer starter that invites you to use vegetables from farm stands, greenmarkets, or your own backyard garden, adding another seasonal staple—grilled beef—for substance. (It's also open to adaptation. Add or substitute other vegetables you might have on hand at this time of year; raw corn kernels scattered about the plate would be an especially nice touch.)

The beef is marinated in a simple mixture of garlic, olive oil, and rosemary. Most marinades feature an acid, but here all of the acid is concentrated in the salad dressing, so the flavor of the beef really stands out. After grilling and resting, the meat is thinly sliced and served with a composed salad of wild arugula, heirloom tomato wedges, and pickled red onion.

Note that the beef must be marinated for at least 6 hours.

8 rosemary branches
¾ cup extra virgin olive oil, plus more for serving
7 large garlic cloves, 6 smashed with the side of a chef's knife and peeled, 1 minced
1 pound skirt steak, trimmed
Kosher salt
Freshly ground black pepper
1 large heirloom tomato or very ripe beefsteak tomato, cut into 8 wedges
¾ cup Pickled Red Onions (recipe follows)
2 cups (loosely packed) wild arugula
¼ cup balsamic vinegar
2 ounces Parmigiano-Reggiano, shaved into shards with a vegetable peeler

Put the rosemary branches on a cutting board and use the back of a heavy chef's knife to bruise them, releasing their essential oils.

Pour ¼ cup of the olive oil into a shallow baking dish and arrange 4 of the rosemary branches and 3 smashed garlic cloves on the bottom. Lay the skirt steak on top, drizzle with another ¼ cup oil, and lay the remaining rosemary branches and smashed garlic cloves on top. Cover and refrigerate for at least 6 hours, or overnight; after 3 hours or so, turn the meat over and press the herbs and garlic onto the meat.

When ready to proceed, remove the steak from the refrigerator and let come to room temperature.

Preheat a grill to high; if using a charcoal grill, let the coals burn until covered with white ash.

Remove the beef from the marinade, flick off any lingering rosemary needles and garlic, and blot up the oil with a paper towel to minimize the chance of flare-ups. Season generously with salt and pepper. Grill over high heat, turning once, until cooked to the desired doneness, about 3 minutes per side for medium-rare. Transfer to a plate and let rest for 5 minutes.

While the steak is resting, put the tomato wedges, pickled onion rings, and arugula in a mixing bowl. Drizzle with the remaining ¼ cup oil and the vinegar, add the minced garlic, season with salt and pepper, and toss gently to coat.

Slice the steak diagonally against the grain into ¼-inch-thick slices and arrange in the center of 4 salad plates, overlapping the slices. (Be sure to slice against the grain to ensure tenderness; this is a distinct concern with skirt steak.) Divide the salad among the plates, arranging it over and around the beef. Scatter some of the Parmigiano slices over each salad and finish with a drizzle of extra virgin olive oil and a few grinds of black pepper.

## PICKLED RED ONIONS

MAKES ABOUT ½ CUP

Scatter these onion rings over other salads and meat dishes, or add them to sandwiches. They can be used whole or chopped.

1 small red onion, sliced crosswise ¼ inch thick and separated into rings
2 tablespoons red wine vinegar
Kosher salt
Freshly ground black pepper

Place the onion rings in a small bowl. Drizzle the vinegar over them, tossing, and season with salt and pepper. Cover with plastic wrap and refrigerate for at least 3 hours or, preferably, overnight. Let come to room temperature before serving.

# P I Z Z A

Like pastas, pizza can be a sort of blank canvas with unlimited possibilities. Here in the United States, contemporary chefs have been reinventing pizza since the heyday of the California Cuisine movement in the late 1970s and early 1980s, so there are often no boundaries when it comes to pizza-making today, and the results can be delicious.

Personally, I apply the same guidelines to my pizza-making that I do to all of my modern Italian cooking, maintaining some connection to traditional Italian cuisine, even in this seemingly casual format; at my pizzeria Nicoletta, the pizzas are unique creations but draw on classic Italian ingredients and combinations, such as the pastas referenced by the puttanesca and carbonara pizzas, or the assortment of cured and cooked meats atop the Sausage, Pepperoni, and Red Onion Pizza (page 231).

You can by all means create your own pizzas following the basic template used to make the pizzas in this chapter, but I urge you to build on Italian themes or at least include an Italian ingredient or two in order to keep the pizzas recognizable and relatable.

# ROASTED SWEET CORN, BURRATA, CHERRY TOMATO, AND BASIL PIZZA

MAKES TWO 12-INCH PIZZAS

Designed as a showcase for the bounty of late summer, this pizza combines the best of America (corn, which rarely takes center stage in Italy) and Italy (fresh, creamy burrata cheese) with fresh tomatoes and a scattering of basil that provides a fragrant lift. This is the perfect recipe to call on when you have a surfeit of fresh produce from a farm stand or your own garden.

If you happen to have your grill fired up within a day of when you plan to make this pizza, grill the corn before slicing off the kernels to add another layer of flavor.

Note that the dough must be removed from the refrigerator about 2 hours before you plan to bake the pizzas.

Pizza Dough (page 50)
1 pint cherry tomatoes, halved
Leaves from 4 thyme sprigs
2 garlic cloves, minced
2 tablespoons finely grated Parmigiano-Reggiano
2 tablespoons fresh basil chiffonade (see page xxx), plus 8 leaves, torn into pieces, for garnish
¼ cup plus 3 tablespoons olive oil
Kosher salt
Freshly ground black pepper
Kernels from 2 large ears of corn
All-purpose flour or 00 flour, for dusting
Cornmeal, for dusting pizza peel
1 cup coarsely grated fresh mozzarella (about 4 ounces)
1 ball burrata cheese (about 1 pound), at room temperature
Extra virgin olive oil, for serving
¼ cup plus 2 tablespoons Seasoned Toasted Bread Crumbs (page xxix)

Remove the dough from the refrigerator about 2 hours before you plan to make the pizzas; this will make it easier to roll.

About 30 minutes before you plan to bake the pizzas, position a rack in the center of the oven and preheat the oven to 450°F.

Put the tomatoes in a bowl. Add the thyme, garlic, Parmigiano, basil chiffonade, and 2 tablespoons of the olive oil, season with salt and pepper, and toss well. Spread the tomatoes out on a rimmed baking sheet and bake until they shrink by about half, about 20 minutes. Remove the pan from the oven and set it aside. Set a pizza stone on the oven rack and raise the temperature to 500°F.

Heat a wide heavy sauté pan over medium-high heat. Add 1 tablespoon of the olive oil and tip and tilt the pan to coat it, heating the oil until it is shimmering and almost smoking. Add the corn, season with salt and pepper, and cook, tossing or stirring with a wooden spoon, until charred, about 8 minutes. Remove the pan from the heat and set aside.

Generously flour a work surface and lightly roll out one piece of the dough with a floured rolling pin, rotating the dough as you roll, until it is about 12 inches in diameter and uniformly ¼ inch thick. In one smooth, deft movement, lift the pizza onto a cornmeal-dusted pizza peel. (If you do not have a peel, use an inverted cookie sheet to transfer the pizza to and from the stone.)

Use a pastry brush to brush the dough with 2 tablespoons of the olive oil. Slide the dough onto the pizza stone and bake until the dough is set but not browned, 3 to 4 minutes. Open the oven, slide out the rack, and scatter half of the mozzarella over the pizza, then scatter half of the tomatoes and corn over it. Bake until the cheese is bubbly and the dough is golden brown around the edges, 3 to 4 more minutes.

Carefully slide the pizza back onto the peel, then transfer it to a cutting board. Tear the burrata into pieces and scatter half of it over the pizza. Drizzle the pizza with extra virgin olive oil and scatter half of the bread crumbs and torn basil leaves over it. Cut the pizza into 6 or 8 slices, transfer to a serving plate or plates, and serve immediately.

Repeat with the remaining dough and toppings.

# MOZZARELLA, SHAVED ASPARAGUS, AND BOTTARGA PIZZA

MAKES TWO 12-INCH PIZZAS

This springtime pizza is all about the contrast between fresh, crisp shavings of asparagus and the salinity of bottarga (gray mullet roe). This is another pizza that can be sliced thin or cut into squares and served as an hors d'oeuvre.

Note that the dough must be removed from the refrigerator about 2 hours before you plan to bake the pizzas.

Pizza Dough (page 50)
6 garlic cloves, minced
¼ cup olive oil
8 ounces large asparagus, tips cut off (reserve for another use), bottom ends trimmed, thinly shaved lengthwise with a vegetable peeler
Kosher salt
Freshly ground black pepper
Red pepper flakes
All-purpose flour or 00 flour, for dusting
Cornmeal, for dusting pizza peel
¼ cup extra virgin olive oil
2 cups shredded fresh mozzarella (about 8 ounces)
2 cups shredded smoked mozzarella (about 8 ounces; or another 2 cups shredded fresh mozzarella)
1 ounce bottarga (salmon roe or trout roe can be substituted; see Sources, page 379)
Seasoned Toasted Bread Crumbs (page xxix)

Remove the dough from the refrigerator about 2 hours before you plan to make the pizzas; this will make it easier to roll.

Position a rack in the center of the oven, set a pizza stone on the rack, and preheat the oven to 500°F.

Put the garlic in a small bowl, add the olive oil, and stir together. Put the asparagus in a large bowl, drizzle with the garlic oil, season with salt, black pepper, and red pepper flakes, and toss well to coat the asparagus.

Generously flour a work surface and lightly roll out one piece of the dough with a floured rolling pin, rotating the dough as you roll, until it is about 12 inches in diameter and uniformly ¼ inch thick. In one smooth, deft movement, lift the pizza onto a cornmeal-dusted pizza peel. (If you do not have a peel, use an inverted cookie sheet to transfer the pizza to and from the stone.)

Use a pastry brush to brush the dough with 2 tablespoons of the extra virgin olive oil. Slide the dough onto the pizza stone and bake until the dough is set but not browned, 3 to 4 minutes. Open the oven, slide out the rack, and arrange half of both mozzarellas over the pizza, then scatter half the asparagus over the pizza and bake until the cheese is bubbly and the dough is golden brown around the edges, 3 to 4 more minutes.

Carefully slide the pizza back onto the peel, then transfer it to a cutting board. Shave some bottarga over the pizza and sprinkle with half the bread crumbs. Cut the pizza into 6 or 8 slices, transfer to a serving plate or plates, and serve immediately.

Repeat with the remaining dough and toppings.

**Note:** When adding smoked mozzarella to a pizza or other recipe, it's often a good idea to combine it with fresh mozzarella to keep the smoke flavor from overwhelming the other ingredients.

# PIZZA PUTTANESCA

MAKES TWO 12-INCH PIZZAS

The primary ingredients of one of Italy's most well-known pastas (see page 77) are relocated to a salty, zesty pizza. This is a wonderful summertime pizza, best washed down with a crisp white wine or ice-cold beer.

Note that the dough must be removed from the refrigerator about 2 hours before you plan to bake the pizzas.

Pizza Dough (page 50)
All-purpose flour or 00 flour, for dusting
Cornmeal, for dusting pizza peel
2 cups Basic Pizza Sauce (page 51)
1 ball (about 1 pound) fresh mozzarella, torn into 1- to 2-inch pieces (buffalo mozzarella can be substituted)
8 oil-packed anchovy fillets, halved lengthwise
3 tablespoons capers, soaked in warm water for 5 minutes and drained
2 teaspoons dried oregano

Remove the dough from the refrigerator about 2 hours before you plan to make the pizzas; this will make it easier to roll.

Position a rack in the center of the oven, set a pizza stone on the rack, and preheat the oven to 500°F.

Generously flour a work surface and lightly roll out one piece of the dough with a floured rolling pin, rotating the dough as you roll, until it is about 12 inches in diameter and uniformly 1/4 inch thick. In one smooth, deft movement, lift the pizza onto a cornmeal-dusted pizza peel. (If you do not have a peel, use an inverted cookie sheet to transfer the pizza to and from the stone.)

Ladle half of the sauce onto the dough, then use the bottom of the ladle to spread it evenly, leaving a 1/2-inch border all around. Slide the dough onto the pizza stone and bake for 3 to 4 minutes. Open the oven, slide out the rack, and arrange half the mozzarella over the pizza, then scatter half of the anchovies, capers, and oregano over it and bake until the cheese is bubbly and the dough is golden brown around the edges, 3 to 4 more minutes.

Carefully slide the pizza back onto the peel, then transfer it to a cutting board. Cut the pizza into 6 or 8 slices, transfer to a serving plate or plates, and serve immediately.

Repeat with the remaining dough and toppings.

# SAUSAGE, PEPPERONI, AND RED ONION PIZZA

MAKES TWO 12-INCH PIZZAS

One of the greatest hits at Nicoletta, our pizzeria on Second Avenue in New York City, is the Calabrese, topped with sausage and pepperoni and two types of cheese.

Note that the dough must be removed from the refrigerator about 2 hours before you plan to bake the pizzas.

Pizza Dough (page 50)
¼ cup extra virgin olive oil
3 garlic cloves, smashed with the side of a chef's knife and peeled
½ cup extra virgin olive oil
All-purpose flour or 00 flour, for dusting
Cornmeal, for dusting pizza peel
2 cups Basic Pizza Sauce (page 51)
1½ cups shredded fresh mozzarella (about 6 ounces)
6 ounces Italian fennel sausage, removed from casings and crumbled into small pieces
6 ounces pepperoni, thinly sliced
1 small red onion, thinly sliced
A wedge of Parmigiano-Reggiano, for grating
¼ cup thinly sliced fresh flat-leaf parsley leaves

Remove the dough from the refrigerator about 2 hours before you plan to make the pizzas; this will make it easier to roll.

Pour the oil into a small bowl, add the garlic, and let infuse for 30 minutes.

Position a rack in the center of the oven, set a pizza stone on the rack, and preheat the oven to 500°F.

Generously flour a work surface and lightly roll out one piece of the dough with a floured rolling pin, rotating the dough as you roll, until it is about 12 inches in diameter and uniformly ¼ inch thick. In one smooth, deft movement, lift the pizza onto a cornmeal-dusted pizza peel. (If you do not have a peel, use an inverted cookie sheet to transfer the pizza to and from the stone.)

Use a pastry brush to brush the dough with half the garlic oil. Ladle half of the sauce onto the dough, then use the bottom of the ladle to spread it evenly, leaving a ½-inch border all around. Slide the dough onto the pizza stone and bake for 3 to 4 minutes. Open the oven, slide out the rack, and arrange half of the mozzarella over the pizza, then scatter half of the sausage, pepperoni, and onions over it and bake until the cheese is bubbly and the dough is golden brown around the edges, 3 to 4 more minutes.

Carefully slide the pizza back onto the peel, then transfer it to a cutting board. Top with some grated Parmigiano and half the parsley, then cut the pizza into 6 or 8 slices, transfer to a serving plate or plates, and serve immediately.

Repeat with the remaining dough and toppings.

# MINTED ZUCCHINI, RICOTTA, AND CHILE OIL PIZZA

MAKES TWO 12-INCH PIZZAS

A springtime pizza topped with fresh mint, thinly sliced zucchini, and fluffy clouds of ricotta cheese, this pie can also be sliced thinner, or into small squares, and served as a passed or plated hors d'oeuvre. To impart an extra counterpoint of char flavor, lightly grill the zucchini (as it's shown in the photograph) before topping the pizzas with it.

Note that the dough must be removed from the refrigerator about 2 hours before you plan to bake the pizzas.

Pizza Dough (page 50)
8 ounces zucchini, thinly sliced
1 cup extra virgin olive oil, plus more for serving
½ cup torn fresh mint leaves
10 large fresh basil leaves, torn into pieces
¼ cup finely grated Pecorino Romano or Parmigiano-Reggiano
Finely grated zest and juice of 1 lemon
Kosher salt
Freshly ground black pepper
2 cups heirloom tomatoes cut into wedges or halved cherry or teardrop tomatoes
All-purpose flour or 00 flour, for dusting
Cornmeal, for dusting pizza peel
1 pound fresh ricotta cheese, at room temperature
1 teaspoon Chile Oil (recipe follows)

Remove the dough from the refrigerator about 2 hours before you plan to make the pizzas; this will make it easier to roll.

Position a rack in the center of the oven, set a pizza stone on the rack, and preheat the oven to 500°F.

Meanwhile, put the zucchini, ½ cup of the olive oil, the mint, basil, Pecorino, lemon zest, and lemon juice in a medium bowl, season with salt and pepper, and toss well to coat the zucchini.

Put the tomatoes in a small bowl and drizzle ¼ cup of the olive oil over them. Season with a pinch of salt and toss to coat the tomatoes.

Generously flour a work surface and lightly roll out one piece of the dough with a floured rolling pin, rotating the dough as you roll, until it is about 12 inches in diameter and uniformly ¼ inch thick. In one smooth, deft movement, lift the pizza onto a cornmeal-dusted pizza peel. (If you do not have a peel, use an inverted cookie sheet to transfer the pizza to and from the stone.)

Use a pastry brush to brush the dough with 2 tablespoons of the olive oil. Slide the dough onto the pizza stone and bake until the dough is golden brown all over, about 8 minutes.

Carefully slide the pizza back onto the peel, then transfer it to a cutting board. Immediately top it with spoonfuls of half the ricotta, half the minted zucchini, and half the tomatoes, then finish with a few grinds of black pepper and a drizzle of extra virgin olive oil and half the chile oil. Cut the pizza into 6 or 8 slices, transfer to a serving plate or plates, and serve immediately.

Repeat with the remaining dough and toppings.

## CHILE OIL

MAKES ABOUT 1 CUP

This oil allows you to control the presence of a very powerful element on the plate, dispersing it exactly where you want it, either over a finished dish or alongside it, allowing people to incorporate the spicy oil into as many bites as they like.

1 cup olive oil
3 tablespoons red pepper flakes

Pour the oil into a small heavy saucepan and heat over medium-high heat until the oil reaches 200°F; to keep the pepper flakes from burning, do not let the oil get hotter than 240°F. Add the pepper flakes, remove the pan from the heat, and let cool, then cover and let the oil infuse at room temperature overnight.

Strain the oil through a fine-mesh strainer, coffee filter, or cheesecloth into a bowl, then use a funnel to pour the strained chile oil into a glass bottle. The chile oil can be kept in a cool dark place for up to 1 week.

# POTATO AND BACON PIZZA

MAKES TWO 12-INCH PIZZAS

Mashed potatoes and Alfredo sauce may seem an unlikely topping for pizza, but when they are baked together, they fuse into a one-of-a-kind sauce that's balanced by sweet caramelized onions and smoky bacon.

Note that the dough must be removed from the refrigerator about 2 hours before you plan to bake the pizzas.

Pizza Dough (page 50)
2 large russet or Idaho potatoes, peeled and quartered
5 tablespoons unsalted butter, at room temperature
Kosher salt
Freshly ground black pepper
2 tablespoons olive oil
1 bay leaf, preferably fresh
2 medium Spanish onions, thinly sliced
6 ounces applewood-smoked bacon, cut crosswise into 2-inch-wide pieces
All-purpose flour or 00 flour, for dusting
Cornmeal, for dusting pizza peel
2 cups Basic Pizza Sauce (page 51)
½ cup shredded fresh mozzarella (about 2 ounces)
A wedge of Parmigiano-Reggiano, for grating
½ cup crème fraîche, lightly beaten
2 tablespoons minced fresh chives

Remove the dough from the refrigerator about 2 hours before you plan to make the pizzas; this will make it easier to roll.

Fill a large pot two-thirds full with water and bring it to a boil over high heat. Add the potatoes and boil until easily pierced with a sharp thin-bladed knife, about 12 minutes. Drain the potatoes, then rice them into a bowl, or transfer them to a heatproof bowl and mash them with a potato masher. Add 4 tablespoons of the butter, season with salt and pepper, and stir together until smooth. Set aside.

Heat a medium skillet over medium heat and add the remaining tablespoon of butter, 1 tablespoon of the olive oil, and the bay leaf. When the butter melts, add the onions, lower the heat to low, and cook, stirring occasionally with a wooden spoon, until the onions are browned and caramelized, 35 to 40 minutes, adding a tablespoon or so of water as necessary to keep them from scorching. Remove from the heat.

Heat a small heavy skillet over medium heat. Add the remaining 1 tablespoon olive oil and tip and tilt the skillet to coat it, warming the oil. Add the bacon and cook, stirring occasionally, until it has rendered some of its fat and is lightly golden brown, about 6 minutes. Drain the bacon on paper towels.

Generously flour a work surface and lightly roll out one piece of the dough with a floured rolling pin, rotating the dough as you roll, until it is about 12 inches in diameter and uniformly ¼ inch thick. In one smooth, deft movement, lift the pizza onto a cornmeal-dusted pizza peel. (If you do not have a peel, use an inverted cookie sheet to transfer the pizza to and from the stone.)

Ladle half of the sauce onto the dough, then use the bottom of the ladle to spread it around evenly, leaving a ½-inch border all around. Slide the dough onto the pizza stone and bake for 3 to 4 minutes. Open the oven, slide out the rack, and arrange half of the mozzarella over the pizza, then top with half of the mashed potatoes, onions, and bacon. Bake until the cheese is bubbly and the dough is golden brown around the edges, 3 to 4 more minutes.

Carefully slide the pizza back onto the peel, then transfer it to a cutting board. Grate some Parmigiano over the top, drizzle with half the crème fraîche, and scatter half the chives over the pizza. Cut the pizza into 6 or 8 slices, transfer to a serving plate or plates, and serve immediately.

Repeat with the remaining dough and toppings.

# CARBONARA PIZZA

MAKES TWO 12-INCH PIZZAS

The defining elements of pasta carbonara—eggs, bacon, onions, Pecorino cheese, and black pepper—prove equally complementary atop a pizza.

Note that the dough must be removed from the refrigerator about 2 hours before you plan to bake the pizzas.

Pizza Dough (page 50)
1 cup heavy cream
1 tablespoon olive oil
8 ounces applewood-smoked bacon, cut crosswise into ½-inch-wide strips
All-purpose flour or 00 flour, for dusting
Cornmeal, for dusting pizza peel
4 large eggs
Kosher salt
Freshly ground black pepper
1 ball (about 1 pound) fresh mozzarella, coarsely grated
½ cup finely grated Pecorino Romano (about 1 ounce)
2 scallions (white and light green parts only), thinly sliced

Remove the dough from the refrigerator about 2 hours before you plan to make the pizzas; this will make it easier to roll.

Position a rack in the center of the oven, set a pizza stone on the rack, and preheat the oven to 500°F.

Bring the cream to a simmer in a small heavy saucepan over medium heat and simmer until reduced by half, about 12 minutes. Remove from the heat and set aside.

Heat a small heavy skillet over medium heat. Add the olive oil and tip and tilt the skillet to coat it, warming the oil. Add the bacon and cook, stirring occasionally, until it has rendered some of its fat and is lightly golden brown, about 6 minutes. Drain the bacon on paper towels.

Generously flour a work surface and lightly roll out one piece of the dough with a floured rolling pin, rotating the dough as you roll, until it is about 12 inches in diameter and uniformly ¼ inch thick. In one smooth, deft movement, lift the pizza onto a cornmeal-dusted pizza peel. (If you do not have a peel, use an inverted cookie sheet to transfer the pizza to and from the stone.)

Slide the dough onto the pizza stone and bake for 3 to 4 minutes. Open the oven, slide out the rack, and use the back of a spoon to press 2 shallow wells toward the center of the pizza, being careful not to tear the crust. Crack 2 of the eggs into a shallow bowl, without breaking the yolks, and use a tablespoon to transfer 1 egg to each well. Season the eggs with salt and pepper. Scatter half the mozzarella and bacon over the pizza and drizzle with half the cream. Bake until the cheese is bubbly and the dough is golden brown around the edges, 3 to 4 more minutes.

Carefully slide the pizza back onto the peel, then transfer it to a cutting board and scatter half the Pecorino over the pizza. Drag a knife through the yolks so they break and ooze all over the surface of the pie. Generously grind black pepper over the pizza and scatter half the scallions over it. Cut the pizza into 6 or 8 slices, transfer to a serving plate or plates, and serve immediately.

Repeat with the remaining dough and toppings.

# SOUPS

Where most traditional Italian soups were born of necessity and economy, the ones in this chapter are more elaborate and elegant, made with slightly more complex techniques and more apt to be finished with a prepared garnish—such as a scattering of sautéed vegetables on the surface, or an island of shellfish in the center—than with simply a drizzle of olive oil or a grinding of black pepper.

What's remarkable to me is that neither approach is superior to the other: the soups in Classico are just as satisfying as the ones here. The question of when to serve which type of soup is a matter of mood, just like selecting what style of restaurant to dine in on a given night. Because they take more time to prepare, and have more components than their Classico counterparts, the following soups seem more appropriate to dinner parties and other special events, but they may be enjoyed as everyday meals, just as those in the preceding section may be served for casual and special occasions as well.

# PEA AND LEEK SOUP WITH RICOTTA CHEESE

SERVES 4

Peas are perennially popular in Italy, where they are braised with leeks, sautéed with cuttlefish, and tossed with prosciutto and cream for a pasta sauce for garganelli, to name just three ways of enjoying them. This soup combines pureed and whole peas and employs one of my favorite high-impact effects, garnishing a milk-free preparation with a lactic dairy product, in this case ricotta cheese, for a stark and compelling contrast.

3 tablespoons olive oil
2 tablespoons unsalted butter
1 cup thinly sliced leeks (white and light green parts only, about 1 large leek)
1 Spanish onion, cut into ¼-inch dice
1 garlic clove, smashed with the side of a chef's knife and peeled
Kosher salt
Freshly ground black pepper
1½ cups (12 ounces) freshly shucked peas (defrosted frozen peas can be substituted), raw, plus ½ cup (4 ounces) peas, blanched, shocked, and drained (see page 367)
2 basil sprigs, plus 12 small leaves for garnish
3 cups Chicken Stock (page 374)
¼ cup extra virgin olive oil
½ cup ricotta cheese

Fill a large bowl halfway with ice water and set a large stainless-steel bowl in it.

Heat a medium heavy pot over medium heat. Add 2 tablespoons of the olive oil and the butter and tip and tilt the pot to coat it and melt the butter. Add the leeks, onions, and garlic and cook, stirring occasionally with a wooden spoon, until the vegetables are softened but not browned, about 4 minutes. Season with salt and pepper, then stir in the 1½ cups raw peas and the basil sprigs. Pour in the stock, bring it to a simmer, and simmer, stirring occasionally, until the peas are tender, 3 to 4 minutes. Pour or ladle the mixture into the bowl set in the ice bath. Let cool, stirring frequently to speed the cooling process and keep the mixture from turning brown.

Once the soup is cooled, ladle it, in batches, into a blender and puree until smooth, transferring the batches to a bowl. Strain the soup through a fine-mesh strainer back into the pot, pressing down on the solids with a wooden spoon or a ladle to extract as much flavorful liquid as possible.

Whisk 2 tablespoons of the extra virgin olive oil into the soup and reheat gently over low heat.

Meanwhile, put the ricotta and the remaining 2 tablespoons extra virgin olive oil in a small bowl and fold together with a rubber spatula until the oil is fully incorporated.

Heat a small saucepan over medium heat. Add the remaining tablespoon olive oil and the blanched peas, season with salt and pepper, toss, and warm the peas through, about 3 minutes. Add the basil leaves and toss briefly.

Divide the peas among 4 shallow bowls, mounding them in the center. Ladle some of the soup over each mound and top with a quenelle or spoonful of the ricotta. Serve.

# PUREED ROOT VEGETABLE SOUP WITH BLACK TRUMPET MUSHROOMS

SERVES 4

When I was cooking and traveling throughout Italy, whenever I visited a home with small children, I'd invariably see them eating pureed vegetables, which, as a parent, I now realize is a terrific way to get kids to start eating healthfully from a young age. That tradition inspired me to develop a soup of pureed root vegetables finished with sautéed black trumpet mushrooms and shavings of ricotta salata cheese.

2 tablespoons unsalted butter
3 tablespoons olive oil
2 large garlic cloves, smashed with the side of a chef's knife and peeled
2 medium Spanish onions, cut into ¼-inch dice
1 bay leaf
1 thyme sprig
2 large carrots, cut into ¼-inch dice
2 large parsnips, peeled and cut into ¼-inch dice
1 small celery root, peeled and cut into ¼-inch dice
8 cups Vegetable Stock (page 371)
1 cup heavy cream
Kosher salt
Freshly ground black pepper
½ cup black trumpet mushrooms
Extra virgin olive oil, for serving
½ cup ricotta salata cheese shavings (shaved with a vegetable peeler)

Heat a large heavy pot over medium heat. Add the butter and 1 tablespoon of the olive oil and tip and tilt the pot to coat it. Once the butter has melted, add the garlic, onions, bay leaf, and thyme and cook, stirring frequently, until the garlic and onions are softened but not browned, 2 to 3 minutes. Stir in the carrots, parsnips, and celery root and cook, stirring, until slightly softened but not browned, 3 to 4 minutes. Pour in the stock and bring it to a simmer, then lower the heat and simmer until the vegetables are tender, 6 to 7 minutes. Remove the pot from the heat.

Transfer the vegetables and some of the broth to a blender, in batches, and blend until smooth (see Blender Safety, page 75), then return the soup to the pot. Bring the soup to a light simmer over medium heat and whisk in the cream. Season with salt and pepper and keep warm over low heat.

Heat a medium skillet over medium heat. Add the remaining 2 tablespoons olive oil and tip and tilt the pan to coat it. Add the mushrooms and cook, stirring frequently, until tender, about 5 minutes. Season with salt and pepper.

Ladle the soup into bowls and top with the mushrooms. Drizzle each portion with extra virgin olive oil, add a grinding of black pepper, top with some of the ricotta salata shards, and serve.

**Variation** You can enrich the soup by making it with chicken stock (see page 374) instead of vegetable stock.

# SEAFOOD AND FREGOLA SOUP

SERVES 4

This recipe is a modern play on couscous Siciliano, a loose seafood and grain soup. It was inspired by my deep and profound love of fregola sarda (sometimes called fregula), a semolina product that resembles a toasted Israeli couscous but whose pearls aren't perfectly round, giving them an appealingly rustic quality.

To enhance the grain's flavor, the fregola is soaked in broth, each pearl swelling with flavor. Then, at the table, the soup is poured over the solids—seafood, herbs, and fregola—a restaurant-style touch that adds a sense of pomp to the proceedings. If desired, serve with crostini (see page 11) alongside.

½ cup olive oil
4 large garlic cloves, smashed with the side of a chef's knife and peeled
1 cup thinly sliced Spanish onion (about 1 small onion)
2 cups thinly sliced leek greens (light green parts only; from about 1 large leek)
½ cup thinly sliced celery
1 medium fennel bulb, trimmed and thinly sliced
Kosher salt
Freshly ground black pepper
1 pound jumbo shrimp (about 16), peeled and deveined, shells reserved
2 cups dry white wine
1 28-ounce can whole tomatoes, preferably Italian San Marzano or organic, crushed by hand, with their juice
An herb sachet (1 bay leaf, 2 thyme sprigs, and 2 tarragon sprigs, tied in a cheesecloth bundle)
Pinch of saffron threads
¾ cup fregola (see Sources, page 379; Israeli couscous can be substituted)
8 ounces bay scallops (quartered diver scallops can be substituted)
8 ounces cleaned calamari bodies, thinly sliced into rings
2 teaspoons minced fresh chives
2 teaspoons minced fresh tarragon
Splash of sambuca or other anise-flavored liquor, such as Pernod or anisette

Heat a large heavy pot over medium heat. Pour in ¼ cup of the olive oil and heat the oil until it is shimmering and almost smoking. Add the garlic, onions, leeks, celery, and fennel, season with salt and pepper, and cook, stirring with a wooden spoon, until softened but not browned, about 3 minutes. Add the shrimp shells and cook, stirring, until they turn red, 1 to 2 minutes.

Turn the heat up to medium-high, pour in the wine, and cook, stirring, until the wine has almost completely evaporated, about 5 minutes. Stir in the tomatoes and their juice, the herb sachet, and saffron, then pour in enough cold water just to cover the solids. Raise the heat to high and bring the liquid to a boil, then lower the heat so the soup is just barely simmering and simmer until it thickens into a hearty soup, about 1 hour, stirring in more liquid as necessary to keep the soup from becoming too thick. After the soup has cooked for 45 minutes, put the fregola in a fine-mesh strainer, lower it into the simmering liquid, and cook until al dente, about 10 minutes, then remove, shaking off the excess liquid. Rinse under cold water, drain, and set aside.

Meanwhile, heat a wide heavy sauté pan over medium-high heat. Pour in the remaining ¼ cup olive oil and heat until the oil is shimmering and almost smoking. Add the shrimp, scallops, and calamari, season with a pinch of salt, and cook, tossing the seafood, until the shrimp are firm and pink and the scallops and calamari are opaque, about 3 minutes. Remove from the heat.

Divide the shrimp, scallops, and calamari among 4 bowls, taking care to include a good mix of all three in each bowl and pushing it to one side of the bowl. Spoon some fregola into each bowl, alongside the seafood. Sprinkle the seafood and fregola with the chives and tarragon.

Strain the soup through a fine-mesh strainer into a bowl, pressing down on the solids with a spoon or a ladle to extract as much flavorful liquid as possible. Wipe out the pot and return the soup to the pot. Heat over high heat until simmering, and finish by stirring in the sambuca. Taste and adjust the seasoning with salt and pepper if necessary.

Finish the dish at the table by ladling or pouring the hot broth over each serving of seafood and fregola.

# MUSSEL SOUP WITH BARLEY AND BROCCOLI RABE

SERVES 4

Founded on a combination that can seem surprising to outsiders, mussel and farro soup is actually a time-honored dish of the Maremma region of Tuscany. Here, I substitute barley for farro and add broccoli rabe, a distinctly southern ingredient, to the bowl. Note that the barley must be soaked overnight.

Kosher salt
½ cup barley, soaked in cold water overnight and drained
6 tablespoons olive oil
2 thyme sprigs
2 bay leaves
3 flat-leaf parsley stems
2 pounds mussels, preferably Prince Edward Island, scrubbed and debearded
4 large garlic cloves, minced
1 strip orange zest, removed with a vegetable peeler (with no white pith attached)
Pinch of red pepper flakes
Pinch of saffron threads
2 cups dry white wine
4 stalks broccoli rabe, cut into florets with ½ inch of stalk attached, blanched, shocked, and drained (see page 367)
2 large tomatoes, peeled, seeded, and cut into small dice (page 367)
Freshly ground black pepper

Fill a small pot about two-thirds full with water, salt it liberally, and bring to a boil. Add the barley and cook until al dente, about 15 minutes. Drain in a colander and rinse under cold running water to stop the cooking. Drain again and set aside.

Heat a large heavy pot over medium heat. Pour in 3 tablespoons of the olive oil and tip and tilt the pot to coat it, heating the oil until it is shimmering and almost smoking. Add the thyme, bay leaves, parsley, mussels, three quarters of the garlic, the orange peel, red pepper flakes, and saffron and stir well. Pour in the wine, bring to a simmer, and cover the pot. Increase the heat to high and simmer just until the mussels open, about 5 minutes, gently shaking the pot once or twice to agitate the mussels. Use a slotted spoon to transfer the mussels to a bowl, discarding any that did not open, and let cool slightly, then remove half of the mussels from their shells, discarding the shells. Cover the remaining mussels to keep them warm.

Strain the mussel broth through a fine-mesh strainer into a bowl. Carefully wipe out the pot and return the broth to the pot. Bring the broth to a simmer and simmer gently until it is slightly reduced and the flavor is concentrated, 5 to 8 minutes.

While the broth is simmering, cook the broccoli rabe: Heat a large skillet over medium heat. Add 2 tablespoons of the olive oil and tip and tilt the pan to coat it. Add the remaining garlic and cook until softened but not browned, about 2 minutes. Stir in the broccoli rabe, tomatoes, and barley and season with salt and pepper. Cook, tossing or stirring with a wooden spoon, until the broccoli rabe is warmed through but still al dente, about 3 minutes.

Season the simmering mussel broth with salt and pepper, return the shucked mussels to the broth, and heat until they are warmed through.

Divide the barley and broccoli rabe among 4 bowls and ladle some broth and mussels over each serving. Garnish with the mussels in the shell and serve immediately.

# WHITE BEAN SOUP WITH SAUTÉED SHRIMP

SERVES 4

A variation on the traditional bean soup featured on page 62, this pairs the snap and salinity of shrimp with white beans. The two seemingly disparate elements are bridged by sautéing the shrimp shells along with the minced vegetables in the soffritto; the beans themselves, which have a distinct ability to absorb other flavors, take on the natural oils released by the shells.

1 cup dried white beans, preferably cannellini
¼ cup olive oil
1 small Spanish onion, cut into ½-inch dice
1 small carrot, cut into ½-inch dice
1 celery stalk, trimmed and cut into ½-inch dice
4 large garlic cloves, thinly sliced
12 ounces large shrimp (about 12 shrimp), peeled and deveined, shells reserved
1 tablespoon tomato paste
½ cup brandy
8 cups Shrimp Stock (page 372)
2 rosemary sprigs, plus 1 teaspoon minced rosemary
Pinch of red pepper flakes
Kosher salt
Freshly ground black pepper
½ cup dry white wine
1 large plum tomato, peeled, seeded, and cut into ½-inch dice (see page 367)
1 teaspoon thinly sliced fresh flat-leaf parsley leaves
Extra virgin olive oil, for serving

Put the beans in a bowl, cover with cold water, and let soak overnight at room temperature. (Alternatively, use the quick-soak method; see page 30.) Drain.

Heat a wide, deep, heavy pot over high heat. Pour in 2 tablespoons of the olive oil, tipping and tilting the pot, and heat the oil until it is shimmering and almost smoking. Add the onions, carrots, celery, and half the garlic and cook, stirring occasionally with a wooden spoon, until the vegetables begin to brown and caramelize, about 7 minutes. Add the shrimp shells and cook, stirring frequently, until they turn bright red and begin to toast lightly, about 3 minutes. Stir in the tomato paste, stirring to coat the other ingredients with the paste, and cook until it turns a shade darker, about 2 minutes.

Pour in the brandy and use the spoon to loosen any flavorful bits cooked onto the bottom of the pot. Bring to a simmer and cook until the brandy has almost completely evaporated, about 5 minutes. Stir in the beans, stock, rosemary sprigs, and red pepper flakes and bring to a simmer, then lower the heat and simmer until the beans are tender, 1 to 1½ hours.

Remove and discard the rosemary. Use a slotted spoon to transfer 1 cup of the beans into a bowl, taking care to include as few vegetables and rosemary needles as possible, and set aside. Using an immersion blender, blend the remaining bean mixture until smooth; or ladle the beans into a standing blender, in batches, and blend until smooth (see Blender Safety, page 75). Strain the mixture through a fine-mesh strainer into a bowl, pressing down on the solids with the ladle to extract as much liquid as possible; discard the solids and return the puree to the pot. Season with salt and pepper and keep warm over low heat.

Heat a medium skillet over medium heat. Pour in the remaining 2 tablespoons olive oil and heat it. Add the remaining garlic and cook, stirring, until lightly toasted, about 4 minutes. Stir in the wine, shrimp, reserved beans, and the tomato and bring to a simmer, then lower the heat and simmer until the shrimp are just cooked through and the wine is reduced by half, about 5 minutes. Stir in the minced rosemary and the parsley and season with salt and pepper.

To serve, divide the shrimp and bean mixture among 4 bowls. Top with the warm soup and finish with a drizzle of extra virgin olive oil.

# GAZPACHO WITH MACKEREL, SEAWEED PESTO, AND CHIVE OIL

SERVES 4

A prime example of free-form contemporary cooking, this soup, dreamt up by Marea's chef di cucina Jared Gadbaw, draws on a variety of influences. The soup itself is modeled on an ajo blanco, a variation of gazpacho made by pureeing almonds and garlic together, which dovetails nicely with the Sicilian tradition of thickening various preparations with ground almonds; the seaweed in the pesto brings a touch of Japanese cuisine to an Italian condiment (it was inspired by the beguiling seaweed fritters served along the Amalfi Coast); and the chive oil is pure modern American cooking.

Ajo blanco is that rare gazpacho that is served warm, and so is this variation.

2 tablespoons olive oil
1 large Spanish onion, cut into ½-inch dice
1 large leek (white and light green parts only), well washed and coarsely chopped
2 shallots, coarsely chopped
3 large garlic cloves, coarsely chopped
1 bay leaf
1 cup slivered blanched almonds, left whole, plus ½ cup slivered blanched almonds, toasted (see page 367) and coarsely chopped
Kosher salt
Pinch of red pepper flakes
4 cups water
1 skin-on mackerel fillet, 10 to 12 ounces
½ cup crème fraîche
½ cup extra virgin olive oil
Seaweed Pesto (page 248)
Chive Oil (page 248)

Heat a large heavy pot over medium-high heat. Add the olive oil and tip and tilt the pot to coat it, heating the oil until it is shimmering and almost smoking. Add the onions, leeks, shallots, and garlic and cook, stirring with a wooden spoon, until softened but not browned, about 4 minutes. Stir in the bay leaf and the 1 cup slivered almonds, season with salt and the red pepper flakes, and add the water. Bring to a simmer, then lower the heat and simmer until the vegetables are very soft and the liquid is slightly reduced, about 40 minutes.

Meanwhile, heat a wide cast-iron skillet over medium-high heat. Add the mackerel, skin side down, and sear until the skin is lightly charred and crispy. Transfer to a cutting board and let cool completely, then cut diagonally into ½-inch-wide pieces.

When the soup is ready, ladle it into a blender, in batches (see Blender Safety, page 75), adding some of the crème fraîche and extra virgin olive oil to each batch, and puree until smooth, then transfer to a bowl. Stir the gazpacho well to blend and season with salt.

Divide the gazpacho among 4 wide shallow bowls and garnish each with a few pieces of mackerel. Sprinkle each portion with a scattering of toasted almonds, add a drizzle of seaweed pesto and chive oil, and serve immediately.

## SEAWEED PESTO

MAKES ABOUT 1½ CUPS

You could also toss this pesto with pasta; for a simple but sublime dish, sauté some sliced garlic in olive oil and toss it with spaghetti, along with a few spoonfuls of the pesto.

¼ cup hijiki seaweed (see Sources, page 379)
1 cup Mushroom Stock (page 371) or store-bought low-sodium mushroom broth
2 tablespoons olive oil
3 large garlic cloves, thinly sliced
1 oil-packed anchovy fillet, minced
2 tablespoons minced fresh chives
2 tablespoons minced fresh flat-leaf parsley
1 cup extra virgin olive oil
Finely grated zest of 1 lemon
Kosher salt
Pinch of cayenne pepper

Put the seaweed in a small heatproof bowl.

Pour the mushroom stock into a medium saucepan and bring to a boil over high heat. Pour the stock over the seaweed and set aside until the seaweed is hydrated, about 20 minutes.

Drain the seaweed in a fine-mesh strainer set over a bowl, pressing down on the solids with a wooden spoon or a ladle to release as much liquid as possible; discard the liquid. Transfer the seaweed to a cutting board and coarsely chop it. Transfer to a small bowl.

Heat a medium heavy sauté pan over medium heat. Add the olive oil and tip and tilt the pan to coat it, heating the oil until it is shimmering and almost smoking. Add the garlic and cook, stirring occasionally, until golden and lightly toasted, about 4 minutes. Set aside to cool.

Add the toasted garlic, anchovy, chives, parsley, extra virgin olive oil, and lemon zest to the seaweed and stir together. Season with salt and the cayenne.

The seaweed pesto can be refrigerated in an airtight container overnight. Let come to room temperature before using.

## CHIVE OIL

MAKES ¼ CUP

2 large bunches of chives, blanched, shocked, and drained (see page 367), then squeezed between paper towels to extract as much water as possible and coarsely chopped
Kosher salt
¼ cup canola oil, chilled

Put the chives in a blender and add an ice cube (this will keep the chives from turning brown when blended). Add a pinch of salt and then, with the motor running, add the canola oil in a thin stream, blending until a smooth green puree forms. Strain the oil through a fine-mesh strainer, coffee filter, or cheesecloth into a bowl.

The chive oil can be refrigerated in an airtight container for up to 2 days.

# CHILLED TOMATO SOUP WITH SHRIMP AND CUCUMBER

SERVES 4

Soup, a small salad, and seafood in one bowl. You can skip the formal step of pouring the soup at the table and compose the bowls in the kitchen, if you like. Note that the soup must be chilled for at least 4 hours.

- 4 medium plum tomatoes, cut into 1-inch dice
- 1 large cucumber, peeled, halved lengthwise, seeded, and cut into 1-inch cubes, plus 1 small cucumber, peeled and sliced lengthwise into ribbons with a vegetable peeler or a mandoline
- 2 medium red bell peppers, cored, seeded, and cut into 1-inch squares
- 1 large garlic clove, minced
- Kosher salt
- Pinch of cayenne pepper
- 2 cups tomato juice
- ½ cup (loosely packed) fresh basil leaves, cut into chiffonade (see page xxx), plus 1 tablespoon chiffonade for garnish
- 3 tablespoons red wine vinegar
- ½ cup plus 2 tablespoons extra virgin olive oil
- 8 ounces large shrimp, peeled and deveined
- ½ cup halved cherry tomatoes
- Freshly ground black pepper
- Nasturtiums, for garnish (optional)

Put the plum tomatoes, diced cucumber, bell peppers, and garlic in a bowl and season with salt and the cayenne. Add the tomato juice, basil, vinegar, and ½ cup of the extra virgin olive oil and stir to incorporate. Cover and refrigerate for 4 to 6 hours.

Meanwhile, fill a medium pot about two-thirds full with water, salt it, and bring to a simmer over medium-high heat. Add the shrimp and cook until firm and pink, 2 to 3 minutes. Drain the shrimp and let cool to room temperature, then transfer to a bowl, cover with plastic wrap, and refrigerate.

When ready to serve, pour the soup into a stand blender and blend just until uniformly smooth (or use an immersion blender and blend right in the bowl); do not overblend.

Put the cucumber ribbons, the remaining basil, and the cherry tomatoes in a small bowl, drizzle with the remaining 2 tablespoons olive oil, and season with salt and black pepper. Toss gently.

Arrange the salad and shrimp in the center of 4 chilled wide shallow bowls. Garnish with nasturtiums, if desired. Pour the soup into a small pitcher or a large measuring cup and carefully pour around the salad and shrimp in each bowl, taking care not to topple them. Serve at once.

# PASTA AND RISOTTO

When I went to work in Italy early in my career, in addition to the Italian language itself, I wanted to become fluent in the language of Italian cuisine. I wanted to be able to express myself on the plate by calling on the existing vocabulary of Italian food—its ingredients, techniques, and traditions—in my own way. From my earliest exposure to real Italian cooking nothing spoke to me quite like pasta, so I suppose it makes perfect sense that pasta has become the medium I'm most known for, the key in which my greatest hits were written.

In addition to my adherence, for the most part, to Italian ingredients, I use the same type of pasta in my contemporary dishes that I do in my traditional cooking, and it's always cooked al dente. And so, while some of these recipes might seem a bit audacious, or call on luxury ingredients, even the most unusual and rarefied of them boast an element of familiarity and comfort. The same is true of the risottos, which are more complex than those in the Classico section but retain the essential charm of more traditional variations.

# POTATO AND TUSCAN KALE AGNOLOTTI

SERVES 6 AS A FIRST COURSE OR 4 AS A MAIN COURSE

Kale has attained newfound popularity in the United States in recent years, hailed for both its appealingly sturdy texture and its nutritional value. It was only a matter of time: The green has been a mainstay of European diets for generations, and other sturdy greens, such as collards, have long been associated with American Southern cooking. Potatoes and greens both show up in a number of ravioli in Italy, including potato ravioli tossed with basil pesto in Tuscany and a spinach and ricotta ravioli in Emilia-Romagna. This agnolotti adapts that tradition to of-the-moment American taste with a potato and kale ravioli made with one of our favorite potato varieties, Yukon Gold.

Note that the filling must be refrigerated for at least 30 minutes before using.

2 pounds Yukon Gold potatoes
2 tablespoons olive oil
3 ounces pancetta or salt pork, cut into ½-inch dice (about ¾ cup)
1 bunch (about 12 ounces) Tuscan kale, stems removed
1 Spanish onion, cut into ⅛-inch dice
2 large garlic cloves, minced
Pinch of red pepper flakes
Kosher salt
Freshly ground black pepper
1 teaspoon minced fresh thyme
1 teaspoon minced fresh rosemary
¼ cup dry white wine
¾ cup freshly grated Parmigiano-Reggiano (about 1½ ounces), plus more for serving
1 large egg, lightly beaten
Pinch of freshly grated nutmeg
All-purpose flour for dusting
Fresh Pasta Sheets (page 72)
Rice flour, for dusting
Tomato and Pork Sauce (page 75)

Put the potatoes in a large pot and cover by 1 inch with cold water. Bring to a simmer over medium-high heat and simmer until the potatoes are easily pierced with a sharp thin-bladed knife, about 20 minutes. Drain the potatoes and let cool slightly.

When they are cool enough to handle, peel the potatoes (the skins should come right off with the aid of a paring knife) and rice them into a bowl, or mash them well with a potato masher.

Heat a large, deep, heavy pot over medium heat. Pour in the olive oil and tip and tilt the pot to coat it, letting the oil warm up. Add the pancetta and cook, stirring occasionally with a wooden spoon, until the pancetta is browned and has rendered much of its fat, about 4 minutes. Add the kale and cook, stirring frequently, until wilted, about 3 minutes. Add the onions, garlic, and red pepper flakes, season with salt and black pepper, and cook, stirring, until the onions have softened but not browned, about 4 minutes. Stir in the thyme and rosemary. Pour in the wine and bring to a simmer over high heat, then lower the heat and simmer until the wine has almost totally evaporated and the onions and kale are tender, about 5 minutes. Remove the pot from the heat and set aside to cool.

Once the kale is cooled, use a slotted spoon to transfer it to a cutting board, saving the cooking liquid. Coarsely chop the kale, then transfer it to the bowl with the potatoes. Add the Parmigiano, egg, and nutmeg and stir until smooth. If the mixture seems dry or crumbly, stir in just enough of the cooking liquid to lightly moisten it.

Spoon the mixture into a pastry bag fitted with a number 7 (⅜-inch) plain tip. (If you do not have a pastry bag, transfer the filling to a large resealable plastic bag, squeeze the air out of the bag, seal it, and snip off a bottom corner to mimic a pastry bag.) Chill the filling in the refrigerator for 30 minutes to 1 hour to firm it.

Set your pasta machine to the thinnest setting and roll the pasta sheets through it a few times, until as thin as possible. Lay the pasta sheets on a floured surface. Use a wheel cutter to cut the pasta sheets into forty to forty-eight 3-inch squares (use a ruler or other straightedge to guide you). Working with 12 squares at a time, and keeping the other squares hydrated under a damp kitchen towel, pipe about 1½ tablespoons of filling into the third of the square closest to you. Fold the square away from you, encasing the filling, then fold it again, like a letter, using your fingers to press out any air. Trim the 2 short sides and the freshly folded long edge with a zigzag cutter, then transfer to the rice-flour-dusted rimmed baking sheet. Repeat with the remaining filling and dough; there may be fewer than 12 squares in the last batch. (The agnolotti can be refrigerated for up to 1 day or frozen for up to 2 months. Wrap the baking sheet in plastic wrap and refrigerate, or freeze the agnolotti on the sheet until frozen hard, then transfer to freezer bags.)

When ready to cook the agnolotti, fill a large pot about two-thirds full with water, salt it liberally, and bring to a gentle boil over medium-high heat. Add the agnolotti to the boiling water and cook until they rise to the surface, 2 to 3 minutes for fresh, or 4 to 5 minute for frozen. Heat the sauce in a medium saucepan over medium heat.

To serve, remove the agnolotti from the pot with a slotted spoon and divide them among plates or wide shallow bowls. Spoon some sauce over each serving and finish with a sprinkling of Parmigiano.

# BAKED CAVATELLI WITH PUREED ZUCCHINI, BUFFALO MOZZARELLA, AND BREAD CRUMBS

SERVES 6 AS AN APPETIZER OR 4 AS A MAIN COURSE

Because they are traditionally paired with hearty sauces, such as the braised lamb neck on page 101, cavatelli are usually served in the fall and winter. This recipe was conceived as a way to use cavatelli in the warmer months, matching it with zucchini, fresh mozzarella, and basil; though baked, the result is so intrinsically light that it feels as if it belongs to the summer.

¼ cup plus 1 tablespoon extra virgin olive oil
2 garlic cloves, 1 minced, 1 thinly sliced
1 small Spanish onion, cut into small dice
3 zucchini (about 1½ pounds total), halved lengthwise, seeds removed, and cut into small dice (about 3 cups)
½ cup Vegetable Stock (page 371)
½ cup fresh basil leaves plus ¼ cup (loosely packed) fresh basil leaves, cut into chiffonade (see page xxx)
Kosher salt
Freshly ground black pepper
1 pound dried cavatelli (penne may be substituted)
1 yellow squash, halved lengthwise, seeds removed, and cut into small dice (about 1 cup)
1 shallot, cut into small dice
8 ounces buffalo mozzarella, drained and cut into small dice
½ cup fresh bread crumbs
Freshly grated Parmigiano-Reggiano cheese (optional)

To make the sauce: Heat a large heavy saucepan over medium-high heat. Add 2 tablespoons of the olive oil and tip and tilt the pan to coat it, heating it until the oil is shimmering and almost smoking. Add the minced garlic, the onions, two thirds of the zucchini, and the stock, bring to a simmer, and simmer until the vegetables are softened, 12 to 15 minutes. Remove the pan from the heat and set aside to cool for about 8 minutes.

Stir the whole basil leaves into the zucchini mixture to wilt them. Transfer the mixture to a blender and puree until smooth. Strain the sauce through a fine-mesh strainer into a bowl and season with salt and pepper. Set aside.

To assemble and bake the pasta: Fill a large pot about two-thirds full with water, salt it liberally, and bring to a boil over high heat. Position a rack in the center of the oven and preheat the oven to 375°F.

Add the pasta to the boiling water and cook until al dente, about 9 minutes. Drain the pasta and set it aside.

Heat a large heavy saucepan over medium-high heat. Pour in the remaining 3 tablespoons olive oil and tip and tilt the pan to coat it. Add the sliced garlic, remaining zucchini, yellow squash, and shallots and cook, stirring with a wooden spoon, until the vegetables are softened but not browned, about 4 minutes. Season with salt and pepper.

Add the sauce to the zucchini mixture and heat until warmed through. Stir in the cavatelli and basil chiffonade, and toss to coat. Pour the pasta into a 9 by 13-inch baking dish. Scatter the diced mozzarella over the pasta and sprinkle the bread crumbs over the top. Cover the dish with aluminum foil and bake for 20 minutes.

Remove the foil and bake until the top is golden brown, about 10 more minutes. Sprinkle with Parmigiano, if desired, and serve.

# TAJARIN WITH WILD MUSHROOMS, BLACK TRUFFLES, AND ANCHOVY

SERVES 6 AS AN APPETIZER OR 4 AS A MAIN COURSE

*Another pasta that grew out of my travels throughout Italy, combining the traditions of two regions: Piedmont's exquisitely thin egg pasta, tajarin (see page 95 for a more traditional treatment), is married with a mushroom-truffle sauce fashioned after the style of Umbria. The inclusion of anchovy is also Umbrian; there it's often stirred into recipes featuring both white and black truffles. The combination of one of the most earthy ingredients with one of the most oceanic might seem surprising, but they come together to produce an intense umami-like effect.*

- Fresh Pasta Sheets (page 72), cut into tajarin (see page 73; store-bought fresh linguine or fettuccine can be substituted)
- ¼ cup olive oil
- 1 pound mixed wild mushrooms, such as cremini, hen-of-the-woods, king oyster, and chanterelle, trimmed and cut into small dice
- Kosher salt
- 2 large garlic cloves, thinly sliced
- 4 oil-packed anchovy fillets, coarsely chopped
- ½ cup dry white wine
- ½ cup cognac or other brandy
- 2 cups Mushroom Stock (page 371)
- ½ cup Chicken Stock (page 374)
- 2 tablespoons cold unsalted butter, cut into 8 cubes
- ¾ cup grated truffled cheese, such as Caseificio, Sottocenere, or Pecorino al tartufo (about 2½ ounces), plus more for serving
- Freshly ground black pepper
- 2 tablespoons extra virgin olive oil
- 1 ounce black truffle

Fill a large pot about two-thirds full with water, salt it liberally, and bring to a boil over high heat. Add the pasta and cook until al dente, 2 to 3 minutes for fresh, or 3 to 4 minutes for frozen. Use a heatproof liquid measuring cup to scoop out and reserve about ½ cup of the cooking liquid, then drain the pasta.

Heat a large wide deep skillet over high heat. Pour in the olive oil and heat the oil until it is shimmering and almost smoking. Add the mushrooms and toss once to coat the mushrooms with the oil, then allow the mushrooms to cook, without stirring, until they have started to brown and soften, 3 to 4 minutes. Toss the mushrooms again and season lightly with salt. Stir in the garlic and cook for 3 minutes, stirring frequently with a wooden spoon to keep the garlic from browning. Stir in the anchovies and use the back of the spoon to mash the anchovies against the bottom of the pan.

Stir in the wine, bring it to a simmer, and simmer and stir until the wine has almost completely evaporated, about 4 minutes. Pour in the cognac, bring it to a simmer, and simmer until the cognac has almost completely evaporated, 3 to 4 minutes. Pour in the mushroom stock, bring it to a simmer, and simmer until the liquid is reduced by half, about 5 minutes. Pour in the chicken stock and simmer for 2 more minutes, then remove the skillet from the heat and cover to keep warm.

Return the pan to the stovetop over medium heat and add the butter to the sauce, a few pieces at a times, stirring until the sauce is completely emulsified. Add the pasta, sprinkle with the cheese, and toss until the cheese melts and the pasta is coated with the sauce. If the sauce seems too thick, thin it with a few drops of the reserved pasta water. Season with salt and pepper.

Divide the pasta among large plates or wide shallow bowls, drizzle with the extra virgin olive oil, and top with more grated cheese. Shave some black truffle over each serving and serve at once.

# SPAGHETTI WITH CRAB AND SEA URCHIN ROE

SERVES 6 AS AN APPETIZER OR 4 AS A MAIN COURSE

In its simplicity, this recalls any number of classic pasta and seafood dishes, including spaghetti with sardines and spaghetti with clams and basil (see page 91). But here the focus is on crabmeat, a prized ingredient in America, and the pairing of it with luxurious sea urchin roe takes this dish to another level entirely. The final scattering of bread crumbs is a traditional touch that needs no updating.

1 pound spaghetti
¼ cup extra virgin olive oil, plus more for serving
4 scallions (white and light green parts only), thinly sliced
3 large garlic cloves, thinly sliced
¼ teaspoon red pepper flakes
1 pound plum tomatoes (3 or 4 tomatoes), cut into ½-inch dice
Kosher salt
½ cup dry white wine
10 ounces (1 ¾ cup) fresh crabmeat, preferably jumbo lump, picked over for shells and cartilage
4 ounces sea urchin roe (see Sources, page 379)
¼ cup Seasoned Toasted Bread Crumbs (page xxix)

Cook the pasta: Fill a large pot two-thirds full with water, salt it liberally, and bring to a boil over high heat. Add the pasta and cook until al dente, about 8 minutes. Use a heatproof liquid measuring cup to scoop out and reserve about ½ cup of the cooking liquid, then drain the pasta.

To make the sauce: Heat a large skillet over medium-high heat. Pour in the olive oil and heat until it is shimmering and almost smoking. Add the scallions, garlic, and red pepper flakes and cook, stirring frequently with a wooden spoon, until the scallions are lightly golden brown, about 1 minute. Stir in the tomatoes and season with salt. Cook, tossing or stirring frequently, until the tomatoes begin to break down, 7 to 8 minutes. Pour in the wine, bring to a simmer, and simmer until the sauce is slightly reduced, 6 to 7 minutes. Stir in the crabmeat and sea urchin roe and season with salt.

Add the pasta to the skillet and toss until well coated with the sauce, adding some of the reserved pasta water if necessary to loosen the sauce. Divide among plates or wide shallow bowls, drizzle with extra virgin olive oil, finish with a scattering of the bread crumbs, and serve.

# RIGATONI WITH SHRIMP AND CUTTLEFISH "SAUSAGE" AND PECORINO FONDUTA

SERVES 6 AS AN APPETIZER OR 4 AS A MAIN COURSE

There's virtually no antecedent for this pasta in the world of Italian cuisine: It began with my observation that shrimp and cuttlefish both have an inherent sweetness. Rather than serve the shellfish in a pasta dish, I decided to grind them and cook them with pepper flakes and garlic to create a sausage effect. The dish also includes a most unconventional cheese sauce. The choice of rigatoni allows the other ingredients to find their way into the center of the pasta in just about every bite.

1 cup heavy cream
1/3 cup finely grated Parmigiano-Reggiano
1/3 cup plus 1/4 cup finely grated Pecorino Romano
1 pound rigatoni
1 pound cleaned cuttlefish, coarsely chopped
1 pound large shrimp, peeled, deveined, and coarsely chopped
1/4 cup extra virgin olive oil, plus more for finishing
1 garlic clove, thinly sliced
2 tablespoons minced leek (white and light green parts only)
Red pepper flakes
1/4 cup dry white wine
1/2 cup Fish Stock (page 373), or as needed
1 tablespoon thinly sliced fresh flat-leaf parsley leaves
Kosher salt
Juice of 1 lemon, or to taste

To make the fonduta: Put the cream in a small heavy saucepan, bring to a simmer over low heat, and reduce by half, about 8 minutes. Whisk in the Parmigiano and 1/3 cup of the Pecorino. Remove the pan from the heat and keep covered and warm.

Fill a large pot about two-thirds full with water, salt it liberally, and bring to a boil over high heat. Add the pasta and cook until al dente, about 9 minutes.

To make the sausage: Put the cuttlefish in the bowl of a food processor and pulse just until coarsely ground, then add the shrimp and pulse a few times to coarsely grind and incorporate it. Set aside.

Heat a large heavy pot over medium heat. Pour in the olive oil and tip and tilt the pot to coat it, heating the oil until it is shimmering and almost smoking. Add the garlic and cook, stirring with a wooden spoon, until softened but not browned, about 2 minutes. Stir in the leeks and cook, stirring occasionally, until softened but not browned, about 3 minutes. Stir in the red pepper flakes and cook for 30 seconds. Stir in the ground shrimp and cuttlefish and cook, using the wooden spoon to break up the mixture, until the shrimp is opaque, about 2 minutes.

When the pasta is done, use a heatproof liquid measuring cup to scoop out and reserve about 1/2 cup of the cooking liquid and drain the pasta.

Pour in the wine and use the wooden spoon to loosen any flavorful bits cooked onto the bottom of the pot. Cook until the pan is almost dry, about 4 minutes, then pour in the stock and bring it to a simmer. Add the fonduta and stir until incorporated.

Add the pasta to the pot, along with the remaining 1/4 cup Pecorino and parsley, and toss well. The sauce should be moist but not soupy. If it is too dry, adjust the consistency with a little of the reserved pasta cooking liquid and/or fish stock; if it is too wet, continue to cook and toss until thickened. Season to taste with salt and lemon juice and finish with a drizzle of olive oil.

Divide the pasta among plates or wide shallow bowls and serve at once.

## COOKING WITH CHEESE

Cheese, usually grated over finished pasta, vegetables, and some meat dishes or served as a coda to a meal in Italy, can also be a potent ingredient in its own right.

When I first arrived in Emilia-Romagna as a young cook, I was almost shocked at how much cheese people there consumed on a daily basis. In addition to grating hard cheeses such as Parmigiano-Reggiano and Pecorino Toscano over soups and pastas, they also ate these and other cheeses at various times of the day, with an affettati misti (see page 13), or alongside fruit at the end of lunch or dinner. Hailing from Wisconsin, America's cheese country, I've always loved cheese, and my affection and appreciation only deepened when I learned more about fine cheeses in the early years of my career. As I became more familiar with Italian food, I was struck that cheese was such a central part of daily life but was rarely cooked into dishes themselves. Breaking that barrier leads to almost limitless possibilities because, considered as an ingredient, cheese is uncommonly complex and complete, adding texture and layers of flavor to a dish.

For example, adding the triple-crème cheese La Tur, via crostini, to a salad of cold duck breast and crushed hazelnuts (page 216) brings a rich, creamy, almost sauce-like addition to the plate. A different effect is conjured up by employing ricotta as a lactic complement to the fresh green flavors in a pea and leek soup (page 240), and yet another by tossing gnocchi with Fontina Fonduta as an accompaniment to braised short ribs (page 337).

Cheese also offers a potent complement to fish and shellfish, which is ironic, because one of the best-known rules of Italian cuisine supposedly forbids such pairings. While that is true in most of Italy's regions, fish and cheese are paired in the south, along La Via Lattea ("Milky Way"), where I first discovered a version of the lobster and burrata dish on page 202. Anchovy and mozzarella also feature prominently in the classic mozzarella en carrozza (page 23) and anchovies are regularly arrayed atop pizzas in the coastal towns along the Amalfi Coast.

The lesson of those dishes is that cheese and fish or shellfish don't just get along well; they can be matches made in heaven. Just consider how the Pecorino fondue enhances the inherent salinity of the shrimp and cuttlefish "sausage" in the rigatoni dish on page 260, or how the smoked ricotta salata brings creaminess, salinity, and smoke to the pasta with Manila clams and broccoli rabe on page 262.

# PACCHERI WITH RICOTTA SALATA, BROCCOLI RABE, AND MANILA CLAMS

SERVES 6 AS AN APPETIZER OR 4 AS A MAIN COURSE

One of the largest pasta shapes, paccheri, a smooth-sided tubular pasta, are about two inches long and an inch or so in diameter, and they are usually served with meat sauces in Italy, especially the Sunday sauces served at large family meals. Here they are the backdrop for a coming together of salty clams, bitter broccoli rabe, and ricotta salata cheese. You want the dish to be moist but not too soupy, and salty but not overwhelmingly so: There's no need to season it with salt, and the cheese should be added judiciously.

- 1 pound paccheri (rigatoni can be substituted)
- 2 tablespoons olive oil
- 3 large garlic cloves, thinly sliced
- 2 pounds Manila clams, scrubbed
- 1 bay leaf
- Pinch of red pepper flakes
- 1 cup dry white wine
- ½ cup thinly sliced leeks (white and light green parts only)
- 4 stalks broccoli rabe, blanched, shocked, and drained (see page 367), and coarsely chopped (about 2 cups)
- 2 tablespoons thinly sliced fresh flat-leaf parsley leaves
- ¼ cup coarsely grated ricotta salata cheese

Fill a large pot about two-thirds full with water, salt it liberally, and bring to a boil over high heat. Add the paccheri and cook until al dente, about 9 minutes.

Meanwhile, heat a large heavy pot over medium heat and pour in the olive oil, tipping and tilting the pot to coat it and heating the oil until shimmering and almost smoking. Add the garlic and cook, stirring, until softened but not browned, about 2 minutes. Stir in the clams, bay leaf, and red pepper flakes, pour in the wine, cover the pot, and cook until the clams begin to open, about 2 minutes. Gently stir in the leeks and broccoli rabe, cover, and cook until the leeks are wilted and translucent and the clams have opened, about 3 minutes. Remove and discard the bay leaf and any clams that did not open.

Use a heatproof liquid measuring cup to scoop out and reserve about ½ cup of the pasta cooking liquid and drain the pasta. Add the pasta to the sauce and toss to combine, adding a little of the reserved pasta liquid if the pasta seems dry.

Use tongs to divide the pasta and clams among wide shallow bowls, then spoon or ladle some broth over each serving. Scatter some parsley and ricotta salata over each portion and serve.

# STROZZAPRETI WITH CALAMARI, GUANCIALE, AND PISTACHIOS

SERVES 4 AS A MAIN COURSE

Pork and shellfish have been cooked together for generations in countries such as Portugal, where the combination defines the seafood stew cataplana, among other dishes. Yet the pairing is all but unheard of in Italy, despite its abundance of pork and shellfish. Here I combine calamari and guanciale (spiced pork jowl) in a dish of strozzapreti, the famous "priest strangler" pasta of Emilia-Romagna, and the result seems perfectly natural, the fat and spice of the guanciale flavoring the rather neutral calamari.

1 pound cleaned calamari, bodies and tentacles separated
Kosher salt
2 tablespoons olive oil
4 ounces thinly sliced guanciale, cut into ½-inch-wide strips
3 large garlic cloves, thinly sliced
½ small Spanish onion, cut into ¼-inch dice
Red pepper flakes
½ cup dry white wine
1 pound Strozzapreti (page 84; gemelli can be substituted)
1 cup Fish Stock (page 373)
1 teaspoon thinly sliced fresh mint leaves
1 tablespoon thinly sliced fresh flat-leaf parsley leaves
2 tablespoons extra virgin olive oil
3 tablespoons coarsely chopped pistachios
Freshly ground black pepper

Use a sharp knife to slice each calamari body open from top to bottom and lay it out flat on your cutting board. Gently score the surface of each body with parallel lines about ¼ inch apart, taking care not to cut through the flesh, then repeat, scoring lines perpendicular to the first set, to create a crosshatch pattern. Cut the bodies into triangles with 1½-inch-long sides. Slice any large clusters of tentacles in half.

Fill a large pot about two-thirds full with water, salt it liberally, and bring to a boil over high heat.

Meanwhile, line a large plate with paper towels. Heat a large skillet over medium heat. Add the olive oil and tip and tilt the pan to coat it, letting the oil warm up. Add the guanciale and cook, stirring with a wooden spoon, until it begins to render some of its fat but has not started to crisp, about 4 minutes. Use tongs or a slotted spoon to transfer the guanciale to the paper-towel-lined plate.

Add the garlic and onions to the pan and cook, stirring occasionally, until softened but not browned, about 4 minutes. Add the calamari and sauté until opaque, about 5 minutes. Season with salt and red pepper flakes. Pour in the wine and stir with the wooden spoon to loosen any flavorful bits cooked onto the bottom of the pan. Cook until the wine has almost completely evaporated, about 4 minutes.

Meanwhile, when the water comes to a boil, add the pasta and cook until al dente, about 2 minutes for fresh, or 4 minutes for frozen. Use a heatproof liquid measuring cup to scoop out and reserve about ½ cup of the cooking liquid and drain the pasta.

Stir the stock into the sauce, bring to a simmer, and simmer until the sauce is nicely thickened and the flavors are balanced, about 4 minutes. Return the guanciale to the skillet, add the pasta, and cook, stirring constantly, for 1 minute, then stir in the mint and parsley. Drizzle with the extra virgin olive oil and sprinkle in 2 tablespoons of the pistachios. Season with salt and pepper and toss well.

Divide the pasta among plates or wide shallow bowls. Top with the remaining tablespoon of pistachios and serve immediately.

# AMATRICIANA RAVIOLI WITH CACIO E PEPE SAUCE

SERVES 6 AS AN APPETIZER OR 4 AS A MAIN COURSE

Starkly beautiful and almost deliriously decadent, this pasta dish unites two of Rome's most famous flavored pastas: A variation on amatriciana sauce (see page 94) is augmented with sausage and ricotta cheese to bind it into a ravioli filling, and then the ravioli is sauced with cacio e pepe, a creamy emulsion of cheese with abundant flecks of black pepper.

- 1 tablespoon olive oil
- 1 pound sweet Italian sausage, removed from its casings
- 1 cup diced (small dice) Spanish onion
- 3 garlic cloves, minced
- 2 tablespoons tomato paste
- 1 15-ounce can crushed tomatoes, preferably Italian San Marzano or organic
- ½ cup fresh ricotta cheese
- 1 cup finely grated Pecorino Romano
- 1 large egg, lightly beaten
- 2 tablespoons thinly sliced fresh flat-leaf parsley leaves
- Fresh Pasta Sheets (page 72)
- All-purpose flour, for dusting
- Rice flour, for dusting
- Kosher salt
- ¼ cup heavy cream
- ¼ cup Chicken Stock (page 374) or store-bought low-sodium chicken broth
- ¾ cup finely grated Parmigiano-Reggiano (about 1½ ounces)
- Freshly ground black pepper
- 4 tablespoons unsalted butter, at room temperature

To make the filling: Heat a wide heavy sauté pan over medium heat. Add the olive oil and tip and tilt the pan to coat it, warming the oil. Add the sausage and cook, breaking it up with a wooden spoon and stirring occasionally, until browned all over, about 7 minutes. Using a slotted spoon, transfer the sausage to a plate.

Add the onions and garlic to the fat in the pan and cook, stirring, until softened but not browned, about 3 minutes. Return the sausage to the pan, add the tomato paste, stirring to coat the other ingredients with the paste, and cook until it turns a shade darker, about 2 minutes. Stir in the tomatoes and bring to a simmer, then lower the heat and simmer, stirring occasionally, until the mixture is moist but not soupy, about 5 minutes. Remove the pan from the heat and let cool.

Stir the ricotta, ¼ cup of the Pecorino, egg, and parsley into the sausage mixture.

To make the ravioli: Set your pasta machine to the thinnest setting and roll the pasta sheets through. Fill a spray bottle with water and set it so that it will produce a fine mist when the trigger is pressed.

Lay the pasta sheets on a work surface dusted with all-purpose flour. Use a wheel cutter or sharp chef's knife to cut the pasta sheets into forty to forty-eight 3-inch squares. (Use a ruler or other straightedge to guide you.) Arrange 12 squares of pasta on the floured work surface, keeping the remaining squares under a damp kitchen towel. Spoon about 1½ tablespoons of filling into the center of each square. Hold the spray bottle a foot or two above the pasta and press once to release a mist of water over the squares. Fold one half of each square over the filling, aligning the edges, and tightly seal the 3 open edges. Trim the freshly sealed edges with a zigzag pasta cutter and transfer the ravioli to a rice-flour-dusted rimmed baking sheet. Repeat with the remaining dough squares and filling; you may have fewer than a dozen squares in the last batch. (The ravioli can be refrigerated for up to 2 days or frozen for up to 2 months. Wrap the baking sheet in plastic wrap and refrigerate, or freeze the ravioli on the sheet until frozen hard, then transfer to freezer bags.)

When ready to cook the ravioli, fill a large pot about two-thirds full with water, salt it liberally, and bring to a gentle boil over medium-high heat.

Meanwhile, make the sauce: Combine the cream and stock in a small pot and bring to a simmer over medium heat. Put an immersion blender in the pot and, with the blender running, sprinkle in the Parmigiano and remaining ¾ cup Pecorino, blending until a smooth sauce forms. Season with salt and a generous grinding of black pepper.

Add the ravioli to the boiling water and cook until they float to the surface, 2 to 3 minutes for fresh, or 4 to 5 minutes for frozen. Carefully drain the ravioli, return them to the pot, and toss with the butter to coat.

Use a kitchen spoon to divide the ravioli among plates or wide shallow bowls. Spoon some sauce over each serving and finish with more freshly ground black pepper. Serve.

# EGG RAVIOLO WITH CHANTERELLES, BASIL, AND TOMATO CONFIT

SERVES 4 AS AN APPETIZER

An aristocratic and visually arresting dish—a single, saucer-size raviolo filled with an egg yolk and bedecked with red, green, and golden accompaniments—this owes more than a passing acknowledgment to San Domenico restaurant, where they still serve a version today. The moment of truth is when the raviolo is cut open and the luscious, golden, molten yolk oozes out, creating a sauce as good as that produced by any recipe.

This is a perfect dish for special occasions.

¼ cup fresh basil leaves, blanched, shocked, and drained (see page 367), plus ½ cup (loosely packed) leaves for garnish
2 tablespoons mascarpone cheese
1¼ cups (10 ounces) ricotta cheese
1 tablespoon finely grated Parmigiano-Reggiano, plus more for serving
1 large egg
Kosher salt
Freshly ground black pepper
Rice flour, for dusting
All-purpose flour, for dusting
2 Fresh Pasta Sheets (page 72), rolled through the thinnest setting, or 8 ounces store-bought fresh pasta sheets
4 large egg yolks
2 tablespoons unsalted butter
8 ounces chanterelle mushrooms
1 cup Tomato Confit (page 369)
½ cup Parmigiano Cream (page 214)

Put the blanched basil and the mascarpone in a blender and blend until very smooth. Transfer to a medium bowl and fold in the ricotta, Parmigiano, and egg. Season with salt and pepper. Transfer the mixture to a pastry bag fitted with a number 7 (⅜-inch) plain tip. (If you do not have a pastry bag, transfer the filling to a large resealable plastic bag, squeeze the air out of the bag, seal, and snip off a bottom corner to mimic a pastry bag.)

Line a rimmed baking sheet with parchment paper and lightly dust with rice flour. Lightly dust a work surface with all-purpose flour and lay the pasta sheets on it. Use a pasta cutter to cut out eight 6-inch squares, keeping the other squares hydrated under a damp kitchen towel. Pipe the filling onto 4 of the squares, starting about 2 inches from the edges and piping it in a circle, to create a receptacle for the egg yolk. Use a spoon to carefully add 1 egg yolk to the center of the filling on each pasta square, without breaking the yolks, and season the yolks with salt and pepper. Use a pastry brush to lightly brush the edges of each square with water, then place the remaining squares on top. Use your fingertips to press the edges of the pasta together, pressing out the air and sealing in the filling. Trim the edges of each square with a zigzag pasta wheel and set on the prepared baking sheet.

Fill a large pot about two-thirds full with water, salt it liberally, and bring to a boil over high heat, then lower the heat so the water is gently simmering. Add the ravioli and cook until they rise to the surface of the water, about 4 minutes. Use a slotted spoon to transfer them to a bowl.

Heat a heavy sauté pan over medium-high heat. Add the butter, melt it, and heat until foaming. Add the chanterelles, season lightly with salt, and cook, stirring, just until tender, 3 to 4 minutes. Add the tomato confit and warm through, about 1 minute. Remove from the heat.

Transfer the ravioli to serving bowls and top with the mushrooms and tomato confit. Spoon some Parmigiano cream around the raviolo on each plate and serve.

## GRAMIGNA WITH DUCK SAUSAGE AND BRUSSELS SPROUTS

SERVES 6 AS AN APPETIZER OR 4 AS A MAIN COURSE

Gramigna is typically served with a hearty, Bolognese-style sauce (such as the sausage and cream with which it's tossed in the recipe on page 97). But here it's combined with a light duck sausage sauce that's bound with a modicum of chicken stock and a grating of Parmigiano-Reggiano. The addition of shaved Brussels sprouts adds color and texture.

If you've never made sausage, there's nothing to be afraid of: This recipe doesn't ask you to stuff the meat into casings, merely to grind it and combine it with a handful of other ingredients. If you don't own a meat grinder, ask your butcher to grind the meat for you. Note that the duck sausage and pork fat must be frozen for 1 hour and the sausage mixture must be chilled for at least 2 hours.

- 1 pound boneless duck legs, cut into 1-inch dice
- 4 ounces pork fat, cut into ½-inch dice
- Kosher salt
- Freshly ground black pepper
- ¼ cup dry red wine
- 3 large garlic cloves, 1 minced, 2 thinly sliced
- Freshly grated nutmeg
- 3 tablespoons olive oil
- 1 Spanish onion, cut into ¼-inch dice
- 10 fresh sage leaves, thinly sliced
- ½ cup dry Marsala or sherry
- 2 cups (loosely packed) shaved Brussels sprouts (about 16 sprouts) ideally shaved on a mandoline, but a sharp heavy knife can also be used
- About ¾ cup Chicken Stock (page 374)
- 1 pound fresh gramigna pasta (see Sources, page 379; dried penne or mezze rigatoni can be substituted)
- A wedge of Parmigiano-Reggiano, for grating

To make the sausage: Put the duck meat and pork fat in a bowl and chill in the freezer for 1 hour.

Remove the bowl from the freezer, transfer the duck to another bowl, and season with 2 teaspoons salt and ½ teaspoon pepper. Process the duck two times through the medium die of a meat grinder and place in the bowl of a stand mixer, then process the pork fat in the same manner and add it to the bowl. Add the wine, minced garlic, and a pinch of nutmeg. Fit the mixer with the paddle attachment, attach the bowl, and mix on low speed until you have a uniformly moist mixture. (You can also knead the mixture with clean hands.) Cover the bowl with plastic wrap and chill the mixture in the refrigerator until very cold, at least 2 hours, or up to 24 hours.

When ready to prepare the dish, remove the bowl from the refrigerator and let the sausage come to room temperature.

Fill a large pot about two-thirds full with water, salt it liberally, and bring to a boil over high heat.

Meanwhile, heat a wide sauté pan over medium-high heat. Pour in the olive oil, tipping and tilting the pan to coat it and heating the oil until it is shimmering and almost smoking. Add the sausage and cook, using a wooden spoon to break up the meat, until browned, about 7 minutes. Add the onions and sliced garlic and cook, stirring, until softened but not browned, about 4 minutes. Stir in the sage, then pour in the Marsala and use the wooden spoon to loosen any flavorful bits cooked onto the bottom of the pan. Bring to a simmer and cook until the Marsala has almost evaporated, 6 to 7 minutes. Add the Brussels sprouts and season with salt and pepper. Stir in ½ cup of the stock and cover the pan with a lid. Cook until the Brussels sprouts are softened, 4 to 5 minutes, adding more stock if necessary to keep the sprouts from drying out.

When the water comes to a boil, add the pasta and cook until al dente, about 3 minutes for fresh, or 10 minutes for dried. Use a heatproof liquid measuring cup to scoop out and reserve about ½ cup of the cooking liquid and drain the pasta.

Add the pasta to the sauce along with some grated Parmigiano and toss, adding a little of the cooking liquid if necessary to keep the mixture nicely moist.

Divide the pasta among large plates or wide shallow bowls, finish with a grating of Parmigiano and a few grinds of black pepper, and serve.

## TROFIE WITH SEAFOOD RAGÙ AND TOASTED BREAD CRUMBS

SERVES 6 AS AN APPETIZER OR 4 AS A MAIN COURSE

This simple seafood pasta, fashioned after the style of Liguria, brings together fresh squid ink pasta and a quick sauté of shrimp, scallops, and squid, punched up with garlic, chiles, white wine, and a pinch of Espelette pepper. To me, it's the epitome of seaside cooking: light, fresh, and quick.

Kosher salt
2 tablespoons olive oil
1 garlic clove, thinly sliced
8 ounces large shrimp, peeled, deveined, and cut into ¼-inch dice
8 ounces cleaned calamari, bodies and tentacles, cut into ¼-inch dice
4 ounces sea scallops, cut into ½-inch dice
¼ cup dry white wine
Pinch of Espelette pepper
½ cup Shrimp Stock (page 372)
Trofie (recipe follows; store-bought squid ink linguine can be substituted)
1 tablespoon unsalted butter
¼ cup thinly sliced fresh herbs, ideally a mix of basil, tarragon, and chives
½ lemon
1 tablespoon extra virgin olive oil
2 tablespoons Seasoned Toasted Bread Crumbs (page xxix)

Fill a large pot two-thirds full with water and season liberally with salt. Bring to a boil over high heat.

Meanwhile, heat a large heavy skillet over medium-high heat. Add the olive oil and tip and tilt the pan to coat it, heating the oil until it is shimmering and almost smoking. Add the garlic and cook, stirring with a wooden spoon, until softened but not browned, about 2 minutes. Add the shrimp, calamari, and scallops and cook until the shrimp is firm and pink and the scallops and calamari are opaque, 2 to 3 minutes. Add the wine, bring to a simmer, and simmer until the wine has almost completely evaporated, about 4 minutes. Add the Espelette pepper and shrimp stock, bring to a simmer, and simmer until slightly reduced, about 2 minutes.

When the water comes to a boil, add the pasta and cook until it rises to the surface, 2 minutes for fresh, or 3 to 4 minutes for frozen.

Drain the pasta and add to the skillet, tossing to combine it with the seafood. Add the butter, herbs, a few drops of lemon juice, and the extra virgin olive oil and toss again.

Divide the pasta among plates or wide shallow bowls, top with the bread crumbs, and serve.

### TROFIE

MAKES ABOUT 1 POUND

This pasta, similar in shape to strozzapreti, can also be served tossed with olive oil, garlic, and red pepper flakes or with Puttanesca Sauce (see page 77).

2¼ cups 00 flour or King Arthur Italian-style flour, plus more for dusting
⅔ cup water
2 teaspoons olive oil
1 tablespoon squid ink (see Sources, page 379)
Pinch of kosher salt
Rice flour, for dusting

Put the 00 flour, water, olive oil, squid ink, and salt in the bowl of a stand mixer fitted with the dough hook. Mix, starting on low speed and gradually increasing to medium, until the ingredients come together in a ball of dough. Remove the bowl from the machine, cover with a damp towel, and let the dough rest for 1 hour.

Lightly flour a work surface and rolling pin and roll the dough out into an even thickness of ⅛ inch. (This can also be done using a hand-crank pasta machine, but because the pieces will be twisted, it's not essential that the pasta be perfectly smooth here.)

Use a wheel cutter to cut the dough into ½-inch-wide strips. Working with one strip at a time, roll it between your fingers, twist the top 3 inches, tear off, and transfer to a rice-flour-dusted rimmed baking sheet. Continue to twist and tear, making about 8 trofie from each strip. The trofie can be refrigerated for up to 1 day or frozen for up to 2 months. Wrap the baking sheet in plastic wrap and refrigerate, or freeze the trofie on the sheet until frozen hard, then transfer to freezer bags.

## FINISHING WITH CRUNCH

Textures are often overshadowed by flavors in discussions of what makes a dish complete, but they're almost as important, and one of the most crucial textural components is crunch.

Many of my contemporary recipes include a crunchy element. Often it's a topping of toasted bread crumbs or crushed nuts. In other dishes, it's more subtle, such as the sprinkling of flaky sea salt that tops several of the crudo dishes. And in others still, it's more dramatic, such as fried slivers of sunchoke (see page 189).

There's not a lot of precedence for this in Italian cuisine, although I vividly remember tucking into my first-ever serving of spaghetti con le sarde (spaghetti with sardines) while traveling in Sicily with my wife, Giovanna, and being taken with the topping of toasted bread crumbs. More recently, our restaurant Al Molo has given me the opportunity to visit Hong Kong, a trip I often complement with jaunts to other Asian cities, and I've noted the prevalence of a crunchy element atop many iconic dishes there, such as the ground peanuts that are scattered over pad thai and several salads of the region.

In all of these instances, the crunch reminds me of nothing so much as nuts on a sundae, something that takes a composition that feels complete and satisfying and adds a fun final flourish that, in its own way, keeps you coming back for more. Just as the presence of acid (see page 211) can prevent a dish from becoming monotonous, crunch can make it more compelling: Think of how difficult it is to resist eating more nuts or potato chips once you've had your first bite.

From a practical standpoint, one of the most appealing aspects of crunch is that it's relatively easy to incorporate it into your cooking. Where a flavor component such as acid requires certain careful decisions—whether to use lemon juice, vinegar, or wine, for example, and how much—generally crunch is more forgiving. Often more than one option will work on a given dish. That said, I do follow a few general guidelines, such as finishing both raw and cooked fish with flaky sea salt (though I use crushed almonds for the shrimp tartare on page 201); topping pastas with bread crumbs or nuts; and complementing dishes that include a creamy or pureed element with larger garnishes such as the garlic chips that adorn the snail risotto with garlic cream on page 287.

# FUSILLI WITH RED WINE–BRAISED OCTOPUS AND BONE MARROW

SERVES 6 AS AN APPETIZER OR 4 AS A MAIN COURSE

This pasta dish, served at Marea, might be the most popular one I've made to date, which is remarkable when you consider that octopus and bone marrow are not especially familiar to American diners. But the way they interact here is sublime, and another argument for the marriage of meat and marine, with the red wine and tomato sauce offering a suitably robust backdrop.

I have to credit one of my chefs, Gordon Finn: Having traveled and cooked in Italy, and being inspired by a cookbook he was reading at the time, he pulled some ingredients from the mise en place at Convivio, most spectacularly, the inspired combination of octopus and bone marrow, and created the template for this pasta. We honed it together in the following weeks to create the version that we serve today.

A note on cooking the bone marrow: Be sure to get your pan very hot, so the marrow sears rather than melts.

¼ cup olive oil
1 large Spanish onion, cut into ¼-inch dice
1 large celery stalk, trimmed and cut into ¼-inch dice
1 large carrot, coarsely grated on a box grater
3 large garlic cloves, thinly sliced
1 bay leaf, preferably fresh
4 thyme sprigs
1½ pounds baby octopus, beaks removed, tentacles halved crosswise, heads coarsely chopped
1 cup dry red wine
3¼ cups tomato puree (from 1 28-ounce can)
Kosher salt
Freshly ground black pepper
Red pepper flakes
8 ounces bone marrow, cut into 1-inch dice (see To Obtain Bone Marrow, page 368)
1 pound dried fusilli (mezze rigatoni can be substituted)
2 tablespoons Seasoned Toasted Bread Crumbs (page xxix)

Heat a deep heavy skillet over medium-high heat. Pour in the olive oil and tip and tilt the pan to coat it, heating the oil until it is shimmering and almost smoking. Add the onions, celery, carrots, and garlic and cook, stirring with a wooden spoon, until softened but not browned, about 4 minutes. Stir in the bay leaf and thyme, add the octopus, and cook, stirring occasionally, until the octopus is opaque and begins to give off its liquid, about 5 minutes.

Pour in the wine, bring to a boil, and cook for 30 seconds, then stir in the tomato puree and season with salt, black pepper, and red pepper flakes. Bring the sauce to a simmer, cover the skillet, and cook until the octopus is tender to the tines of a fork, about 1 hour; check the liquid periodically to be sure that it is just barely simmering—you are looking for a slight, almost imperceptible bubbling on the surface. If it is not simmering at all, raise the heat slightly; if it's simmering too assertively, lower the heat slightly. Use tongs or a slotted spoon to fish out and discard the thyme and bay leaf. Set aside. (The sauce can be made to this point, cooled, and refrigerated in an airtight container for up to 2 days. When ready to proceed, reheat it in a skillet over medium heat.)

Line a plate with paper towels. Season the bone marrow with salt and black pepper. Heat a medium skillet over high heat. When the skillet is very hot, add the bone marrow and sear it, stirring vigorously with a wooden spoon. Sear evenly all over, about 1 minute. Carefully transfer the marrow to the paper-towel-lined plate; reserve any liquefied bone marrow in a small bowl.

Fill a large pot about two-thirds full with water, salt it liberally, and bring to a boil over high heat. Add the pasta and cook until al dente, about 7 minutes.

Use a heatproof liquid measuring cup to scoop out and reserve about ½ cup of the cooking liquid and drain the pasta.

Meanwhile, bring the sauce to a simmer. Stir in the reserved bone marrow, then add the pasta and stir until well incorporated. Gently stir in the reserved melted bone marrow, if you have it, and season with salt and pepper.

Divide the pasta and sauce among large plates or wide shallow bowls, sprinkle with bread crumbs, and serve immediately.

# LUMACHE WITH BRAISED LAMB NECK AND FAVA BEANS

SERVES 6 AS AN APPETIZER OR 4 AS A MAIN COURSE

Cooked in the style of Molise, with white wine and no tomato, braised lamb neck proves an apt co-star for fava beans in this springtime dish, a modern riff on the pasta recipe on page 101. If possible, use a peppery extra virgin olive oil to complement the hearty lamb and gentle favas.

¼ cup canola oil
1 bone-in lamb neck, about 2½ pounds, blotted dry with paper towels
Kosher salt
Freshly ground black pepper
2 garlic cloves, minced
1 Spanish onion, minced
1 carrot, minced
1 celery stalk, trimmed and minced
2 oil-packed anchovy fillets, minced
1 cup dry white wine
1 rosemary sprig
1 sage sprig
1 bay leaf, preferably fresh
Pinch of red pepper flakes
4 cups Chicken Stock (page 374), Vegetable Stock (page 371), or store-bought low-sodium chicken or vegetable broth, plus more as needed
1 pound fava beans in the pod, shelled
1 pound dried lumache or cavatappi pasta
¼ cup extra virgin olive oil
A wedge of Oro Antico cheese, or Pecorino Romano

Position a rack in the center of the oven and preheat the oven to 350°F.

Heat a Dutch oven or other large heavy pot over medium-high heat. Add 2 tablespoons of the canola oil and tip and tilt the pot to coat it, heating the oil until it is shimmering and almost smoking. Season the lamb neck with salt and pepper, add to the pot, and brown well on all sides, about 10 minutes. Use tongs to transfer the neck to a plate and set it aside.

Add the remaining 2 tablespoons canola oil to the pot and heat it. Add the garlic, onions, carrots, celery, and anchovies and cook, stirring and breaking the anchovies up with a wooden spoon, until the vegetables are softened but not browned, about 4 minutes. Return the lamb neck to the pot and stir to coat it with the soffritto. Add the wine, stirring with the wooden spoon to loosen any flavorful bits cooked onto the bottom of the pot, then bring to a simmer and simmer until the wine has almost completely evaporated, about 5 minutes. Stir in the rosemary, sage, bay leaf, and red pepper flakes, add the stock, and bring it to a simmer.

Cover the pot and place in the oven. Braise until the lamb is tender to the tines of a fork and almost falling off the bone, 2 to 2½ hours; check the liquid periodically to be sure that it is just barely simmering—you are looking for a slight, almost imperceptible bubbling on the surface. If it is not simmering, raise the heat to 375°F; if it's simmering too assertively, lower the heat to 325°F. When you check on the liquid, baste the neck with it. If the level of the braising liquid falls below halfway up the sides of the neck or the liquid starts to become syrupy, stir in more stock.

Meanwhile, prepare the fava beans: Fill a large pot about two-thirds full with water, salt it liberally, and bring to a boil over high heat. Fill a medium bowl halfway with ice water. Add the favas to the boiling water and blanch for 1 minute. Drain and transfer to the ice water to stop the cooking and preserve their color. Allow to cool completely, then drain and force the beans from their pale skins by pinching the skin between your thumb and forefinger.

Fill the pot with fresh water, salt it liberally, and bring it to a boil.

When the lamb is done, remove the pot from the oven and carefully remove the lamb; keep the pot warm over very low heat. Let the lamb rest until cool enough to handle, then pull the meat from the neck, discarding the bones, and cut the meat into bite-size pieces. Return the meat to the vegetables and sauce in the pot and stir to coat with the sauce.

Meanwhile, add the pasta to the boiling water and cook until al dente, about 8 minutes. Drain the pasta, transfer to a medium mixing bowl, and toss with 2 tablespoons of the olive oil.

To serve, toss the pasta with the ragù. Add the favas and toss again. Divide the pasta among plates or bowls, drizzle with the remaining 2 tablespoons olive oil, and finish with a few grinds of black pepper and shards of the cheese.

# RICOTTA AND SWISS CHARD TORTELLI WITH WILD MUSHROOMS AND BLACK TRUFFLE–VEAL SAUCE

SERVES 6 AS AN APPETIZER OR 4 AS A MAIN COURSE

Ricotta-and-spinach-filled pastas, such as ravioli or tortelli, are a homemade convenience food in Italy, pulled from freezers and cooked on a moment's notice, usually sauced with butter and sage. (See page 280 for a more traditional recipe.) In this recipe, the spinach is replaced with Swiss chard, and the tortelli are sauced with a rich and sophisticated veal stock reduction. The dish is made all the more special with a last-second addition of shaved black truffle.

- 2 tablespoons olive oil
- 3 large garlic cloves, smashed with the side of a chef's knife and peeled
- 1 pound mixed wild mushrooms, such as cremini, chanterelle, hen-of-the-woods, and black trumpet, trimmed and minced
- Kosher salt
- Freshly ground black pepper
- 1 cup dry white wine
- 4 cups Veal Stock (page 375)
- 1 rosemary sprig
- 2 tablespoons unsalted butter, at room temperature
- Ricotta and Swiss Chard Tortelli (page 280)
- 1 ounce black truffle
- 1 teaspoon fresh thyme leaves
- A wedge of Parmigiano-Reggiano, for grating

Heat a large heavy skillet over medium-high heat. Pour in the olive oil and tip and tilt the pan to coat it, heating the oil until it is shimmering and almost smoking. Add the garlic and cook, stirring frequently with a wooden spoon, until softened and just beginning to brown, about 2 minutes. Stir in the mushrooms, season with salt and pepper, and cook just until the mushrooms begin to soften and give off some liquid, about 2 minutes.

Raise the heat to high and stir in the wine. Bring the mixture to a simmer, lower the heat, and cook until the liquid is reduced by half, about 6 minutes. Pour in the stock, add the rosemary sprig, and bring the liquid to a boil over high heat. Lower the heat and gently simmer the sauce until it has thickened enough to coat the back of a spoon, about 45 minutes. Use tongs or a slotted spoon to fish out and remove the rosemary. Season the sauce with salt and pepper, remove from the heat, and cover to keep warm. Whisk in 1 tablespoon of the butter.

Fill a large pot about two-thirds full with water, salt it liberally, and bring to a boil over high heat. Add the pasta and cook until the tortelli rise to the surface, 2 to 3 minutes for fresh, or 4 to 5 minutes for frozen. Carefully drain the pasta and return it to the pot. Add the remaining tablespoon of butter and gently toss to melt the butter and coat the tortelli with it.

Spoon some mushrooms and sauce into each wide shallow bowl and shave some truffle over the mushrooms. Divide the tortelli among the bowls. Finish with a scattering of the thyme and a grating of Parmigiano and serve.

## RICOTTA AND SWISS CHARD TORTELLI

SERVES 6 AS AN APPETIZER OR 4 AS A MAIN COURSE

For a more traditional treatment of this tortelli, sauce it with a reduction of heavy cream, adding some finely diced prosciutto just before tossing, or ladle some beef ragù (page 99) into serving bowls, top with the tortelli, and finish with a grating of Parmigiano-Reggiano.

1 pound Swiss chard, stalks removed and discarded, tough center ribs cut out, leaves blanched, shocked, and drained (see page 367), then squeezed free of excess liquid, and coarsely chopped
1¼ cups (about 10 ounces) fresh whole-milk ricotta cheese
¾ cup freshly grated Parmigiano-Reggiano (about 1½ ounces)
1 large egg, lightly beaten
Pinch of freshly grated nutmeg
Kosher salt
Freshly ground black pepper
Fresh Pasta Sheets (page 72)
Rice flour, for dusting the baking surface
All-purpose flour, for dusting the work surface

Put the chard, ricotta, Parmigiano, egg, and nutmeg in a medium mixing bowl, season with salt and pepper, and stir together until well blended. Set aside.

Line a rimmed baking sheet with parchment paper and lightly dust it with rice flour.

Set your pasta machine to the thinnest setting and roll the pasta sheets through it. Lay the pasta sheets on a work surface dusted with all-purpose flour. Use a wheel cutter or sharp chef's knife to cut the pasta sheets into forty to forty-eight 3-inch squares. (Use a ruler or other straightedge to guide you.) Arrange 12 squares on the floured work surface, keeping the remaining squares hydrated under a damp towel. Spoon about 1 tablespoon of filling into the center of each square. Use a pastry brush or a clean finger to brush the edges with water. (I don't use a spray bottle for this recipe because the cheese filling is especially delicate and could become watery.) One at a time, place a filling-topped square in the palm of your hand with one corner of the square facing you. Fold the corner over the filling to make a triangle, pressing tightly to seal the edges. Then bring the two short ends of the triangle to a point, crimp them together, and transfer to a rice-flour-dusted baking sheet. Repeat with the remaining pasta squares and filling. (The tortelli can be refrigerated for up to 2 days or frozen for up to 2 months. Wrap the baking sheet in plastic wrap and refrigerate, or freeze the tortelli on the sheet until frozen hard, then transfer to freezer bags.)

When ready to cook the tortelli, fill a large pot about two-thirds full with water, salt it liberally, and bring to a boil over high heat. Lower the heat slightly so the water is at a gentle boil and gingerly deposit the tortelli in the water, a few at a time. Stir carefully once to keep them from sticking together, taking care not to break them, and cook until they float to the surface, 2 to 3 minutes for fresh, or 4 to 5 minutes for frozen. Remove with a slotted spoon, letting the excess water run off, and transfer to a bowl, or very gently drain in a colander.

# AGNOLOTTI WITH PARMIGIANO CREAM, BUTTERNUT SQUASH PUREE, AND WHITE TRUFFLE

SERVES 6 AS AN APPETIZER OR 4 AS A MAIN COURSE

Veal-Stuffed Agnolotti (page 103), one of the simplest, most unadorned pastas in Classico, becomes the center of dramatic attention in this modern spectacle of a dish. Any of the three distinct yet complementary components would have been enough to take the agnolotti to another level, but when all three meet in a mouthful, there's an unforgettable interplay of salty, sweet, and earthy effects.

Note that the filling mixture must be refrigerated for 1 hour before using.

¼ cup canola oil
6 tablespoons unsalted butter
1 pound skinless, boneless chicken thighs, cut into 1-inch cubes
12 ounces boneless veal breast or shoulder, cut into 1-inch cubes
1 large Spanish onion, cut into ¼-inch dice
1 celery stalk, trimmed and cut into ¼-inch dice
1 small leek (white and light green parts only), well washed and cut into ¼-inch dice
2 garlic cloves, 1 smashed with the side of a chef's knife and peeled, 1 thinly sliced
¼ cup long-grain white rice
1 cup dry red wine
About 4 cups Dark Chicken Stock (page 374)
An herb sachet (1 thyme sprig, 1 sage sprig, 1 rosemary sprig, and 1 bay leaf, tied in a cheesecloth bundle)
Kosher salt
Freshly ground black pepper
1 small bunch of spinach, trimmed and coarsely chopped
½ cup finely grated Parmigiano-Reggiano (about 1 ounce), plus a wedge for grating
2 large eggs, lightly beaten
2 tablespoons truffle paste (see Sources, page 379; optional)
1 tablespoon thinly sliced fresh flat-leaf parsley leaves
All-purpose flour, for dusting the work surface
Fresh Pasta Sheets (page 72), rolled through the thinnest setting, or 1 pound store-bought fresh pasta sheets
Rice flour, for dusting the baking sheet
4 tablespoons unsalted butter
1 tablespoon olive oil
2 cups 1-inch cubes butternut squash (from ½ small squash)
1 cup Chicken Stock (page 374), Vegetable Stock (page 371), or store-bought low-sodium chicken or vegetable broth
Parmigiano Cream (page 214)
¼ cup Red Wine Sauce (page 370; optional)
1 ounce white truffle

Heat a large heavy skillet over medium-high heat. Add the canola oil and 2 tablespoons of the butter, tipping and tilting the pan to coat it with the melting butter and oil. Add the chicken and veal and cook, stirring occasionally with a wooden spoon, until browned on all sides, about 8 minutes. Add half of the onions, the celery, leeks, and smashed garlic and cook until the vegetables begin to brown and caramelize, about 7 minutes. Carefully drain the excess fat from the pan.

Scatter the rice over the vegetables and stir well, then add the wine and use the wooden spoon to scrape up any flavorful bits cooked onto the bottom of the pan. Bring to a simmer and simmer until the wine has almost completely evaporated, about 6 minutes. Add enough dark chicken stock to cover the meats, then add the herb sachet, season with salt and pepper, and bring to a simmer. Cover and simmer until the veal is almost falling apart, about 1½ hours.

Use a heatproof liquid measuring cup to scoop out and reserve 1 cup of the cooking liquid, then add the spinach to the pan, stirring until wilted. Remove from the heat and remove and discard the herb sachet.

Transfer the contents of the pan to the bowl of a food processor and pulse just to a coarse puree, not to a paste. Transfer the mixture to a medium mixing bowl and season with salt and pepper. Let cool.

Add the Parmigiano, eggs, truffle paste, and parsley, if using, to the veal mixture and stir together with a rubber

*(continued on page 284)*

spatula; the mixture will be moist. Cover the bowl with plastic wrap and refrigerate for 1 hour to firm it up.

Set your pasta machine to the thinnest setting and roll the pasta sheets through it a few times, until as thin as possible. Lay the pasta sheets on a floured surface. Use a wheel cutter to cut the pasta sheets into forty to forty-eight 3-inch squares (use a ruler or other straightedge to guide you). Working with 12 squares at a time, and keeping the other squares hydrated under a damp kitchen towel, pipe about 1½ tablespoons of filling into the third of the square closest to you. Fold the square away from you, encasing the filling, then fold it again, like a letter, using your fingers to press out any air. Trim the 2 short sides and the freshly folded long edge with a zigzag cutter, then transfer to the rice-flour-dusted rimmed baking sheet. Repeat with the remaining filling and dough; there may be fewer than 12 squares in the last batch. (The agnolotti can be refrigerated for up to 2 days or frozen for up to 2 months. Wrap the baking sheet in plastic wrap and refrigerate, or freeze the agnolotti on the sheet until frozen hard, then transfer to freezer bags.)

Fill a large pot two-thirds full with water, salt it liberally, and bring to a boil over high heat.

Meanwhile, heat a medium pot over medium-high heat. Add 1 tablespoon of the butter and the olive oil and heat until the butter is melted, tipping and tilting the pot to coat it. Add the remaining diced onions and the sliced garlic and cook, stirring with a wooden spoon, until softened but not browned, about 4 minutes. Season with salt and pepper, add the squash, and cook, stirring, until the cubes are softened but still hold their shape, 3 to 4 minutes. Pour in the 1 cup chicken stock, bring to a simmer, cover, and simmer until the squash is soft to a knife tip, 10 to 12 minutes.

Use a slotted spoon to transfer the squash to the bowl of a food processor and process to a smooth puree, adding a few tablespoons of the reserved cooking liquid if necessary to make it spreadable. Pass the puree through a fine-mesh strainer into a bowl, pressing down on the puree with a rubber spatula. Whisk in 1 tablespoon of the butter to enrich the puree. Cover to keep warm.

Melt the remaining 2 tablespoons butter in a medium heavy pot over medium heat. Remove the pot from the heat and set aside.

Add the agnolotti to the boiling water and cook until they rise to the surface, 2 to 3 minutes for fresh, or 4 to 5 minutes for frozen. Carefully drain the pasta.

To serve, toss the agnolotti with ¼ cup of the Parmigiano cream and spoon them onto plates. Spoon the butternut squash alongside and drizzle with the remaining Parmigiano cream. If using, spoon droplets of the red wine sauce around each plate. Shave the white truffle over and around the pasta and grate some Parmigiano over the top.

# STEWED SEAFOOD RISOTTO

SERVES 6 AS AN APPETIZER OR 4 AS A MAIN COURSE

This bread-crumb-topped seafood risotto was inspired by my time cooking in the South of France. On my days off, I often purchased my lunch from a paella stand outside the local supermarket; my favorite part was the crusty bits in the corners of the vendor's pan, which I'd point to and ask the vendor to include in my portion.

¼ cup olive oil
1 large garlic clove, smashed with the side of a chef's knife and peeled
Pinch of red pepper flakes, or to taste
6 ounces large shrimp, peeled, deveined, and cut into ½-inch dice
6 ounces sea scallops, cut into ½-inch dice
6 ounces cleaned calamari, tentacles and bodies, cut into ½-inch dice
¾ cup dry white wine
1 plum tomato, peeled (see page 367) and cut into ¼-inch dice
Kosher salt
8 cups Shrimp Stock (page 372)
4 tablespoons unsalted butter
1 small Spanish onion, minced
2½ cups risotto rice, such as arborio
½ cup finely grated Parmigiano-Reggiano (about 1 ounce)
1 cup Seasoned Toasted Bread Crumbs (page xxix)

To make the seafood ragù: Heat a wide, deep, heavy skillet over medium heat. Add 2 tablespoons of the olive oil, tipping and tilting the pan to coat it and heating the oil until it is shimmering and almost smoking. Add the garlic and red pepper flakes and cook, stirring with a wooden spoon, until the garlic is softened but not browned, about 2 minutes. Stir in the shrimp, scallops, and calamari and cook, stirring frequently, until the shrimp are firm and pink and the scallops and calamari are opaque, 2 to 3 minutes. Pour in ¼ cup of the wine and use the spoon to loosen any flavorful bits cooked onto the bottom of the pan. Bring to a simmer and cook until the wine is reduced by half, about 2 minutes. Use a slotted spoon to remove and discard the garlic. Stir in the tomato, taste the ragù, and correct the seasoning with salt and more red pepper flakes if necessary. Remove the pan from the heat and cover to keep warm.

Pour the stock into a large saucepan and bring it to a simmer over medium-high heat. Reduce the heat as necessary to keep the stock at a simmer.

Heat a large wide heavy pot over medium heat. Add 2 tablespoons of the butter and the remaining 2 tablespoons olive oil and tip and tilt the pot to coat it with the oil and melting butter. Add the onions and cook, stirring frequently with a wooden spoon, until softened but not browned, about 4 minutes. Add the rice and cook, stirring to coat it with the fat, until the grains turns opaque at the center, about 3 minutes. Pour in the remaining ½ cup wine and cook, stirring constantly, until it has evaporated, about 5 minutes.

Ladle in about 1 cup of the stock and cook, stirring constantly in alternating wide and narrow circles, until the stock is absorbed by the rice. Then continue to add the stock in ½-cup increments, stirring constantly and only adding the next addition after the previous one has been completely absorbed. If the rice begins to scorch or stick to the bottom of the pot, lower the heat slightly. After about 15 minutes, when there is only about a cup of simmering stock remaining in the saucepan, begin adding it more judiciously, just a few tablespoons at a time. Stop adding stock when the risotto is nicely moist and the grains are al dente. (Remove a couple of grains with a teaspoon and taste them; they should offer some resistance but not taste undercooked.)

Remove the pot from the heat and stir in the remaining 2 tablespoons butter and the cheese. Taste and, if necessary, adjust the seasoning with salt. Fold in the seafood ragù.

Preheat the broiler. Transfer the risotto to an ovenproof serving dish, such as an enameled or earthenware casserole dish. Top with the bread crumbs and broil just until the crumbs are hot, about 1 minute. Serve.

# SNAIL RISOTTO WITH PARSLEY PESTO, GARLIC CREAM, AND GARLIC CHIPS

SERVES 6 AS AN APPETIZER OR 4 AS A MAIN COURSE

In this over-the-top risotto, the classic flavors of a French escargot dish, namely the liberal use of garlic and parsley, are relocated to a snail risotto, with the garlic present both in a cream and in fried chips, and the parsley in a quick pesto. The flavors are so powerful and satisfying that you could omit the snails and still have a wonderful risotto.

For a more traditional treatment of snails, see the recipe on page 39.

- 2 bunches of flat-leaf parsley, 1 bunch blanched, shocked, and drained (see page 367)
- ¼ cup olive oil
- Kosher salt
- ¼ cup garlic cloves (from about 1 large head)
- ½ cup whole milk
- 8 cups Chicken Stock (page 374)
- 5 tablespoons unsalted butter
- 1 6-ounce can snails (see Sources, page 379)
- 1 small Spanish onion, minced
- 2½ cups risotto rice, such as arborio
- ½ cup dry white wine
- ½ cup finely grated Parmigiano-Reggiano (about 1 ounce)
- Garlic Chips (page 288)

To make the pesto: Put the blanched and fresh parsley in a blender. Add 2 tablespoons of the olive oil and 1 teaspoon salt and blend until smooth. Using a rubber spatula, scrape the pesto into a small bowl. Rinse and dry the blender jar.

To make the garlic cream: Combine the garlic cloves and milk in a small heavy saucepan and bring to a gentle simmer, then lower the heat and simmer until the garlic is easily pierced with the tip of a sharp thin-bladed knife, about 40 minutes. Transfer the mixture to a blender and puree until smooth.

Pour the stock into a large saucepan and bring it to a simmer over medium-high heat. Reduce the heat as necessary to keep the stock at a simmer.

Meanwhile, cook the snails: Melt 1 tablespoon of the butter in a small heavy skillet over medium heat. Add the snails and cook, stirring or tossing, just until warmed through, about 4 minutes. Remove the skillet from the heat and cover the snails to keep warm.

Heat a large wide heavy pot over medium heat. Add 2 tablespoons of the butter and the remaining 2 tablespoons olive oil and tip and tilt the pot to coat it with the oil and melting butter. Add the onions and cook, stirring frequently with a wooden spoon, until softened but not browned, about 4 minutes. Add the rice and cook, stirring to coat it with the fat, until the grains turns opaque at the center, about 3 minutes. Pour in the wine and cook, stirring constantly, until it has evaporated, about 5 minutes.

Ladle in about 1 cup of the stock and cook, stirring constantly in alternating wide and narrow circles, until the stock is absorbed by the rice. Then continue to add the stock in ½-cup increments, stirring constantly and adding the next addition only after the previous one has been completely absorbed. If the rice begins to scorch or stick to the bottom of the pot, lower the heat slightly. After about 15 minutes, when there is only about a cup of simmering stock remaining in the saucepan, begin adding it more judiciously, just a few tablespoons at a time. Stop adding stock when the risotto is nicely moist and the grains are al dente. (Remove a few grains with a teaspoon and taste them; they should offer some resistance but not taste undercooked.) Taste and, if necessary, adjust the seasoning with salt.

Remove the pot from the heat and stir in the pesto, the remaining 2 tablespoons butter, the cheese, and the snails.

Divide the risotto among wide plates or shallow bowls, drizzle with the garlic cream, garnish with the garlic chips, and serve.

## GARLIC CHIPS

MAKES ABOUT 30 CHIPS

Sautéed into the base of a recipe, toasted garlic can sometimes overwhelm the other ingredients. These fried slivers harness the flavor of toasted garlic in a way that lets you contain and manage its impact. They also add an element of crunch to soups, salads, risottos, and other dishes.

A few cups of canola oil or other neutral oil for deep frying
3 large garlic cloves, thinly sliced
Kosher salt

Line a plate with paper towels. Pour the oil into a small heavy pot to a depth of 2 inches. Place the pan over medium heat and slowly heat it, gently frying the garlic until the slices are golden brown and crisp and stop bubbling, which indicates they have given up all their moisture, 4 to 5 minutes.

Use a slotted spoon to transfer the garlic to the paper-towel-lined plate and season immediately with salt. Serve right away, or within an hour.

# RISOTTO WITH SWEET SAUSAGE AND BLACK TRUFFLE

SERVES 6 AS AN APPETIZER OR 4 AS A MAIN COURSE

Alla Norcina means "in the style of Norcia," an Umbrian town where sausage and truffles rule. This risotto incorporates both in a lusty preparation freshened by the inclusion of sautéed leeks. As with all black truffle dishes, serve this in December and January, the height of their season.

¼ cup olive oil
8 ounces sweet Italian sausage, preferably without fennel seeds
1 large leek (white and light green parts only), well washed and cut into ¼-inch dice
8 cups Chicken Stock (page 374)
4 tablespoons unsalted butter
1 small Spanish onion, minced
2½ cups risotto rice, such as arborio
½ cup dry white wine
½ cup finely grated Parmigiano-Reggiano (about 1 ounce)
Kosher salt
1 ounce black truffle

Heat a medium heavy skillet over medium heat. Add 1 tablespoon of the olive oil and warm it. Add the sausage and cook, using a wooden spoon to break it up, until the sausage is cooked through and browned all over, about 7 minutes. Remove the pan from the heat and set aside.

Heat another medium skillet over medium heat. Add 1 tablespoon of the olive oil and tip and tilt the pan to coat it. Add the leeks and cook, stirring occasionally, until softened but not browned, about 4 minutes. Remove the pan from the heat and set aside.

Pour the stock into a large saucepan and bring it to a simmer over medium-high heat. Reduce the heat as necessary to keep the stock at a simmer.

Heat a large wide heavy pot over medium heat. Add 2 tablespoons of the butter and the remaining 2 tablespoons olive oil and tip and tilt the pot to coat it with the oil and melting butter. Add the onions and cook, stirring frequently with a wooden spoon, until softened but not browned, about 4 minutes. Add the rice and cook, stirring to coat it with the fat, until the grains turns opaque at the center, about 3 minutes. Pour in the wine and cook, stirring constantly, until it has evaporated, about 5 minutes.

Ladle in about 1 cup of the stock and cook, stirring constantly in alternating wide and narrow circles, until the stock is absorbed by the rice. Then continue to add the stock in ½-cup increments, stirring constantly and only adding the next addition after the previous one has been completely absorbed. If the rice begins to scorch or stick to the bottom of the pot, lower the heat slightly. After about 15 minutes, when there is only about a cup of simmering stock remaining in the saucepan, begin adding it more judiciously, just a few tablespoons at a time. Stop adding stock when the risotto is nicely moist and the grains are al dente. (Remove a few grains with a teaspoon and taste them; they should offer some resistance but not taste undercooked.)

Remove the pot from the heat and stir in the remaining 2 tablespoons butter, the cheese, sausage, and leeks. Taste and, if necessary, adjust the seasoning with salt.

Divide the risotto among wide plates or shallow bowls, use a truffle slicer to shave some truffle over each serving, and serve.

# FISH AND SHELLFISH

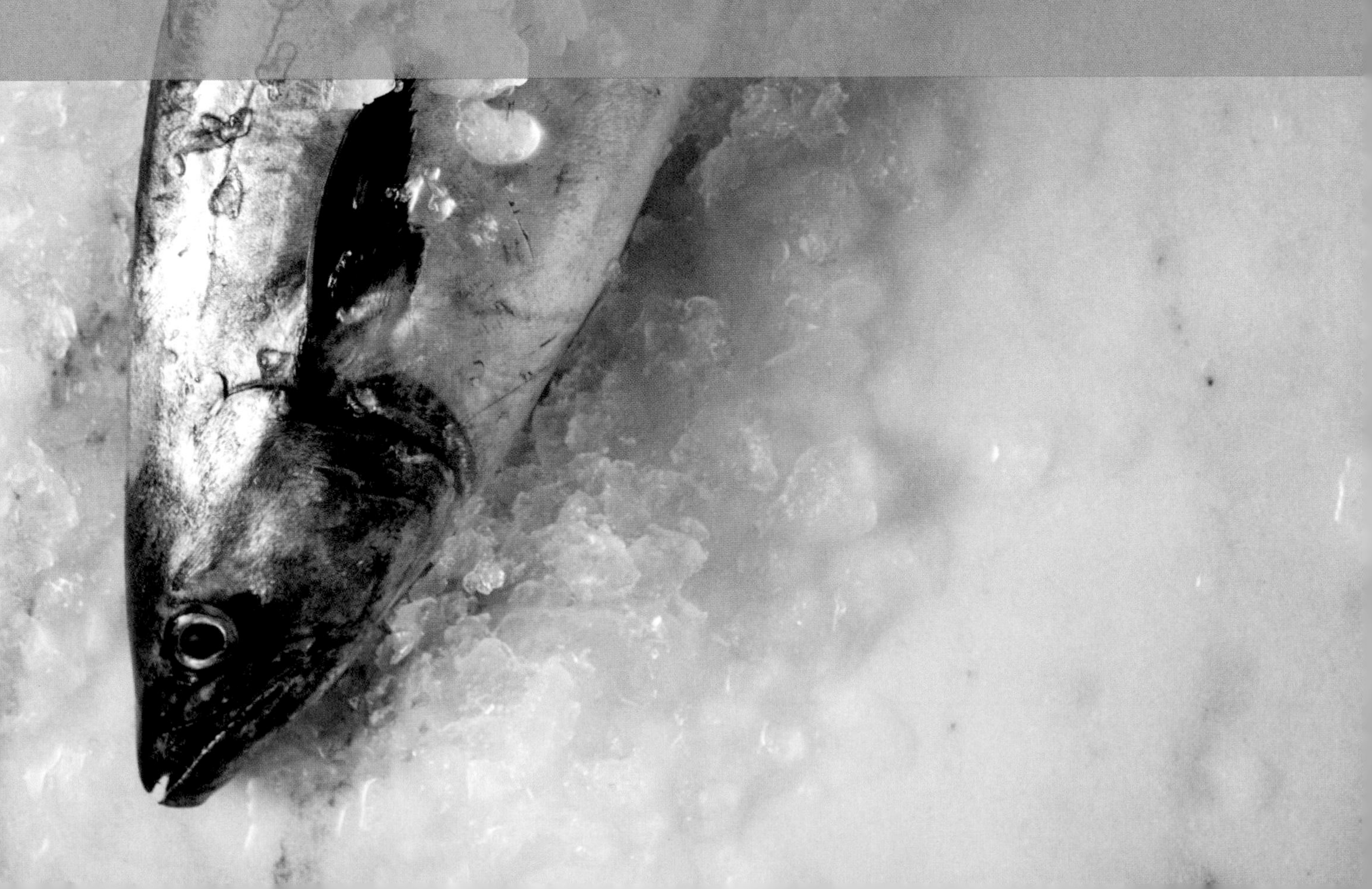

Most chefs would name fish and shellfish as their favorite proteins with which to cook and create, because they offer the greatest range of flavors and textures. I think this is especially true with contemporary Italian food in America, because it allows the cook to draw on both traditional fish preparations and on the vast array of world-class seafood available far and wide in the United States today. Generally speaking, fish and shellfish are also less dominating presences on the plate, so they can be more influenced by accompaniments and sauces than poultry and, especially, meats.

Two stylistic tendencies flow through my contemporary Italian seafood entrees. One is introducing pork products, from salt pork to sausage to soppressata to guanciale, into seafood dishes. The other is the elimination of the demarcation between earth and sea, with ingredients and elements Italians would usually serve alongside poultry and meats freely paired with fish and shellfish: chestnuts, wild mushrooms, and root vegetable purees, among others. Such pairings are not especially revolutionary by contemporary American dining standards but are virtually unheard of in traditional Italian cuisine.

# STEWED CALAMARI WITH WHITE POLENTA

SERVES 4

It's the little details that take this Venetian-style entrée from traditional to contemporary such as the use of shrimp stock, instead of chicken stock, to make a seafood-friendly polenta (the gentle flavor of white cornmeal is also more appropriate than yellow for seafood), and the inclusion of salt pork in a shellfish dish.

9 cups Shrimp Stock (page 372)
1 cup white cornmeal
Kosher salt
Freshly ground black pepper
¼ cup extra virgin olive oil
2 large garlic cloves, thinly sliced
1 small Spanish onion, cut into ½-inch dice
1 ½ pounds cleaned calamari, bodies sliced open and cut into 1-inch rectangles
Pinch of red pepper flakes
½ cup dry white wine
2 tomatoes, peeled, seeded, and cut into ½-inch dice (see page 367)
2 basil sprigs
2 cups fresh or defrosted frozen peas
¼ cup Seasoned Toasted Bread Crumbs (page xxix)

Bring 6 cups of the shrimp stock to a boil in a large heavy pot over high heat. Gradually sift the cornmeal into the boiling stock, stirring constantly with a wooden spoon, then lower the heat to low. Cover the pot with a tight-fitting lid and simmer gently, stirring occasionally, until the polenta is smooth and creamy, 1¼ to 1½ hours. Season with salt and pepper. Drizzle in 2 tablespoons of the olive oil and stir vigorously to incorporate. (The polenta can be kept warm, covered, in the top of a double boiler over gently simmering water for up to 2 hours.)

Meanwhile, heat a medium heavy pot over medium-high heat. Pour in the remaining 2 tablespoons olive oil, tilting and tipping the pan to coat it with oil, and heat until the oil is shimmering and almost smoking. Add the garlic and onions and cook, stirring frequently with a wooden spoon, until softened but not browned, about 4 minutes.

Add the calamari and cook, stirring constantly, until it turns opaque, 3 to 4 minutes. Stir in the red pepper flakes. Pour in the wine and use the wooden spoon to loosen any flavorful bits cooked onto the bottom of the pot, then bring to a simmer and cook until the wine has almost completely evaporated, about 5 minutes. Stir in the tomatoes and their juices, the basil sprigs, and the remaining 3 cups stock and bring to a simmer. Cover the pot, lower the heat, and simmer until the calamari is tender, 20 to 25 minutes. Stir in the peas and simmer, uncovered, until they are tender, about 10 minutes for fresh, or 5 minutes for frozen.

To serve, spoon some polenta into the center of each of 4 wide shallow bowls. Spoon some calamari stew over the polenta in each bowl and finish with a scattering of bread crumbs.

# PAN-ROASTED SEA SCALLOPS WITH CELERY ROOT PUREE, CHESTNUT RAGÙ, AND PORCINI MUSHROOMS

SERVES 4

This composed sea scallop dish evokes autumn in Tuscany with the chestnuts and porcini, though you'd be more likely to encounter those ingredients alongside poultry or meat than something from the sea (see page 295).

¼ cup sugar
1 tablespoon water
7 tablespoons unsalted butter
7 celery stalks, trimmed, 2 cut into ¼-inch dice
6 ounces chestnuts, peeled (about 1 cup peeled; defrosted, frozen chestnuts may be substituted)
½ cup Chicken Stock (page 374)
Kosher salt
Freshly ground black pepper
1 teaspoon freshly squeezed lemon juice
1 tablespoon plus 2 teaspoons extra virgin olive oil
2 tablespoons canola oil
12 large sea scallops (about 1½ pounds)
2 thyme sprigs
1 garlic clove, smashed with the side of a chef's knife and peeled
8 ounces porcini mushrooms, ends trimmed, halved lengthwise
Celery Root Puree (page 294)
2 tablespoons minced fresh chives

Put the sugar in a medium saucepan, stir in the water until the sugar is evenly moistened, and bring to a boil over medium heat, stirring with a wooden spoon until the sugar is dissolved, then cook, without stirring, until caramelized, about 5 minutes. Add 4 tablespoons of the butter and stir until it melts, turns foamy, and browns, about 2 minutes. Stir in the diced celery and the chestnuts, pour in the stock, and use the wooden spoon to scrape up any bits of hardened caramel from the bottom of the pan and dissolve it completely. Bring to a simmer and cook until the chestnuts are tender, about 8 minutes. With a slotted spoon, remove the chestnuts and the celery. Remove from the heat and season to taste with salt and pepper.

Cut the remaining 5 celery stalks into 5-inch pieces and use a vegetable peeler to shave the celery into ribbons. Put the ribbons in a medium bowl, add the lemon juice, and drizzle with 2 teaspoons of the olive oil, tossing to coat. Season with salt.

Heat a large skillet over high heat, then add the canola oil, tipping and tilting the pan to coat it and heating the oil until it begins to smoke. Add the scallops and sear until nicely golden and crispy on the bottom, 2 to 3 minutes. Turn the scallops over, lower the heat to medium-high, and add 2 tablespoons of the butter, the thyme, and the garlic. Cook the scallops, using a pastry brush or spoon to baste them with the butter and herbs, until they are opaque throughout, about 3 more minutes. Transfer the scallops to a plate and tent loosely with foil to keep them warm.

Pour off and discard the fat, thyme, and garlic from the pan. Carefully wipe it out, add the remaining 1 tablespoon butter and 1 tablespoon olive oil, and heat over high heat until the butter melts. Add the porcini, cut side down, and sear until golden, 2 to 3 minutes. Turn them over and cook for another 2 to 3 minutes until golden on the other side. Season with salt and pepper and remove from the heat.

Reheat the caramel sauce.

Spoon a dollop of the celery root puree onto each plate. Arrange the mushrooms and chestnuts alongside the celery root puree and spoon some of the caramel sauce onto each plate. Place 3 scallops on each plate and garnish with the sauce and celery ribbons. Scatter the chives over the top and serve immediately.

## Roasting and Peeling Chestnuts

To peel chestnuts, preheat the oven to 400°F. Cut a small shallow X in the flat side of each chestnut and spread on a rimmed baking sheet. Roast for about 20 minutes, or until the shells begin to curl up at the cut. Peel off both the outer shells and inner skins. Let cool, then peel.

## CELERY ROOT PUREE

SERVES 4 TO 6

Celery root has a more gentle flavor than celery, and it makes a wonderful puree that gets along with seafood and meats and positively drinks up sauces. It can be spooned onto dinner plates, served in a bowl, or even piped from a pastry bag. This recipe can also be made with an equal amount of parsley root or parsnips.

2 tablespoons olive oil
1 garlic clove, smashed with the side of a chef's knife and peeled
1 small celery root (about 1½ pounds), peeled and cut into ¼-inch dice
Kosher salt
Freshly ground black pepper
2 cups whole milk
1 thyme sprig
1 bay leaf
2 tablespoons unsalted butter
¼ cup extra virgin olive oil

Heat a medium heavy pot over medium heat. Add the olive oil and tip and tilt the pot to coat it, heating the oil until it is shimmering and almost smoking. Add the garlic and cook, stirring with a wooden spoon, until softened but not browned, about 2 minutes. Add the celery root, season with salt and pepper, and cook, stirring, for 2 minutes, without letting it brown.

Stir in the milk, thyme, bay leaf, and butter, bring the liquid to a simmer, and simmer until the celery root is very tender, about 25 minutes.

Transfer the mixture to a blender, in batches (see Blender Safety, page 75), and puree, adding the extra virgin olive oil in a thin stream, until smooth. Taste and adjust the seasoning with salt and pepper. Pass the puree through a fine-mesh strainer into a bowl, pressing down on the puree with a rubber spatula to yield as much puree as possible.

The puree can be kept warm in a double boiler over simmering water for up to 2 hours.

## LAND AND SEA

Incorporating meat and earthy elements into seafood recipes anchors dishes that are traditionally thought of as delicate with substantial flavors and textures and opens up new possibilities.

The natural tendency for cooks is to treat fish and shellfish with kid gloves: Look at the recipes in Classico, and you'll see that they either present the seafood in a broth or light sauce or serve it with a composition of tomatoes and/or vegetables.

But fish and shellfish get along surprisingly well with a great many assertively flavored, texturally rich accompaniments. The sea scallop dish with celery root puree, chestnut ragù, and porcini mushrooms on page 293 is a fine example, as is the salmon on page 317, with similar components and a red wine sauce.

Incorporating a meat element into a seafood context can also pay big dividends, bringing a sort of culinary gravitas to the plate, as the lardo does in the sea urchin toasts on page 207, the bone marrow does in the fusilli with braised octopus on page 274, and the guanciale does in the strozzapreti with squid on page 263 and the halibut dish on page 313.

Many diners prefer to drink red wine with Italian food, so an added benefit from incorporating these and similar elements into fish and shellfish dishes is that it makes them more red wine friendly.

# BUTTER-POACHED LOBSTER WITH ASPARAGUS AND MORELS

SERVES 4

This lobster preparation, an Ai Fiori favorite lauded by a number of top critics—including Sam Sifton of the *New York Times* and the *New York Post*'s Steve Cuozzo, who called it "the best dish in the world"—is pure decadence. The crustacean is poached in a mixture of butter and cream, then served with asparagus, morel mushrooms, and a butter sauce of tarragon, black pepper, and shallot that resembles an eggless hollandaise, with the French white wine Vin Jaune, which has an elegant flavor reminiscent of sherry, standing in for the vinegar.

Kosher salt
1 pound large asparagus, ends trimmed
2 tablespoons olive oil
1 large garlic clove, smashed with the side of a chef's knife and peeled
2 thyme sprigs
15 morel mushrooms, checked for small stones
¼ cup dry white wine
4 tablespoons unsalted butter, plus 2 sticks unsalted butter, cut into 1-inch dice
4 large lobsters, about 1½ pounds each
¼ cup heavy cream
2 teaspoons freshly squeezed lemon juice
A pinch of Espelette pepper (see Sources, page 379)
Vin Jaune Sauce (page 298)

Fill a large pot about two-thirds full with water, salt it, and bring to a boil over high heat. Fill a medium bowl and a large bowl halfway with ice water.

Meanwhile, cut the tips off the asparagus stalks. Use a vegetable peeler to shave 4 of the asparagus stalks into thin strips and place in the medium bowl of ice water. Cut the rest of the asparagus stalks into 1½-inch pieces. Add the asparagus tips and segments to the boiling water and blanch until bright green, about 2 minutes. Using a slotted spoon, transfer the asparagus to the large bowl of ice water to stop the cooking and preserve their color. Drain the asparagus and pat dry with paper towels.

Heat a large skillet over medium heat and add the olive oil. Add the garlic and thyme and cook, stirring with a wooden spoon, until the garlic is fragrant but not browned, about 2 minutes. Add the asparagus tips, segments, and morels. Cook until the asparagus is tender, about 3 minutes. Pour in the wine, bring to a simmer, and continue to simmer until the wine is reduced by half, about 5 minutes. Reduce the heat to low and add the 4 tablespoons of butter. Toss to melt the butter and glaze the vegetables. Remove the thyme sprigs and the garlic and season with salt.

Refill the large bowl halfway with fresh ice water. Fill a large pot about two-thirds full with water, salt it liberally, and bring to a boil over high heat. Add the lobsters, turn off the heat, cover the pot, and cook for 5 minutes. Using tongs or a slotted spoon, transfer the lobsters to a cutting board and let them rest until cool enough to handle. When cool enough to handle, twist the lobsters to separate the bodies from the head. Breaking off the claws, remove all the meat from the lobster in single large pieces from the body and claws.

Put the cream in a medium saucepan set over medium-high heat and bring to a simmer. Reduce the heat to low and slowly add the diced butter, a few pieces at a time, whisking constantly, until the sauce has emulsified. Whisk in the lemon juice and Espelette pepper, and season with salt. Add the lobster tails and claws to the sauce and heat until warmed through, 3 to 4 minutes. Meanwhile, reheat the asparagus and morels over very low heat.

To serve, spoon some Vin Jaune sauce in the center of each of 4 plates. Set a poached lobster body on the sauce. Arrange the lobster claw meat to one side. Spoon the asparagus and morels on the other side of the lobster and serve.

## VIN JAUNE SAUCE

MAKES ABOUT 1 CUP

This is also delicious over any light fish such as halibut and over poached shrimp.

17 tablespoons (2 sticks plus 1 tablespoon) unsalted butter
2 shallots, minced
1 sprig tarragon
1 bay leaf, preferably fresh
1 cup Vin Jaune (sauternes or other sweet white wine may be substituted)
3 tablespoons heavy cream
Half a lemon
½ ounce black truffle, grated on a Microplane

Heat a medium heavy saucepan over medium-high heat. Add 1 tablespoon of the butter and melt it. Add the shallots, tarragon, and bay leaf and cook, stirring with a wooden spoon, until the shallots have softened but not browned, about 3 minutes. Add the Vin Jaune, bring to a simmer, and reduce until almost completely evaporated, about 6 minutes. Stir in the heavy cream and bring the sauce to a simmer, then whisk in the remaining butter, a few pieces at a time, moving the pan on and off the heat to prevent the butter from separating. Squeeze a few drops of lemon juice into the pan, stirring to incorporate, then pass the sauce through a fine-mesh strainer. Keep the sauce covered and warm until ready to serve, but use it as soon as possible. If necessary, reheat over low heat before serving, stirring in the black truffle.

## HALIBUT WITH SPRING VEGETABLE STEW

SERVES 4

For all of their devotion to cooking with what's growing at the moment, most traditional Italian recipes confine themselves to celebrating one main vegetable, as in the Halibut with Broccoli Rabe Sauce on page 119. But this dish, one chef's answer to spring fever, with its stew, or stufato, of seasonal vegetables, includes asparagus, peas, leeks, and morel mushrooms. As familiar as that combination might be in American homes and restaurants, it's something you simply wouldn't see in Italy.

Sweet-and-Sour Baby Onions (page 164) would make a wonderful addition to the plate.

5 tablespoons unsalted butter
¼ cup plus 1 tablespoon olive oil
2 thyme sprigs
1 shallot, minced
10 ounces morel mushrooms, trimmed, halved lengthwise, and thoroughly washed
1 large leek (white and light green parts only), well washed and cut into ½-inch dice
1 spring (green) garlic stalk, thinly sliced (regular garlic can be substituted)
Kosher salt
Freshly ground black pepper
1 small bunch of asparagus, trimmed, blanched, shocked, and drained (see page 367), then cut into 1-inch pieces
1 cup fresh or defrosted frozen peas, blanched, shocked, and drained (see page 367)
10 fresh basil leaves, torn into pieces, plus 1 whole sprig
4 skinless halibut fillets, 6 ounces each
2 large garlic cloves, smashed with the side of a chef's knife and peeled
Grated zest of 1 lemon

Heat a medium heavy sauté pan over medium-high heat. Add 2 tablespoons of the butter and 1 tablespoon of the olive oil and tip and tilt the pan to coat it, melting the butter. Add 1 of the thyme sprigs and the shallots, stir with a wooden spoon, and cook until the shallots are softened but not browned, about 2 minutes. Stir in the morels and cook, stirring frequently, until they are tender and have started to give off their liquid, about 6 minutes. Transfer the mushrooms to a bowl and set aside.

Carefully wipe out the pan and return it to medium heat. Add 1 tablespoon of the butter and 2 tablespoons of the olive oil and tip and tilt the pan to coat it. Add the leeks and the garlic stalk, season with salt and pepper, and cook, stirring occasionally, until softened but not browned, about 2 minutes. Stir in the asparagus and peas and cook until the asparagus is just tender, 1 to 2 minutes, Stir in the torn basil leaves and the reserved mushrooms and season with salt and pepper. Remove from the heat and set aside.

Line a large plate with paper towels. Heat a large skillet over medium-high heat. Add the remaining 2 tablespoons olive oil and tip and tilt the pan to coat it, heating the oil until it is shimmering and almost smoking. Season the halibut fillets with salt and add them to the pan, skinned side down. Cook until the halibut is golden brown, 3 to 4 minutes. Carefully pour out the oil and add the remaining 2 tablespoons butter, along with the basil sprig, the remaining thyme sprig, and the smashed garlic, to the pan. Cook, using a pastry brush or a tablespoon to baste the fillets with the foaming butter, until the halibut is flaky and just cooked through, about 3 minutes. Stir in the lemon zest and transfer the halibut to the paper-towel-lined plate to drain briefly.

To serve, reheat the vegetable stew, divide it among 4 dinner plates, and top with the fillets.

# JOHN DORY WITH CRAB AND ZUCCHINI FLOWERS

SERVES 4

In this light, summery dish, one of the most iconic of all antipasti, fried squash blossoms are stuffed with a rich crabmeat filling and used as a garnish for sautéed fish fillets sauced with a quick stew of tomato and basil. I love serving meaty John Dory, but this would also be delicious with firm white-fleshed fish such as halibut or cod.

Note that the filling has to chill for 1 hour.

3 tablespoons unsalted butter
2 large eggs
6 ounces fresh jumbo lump crabmeat, picked over for shells and cartilage
2 tablespoons mayonnaise, preferably Hellmann's
1 tablespoon thinly sliced fresh basil, tarragon, or chervil leaves
¾ cup fresh bread crumbs
Kosher salt
Freshly ground black pepper
¼ cup olive oil
2 garlic cloves, thinly sliced
6 plum tomatoes, peeled, seeded, and cut into ½-inch dice (see page 367)
1 basil sprig
Pinch of red pepper flakes
Pinch of sugar (optional)
A few cups of canola oil or other neutral oil, for deep-frying
8 large zucchini flowers, stamens removed
All-purpose flour, for dusting
4 skinless John Dory fillets, 6 ounces each
1 thyme sprig
2 tablespoons thinly sliced fresh flat-leaf parsley leaves

Melt 1 tablespoon of the butter in a small sauté pan over low heat. Meanwhile, lightly beat 1 of the eggs in a medium bowl. Add the crabmeat, mayonnaise, herbs, and bread crumbs, season with salt and black pepper, and stir gently to mix. Stir in the melted butter. Cover the bowl with plastic wrap, transfer to the refrigerator, and chill for 1 hour.

When ready to cook the dish, heat a medium heavy sauté pan over medium-high heat. Add 2 tablespoons of the olive oil and tip and tilt the pan to coat it, heating the oil until it is shimmering and almost smoking. Add half the garlic and cook, stirring with a wooden spoon, until softened but not browned, about 2 minutes. Add the tomatoes, basil, and red pepper flakes, season with salt and black pepper, and cook, stirring occasionally, until the tomatoes have broken down and the juices are reduced slightly, about 5 minutes. Taste and season with salt if necessary and with a pinch of sugar if the tomatoes lack vibrancy. Remove from the heat.

Pour enough canola oil into a medium heavy pot to come halfway up the sides and heat until the oil reaches 350°F.

Meanwhile, set a wire rack over a baking tray. Lightly beat the remaining egg in a small bowl. Use a teaspoon to fill each zucchini flower about three-quarters full with the crab mixture, then twist the tops of the petals together to close the flower. Dust the flowers gently but uniformly with the flour and use a pastry brush to brush the flowers with the egg wash. Place on the rack. Line a large plate with paper towels.

Working quickly, holding each flower by the stem, carefully lower half the flowers into the oil, without crowding. Fry just until lightly golden, gently turning them with a slotted spoon, about 2 minutes. Use the slotted spoon to transfer the flowers to the paper-towel-lined plate to drain. Season immediately with salt. Repeat with the remaining zucchini flowers.

Heat a large skillet over medium-high heat. Pour in the remaining 2 tablespoons olive oil and tip and tilt the pan to coat it, heating the oil. Season the fish fillets with salt and add them to the pan, skinned side down. Cook until browned, 3 to 4 minutes. Carefully pour out and discard the oil and lower the heat to medium, then add the remaining 2 tablespoons butter, the thyme, and the remaining garlic. Cook, using a pastry brush or a spoon to occasionally baste the fish with the foaming butter, until it is flaky and just cooked through, about 3 more minutes.

To serve, reheat the sauce. Set 1 fillet on each of 4 dinner plates, spoon some tomato sauce over the fish, and set 2 zucchini flowers alongside. Scatter some parsley over each serving and serve at once.

# GRILLED MACKEREL WITH SPINACH, POTATO, AND SOPPRESSATA SALAD

SERVES 4

This summertime dish is a meal unto itself, featuring fish, potatoes, and greens on one plate. It's more an Italian adaptation of a familiar American combination—grilled fish and potato salad—than the other way around, thanks to the garlic, rosemary, and thyme in the fish's marinade and the soppressata in the salad.

At home, I usually avoid recipes that call for both indoor and outdoor cooking, but in this case, the steps break down neatly: You can marinate the fish, roast the potatoes, and make the vinaigrette inside, then take all of your prepared elements out to the grill when it's time to cook and serve the dish. Note that the fish must marinate for at least 2 hours.

2/3 cup olive oil
2 large garlic cloves, smashed with the side of a chef's knife and peeled
2 rosemary sprigs
2 thyme sprigs
4 skin-on mackerel fillets, 6 ounces each
1 pound fingerling potatoes, scrubbed and patted dry with paper towels
Kosher salt
Freshly ground black pepper
1/4 cup red wine vinegar
2 to 3 tablespoons Dijon mustard
1/3 cup extra virgin olive oil
2 cups (loosely packed) baby spinach leaves
2 ounces soppressata, cut into 1/4-inch dice
Canola oil or other neutral oil, for grilling
2 teaspoons Chile Oil (page 232; optional)

Put 1/3 cup of the olive oil, the garlic, rosemary, and thyme in a baking dish large enough to hold the mackerel fillets in one layer without crowding. Add the fillets, skin side down, and turn to coat in the oil. Cover the dish with plastic wrap and refrigerate for at least 2 hours, or up to 4 hours.

Meanwhile, roast the potatoes: Position a rack in the center of the oven and preheat the oven to 350°F.

Put the potatoes in a medium bowl, drizzle with the remaining 1/3 cup olive oil, and season with salt and pepper. Toss to coat the potatoes, spread them out in a single layer on a rimmed baking sheet, and roast until easily pierced with a sharp thin-bladed knife, 30 to 35 minutes. Remove from the oven and set aside.

Put the vinegar and mustard in a small bowl and whisk together. Slowly drizzle in the extra virgin olive oil, a few drops at a time at first and then in a thin, steady stream, whisking constantly to form an emulsified vinaigrette.

Put the roasted potatoes, spinach, and soppressata in a medium bowl. Drizzle with about two thirds of the vinaigrette and toss to coat. Divide the salad among 4 dinner plates, leaving space for the fish.

Preheat a grill to high (make sure the grates are very clean); if using a charcoal grill, let the coals burn until covered with white ash. Wipe the grates with a paper towel soaked in canola oil.

Remove the mackerel fillets from the baking dish and wipe off any herbs and garlic. Add the fillets, skin side down, to the grill and grill until the skin is charred, about 3 minutes. Use a spatula or tongs to gently turn the fillets over and grill until they are cooked through, 2 to 3 more minutes.

To serve, transfer 1 mackerel fillet to each plate, setting it alongside the salad, and drizzle with the remaining vinaigrette. If using, drizzle some chile oil over the plates.

# SNAPPER WITH ARTICHOKE PUREE AND BASIL OIL

SERVES 4

This composed dish takes artichokes and basil, two essential Italian ingredients, and modernizes them, presenting the artichoke in a puree and the basil in a beguiling green infused oil. It isn't a terribly complicated recipe, but the presentation makes an impact that recommends it for dinner parties and other special occasions.

½ lemon
7 small artichokes
¼ cup olive oil
3 garlic cloves, thinly sliced
½ small white onion, cut into ¼-inch dice
Kosher salt
Freshly ground black pepper
Leaves from 1 small bunch of basil
Pinch of red pepper flakes
½ cup dry white wine
1½ cups Vegetable Stock (page 371) or water, or as needed
4 medium heirloom tomatoes, quartered
2 tablespoons extra virgin olive oil
2 tablespoons canola oil
4 skin-on red snapper fillets, about 7 ounces each
¼ cup Basil Oil (page 306)

Position a rack in the center of the oven and preheat the oven to 350°F.

To make the artichoke puree: Fill a large bowl halfway with cold water and squeeze the juice of the lemon into it, catching the seeds in your hands and discarding them. Trim 4 of the artichokes: Working with 1 artichoke at a time, pull off the tough outer leaves. Use a chef's knife to remove the stem, if any. Cut the choke about 1½ inches from the top. Then, using a paring knife, trim away the green leaves until you get down to the yellow part (the heart). Halve the artichokes lengthwise, and remove the chokes; add the halves to the acidulated water as you go. Trim and halve the remaining 3 artichokes, remove the chokes, and cut each half lengthwise into 3 pieces, adding the pieces to the water.

Heat a wide heavy pot over medium heat. Add the olive oil and tip and tilt the pot to coat it, heating the oil until it is shimmering and almost smoking. Add the garlic and cook, stirring with a wooden spoon, until softened but not browned, about 2 minutes. Add the onions and cook, stirring occasionally, until softened but not browned, about 4 minutes. Drain the artichokes, add them to the pot, season with salt and pepper, and cook, stirring, for 2 minutes.

Reserve 12 small basil leaves for garnish. Stir the remaining basil and the red pepper flakes into the pot. Pour in the wine, bring to a simmer, and simmer until slightly reduced, about 4 minutes. Pour in the stock and bring to a simmer, then lower the heat, cover the pot with a tight-fitting lid, and simmer for 10 minutes. Use a slotted spoon to remove the 18 small artichoke pieces and set them aside in a bowl, covered to keep warm. Continue to simmer the artichoke halves until very tender; a paring knife inserted into an artichoke should pierce easily to the center. (Periodically lift the lid to make sure the artichokes are covered with liquid; if not, add just enough stock to cover them.)

Meanwhile, put the tomatoes in a medium mixing bowl. Drizzle the extra virgin olive oil over them, season with salt and pepper, and toss to coat the tomatoes with the oil and seasonings. Set aside.

When the artichoke halves are just about done, heat a wide heavy ovenproof sauté pan over medium-high heat. Add the canola oil and tip and tilt the pan to coat it, heating the oil until it is shimmering and almost smoking. Season the snapper fillets with salt and pepper. Add the fillets to the pan, skin side down, and cook for 3 minutes, then put the pan in the oven and cook until the fillets are cooked through, about 3 more minutes. Remove the pan from the oven and let the fillets rest for 5 minutes. Meanwhile, transfer the artichoke and onion mixture to a blender and blend on high speed until smooth (see Blender Safety, page 75). Strain the puree through a fine-mesh strainer into a bowl, pressing on the solids with a wooden spoon or ladle to obtain as much puree as possible.

To serve, spread some artichoke puree in the center of each of 4 plates. Set the fillets on top and garnish with the tomatoes (removing them from their marinade with a slotted spoon), reserved artichoke halves, and reserved basil leaves. Finish with a drizzle of basil oil and serve at once.

## BASIL OIL

MAKES ABOUT 1½ CUPS

3 cups (loosely packed) fresh basil leaves, blanched, shocked, and drained (see page 367), then patted dry with paper towels
1 cup canola oil or other neutral oil, chilled
Kosher salt

Put the basil in a blender, add an ice cube (this will keep the basil from turning brown when blended), and blend on high speed for just a few seconds. Add the canola oil and a pinch of salt and continue to blend until the mixture is completely smooth, about 1 minute. Strain the oil through a fine-mesh strainer, coffee filter, or cheesecloth into a bowl.

The basil oil can be refrigerated in an airtight container for up to 2 days.

# OLIVE-OIL-POACHED DOVER SOLE ON MIXED GREENS WITH THYME AND BOTTARGA

SERVES 4

Originally created as a starter, this room-temperature salad is so satisfying that it makes a wonderful light lunch. It's a very efficient recipe, in which a portion of the fish's poaching oil, along with the garlic cloves, becomes a dressing for the greens. The dish is finished with bottarga, the exquisitely briny dried gray mullet roe.

2 Dover sole, 20 to 22 ounces each, cleaned and filleted (4 fillets from each fish) by your fishmonger
2 to 3 cups extra virgin olive oil, or as needed
3 large garlic cloves, smashed with the side of a chef's knife and peeled
3 fresh thyme sprigs
Juice of 1 large lemon
Kosher salt
Freshly ground black pepper
1 tablespoon thinly sliced fresh flat-leaf parsley leaves
2 cups (loosely packed) mesclun greens
1 ounce bottarga (see Sources, page 379)
1 tablespoon minced scallions (white and light green parts only)

Line a rimmed baking sheet with paper towels. Set a deep heavy pot wide enough to comfortably hold the sole in a single layer over medium heat, add 2 cups of the olive oil, the garlic, and thyme, and heat until the oil is warm. Remove the pot from the heat and set it aside for 3 minutes to allow the garlic and thyme to infuse the oil, then use tongs or a slotted spoon to fish out and discard the thyme.

Return the pot to medium heat to warm the oil, making sure it does not simmer, and add the sole; it should be submerged. If it is not, add enough oil to cover it. Poach until the fish is cooked through, about 5 minutes. (The best way to check for doneness is to carefully remove 1 fillet from the oil with a slotted fish spatula or slotted spoon and pry apart the flakes with a fork to make sure the fish is opaque and warm in the center.) Remove the fish from the pot and drain on the paper-towel-lined baking sheet.

Transfer ¾ cup of the poaching oil and the garlic cloves to a blender. Add the lemon juice and puree until smooth. Transfer the vinaigrette to a small bowl, season with salt and pepper, and stir in the parsley.

Put the greens in a medium mixing bowl, drizzle the vinaigrette over the greens, and toss to coat.

Divide the greens among 4 dinner plates, mounding them in the center. Top with the poached sole, garnish with a shaving of bottarga, scatter the scallions over the top, and serve.

# FENNEL-CRUSTED TUNA WITH BEAN PUREE AND CRISPY PICKLED ONIONS

SERVES 4

This modern take on the tuna dish on page 30 separates the components of the salad, recasting the beans as a puree, pickling the onions, and crusting the tuna with fennel; the core ingredients are the same, but the effect is radically different.

1 cup dried white beans, such as cannellini or gigante
4 cups Vegetable Stock (page 371) or store-bought low-sodium vegetable broth
1 rosemary sprig
1 garlic clove, smashed with the side of a chef's knife and peeled
Kosher salt
Freshly ground black pepper
1 tablespoon plus 1 teaspoon extra virgin olive oil
2 tablespoons fennel seeds, toasted and ground (see page 367)
2 tablespoons coriander seeds, toasted and ground (see page 367)
2 tablespoons yellow mustard seeds, toasted and ground (see page 367)
4 tuna steaks, 6 ounces each, ideally 1 inch thick
2 tablespoons canola oil
1 cup (loosely packed) wild arugula
1 teaspoon freshly squeezed lemon juice
Pickled Red Onions (page 225)
1 tablespoon lemon oil (see Sources, page 379; additional extra virgin olive oil can be substituted)

Soak the beans overnight in cold water. (Alternatively, use the quick-soak method; see page 30.) Drain.

Add the beans, vegetable stock, rosemary, and garlic to a large heavy saucepan, bring to a simmer over medium heat, and simmer until the beans are tender, 1 to 1½ hours. Season with salt and pepper, remove the pan from the heat, and discard the rosemary and garlic. Let the beans cool. (The beans can be cooled and refrigerated in an airtight container for up to 24 hours. Let come to room temperature before proceeding.)

Drain the beans in a strainer set over a bowl; reserve the cooking liquid. Transfer 1 cup of the beans and ½ cup of the cooking liquid to a medium heavy saucepan. Transfer the remaining beans to a small saucepan, add the remaining cooking liquid, and set aside.

Bring the medium saucepan of beans to a simmer over medium heat. Add 1 tablespoon of the extra virgin olive oil and season with salt and pepper, blend with an immersion blender until a smooth puree is formed, adding more cooking liquid (from the small saucepan) if necessary, and remove from the heat; or transfer to a stand blender and puree, then return to the saucepan. Cover the puree to keep warm.

Put the ground fennel, coriander, and mustard seeds in a small bowl and mix well. Pat the tuna dry with paper towels and season with salt and pepper. Rub the ground spices onto the tuna. Heat a large skillet over high heat, then add the canola oil and tip and tilt the pan to coat it, heating the oil until it is shimmering and almost smoking. Add the tuna and cook for 1½ minutes per side, on each of 4 sides: Cook on both sides, then stand on end and cook the two opposite sides. Transfer the tuna to a cutting board and let rest briefly.

Meanwhile, heat the remaining beans over medium heat just until warmed through.

Put the arugula in a small bowl and drizzle the lemon juice and the remaining teaspoon of extra virgin olive oil over it. Season with a pinch of salt and toss.

To serve, cut each piece of tuna crosswise into 3 blocks. Spoon some of the bean puree into the center of each of 4 plates and arrange the tuna over the puree. Scatter some beans, arugula, and pickled onions around the tuna on each plate and finish with a drizzle of lemon oil and a few grinds of black pepper.

## ROASTED COD WITH LIVORNESE-STYLE SAUCE

SERVES 4

Braising whole fish, such as red mullet, in a tomato-caper sauce is a popular cooking method in the Northern Italian region of Livorno. I love the flavors but find eating the fish to be a bit of a chore, because you have to navigate the bones, and the fish often doesn't cook evenly. Here fish fillets are roasted and then topped with a Livornese-style sauce. Cod has a high water content and large flake, which can cause it to break apart when cooked. Quick-curing it draws out the excess moisture, and keeping it cold firms it up. Chickpeas add a starch, and a distinctly Tuscan element that gets along very well in this context.

1 small carrot, cut into ½-inch dice
1 small Spanish onion, cut into ½-inch dice
1 celery stalk, trimmed and cut into ½-inch dice
¼ cup olive oil
4 large garlic cloves, thinly sliced
1 cup dry white wine
1 14-ounce can whole tomatoes, crushed by hand, with their juice
Kosher salt
Freshly ground black pepper
Red pepper flakes
4 skinless cod fillets, 6 ounces each
½ cup capers, soaked in warm water for 5 minutes and drained
¾ cup taggiasca olives, pitted
Pinch of dried oregano
2 cups canned chickpeas, drained and rinsed
Freshly squeezed lemon juice, for serving
Flaky sea salt, such as Maldon
Extra virgin olive oil, for serving

To make the sauce: Put the carrots, onions, and celery in the bowl of a food processor and pulse until all the vegetables are finely minced, removing the cover to scrape down the sides of the bowl with a rubber spatula once along the way.

Heat a medium heavy skillet over medium heat. Add 2 tablespoons of the olive oil and tip and tilt the pan to coat it, heating the oil until it is shimmering and almost smoking. Add the garlic and cook, stirring with a wooden spoon, until softened but not browned, about 2 minutes. Add the minced vegetables and cook, stirring occasionally, until they start to soften but do not brown, 4 to 5 minutes. Pour in the wine and use the wooden spoon to loosen any flavorful bits cooked onto the bottom of the pan. Bring to a simmer, lower the heat, and simmer until the liquid is reduced by half, about 7 minutes.

Add the tomatoes and bring back to a simmer. Season lightly with salt, black pepper, and red pepper flakes and simmer, uncovered, until the sauce has thickened and the flavors are concentrated, about 1 hour.

Meanwhile, generously season the cod fillets all over with salt and set in a small baking pan. Refrigerate for 40 minutes, but no longer. After the sauce has simmered about 50 minutes, position a rack in the center of the oven and preheat the oven to 450°F.

Using a potato masher, break up any large tomato chunks but leave the sauce somewhat chunky. Stir in the capers, olives, and oregano and simmer for 8 to 10 minutes, then remove the pan from the heat, cover to keep warm, and set aside.

Remove the cod fillets from the pan, brushing off the excess salt, rinse well under cold running water, and pat dry with paper towels.

Heat a large heavy ovenproof skillet over high heat. Add the remaining 2 tablespoons olive oil and tip and tilt the pan to coat it, heating the oil until it is shimmering and almost smoking. Add the fish fillets, skinned side down, lower the heat to medium, and cook for 3 minutes. Transfer the skillet to the oven and cook until the fish is cooked through, 3 to 5 minutes. Remove the skillet from the oven and set aside.

Add the chickpeas to the sauce, season with salt and pepper, and heat over medium heat until the chickpeas are warmed through, 5 to 7 minutes.

Divide the sauce among 4 shallow bowls and top with the cod fillets. Sprinkle with lemon juice, sea salt, and a drizzle of extra virgin olive oil. Serve immediately.

# HALIBUT WITH BABY ROMAINE, GUANCIALE, AND PARSNIP PUREE

SERVES 4

When you get right down to it, this is a simple dish of seared halibut, an elemental stew of guanciale and vegetables, wilted romaine lettuce, and parsnip puree. But the presentation elevates it to another level, with the romaine acting as cups for the guanciale and the puree separating the components on the plate.

¼ cup olive oil
1 8-ounce piece guanciale, cut into ¼-inch dice
1 large carrot, cut into ⅛-inch dice
½ medium Spanish onion, cut into small dice
1 large celery stalk, trimmed and cut into ⅛-inch dice
4 skinless halibut fillets, 6 ounces each
Kosher salt
Freshly ground black pepper
4 cup-shaped romaine lettuce leaves
Parsnip Puree (page 294)
1 tablespoon freshly squeezed lemon juice

Position a rack in the center of the oven and preheat the oven to 350°F.

Line a plate with paper towels. Heat a large heavy skillet over low heat and add 1 tablespoon of the olive oil, warming it. Add the guanciale and cook, stirring occasionally with a wooden spoon, until the guanciale has rendered its fat and is browned and crisp, 10 to 12 minutes. Transfer the guanciale to the paper-towel-lined plate.

Drain all but about 2 tablespoons of the fat from the pan and add the carrots, onions, and celery. Cook, stirring frequently, until the vegetables are softened but not browned, about 6 minutes. Remove the pan from the heat and set aside.

Heat a large heavy ovenproof skillet over high heat. Add 2 tablespoons of the olive oil and tip and tilt the pan to coat it, heating the oil until it is shimmering and almost smoking. Season the halibut with salt and pepper, add the fillets to the pan, skinned side down, and cook until golden brown, 3 to 4 minutes. Transfer the skillet to the oven and bake until the halibut is just cooked through, about 4 more minutes.

While the halibut is in the oven, return the guanciale to the pan with the vegetables, set over medium-high heat, season with salt and pepper, and toss to rewarm the guanciale and integrate the flavors. Transfer the mixture to a heatproof bowl.

Add the remaining 1 tablespoon olive oil to the pan, add the romaine cups, and cook briefly, turning with tongs, to wilt them and flavor them with the lingering fat in the pan, about 1 minute. Remove from the heat.

Spoon a line of parsnip puree down the center of each of 4 dinner plates. Set a halibut fillet on one side of the puree and a romaine cup on the other. Spoon the guanciale mixture into the romaine cups, drizzle the fish with the lemon juice, and serve.

# SWORDFISH STEAKS WITH BLACK PEPPERCORN SAUCE

SERVES 4

Here swordfish gets treated as a beefsteak, with a wine and peppercorn sauce reminiscent of the French preparation known as steak au poivre. Though the dish is not inherently Italian, because of the simplicity of the preparation, and the white-wine-based sauce, it would be right at home in any of the coastal towns of Southern Italy.

Serve this with sautéed broccoli rabe (page 165).

1½ cups dry white wine
3 tablespoons white wine vinegar or champagne vinegar
3 shallots, minced
1 thyme sprig
1 bay leaf
1 garlic clove, smashed with the side of a chef's knife and peeled
Pinch of red pepper flakes
¼ cup heavy cream
5 tablespoons cold unsalted butter, cut into 5 pieces
Kosher salt
Freshly ground black pepper
Finely grated zest of 1 lemon, plus ½ lemon (optional)
4 swordfish steaks, about 8 ounces each
Canola oil or other neutral oil, for brushing
Extra virgin olive oil
1 tablespoon thinly sliced fresh flat-leaf parsley leaves

Put the wine, vinegar, shallots, thyme, bay leaf, garlic, and red pepper flakes in a large wide pot and bring to a simmer over high heat, then lower the heat and simmer until the wine is reduced by half, about 12 minutes.

Stir in the cream, then whisk in the butter 1 tablespoon at a time until it is incorporated and the sauce is creamy. Strain the sauce through a fine-mesh strainer into a bowl. Season with salt, a few grinds of black pepper, and a few drops of lemon juice, if desired. Cover to keep warm while you cook the fish.

Heat a ridged grill pan over high heat and brush it with canola oil.

Season the swordfish with salt and pepper. Set the fillets in the pan and grill, turning once, until nicely charred with defined grill marks on both sides, about 3 minutes per side (a bit less if the fillets are thin).

Transfer 1 fillet to each of 4 plates and top with some of the lemon zest, a drizzle of extra virgin olive oil, and some of the parsley. Spoon the sauce over the fish and serve at once.

# COD WITH BACCALÀ AND STEWED ARTICHOKES

SERVES 4

A variation on the salt cod classic baccalà (page 9), made with fresh cod and served as a kind of sauce for sautéed cod fillets, is paired with stewed artichokes based not on an Italian dish but rather on the French barigoule. This hearty fish dish is perfect for the autumn and winter. Note that the cod must be salted, then soaked, for a total of about 3 hours.

- 6 skinless cod fillets, about 6 ounces each, 2 cut into 2-inch dice, 4 left whole
- ¼ cup kosher salt plus more for seasoning
- 5 large garlic cloves, 3 smashed with the side of a chef's knife and peeled, 2 thinly sliced
- 8 ounces Idaho or russet potatoes, peeled and cut into 1-inch cubes
- 2 cups whole milk
- 1 cup heavy cream
- 8 thyme sprigs
- 2 bay leaves, preferably fresh
- 1¼ cups plus 3 tablespoons extra virgin olive oil
- 2 medium shallots, thinly sliced
- 2 cups dry white wine
- 1 tablespoon whole black peppercorns
- 2 tablespoons freshly squeezed lemon juice
- 8 baby artichokes, trimmed
- 1 tablespoon unsalted butter
- 1 cup Dark Chicken Stock (page 374)
- 1 teaspoon sherry vinegar
- 2 tablespoons plus 1 teaspoon minced black truffles (about 1 ounce)
- 8 ounces porcini mushrooms, trimmed
- 2 tablespoons canola oil
- Freshly ground black pepper
- 2 teaspoons minced fresh chives
- Tender yellow leaves from the center of a bunch of celery

Put the diced cod and salt in a large bowl and toss to coat the fish. Cover the bowl with plastic wrap and refrigerate for 1 hour.

Transfer the diced cod to a strainer and rinse well with gently running cold water. Fill a large bowl with ice water and add the diced cod. Cover the bowl with plastic wrap and refrigerate for 2 hours.

Toward the end of the cod's soaking time, combine the smashed garlic, potatoes, milk, cream, 3 thyme sprigs, and 1 bay leaf in a medium pot and bring the liquid to a simmer over medium heat, then lower the heat and simmer until the potatoes can be easily pierced with a sharp thin-bladed knife, about 12 minutes.

Drain the diced cod and add it to the pot, stirring it in with a wooden spoon. Simmer until the cod is cooked through, about 5 minutes. Set a colander over a large heatproof bowl and drain the cod mixture; reserve the cooking liquid. Use a fork to fish out and discard the bay leaf and thyme sprigs.

Transfer the potato-cod mixture to a blender and blend on high speed (see Blender Safety, page 75), slowly pouring in 3 tablespoons of the olive oil and 2 tablespoons of the reserved cooking liquid in a steady stream, then blending until the mixture is smooth. Set the baccalà aside to cool.

Heat a medium pot over medium-high heat. Add 2 tablespoons of the olive oil and tip and tilt the pan to coat it. Add the sliced garlic and shallots and cook, stirring with a wooden spoon, until softened but not browned, about 3 minutes. Stir in the wine, add the remaining bay leaf, 4 of the thyme sprigs, and the peppercorns, and bring to a simmer, then lower the heat and simmer until the wine is reduced by half, about 12 minutes.

Stir in 1 cup of the olive oil and the lemon juice. Season with salt. Bring the liquid to a boil, then lower the heat so the liquid is simmering, add the artichokes, and simmer until they are easily pierced with a sharp thin-bladed knife, about 25 minutes.

Meanwhile, make the sauce: Melt the butter in a small saucepan over medium heat and continue to heat it until it starts to turn brown. Add the stock, vinegar, and 1 teaspoon of the black truffles and heat, whisking occasionally, until hot. Season to taste with salt. Set the sauce aside and cover to keep warm.

Position a rack in the center of the oven and preheat the oven to 350°F.

Heat a medium pot over medium heat and pour in the remaining 2 tablespoons olive oil. Tip and tilt the pan to coat it, then add the mushrooms and cook until lightly

*(continued)*

browned, about 5 minutes. Add the sauce, bring to a simmer, and cook, stirring occasionally, until the mushrooms are tender, about 5 more minutes. Remove from the heat.

Heat a large ovenproof skillet over medium-high heat. Add the canola oil and tip and tilt the pan to coat it. Season the cod fillets with salt and pepper. When the oil is shimmering, add the cod fillets to the pan, skinned side down, and sear until golden brown, 3 to 4 minutes. Transfer the skillet to the oven and bake until the cod is cooked through, about 5 minutes.

While the cod is cooking, transfer the baccalà to a small pot and heat, stirring occasionally, until warmed through, adjusting the consistency with additional reserved cooking liquid if necessary. Stir in the remaining 2 tablespoons black truffles and the chives and mix to incorporate.

To serve, spoon some baccalà into the center of each of 4 dinner plates. Set a cod fillet on top, spoon some artichokes, sauce, and mushrooms alongside, and garnish with the celery leaves.

# SALMON WITH CHESTNUT PUREE, WILD MUSHROOMS, AND RED WINE SAUCE

SERVES 4

For years, I was reluctant to serve salmon in my restaurants because I associate it much more with France than with Italy. But, in time, I realized that certain fish have become so ubiquitous in today's world that there really wasn't any reason not to use them freely in my modern Italian cooking, and this dish *feels* inherently Italian, thanks to the combination of chestnuts, Brussels sprouts, and wild mushrooms. Pureeing the chestnuts is a distinctly contemporary touch, as is the red wine sauce.

The puree and Brussels sprouts can be made in advance, so this is an especially good dish for entertaining. For a simpler preparation and presentation, replace the salmon steak with skinless salmon fillets.

4 skin-on salmon steaks, about 6 ounces each
2¼ cups water
¾ cup sugar
8 ounces chestnuts, roasted and peeled (about 1¼ cups peeled; defrosted, frozen chestnuts may be substituted; see page 293), or 16 defrosted frozen chestnuts
2 celery stalks, trimmed and cut into ½-inch dice
1 small Spanish onion, cut into ½-inch dice
7 large garlic cloves, 4 smashed with the side of a chef's knife and peeled, 3 thinly sliced
1¼ cups cognac or other brandy
An herb sachet (6 thyme sprigs, 3 bay leaves, preferably fresh, and 1 teaspoon whole black peppercorns, tied in a cheesecloth bundle)
2 cups Chicken Stock (page 374)
Kosher salt
Freshly ground black pepper
Pinch of red pepper flakes
¼ cup olive oil
1 pound mixed wild mushrooms, such as cremini, hen-of-the-woods, royal trumpet, and chanterelle, trimmed and cut into ½-inch dice
2 tablespoons unsalted butter
2 cups Brussels sprout leaves (from 8 to 10 large sprouts), blanched, shocked, and drained (see page 367)
Juice of 1 lemon
Flaky sea salt, such as Maldon
Extra virgin olive oil, for serving (optional)
¾ cup Red Wine Sauce (page 370)

To prepare the salmon steaks: Make a small incision on either side of the bone in the center of 1 steak and remove it, then remove any remaining pin bones with tweezers. Cut 2 inches of the skin away from the flesh on one protruding end (belly side) of the steak, then tuck that end into the center of the steak and wrap the other end around it, to create a round salmon steak completely surrounded by skin. Tie the steak firmly but not too tight with a piece of kitchen string to hold the shape. Repeat with the other steaks and set aside.

Pour ¼ cup of the water into a medium heavy pot, add the sugar, and stir until the sugar is thoroughly moistened. Set the pot over medium heat and cook, stirring frequently with a wooden spoon, until the sugar is dissolved. Then cook, without stirring, until the sugar becomes a medium-brown caramel, 5 to 6 minutes. Carefully add the chestnuts, stirring them in with the spoon to coat them with the caramel. Cook, stirring occasionally, until they are nicely glazed, about 3 minutes, then stir in the celery, onions, and smashed garlic and continue cooking and stirring until the onions are softened, about 3 minutes,

Pour in ¾ cup of the cognac and cook, stirring to dissolve any hardened lumps of caramel. Continue to cook and stir until the liquid has almost completely evaporated, about 5 minutes. Add the herb sachet, stock, and the remaining 2 cups water to the pot, season with salt, black pepper, and the red pepper flakes, and bring to a boil. Reduce the heat to a simmer and cook, stirring occasionally, until the chestnuts are soft to a knife tip, about 20 minutes. Remove and discard the sachet.

Transfer the mixture to a blender, in batches, and blend until smooth (see Blender Safety, page 75). Strain the puree through a fine-mesh strainer into a large bowl, pressing down on the solids with the wooden spoon or a ladle. Set the puree aside. (The puree can be refrigerated in an airtight container for up to 24 hours. Gently rewarm it in a small heavy pot over medium heat before serving.)

*(continued on page 319)*

Position a rack in the center of the oven and preheat the oven to 350°F.

Heat a large heavy skillet over high heat. Add 2 tablespoons of the olive oil and tip and tilt the pan to coat it with the oil, heating it until it is shimmering and almost smoking. Add the mushrooms and toss once to coat the mushrooms with the oil, then cook the mushrooms, without stirring, until they have started to brown and soften, about 5 minutes. Toss the mushrooms again and season lightly with salt. Add the sliced garlic and cook, stirring with a wooden spoon, until it is softened but not browned, about 3 minutes. Pour in the remaining ½ cup cognac and use the wooden spoon to loosen any flavorful bits cooked onto the bottom of the skillet. Cook until the liquid has almost completely evaporated, about 5 minutes, then stir in 1 tablespoon of the butter, melting it, and season with salt and pepper. Remove from the heat and set aside.

Heat a medium skillet over high heat and add the remaining tablespoon of butter. Tip and tilt the pan and heat until the butter has melted and begins to lightly brown. Add the Brussels sprout leaves and cook, stirring occasionally, until heated through, 1 to 2 minutes. Season with salt and pepper, remove from the heat, and cover to keep warm.

Heat a wide deep ovenproof skillet over high heat. Add the remaining 2 tablespoons olive oil and tip and tilt the pan to coat it. Add the salmon steaks, lower the heat to medium, and cook for 3 minutes. Transfer the skillet to the oven and cook until the fish is cooked through, 3 to 5 minutes. Remove from the oven.

To serve, divide the mushrooms among 4 dinner plates and top with the Brussels sprout leaves. Place a salmon steak on each plate and sprinkle with lemon juice, then finish with a scattering of sea salt and a drizzle of extra virgin olive oil, if using. Spoon some red wine sauce alongside the salmon on each plate and spoon a streak of chestnut puree across each plate.

# POULTRY AND MEATS

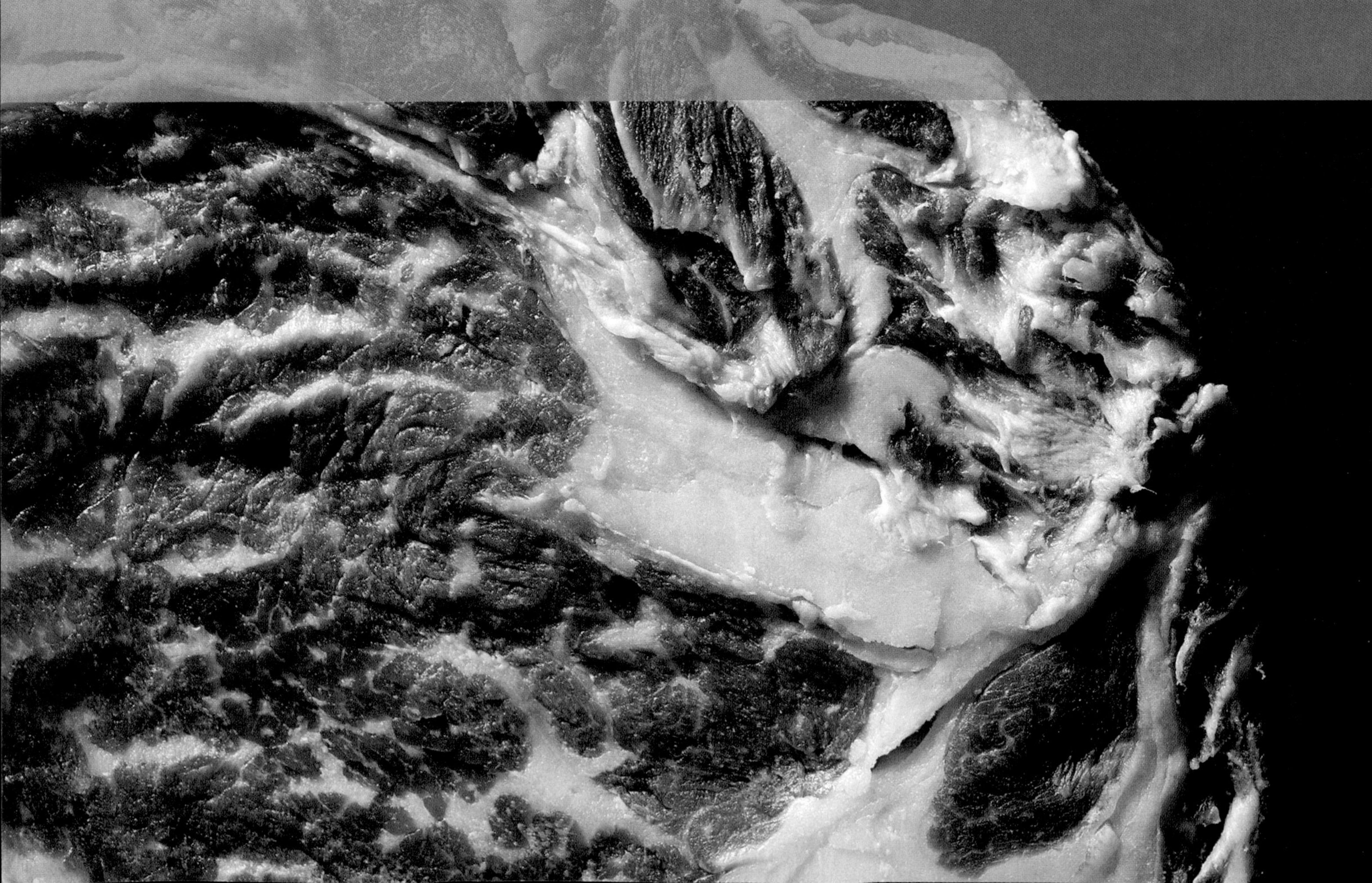

This chapter features the dishes in my repertoire that veer most dramatically from the traditional Italian, because meat cookery in Italy is such an elemental affair. The most famous meat dish in the country is probably bistecca alla Fiorentina (page 144), which is nothing more than a seasoned grilled porterhouse. Although delicious and immensely satisfying, it bears no resemblance to the composed plates on the following pages.

Part of the joy of creating modern Italian dishes is the opportunity it provides to view the classics through a new lens; separating, then reassembling their elements, such as the re-imagining of osso buco with risotto Milanese on page 345, or the contemporary coming together of the steak and the bread salad panzanella (united with the beef by the addition of bone marrow) on page 342, that reminds us of just how sound the building blocks of the cuisine, the primary flavors and preparations that have defined it for generations, are.

Diners equate formal with "restrained," so one of my favorite aspects of these dishes is that because they are precisely plated, rather than rustic, they pleasantly surprise with their unabashedly bold flavors.

# CHICKEN WITH SAVOY CABBAGE, PORCINI MUSHROOMS, AND PANCETTA

SERVES 4

One of the first contemporary Italian dishes I ever laid eyes on was a version of this dish made with guinea hen at Spiaggia restaurant. It was one of my initial windows into the fact that Italian food was more than chicken scaloppine with a wedge of lemon alongside. There was no oregano, and it used cabbage, an ingredient I associated with one thing and one thing only back in Wisconsin: coleslaw. When I went to cook at San Domenico in Imola, I learned that Spiaggia's chef, Paul Bartolotta, had based his recipe on one served there. This rendition uses garlic, rosemary, and red pepper flakes—the central triumvirate in my Italian cooking—to set the tone.

Kosher salt
1 head of Savoy cabbage (about 2 pounds), cored, separated into leaves, and leaves sliced crosswise into 3 equal pieces each
4 bone-in, skin-on chicken breasts, about 8 ounces each
3 tablespoons olive oil
5 tablespoons unsalted butter
4 large garlic cloves, smashed with the side of a chef's knife and peeled
3 rosemary sprigs
4 ounces pancetta, unrolled and cut into ½-inch-wide strips (bacon can be substituted)
8 ounces porcini mushrooms, trimmed and cut into ½-inch dice (cremini mushrooms can be substituted)
Pinch of red pepper flakes
½ cup dry white wine
1½ cups Dark Chicken Stock (page 374)
Extra virgin olive oil, for serving

Position a rack in the center of the oven and preheat the oven to 400°F.

Fill a medium pot about two-thirds full with water, salt it liberally, and bring it to a boil over high heat. Fill a medium bowl halfway with ice water.

Blanch the cabbage in the boiling water until wilted and bright green, 1 to 2 minutes. Drain and add it to the ice water to stop the cooking. Drain again and set aside.

Season the chicken breasts liberally on both sides with salt. Heat a wide, deep, heavy ovenproof skillet over medium-high heat. Pour in 2 tablespoons of the olive oil and tip and tilt the pan to coat it, heating the oil until it is shimmering and almost smoking. Add the chicken breasts to the pan, skin side down, and cook, periodically removing and discarding the fat that renders from the skin, for 3 minutes.

Turn the breasts over, transfer the pan to the oven, and cook until the chicken is just cooked through, about 18 minutes. Remove the pan from the oven and return to the stovetop over medium heat. Add 4 tablespoons of the butter, 2 of the garlic cloves, and 1 rosemary sprig. Use a pastry brush or a spoon to baste the chicken breasts with the butter for 1 minute, then transfer the chicken breasts to a cutting board and tent loosely with foil.

Pour off the fat from the skillet, carefully wipe it out, and heat over medium heat. Add the remaining tablespoon of olive oil and tip and tilt the pan to coat it, gently warming the oil. Add the pancetta and cook, stirring occasionally with a wooden spoon, until it starts to render some of its fat but has not started to crisp, about 4 minutes. Add the porcini mushrooms and toss lightly to coat them with the fat, then cook, stirring occasionally, until they start to turn golden brown, about 3 minutes. Add the remaining 2 garlic cloves and 2 rosemary sprigs and season the mushrooms with salt and the red pepper flakes. Pour in the wine and use the wooden spoon to loosen any flavorful bits cooked onto the bottom of the pan. Cook until the wine has almost completely evaporated, about 5 minutes, then stir in the cabbage leaves and cook, stirring or tossing, for 2 minutes.

Pour in the stock and bring to a simmer, then lower the heat and simmer until the liquid is reduced by about one third, about 8 minutes. Stir in the remaining tablespoon of butter, melting it. Use the spoon to fish out and discard the garlic cloves and rosemary sprigs.

Using the point of a sharp chef's knife, carefully tease the breast plate from the flesh of each chicken breast and remove it. Divide the mushroom-cabbage mixture among 4 dinner plates, drizzle with extra virgin olive oil, and top with the chicken breasts. Serve immediately.

# CACCIATORE-STYLE CHICKEN

SERVES 4

This recipe recasts the famous "hunter's style" stew as a composted plate of chicken, vegetables, and sauce.

Note that the chicken must marinate for at least 3 hours.

4 boneless chicken breasts, skin-on, about 8 ounces each
⅓ cup plus ¼ cup olive oil
4 garlic cloves, 2 smashed with the side of a chef's knife but not peeled, 1 sliced, 1 minced
¼ cup plus 3 tablespoons red wine vinegar
2 tablespoons freshly squeezed lemon juice
3 rosemary sprigs, needles removed from 1 sprig and minced
2 bay leaves, preferably fresh
Pinch of red pepper flakes
Kosher salt
Freshly ground black pepper
3 tablespoons canola oil
3 tablespoons unsalted butter
8 cipollini onions, quartered
10 ounces porcini mushrooms, trimmed (cremini or oyster mushrooms can be substituted)
10 ounces spinach, trimmed, washed, and spun dry
½ cup diced jarred or canned piquillo peppers (about 4 peppers)
1 shallot, minced
2 cups Dark Chicken Stock (page 374)
½ tablespoon Dijon mustard
½ teaspoon thyme

Put the chicken breasts into a resealable plastic bag. Add ⅓ cup of the olive oil, the smashed garlic gloves, 3 tablespoons of the vinegar, 1 tablespoon of the lemon juice, 1 of the rosemary sprigs, the bay leaves, and the red pepper flakes and shake to coat the chicken well with the marinade. Cover and refrigerate for at least 3 hours, or up to 24 hours.

When ready to cook the chicken, position a rack in the center of the oven and preheat the oven to 400°F.

Remove the chicken breasts from the bag (discard the marinade) and pat them dry with paper towels. Season with salt and black pepper.

Heat a large ovenproof sauté pan over medium-high heat. Add the canola oil, heating the oil until it is shimmering and almost smoking. Add the chicken breasts, skin side down, to the pan and sear for 5 minutes. Turn the breasts over. Drizzle with 1 tablespoon of the olive oil, add 1 tablespoon of the butter, the remaining rosemary sprig, and the sliced garlic, and cook, basting the breasts with the butter, for 2 minutes. Transfer the pan to the oven and roast the chicken until the juices run clear when pierced with a knife, 10 to 12 minutes. Remove the pan from the oven, transfer the chicken breasts to a plate, skin side up, tent them with foil, and let them rest. Set the pan aside.

Meanwhile, make the garnish: Heat a large sauté pan over medium-high heat. Add 2 tablespoons of the olive oil and tip and tilt the pan to coat it, heating the oil until it is shimmering and almost smoking. Add the cipollini onions, season with salt and black pepper, and cook, stirring with a wooden spoon, until lightly caramelized, 5 to 6 minutes. Transfer the onions to a plate; pour off and discard the oil.

Add the remaining 1 tablespoon olive oil and 1 tablespoon of the butter to the pan and heat over medium heat, melting the butter. Add the minced garlic and rosemary and cook, stirring, for 1 minute, then add the porcini, season with salt, and cook until the mushrooms begin to give off their liquid, 5 to 6 minutes. Add the spinach and piquillo peppers and cook just until wilted, about 2 minutes. Return the onions to the pan, season with salt and black pepper, and stir. Remove from the heat and cover the vegetables to keep warm while you make the sauce.

Pour off and discard all but 1 tablespoon of the fat from the pan you used for the chicken; discard the rosemary sprig and garlic. Set the pan over medium heat, add the shallots and cook, stirring, until softened but not browned, about 2 minutes. Add the remaining tablespoon of lemon juice and the remaining ¼ cup of vinegar and cook, stirring, until the liquid has evaporated, about 1 minute. Add the stock and bring to a simmer, then lower the heat and simmer until it is reduced by half and the sauce coats the back of the spoon, 10 to 12 minutes. Stir in the mustard, thyme, and the remaining 1 tablespoon butter and remove from the heat.

To serve, mound some of the vegetables in the center of each of 4 plates, top with a chicken breast, and spoon some sauce over and around the chicken and vegetables.

## LIGURIAN-STYLE CHICKEN WITH OLIVES, BASIL, AND PEPPER

SERVES 4

Fennel, tomato, and olives are among the most popular ingredients in the Mediterranean, featuring centrally in cuisines from the South of France to Sicily. Were they to be served with chicken in either of those two locales, it would be in a stew. Here they are recombined as the building blocks of a composed main course.

¼ cup canola oil
2 chickens, 3½ pounds each, split and deboned by your butcher, with only the wing bones remaining
Kosher salt
Freshly ground black pepper
2 cups Dark Chicken Stock (page 374)
1 tablespoon unsalted butter
2 tablespoons olive oil
8 baby fennel bulbs, trimmed, blanched, shocked, and drained (see page 367; 1 regular fennel bulb, trimmed and cut into 8 wedges, can be substituted)
12 taggiasca olives
12 Castelvetrano olives
Garlic Confit (page 370)
Tomato Confit (page 369)
Parsley Root Puree (see page 294)

Position a rack in the center of the oven and preheat the oven to 400°F.

Heat 2 large ovenproof skillets over high heat and add half the canola oil to each one, tipping and tilting the pans to coat them and heating the oil until it is shimmering and almost smoking. Season the chicken halves with salt and pepper and add the halves of 1 chicken to each pan, skin side down. Cook until the skin is nicely golden, 3 to 4 minutes.

Carefully pour out the fat from each pan and transfer the pans to the oven. Roast until the chicken reaches an internal temperature of 160°F when pierced in the thigh, 14 to 16 minutes. Transfer the chicken to a cutting board, skin side up, tent loosely with foil, and let rest while you finish the rest of the dish.

Pour the stock into a small saucepan, bring to a boil over high heat, and boil until reduced by half, about 6 minutes. Off the heat, swirl in the butter to enrich the sauce. Cover the pan and keep warm over very low heat.

While the stock is reducing, heat the olive oil in a large sauté pan over medium heat. Add the fennel, olives, garlic confit, and tomato confit and briefly heat them.

To serve, cut the chicken thighs from the breasts. Spoon some parsley root puree into the center of each of 4 plates. Top with the chicken pieces and spoon the sauce around the puree and chicken. Finish by scattering the fennel, olives, garlic confit, and tomato confit around the plates. Serve.

# DUCK WITH PEACHES AND VIN SANTO

SERVES 4

When I'm devising a new dish, one flight of culinary fancy can lead to another. In this case, I wanted to play around with the tradition of pairing duck and other game birds with fruits that cut their richness with essential sweetness. The most famous example is the French duck à l'orange, but I selected peaches. Rather than deglazing the pan in which the duck is cooked with wine or Madeira, I decided to use the sweet Tuscan dessert wine vin santo, which is usually served with biscotti for dipping.

3 tablespoons olive oil
¼ cup peeled, crushed hazelnuts (crushed with the bottom of a heavy pan)
Kosher salt
4 duck breasts, about 8 ounces each
Freshly ground black pepper
5 tablespoons unsalted butter
2 garlic cloves, smashed with the side of a chef's knife and peeled
2 rosemary sprigs
2 bay leaves, preferably fresh
¼ cup honey
4 firm but ripe peaches, pitted and cut into eighths
¼ cup red wine vinegar
¼ cup vin santo
2 cups Dark Chicken Stock (page 374)
2 cups (loosely packed) spinach leaves

Heat a small skillet over medium-high heat. Add the olive oil and heat it, tipping and tilting the pan to coat it with the oil. Add the hazelnuts, season with salt, and cook, tossing, until slightly crisped and fragrant, about 3 minutes. Remove from the heat and set aside.

Use a sharp thin-bladed knife or a razor blade to score a crosshatch pattern in the skin of each duck breast, taking care not to cut into the flesh; this will help render the fat and turn the skin crispy. Season the breasts with salt and pepper. Heat a wide heavy sauté pan over high heat, add the breasts, skin side down, and sear for 6 to 8 minutes, until they have rendered much of their fat and are nicely golden brown. Gently turn the breasts over and cook until golden brown on the other side, another 3 to 4 minutes. Transfer the breasts to a plate and set aside.

Pour off and discard the fat from the pan and return the pan to medium heat. Add 2 tablespoons of the butter and melt it, tipping and tilting the pan to coat it, then add the garlic, 1 of the rosemary sprigs, the bay leaves, and the duck breasts, skin side up. Cook, basting the breasts with the butter, until the skin is burnished and crispy, about 4 minutes. Transfer the breasts to a cutting board, tent with foil, and let rest while you make the sauce.

Return the pan to medium-high heat. Add 2 tablespoons of the butter and cook until it foams, begins to turn brown, and gives off a nutty fragrance, about 4 minutes. Add the remaining rosemary sprig and stir in the honey. Add the peaches, toss or stir, and cook until tender, 4 to 5 minutes. Use a slotted spoon to transfer the peaches to a plate.

Add the vinegar to the pan, stirring with a wooden spoon to loosen any flavorful bits stuck to the bottom of the pan, bring to a simmer, and simmer until the mixture thickens, about 2 minutes. Stir in the vin santo, bring to a simmer, and simmer for 2 minutes. Stir in the stock, bring to a simmer, and simmer until reduced by about half, about 5 minutes. Strain the sauce through a fine-mesh sieve into a bowl and cover it to keep warm.

Heat a small sauté pan over medium-high heat. Add the remaining tablespoon of butter and let it melt, then add the spinach and sauté until nicely wilted, about 2 minutes. Remove from the heat.

To serve, slice the duck breasts diagonally into thin slices and arrange on 4 dinner plates. Spoon some peaches and sauce alongside. Arrange the spinach on the plates, scatter some hazelnuts over each serving, and serve at once.

**Variations** For a fun play on the inclusion of vin santo, replace the hazelnuts with crumbled biscotti.

You can build out this dish by adding red sorrel and a starchy puree, such as parsnip (see page 294), as pictured.

# BACON-WRAPPED RABBIT LOIN WITH BABY VEGETABLES AND BLACK OLIVES

SERVES 4

The rabbit in this dish is prepared in the style of porchetta, a gargantuan herb-and-garlic-stuffed pork roast. It's a traditional dish, but today many Italians enjoy it only on occasion, when they purchase it as a treat from a roadside vendor. Wrapping rabbit loins in bacon results in a similar combination of flavors and textures but on a more manageable scale. The vegetables and sauce further elevate the rustic dish into something appropriate for even the most formal occasion.

4 rabbit loins, about 8 ounces each
Kosher salt
Freshly ground black pepper
1 tablespoon minced fresh rosemary
10 slices bacon
2 tablespoons canola oil
2 tablespoons olive oil
1 tablespoon unsalted butter
1 garlic clove, minced
1 cup small chanterelle mushrooms, trimmed (or quartered larger mushrooms)
2 tablespoons dry vermouth
1 cup Dark Chicken Stock (page 374)
12 baby carrots, blanched, shocked, and drained (see page 367)
8 baby turnips, quartered, blanched, shocked, and drained (see page 367)
5 large fresh basil leaves, torn into pieces
½ cup black olives, such as Niçoise or taggiasca, pitted

Position a rack in the center of the oven and preheat the oven to 400°F.

Season the rabbit loins with salt, pepper, and the rosemary. Lay 5 strips of bacon vertically side by side and slightly overlapping on a work surface. Set 1 rabbit loin across the end of the strips closest to you and roll up the loin tautly in the bacon, slightly overlapping the strips at the end to completely encase the rabbit. Cut the bacon at the "seam," then roll a second loin in the remaining bacon. Repeat with the remaining bacon and loins.

Heat a large ovenproof skillet over medium-high heat. Pour in the canola oil and tip and tilt the pan to coat it, heating the oil until it is shimmering and almost smoking. Add the rabbit loins, seam side down, and cook until the seams are fused closed, then continue to cook, rolling the loins as the bacon browns, until the bacon is crispy, 6 to 8 minutes total. Transfer the pan to the oven and cook until the rabbit is cooked through, about 10 minutes.

Meanwhile, heat the olive oil and butter in a sauté pan over medium-high heat until the butter melts. Add the garlic and cook, stirring, until softened, about 1 minute. Add the mushrooms, season with salt, and cook, stirring, until they begin to give off their liquid, about 5 minutes. Add the vermouth, bring to a simmer, and simmer until the vermouth is almost completely evaporated, about 1 minute. Add the stock and bring it to a simmer, then add the carrots and turnips and warm through, about 3 minutes. Stir in the basil and olives and keep the sauce warm over very low heat.

Remove the pan with the rabbit from the oven and transfer the loins to a cutting board. Tent them with foil to keep warm and let rest for 3 to 4 minutes.

To serve, cut the loins crosswise into 3 pieces each. Arrange 3 pieces of rabbit loin on one side of each plate and spoon the vegetables and sauce onto the other side of the plate.

# PORK LOIN WITH CHICKPEAS AND RICOTTA SALATA

SERVES 4

Rather than slow-roasting a larger cut, this quick, contemporary rendering of the quintessential Tuscan pairing of pork and legumes uses pork loin, setting it atop a base of chickpeas. Lemon zest and an unconventional scattering of ricotta salata over the finished dish add tart, tangy flavors that provide an essential lift.

¼ cup canola oil
1 boneless pork loin roast, about 2 pounds, trimmed of excess fat and tied
Kosher salt
Freshly ground black pepper
1 head of garlic, halved horizontally, plus 3 large garlic cloves, thinly sliced
1 Spanish onion, cut into ½-inch dice
1 carrot, cut into ½-inch dice
1 celery stalk, trimmed and cut into ½-inch dice
5 sage sprigs
5 bay leaves, preferably fresh
1½ cups dry white wine
¼ cup extra virgin olive oil, plus more for serving
Juice of 1 lemon
4 cups canned chickpeas
1 to 2 cups Chicken Stock (page 374)
About 4 ounces ricotta salata cheese, shaved with a vegetable peeler

Position a rack in the center of the oven and preheat the oven to 400°F.

Heat a wide heavy pot over high heat. Pour in the canola oil and tip and tilt the pot to coat it, heating the oil until it is shimmering and almost smoking. Season the pork loin with salt and pepper, add it to the pot, and cook, using tongs to turn it occasionally, until it is browned on all sides, about 8 minutes. Transfer the pork to a large plate.

Add the halved garlic head, onions, carrots, celery, 2 of the sage sprigs, and 3 of the bay leaves to the pot and cook, stirring occasionally with a wooden spoon, until the vegetables are softened and lightly browned, about 6 minutes. Use a slotted spoon to transfer the vegetables to a small roasting pan and place the pork loin on top.

Discard the oil from the skillet, pour in 1 cup of the wine, and use the wooden spoon to loosen any flavorful bits cooked onto the bottom of the pot. Pour the wine over the pork loin and place the roasting pan in the oven. Roast until an instant-read thermometer inserted in the center of the roast reads 150° to 160°F. Remove from the oven and transfer the pork loin to a cutting board. Cover the pork loosely with aluminum foil and let rest for 20 minutes.

Meanwhile, heat a medium saucepan over medium-high heat. Pour in the olive oil and tip and tilt the pan to coat it. Add the sliced garlic cloves and cook, stirring occasionally, until fragrant. Add the remaining ½ cup wine, the lemon juice, and the remaining 3 sage sprigs and 2 bay leaves, bring to a simmer, and continue to simmer until the liquid is reduced by half, about 5 minutes. Add the chickpeas and enough stock just to cover them, bring to a simmer, and continue to simmer until the chickpeas are warmed through and the sauce is slightly thickened, about 5 minutes.

To serve, carve the pork loin diagonally into thin slices. Divide the chickpeas among 4 plates, top with the pork, and drizzle with olive oil. Sprinkle with pepper and top with the ricotta salata shavings.

# PORK AND CABBAGE ROLLS

SERVES 4

Yet another example of the influence of Germany and Austria on the cuisine of Northern Italy. These ground-pork-filled cabbage rolls are perfect for entertaining, or for busy households, because they can be prepared a day ahead and then quickly heated and served.

1½ pounds ground pork
½ cup finely grated Parmigiano-Reggiano (about 1 ounce), plus more for serving
3 garlic cloves, 2 minced, 1 smashed with the side of a chef's knife and peeled
½ cup dried bread crumbs
¼ cup heavy cream
2 tablespoons chopped fresh flat-leaf parsley
1 tablespoon paprika
Kosher salt
Freshly ground black pepper
16 leaves Savoy cabbage, tough ribs cut out, blanched, shocked, and drained (see page 367)
2 tablespoons olive oil
2 tablespoons unsalted butter
4 ounces slab bacon, cut into ¼-inch dice
1 small Spanish onion, minced
1 small carrot, finely diced
1 celery stalk, trimmed and minced
1 thyme sprig
1 bay leaf
1 tablespoon tomato paste
2 cups Chicken Stock (page 374)
Polenta (page 168)

Put the pork, Parmigiano, minced garlic, bread crumbs, cream, parsley, and paprika in a bowl. Season with salt and pepper and mix together with a wooden spoon just until combined, making sure not to overwork the mixture.

Lay out the cabbage leaves on a work surface. Using a spoon, place a meatball-size ball of filling on the bottom end of 1 leaf and roll it over one time, then tuck in the sides and roll up tightly. Set seam side down on a plate and repeat with the remaining cabbage and filling.

Heat the olive oil and 1 tablespoon of the butter in a wide heavy pot over medium-high heat until the butter melts. Add the bacon and cook, stirring with a wooden spoon, until lightly browned, about 5 minutes. Add the onions, carrots, celery, smashed garlic, thyme, and bay leaf and cook, stirring, until the vegetables are softened but not browned, about 4 minutes. Add the tomato paste, stirring to coat the other ingredients, and cook until it turns a shade darker, about 2 minutes.

Add the stock and bring to a simmer, then gently lower the rolls into the pot in a single layer. Cook, basting the rolls with the braising liquid, until the filling is cooked through and the cabbage is tender and well glazed, 30 to 35 minutes. Swirl in the remaining tablespoon of butter.

To serve, spoon some polenta into the center of each of 4 plates. Top with 4 cabbage rolls and spoon some braising liquid over the cabbage and polenta. Top each serving with some grated Parmigiano.

# LAMB CHOPS WITH SWEET PEPPERS

SERVES 4

This visually dramatic double chop of lamb is one of the most popular dishes at Ai Fiori. It's intensely rich, with the lamb encased in a sort of external stuffing of ground lamb, herbs, and spices. Long, narrow red and yellow Padrón peppers offer a sweet and slightly spicy counterpoint. Note that the stuffing mixture must be refrigerated for at least 4 hours and the prepared lamb chops must chill for at least 2 hours.

One 8-bone rack of lamb, 1¾ to 2 pounds, trimmed of excess fat and silverskin and frenched (by your butcher)
Kosher salt
Freshly ground black pepper
¼ cup canola oil
¼ cup olive oil
4 tablespoons unsalted butter
¼ cup minced shallots
2 large garlic cloves, minced
1 cup minced white button mushrooms (about 3 ounces mushrooms)
1 teaspoon minced fresh thyme
1 teaspoon minced fresh rosemary
¼ cup dry vermouth
10 ounces ground lamb
1 large egg, lightly beaten
½ cup fresh bread crumbs
¼ cup plus 2 tablespoons heavy cream
1 ounce black truffle, thinly shaved (optional)
4 sheets (8 inch squares, about ½ pound total) caul fat (see Sources, page 379; if it is salted, rinse in a bowl under gently running cold water for at least 1 hour to remove the salt and blot dry with paper towels)
½ cup Red Wine Lamb Sauce (page 384)
Pan-Charred Padrón Peppers (page 334)

Cut the lamb between the bones into 4 double chops. Use a cleaver or poultry shears to cut one bone off each double chop (use the bones in the Red Wine Lamb Sauce; page 334). Working with one double chop at a time, set the chop between 2 pieces of plastic wrap and gently pound with a meat mallet or the bottom of a small heavy pan, maintaining the chop's shape, until the meat is about ¾ inch thick.

Set a wire rack on a baking sheet. Season the chops on both sides with salt and pepper. Heat a large heavy skillet over high heat and add the canola oil, tipping and tilting the pan to coat it and heating the oil until it is shimmering and almost smoking. Add the lamb chops and sear for 1 minute on each side. Transfer the lamb chops to the rack (set the skillet aside) and let cool, then wrap individually in plastic wrap and refrigerate while you make the filling.

Carefully wipe out the skillet and return it to medium heat. Add 2 tablespoons of the olive oil and 2 tablespoons of the butter and heat to melt the butter, tipping and tilting the pan to coat it. Add the shallots and garlic and cook, stirring with a wooden spoon, until softened but not browned, about 2 minutes. Stir in the mushrooms, thyme, and rosemary and cook, stirring often, just until the mushrooms begin to give off their liquid, about 4 minutes. Pour in the vermouth and use the spoon to loosen any flavorful bits cooked onto the bottom of the pan, then bring to a simmer and simmer until the vermouth is reduced by half, about 3 minutes. Season with salt and pepper and set aside to cool.

Put the ground lamb, egg, bread crumbs, heavy cream, and truffle, if using, in a large bowl. Stir to mix, then add the cooled mushroom mixture and stir to incorporate. Form the stuffing mixture into 4 balls and place on a large plate. Cover loosely with plastic wrap and refrigerate until completely chilled, at least 4 hours. Once the balls are chilled, press 1 portion of meat stuffing around each chop, leaving the bones exposed. Return the chops to the refrigerator and chill for 15 minutes.

Wrap the chops in caul fat: Lay a sheet of caul fat on a work surface, set a "stuffed" chop in the center, and wrap the fat around it, making sure all the folds are on one side; trim any excess fat. Repeat with the remaining chops and sheets of fat, then put the chops on a large plate, cover loosely with plastic wrap, and chill until the meat mixture is firm, at least 2 hours, or overnight.

When ready to cook the lamb, position a rack in the center of the oven and preheat the oven to 325°F. Set a rack on a rimmed baking sheet.

Heat a large heavy skillet over medium heat and add the remaining 2 tablespoons olive oil and 2 tablespoons butter,

*(continued on page 334)*

tipping and tilting the pan to coat it. Gently add the wrapped lamb chops, seam side down (to sear and seal the seam closed), and cook until lightly golden brown, about 2 minutes, then turn the chops over and cook on the other side until lightly golden brown, about 2 minutes.

Transfer the chops to the rack on the baking sheet. Use a pastry brush or tablespoon to brush the chops with enough of the red wine lamb sauce to glaze them, then roast until the interior of the chops reads 125° to 130°F on an instant-read thermometer, about 20 minutes.

Put 1 chop on each of 4 serving plates and drizzle with some of the remaining red wine lamb sauce. Arrange the peppers alongside and serve.

## RED WINE LAMB SAUCE

MAKES ABOUT 1 CUP

3 tablespoons unsalted butter
¼ cup canola oil
6 to 8 ounces lamb trimmings and bone (such as the trimmings and bone from the rack of lamb) or lamb blade chopped with a cleaver or by your butcher
1 small Spanish onion, cut into ¼-inch dice
4 large garlic cloves, smashed with the side of a chef's knife and peeled
2 thyme sprigs
2 rosemary sprigs
2 bay leaves, preferably fresh
1 teaspoon whole black peppercorns
1 cup dry red wine
2 cups Veal Stock (page 375)

Heat a wide heavy pot over medium-high heat and add 2 tablespoons of the butter. Once the butter is melted and beginning to foam, add 2 tablespoons of the canola oil and tip and tilt the pot to coat it. Add the lamb trimmings and bones and cook, stirring with a wooden spoon, until the trimmings are browned on all sides, about 8 minutes. Remove the trimmings and bones, discard the trimmings, and set the bones aside on a plate. Carefully pour out and discard the oil from the pot.

Add the remaining 2 tablespoons canola oil to the pot and tip and tilt the pot to coat it. Add the onions, garlic, thyme, rosemary, bay leaves, and peppercorns and cook, stirring, until the onions are softened and lightly browned, about 5 minutes. Carefully pour out and discard the oil. Add the reserved bones and the wine to the pot and bring to a simmer, then lower the heat and simmer until the wine is reduced slightly, about 4 minutes. Pour in the stock and bring to a simmer. Cook, using a kitchen spoon or tablespoon to skim any fat or scum from the surface frequently, until the sauce is reduced and thickened and coats the back of the spoon, 12 to 15 minutes. Discard the bay leaves and the rosemary and thyme sprigs. Whisk in the remaining tablespoon of butter. The sauce can be kept warm in the top of a double boiler over simmering water for up to 1 hour.

## PAN-CHARRED PADRÓN PEPPERS

SERVES 4

Serve these sweet peppers alongside meats and game. Be sure to cook them in a well-ventilated area as they create a good deal of smoke.

1 pound whole Padrón peppers, ideally a mix of red and green (sliced red and green bell peppers can be substituted)
2 tablespoons olive oil
Kosher salt
½ lemon

Heat a large cast-iron skillet over high heat. Put the peppers in a large bowl, drizzle with the olive oil, season with salt, and toss to coat. Add the peppers to the hot pan and vigorously shake, then cook, tossing the peppers frequently, until lightly charred and slightly softened, 3 to 4 minutes. Drizzle with lemon juice and serve.

## BRAISED LAMB SHANKS WITH FARROTTO

SERVES 4

This recipe transforms meaty braised lamb shanks (a recipe for a traditional version of this rustic classic is on page 140) into boneless rounds, bursting with flavor, and sets them atop a vegetable farrotto.

Note that the cooked and shaped lamb shank meat must be refrigerated for at least 8 hours.

4 lamb shanks, preferably American, about 1 pound each, trimmed
Kosher salt
Freshly ground black pepper
½ cup plus 1 tablespoon canola oil
3 tablespoons unsalted butter
1 small Spanish onion, coarsely chopped
1 small carrot, coarsely chopped
1 small celery stalk, trimmed and coarsely chopped
1 head of garlic, halved horizontally
3 rosemary sprigs, plus 2 tablespoons minced rosemary
2 sage sprigs, plus 2 tablespoons minced sage
2 bay leaves
1½ teaspoons whole black peppercorns
2 cups dry red wine
3 cups Veal Stock (page 375) or Dark Chicken Stock (page 374)
Grated zest of 1 large lemon
Farrotto (page 336)

Position a rack in the center of the oven and preheat the oven to 325°F.

Season the shanks all over with salt and pepper and set them aside.

Heat a Dutch oven or other large heavy pot over medium-high heat. Pour in ¼ cup of the canola oil and heat it until shimmering and almost smoking. Add the shanks and sear on all sides, 4 to 5 minutes per side, turning them with tongs as they brown. Transfer the shanks to a large plate and set aside.

Pour off and discard the oil from the pot. Add ¼ cup of the canola oil and 2 tablespoons of the butter to the pot and heat until the butter melts. Add the onions, carrots, celery, and garlic and cook, stirring with a wooden spoon, until softened but not browned, 6 to 7 minutes. Stir in 2 of the rosemary sprigs, the sage sprigs, bay leaves, and peppercorns and cook for 1 minute. Pour in the wine and use the wooden spoon to scrape up any flavorful browned bits cooked onto the bottom of the pot. Bring to a simmer and simmer until reduced by half, 8 to 10 minutes.

Pour in the stock and bring to a simmer, then return the shanks to the pot and let the liquid return to a simmer. Cover, place in the oven, and braise until the meat is tender and falling off the bone, about 1½ hours, basting the shanks occasionally with the braising liquid. During this time, check the liquid periodically to be sure that it is just barely simmering; you are looking for a slight, almost imperceptible bubbling on the surface. If it is not simmering at all, raise the heat to 350°F; if it's simmering too assertively, lower the heat to 300°F. When the shanks are done, remove the pot from the oven and use tongs to transfer the shanks to a large plate.

Strain the braising liquid through a fine-mesh strainer into a medium heavy pot, pressing down on the solids with the spoon or a ladle to extract as much flavorful liquid as possible. Discard the solids, add the remaining sprig of rosemary to the pot, and bring the liquid to a simmer over high heat. Continue to simmer until reduced and slightly thickened to a sauce consistency, 6 to 8 minutes, skimming any impurities and fat that rise to the surface. Remove the pot from the heat and set the sauce aside to cool.

By now the shanks should be cool enough to handle. Remove and discard the bones (they should come right out), and trim any discolored or stringy meat where the shanks surrounded the bones. Working with 1 shank at a time, lay the meat on a piece of plastic wrap, scatter one quarter of the lemon zest, minced rosemary, and minced sage over the top. Wrap in the plastic, gathering the ends of the plastic together and twisting them, as though wringing out a towel, until the plastic tightens around the meat and it forms a sausage-like shape. Knot the ends. Put the wrapped meat on a plate.

Pour the cooled braising liquid into an airtight container and refrigerate the shanks and liquid for at least 8 hours or, preferably, overnight.

When ready to cook the dish, position a rack in the center of the oven and preheat the oven to 350°F.

*(continued)*

Pour the sauce into a medium heavy saucepan and warm it over low heat.

Meanwhile, cut the still-wrapped shanks crosswise into ¾-inch slices and remove the plastic wrap from each piece, taking care to remove any small bits. Tie each slice around the equator with kitchen twine to keep it from falling apart when cooked.

Rub the bottom of a baking dish with the remaining tablespoon of canola oil. Lay the shank rounds in a single layer in the dish and pour enough sauce over them just to cover. Bake just until the rounds are warmed through, about 8 minutes.

To serve, spoon the farrotto onto the center of 4 dinner plates and arrange the shank rounds decoratively over it. Spoon some sauce over the rounds and farrotto and serve.

## FARROTTO

SERVES 4

3 tablespoons unsalted butter
1 tablespoon extra virgin olive oil
1 small Spanish onion, minced
1 large carrot, peeled and minced
1 celery stalk, trimmed and minced
1 small garlic clove, minced
1 bay leaf, preferably fresh
1 cup farro
½ cup dry white wine
3 cups Chicken Stock (page 374)
½ cup finely grated Parmigiano-Reggiano (about 1 ounce)
1 tablespoon thinly sliced fresh flat-leaf parsley leaves
Kosher salt
Freshly ground black pepper

Heat a large heavy saucepan over medium-high heat. Add 1 tablespoon of the butter and the olive oil and tip and turn the pan to coat it. Once the butter has melted, add the onions, carrots, celery, and garlic and cook, stirring occasionally with a wooden spoon, until softened but not browned, about 4 minutes. Add the bay leaf and farro and cook, stirring constantly, for 2 minutes.

Stir in the wine, bring to a simmer, and simmer until it has almost completely evaporated, about 4 minutes. Pour in the stock, bring to a simmer, and cook, stirring frequently, until the farro is tender, 35 to 40 minutes. Stir in the remaining 2 tablespoons butter, the Parmigiano, and parsley, season with salt and pepper, and remove from the heat. Discard the bay leaf and serve.

# BRAISED SHORT RIBS WITH GNOCCHI, FONTINA FONDUTA, AND RED BELGIAN ENDIVE

SERVES 4

Pasta and meat, traditionally served as two distinct courses in Italy, are combined on the same plate here: Gnocchi is tossed in a decadent Fontina sauce and paired with luscious braised short ribs, with a quick sauté of endive bringing a touch of bitterness and crunch that offsets the richness. Note that the ribs need to marinate for 24 hours.

6 pounds beef short ribs, cut into individual ribs by your butcher
2 Spanish onions, coarsely chopped
3 large celery stalks, trimmed and cut into large dice
2 large carrots, cut into large dice
1 28-ounce can whole tomatoes, crushed by hand, with their juice
2 bay leaves
2 thyme sprigs
2 rosemary sprigs
2 teaspoons whole black peppercorns
About 3 cups dry red wine
Kosher salt
Freshly ground black pepper
¼ cup canola oil
4 tablespoons unsalted butter
6 cups Veal Stock (page 377)
Gnocchi (page 90)
Fontina Fonduta (page 338), just made or kept warm in a double boiler over simmering water
Pan-Seared Red Belgian Endive (page 338)

Put the short ribs in a roasting pan. Scatter the onions, celery, carrots, tomatoes, bay leaves, thyme, rosemary, and peppercorns over them and pour in enough wine to cover the ribs. Cover the dish with plastic wrap, transfer to the refrigerator, and marinate for 24 hours.

Position a rack in the center of the oven and preheat the oven to 325°F. Line a platter with paper towels.

Remove the short ribs from the marinade, brushing any solids back into the roasting pan, and transfer them to the paper-towel-lined platter. Strain the marinade through a fine-mesh strainer into a bowl and reserve the liquid and vegetables separately.

Pat the ribs dry with paper towels and season with salt and pepper. Heat a Dutch oven or other large heavy pot over medium-high heat, then add the canola oil and heat until it is shimmering and almost smoking. Add the short ribs and cook, turning occasionally with tongs, until nicely seared on all sides, 8 to 10 minutes. Transfer the ribs to a platter.

Pour out all but 2 tablespoons of the oil from the pot and add 2 tablespoons of the butter. Once the butter is melted, add the reserved marinade vegetables and herbs and cook, stirring with a wooden spoon, until the vegetables are softened and lightly browned, about 5 minutes. Pour in the reserved marinade and use the spoon to loosen any flavorful bits cooked onto the bottom of the pot. Bring to a simmer and cook until the liquid is reduced by half, about 12 minutes.

Pour in the stock, return the short ribs to the pot, and bring the stock to a simmer. Place in the oven, uncovered, and braise until the ribs are almost falling from the bone, 1½ to 2 hours; check the liquid periodically to be sure that it is just barely simmering—you are looking for a slight, almost imperceptible bubbling on the surface. If it is not simmering at all, raise the heat to 350°F; if it's simmering too assertively, lower the heat to 300°F.

Meanwhile, toward the final 15 minutes of the ribs' braising time, fill a large pot about two-thirds full with water, season liberally with salt, and bring to a boil.

Remove the ribs from the braising liquid and transfer to a large platter. Cover loosely with aluminum foil and set aside.

Strain the braising liquid through a fine-mesh strainer into a bowl, pressing on the vegetables with the back of a wooden spoon or a ladle to extract as much flavorful liquid as possible. Return the liquid to the Dutch oven, bring to a simmer over medium heat, and cook until reduced to about 1 cup, using a spoon to skim off and discard any fat that rises to the surface. Whisk in the remaining 2 tablespoons butter to enrich the sauce, then return the short ribs to the pot and heat through.

Meanwhile, when the water come to a boil, add the gnocchi and cook until they rise to the surface, about 2 minutes for fresh, or 4 minutes for frozen. Drain the gnocchi, transfer to the pan with the fondue, and toss to coat.

To serve, spoon the gnocchi onto 4 dinner plates and arrange the short ribs alongside. Fan some endive on each plate and serve.

## FONTINA FONDUTA

MAKES ABOUT 3 CUPS

Fontina is one of the great melting cheeses, and whisking it, along with egg yolks, into warm milk and cream makes a rich and satisfying sauce. You could also toss this with bite-size pastas or spoon over green vegetables such as asparagus. For an especially delicious starter, stir diced prosciutto or speck (smoked prosciutto) into reheated leftover fonduta and spoon onto crostini.

½ cup whole milk
½ cup heavy cream
6 ounces Fontina cheese, coarsely grated
6 large egg yolks

Pour the milk and cream into a small heavy pot and bring to a simmer over medium heat, then gradually whisk in the cheese and cook, whisking constantly, until the cheese is melted and the mixture is smooth, about 1 minute. Remove the pot from the heat and whisk in the yolks, then cook, whisking frequently and moving the pot away from the heat as necessary to avoid scrambling the yolks, until the mixture thickens. Remove from the heat and serve.

## PAN-SEARED RED BELGIAN ENDIVE

SERVES 4

Red Belgian endive, a stunning and slightly bitter chicory, is sturdy and flavorful enough that it needs little more than a quick sauté in olive oil and salt to become a compelling side dish.

2 tablespoons olive oil
2 red Belgian endive, core removed and separated into leaves
(regular Belgian endive or radicchio can be substituted)
Kosher salt

Heat a wide sauté pan over medium-high heat. Add the olive oil and tip and tilt the pan to coat it, heating the oil until it is shimmering and almost smoking. Add the endive, season with salt, and cook it just until wilted, about 30 seconds, tossing to keep it from scorching.

Use tongs to transfer the endive to plates or a serving bowl.

# PIZZA-MAKER-STYLE STEAK WITH EGGPLANT VARIATIONS

SERVES 4

A formalized, contemporary, restaurant-style version of the classic carne alla pizzaiola, or pizza-maker-style steak. Rather than a stew of tomato, garlic, and other pizza-topping ingredients, this version starts with the idea of an eggplant-topped pizza, then separates the components into a composed plate featuring grilled marinated eggplant, tomato-eggplant puree, and tender beef fillet.

Note that the marinated eggplant needs to marinate for at least 3 hours.

1 tablespoon thinly sliced flat-leaf parsley
1 tablespoon thinly sliced mint
1 large garlic clove, thinly sliced, plus 4 garlic cloves, smashed with the side of a chef's knife and peeled
1 tablespoon capers, soaked for 5 minutes in warm water, drained, and coarsely chopped
3 tablespoons red wine vinegar
Pinch of red pepper flakes
⅔ cup plus 2 tablespoons olive oil
3 Japanese eggplants
Kosher salt
Freshly ground black pepper
1½ cups Tomato Sauce with Basil (page 74)
1 center-cut filet of beef, about 24 ounces
¼ cup canola oil
4 tablespoons unsalted butter
3 bay leaves, preferably fresh
2 rosemary sprigs
½ cup Red Wine Sauce (page 370)

Make the marinated eggplant: Put the parsley, mint, sliced garlic, capers, vinegar, red pepper flakes, and ⅓ cup of the olive oil in a large mixing bowl and stir together.

Cut the ends and sides off 2 of the eggplants and discard the trimmings. Thinly slice the eggplants lengthwise into 4 rectangular slices each.

Heat a grill or grill pan over high heat. Brush the sliced eggplants with ⅓ cup of the olive oil and season with salt and pepper. Add the eggplant slices to the grill until well-marked on each side, about 3 minutes per side. Immediately transfer the eggplant slices to a baking dish and drizzle with the marinade. Cover and let marinate for at least 3 hours or overnight.

When ready to prepare and serve the dish, position a rack in the center of the oven and preheat the oven to 425°F.

Make the tomato braised eggplant: Cut the ends off the remaining eggplant and discard the ends. Cut the remaining eggplant crosswise into eight ½-inch rounds. Heat an ovenproof sauté pan over medium-high heat. Add the remaining 2 tablespoons of olive oil and tip and tilt the pan to coat it, heating the oil until it is shimmering and almost smoking. Add the eggplant discs to the pan, season with salt and pepper, and cook until the eggplant is lightly golden-brown. Spoon 2 tablespoons of the Tomato Sauce with Basil over each disc and set aside.

Make the filet of beef: Using a paper towel, pat the filet of beef dry, rub with the canola oil, and season with salt and pepper. Heat a large cast-iron pan over high heat. Add the filet and sear until all sides are browned, using a pair of tongs to carefully turn the filet, about 3 minutes per side. Place the pan with the beef filet and the pan with the eggplant rounds in the oven and cook, turning the filet over every 4 to 5 minutes, until the filet is medium-rare, 8 to 10 minutes. Turn off the oven and remove the beef filet, leaving the tomato-topped eggplant to keep warm in the oven.

Return the pan with the filet to the stovetop and add the butter, the 4 garlic cloves, bay leaves, and rosemary sprigs. Using a spoon or a pastry brush, baste the filet with the herbs and butter for 2 minutes over medium-high heat. Transfer the filet to a cutting board and cover loosely with aluminum foil and let rest for at least 10 minutes.

To serve, cut the filet crosswise into 4 equal pieces and divide the slices among 4 plates. Arrange 2 slices of marinated eggplant and 2 tomato-braised eggplant discs alongside, drizzle with the red wine sauce, and serve.

# NEW YORK STRIP STEAK WITH WARM BONE-MARROW PANZANELLA

SERVES 4

The bread salad panzanella is one of those taken-for-granted staples that Italians turn to when they need to use up an abundance of fresh vegetables, dicing them and tossing them with stale bread that's reinvigorated with a light soaking in water and dressed with a vinaigrette. Here cubes of fresh country bread are toasted in butter, then tossed with bone marrow, caramelized shallots, romaine quarters, and spinach for a decidedly dressed-up version that's the perfect accompaniment to a steak. Note that the bone marrow must be soaked overnight.

¼ cup plus 2 tablespoons olive oil
6 large shallots, thinly sliced
Kosher salt
2 cups bone marrow (see page 368) cut into ½-inch dice and soaked overnight in ice water
2 large garlic cloves, minced
2 teaspoons minced fresh summer savory (thyme can be substituted)
4 New York strip steaks, 1 pound each, ideally 1 inch thick
3 tablespoons unsalted butter
1 large loaf country bread, such as Pugliese, crusts removed and discarded, cut into 1-inch cubes
2 heads of baby romaine, quartered through the root end
3 tablespoons thinly sliced spinach leaves
Freshly ground black pepper
2 tablespoons balsamic vinegar

Heat a medium heavy skillet over medium heat. Add 2 tablespoons of the olive oil and tip and tilt the pan to coat it, heating the oil. Add the shallots and cook, stirring frequently, until nicely caramelized, 35 to 40 minutes; stir in a tablespoon of water now and then if necessary to keep the shallots from drying out or scorching. Season with salt and set aside.

Put the bone marrow, garlic, and savory in a medium bowl and toss well.

Season the steaks generously with salt and drizzle with 2 tablespoons of the olive oil. Heat a wide cast-iron skillet over medium-high heat. Add the steaks and cook for about 6 minutes on each side for medium-rare, a bit longer for more well done. Transfer the steaks to a large plate or platter, tent with foil to keep warm, and let rest for 5 minutes.

Meanwhile, heat a large skillet over medium heat and add the remaining 2 tablespoons oil and the butter. Once the butter has melted and is foaming, add the bread cubes and season with salt, tossing to coat the cubes with the fat. Cook, tossing frequently, until the bread is toasted on all sides, about 8 minutes. Add the romaine quarters, caramelized shallots, and bone marrow mixture, toss, and cook until the lettuce starts to wilt and the marrow is heated through, 2 to 3 minutes. Add the spinach, toss, and season with salt and pepper.

Mound some panzanella on each of 4 dinner plates. Slice each steak into about 6 slices and drape the slices over the panzanella. Drizzle the steak and panzanella with the vinegar and serve.

# FILET MIGNONS TOPPED WITH BUTTER-HERB CRUST WITH A BARBERA WINE SAUCE

SERVES 4

Every once in a while, every carnivore is subject to an intense and urgent longing for red meat and red wine. If you ever find yourself in the throes of such a compulsion, make this dish: The signature flourish is the herb crust, which is something usually found on roasted pork or lamb, incorporated here as a last-second topping that is finished under the broiler. This is best made with a Barbera, but you can also make it with Valpolicella or another robust red. Serve the dish with whatever wine you used in the sauce.

1 cup Seasoned Toasted Bread Crumbs (page xxix)
9 tablespoons (1 stick plus 1 tablespoon) unsalted butter, at room temperature
2 teaspoons thinly sliced fresh flat-leaf parsley leaves
1 teaspoon minced fresh thyme
2 tablespoons canola oil
4 beef filet mignons, 6 ounces each
Kosher salt
Freshly ground black pepper
1 small shallot, minced
¼ cup dry red wine (see the headnote)
½ cup Veal Stock (page 375)

Put the bread crumbs, 8 tablespoons of the butter, the parsley, and thyme in a medium bowl and stir together with a rubber spatula until well blended. Transfer to a large piece of parchment paper and top with another piece of parchment paper. Use a rolling pin to roll the mixture out to a rectangle about 3 inches by 12 inches and about ⅛ inch thick. Transfer the parchment-paper-encased crust to a baking sheet and place in the freezer until firm, about 30 minutes.

Cut the crust mixture into 3-inch squares (roughly the same size as the filet mignon pieces), cutting through the paper and leaving it intact. Set aside.

Position a rack in the center of the oven and preheat the oven to 400°F.

Heat a large heavy skillet over high heat. Add 1 tablespoon of the canola oil and tip and tilt the pan to coat it, heating the oil. Season the steaks with salt and pepper, add them to the pan, and sear, turning once, until golden brown on both sides, about 3 minutes per side.

Transfer the steaks to a baking sheet or an ovenproof sauté pan (set the skillet aside), set in the oven, and cook for 4 minutes for medium-rare, or a bit longer for more well done.

Meanwhile, make the sauce: Return the pan in which the steaks were seared to medium-high heat, add the remaining tablespoon of canola oil, and tip and tilt the pan to coat it with the oil, warming it. Lower the heat to medium-low, add the shallots, and cook, stirring frequently with a wooden spoon, until softened but not browned, about 3 minutes. Pour in the wine and use the spoon to loosen any flavorful bits cooked onto the bottom of the pan. Bring to a simmer and cook until the wine is slightly reduced, about 2 minutes. Stir in the stock, bring to a simmer, and simmer until the sauce has thickened enough to coat the back of the spoon and the flavors are nicely concentrated, about 6 minutes. Swirl in the remaining tablespoon of butter until it is melted and season with salt and pepper. Strain the sauce through a fine-mesh strainer into a bowl and cover to keep warm.

When the steaks are done, remove the baking sheet from the oven and preheat the broiler. Top each piece of beef with one of the prepared crusts, removing the parchment paper, then return the baking sheet to the oven and broil until the crust is golden brown, 1 to 2 minutes.

Arrange the steaks on 4 dinner plates, drizzle with the wine sauce, and serve.

# BRAISED VEAL BREAST WITH RISOTTO MILANESE

SERVES 4

Risotto Milanese, meaning "in the style of Milan," is a dish that transcends Italy. It is instantly recognizable by its golden hue, created by saffron, and is *always* served as a complement to, and pedestal for, osso buco, braised veal shanks. This contemporary riff on that dynamic duo substitutes more gelatinous veal breast for the shanks and presses the cooked veal so that it can be cut and shaped into neat blocks. Note that the veal must be braised for about 2 hours and then pressed for another 2 to 4 hours.

¼ cup olive oil
1 bone-in veal breast, about 3 pounds
2 large carrots, cut into ½-inch dice
2 medium Spanish onions, cut into ½-inch dice
2 large celery stalks, trimmed and cut into ½-inch dice
6 thyme sprigs
4 bay leaves, preferably fresh
2 rosemary sprigs
2 cups dry white wine
4 cups Chicken Stock (page 374)
Risotto Milanese (page 346)
Gremolata (page 102)

Position a rack in the center of the oven and preheat the oven to 325°F.

Heat a large Dutch oven over medium-high heat. Add the olive oil and heat it until it is shimmering and almost smoking. Add the veal breast and sear, turning it with tongs, until golden brown on all sides, 8 to 10 minutes. Transfer the veal to a large plate or platter.

Add the carrots, onions, celery, thyme, bay leaves, and rosemary to the Dutch oven and cook, stirring with a wooden spoon, until the vegetables are softened but not browned, about 4 minutes. Pour in the wine and use the spoon to loosen any flavorful bits cooked onto the bottom of the pot, then bring to a simmer and simmer until reduced by half, about 8 minutes.

Pour in the stock and bring it to a simmer. Return the veal to the pot, cover with a lid, and braise in the oven for 1 hour. Remove the lid and braise until the veal is tender, about 1 more hour. As the veal cooks, check the liquid periodically to be sure that it is just barely simmering—you are looking for a slight, almost imperceptible bubbling on the surface. If it is not simmering at all, raise the heat to 325°F; if it's simmering too assertively, lower the heat to 275°F. Transfer the veal breast to a rimmed baking sheet, brushing off any solids. Set the pot aside.

As soon as the veal is cool enough to handle, remove the bones, which should come out easily with just a tug. Place another baking sheet on top and weight it with heavy objects such as cans of tomatoes, to press the veal and extract excess fat. Refrigerate until chilled, at least 2 hours, but no more than 4 hours.

Meanwhile, strain the cooking liquid through a fine-mesh strainer into a small heavy pot, pressing down on the solids with a wooden spoon or a ladle to extract as much flavorful liquid as possible. Set the pot over medium-high heat and bring to a simmer. Simmer until thickened and reduced to a sauce consistency, about 8 minutes. Let cool completely, then cover and refrigerate. About 10 minutes before serving, gently reheat over low heat.

For a formal presentation, cut the pressed veal into 4 rectangular portions and add them to the pot with the sauce. Spoon the sauce over the top and gently warm, continuing to spoon the sauce over the meat, until the meat is warmed through and coated with sauce. Create a "trail" of gremolata across the center of each of 4 plates. Set 1 piece of veal to one side of the gremolata. Spoon some risotto into a 1-cup mold or other vessel and carefully unmold on the other side of the gremolata. Repeat with the remaining risotto.

For a simpler presentation, cut the veal breast into 1-inch pieces. Add the veal to the sauce and heat until it is warmed through and lightly glazed with sauce. Spoon the risotto into 4 wide bowls, top with the veal, and drizzle with the sauce. Serve.

## RISOTTO MILANESE

SERVES 4 AS AN ACCOMPANIMENT

This classic osso buco accompaniment is also delicious on its own.

4 cups Chicken Stock (page 374)
1 teaspoon saffron threads
3 tablespoons unsalted butter
1 tablespoon olive oil
¼ cup diced Spanish onion
1 cup risotto rice, such as arborio
¼ cup dry white wine
3 tablespoons finely grated Parmigiano-Reggiano
Kosher salt

Pour the stock into a medium saucepan and bring it to a simmer over medium-high heat. Stir in the saffron and reduce the heat as necessary to keep the stock at a simmer.

Heat a large wide heavy pot over medium heat. Add 2 tablespoons of the butter and the olive oil and tip and tilt the pot to coat it with the oil and melting butter. Add the onions and cook, stirring frequently with a wooden spoon, until softened but not browned, about 4 minutes. Add the rice and cook, stirring to coat it with the fat, until the grains turn opaque at the center, about 3 minutes. Pour in the wine and cook, stirring constantly, until it has evaporated, about 5 minutes.

Ladle in about 1 cup of the stock and cook, stirring constantly in alternating wide and narrow circles, until the stock is absorbed by the rice. Then continue to add the stock in ½-cup increments, stirring constantly and only adding the next addition after the previous one has been completely absorbed. If the rice begins to scorch or stick to the bottom of the pot, lower the heat slightly. After about 15 minutes, when there is only about a cup of simmering stock remaining in the saucepan, begin adding it more judiciously, just a few tablespoons at a time. Stop adding stock when the risotto is nicely moist and the grains are al dente. (Remove a few grains with a teaspoon and taste them; the rice should offer some resistance but not taste undercooked.)

Remove the pot from the heat and stir in the remaining tablespoon of butter and the cheese. Taste and, if necessary, adjust the seasoning with salt. Serve.

# VEAL CHOPS WITH ROASTED ENDIVE AND PANCETTA CREAM SAUCE

SERVES 4

This riff on the veal with smoked pancetta cream sauce on page 153 features a more nuanced sauce, made with regular pancetta instead of smoked and wine instead of vodka, and leaving out the coarsely ground black pepper. The accompaniment of roasted Belgian endive is also a departure from the traditional, all the more so with the orange juice in its cooking liquid. This is also delicious with the sweet-and-sour cipollini onions on page 350, in addition to or in place of the endive.

1 tablespoon canola oil or other neutral oil
¼ cup diced (small dice) pancetta (about 2 ounces)
1 small Spanish onion, minced
5 large garlic cloves, 1 minced, 4 smashed with the side of a chef's knife and peeled
5 thyme sprigs
¼ cup dry white wine
1½ cups heavy cream
½ lemon
Kosher salt
Freshly ground black pepper
4 bone-in center-cut veal rib chops, about 12 ounces each
¼ cup olive oil
4 tablespoons unsalted butter
Roasted Belgian Endive (recipe follows)

Heat a small heavy skillet over medium heat. Add the canola oil and warm it, then add the pancetta and cook, stirring often with a wooden spoon, until it is crispy and has rendered enough of its fat to coat the bottom of the pan, about 6 minutes. Add the onions, minced garlic, and 1 thyme sprig and cook, stirring occasionally, until the onions are softened but not browned, about 4 minutes.

Pour in the wine, stirring to loosen any flavorful bits cooked onto the bottom of the pan, bring to a simmer, and simmer until the wine has completely evaporated, about 4 minutes. Pour in the heavy cream, bring to a simmer, and reduce until the sauce is thick enough to coat the back of the spoon, 8 to 10 minutes. Add a few drops of lemon juice and season with salt and pepper. Remove from the heat and cover to keep warm.

Rub the chops on both sides with the olive oil and season liberally with salt and pepper.

Heat a large cast-iron skillet over medium-high heat. Add the veal chops and sear, turning once, until golden brown, 4 to 5 minutes on each side. Just before you remove the veal, add the smashed garlic cloves, butter, and the remaining 4 thyme sprigs. Let the butter melt, and use a pastry brush to baste the chops with the butter. Transfer the chops to a platter, tent loosely with aluminum foil, and set aside to rest for 10 minutes.

Meanwhile, reheat the sauce over medium heat.

To serve, set 1 chop on each of 4 dinner plates, spoon some sauce over it, and set 2 endive halves alongside.

## ROASTED BELGIAN ENDIVE

SERVES 4

Serve this versatile accompaniment with white-fleshed fish and other white meats, such as roasted pork.

4 heads of Belgian endive, halved lengthwise
¼ cup freshly squeezed orange juice
½ cup Chicken Stock (page 374)
2 thyme sprigs
1 tablespoon unsalted butter

Heat a wide heavy sauté pan over medium-high heat. Add the endive, cut side down, and sear, without moving, until the bottom is golden brown, about 2 minutes. Pour in the orange juice and stock and add the thyme and butter. Reduce the heat to low and cook gently until the endive is tender to the tines of a fork and the liquid is reduced to a thick glaze, about 20 minutes.

Serve, or transfer the endive to a plate and keep covered and warm until ready to serve.

# VENISON MEDALLIONS WITH QUINCE PUREE AND JUNIPER SAUCE

SERVES 4

One of the first lessons I learned at San Domenico was the importance of pairing venison with ingredients that offset its gaminess. The two most oft-called-on agents in that mission are juniper as a seasoning and quince as an accompaniment, usually in the form of a mostarda (see page 149). When dining throughout Italy, though, I find that all too often these elements are incorporated almost by rote, rather than with true passion and finesse. Here the quince takes the form of a puree and the juniper is made the focal point of both the marinade and the sauce. Note that the venison must be marinated overnight. Sweet-and-Sour Cipollini Onions (recipe follows on page 350) may be added to or substituted for the prune compote.

1 tablespoon juniper berries, lightly crushed with the side of a chef's knife, plus 1 tablespoon whole juniper berries
3 garlic cloves, smashed with the side of a chef's knife and peeled
2 thyme sprigs
6 bay leaves, preferably fresh
2 fresh sage leaves
1/3 cup canola olive oil
2 pieces venison loin, 12 ounces each
Freshly ground black pepper
1 cup dry red wine
1 cinnamon stick
2 tablespoons sugar
8 ounces pitted prunes
Kosher salt
Red Wine Sauce (page 370)
1 teaspoon cocoa powder
1 tablespoon unsalted butter
Quince Puree (page 350)

Marinate the venison medallions: Place the bruised juniper berries in a baking dish with the garlic cloves, thyme, 5 bay leaves, and the sage, and drizzle with half the oil. Add the venison medallions in a single layer. Season the medallions with the pepper and drizzle with the remaining olive oil. Cover the dish with plastic wrap and refrigerate for 2 hours. Turn the medallions over, recover the dish and refrigerate overnight.

Make the prune compote: Place the wine, cinnamon, sugar, and remaining bay leaf in a small saucepan. Bring to a simmer, stirring, until the sugar is dissolved and the liquid is reduced by about 25 percent, about 4 minutes. Add the prunes and simmer for 5 minutes, then remove the pan from the stove and let the prunes steep for 1 hour; during that time they will absorb most of the liquid. Break up the prunes with a wooden spoon to make the compote, drain the remaining liquid, and discard the bay leaves and cinnamon. The compote can be refrigerated in an airtight container for up to 24 hours; reheat gently before serving.

When ready to prepare and serve the dish, remove the venison medallions from the marinade. Place the medallions on a large plate and let come to room temperature.

Heat the red wine sauce in a small heavy saucepan over medium heat. Whisk in the whole juniper berries and cocoa powder. Swirl in the butter and keep covered and warm over very low heat.

Position a rack in the center of the oven and preheat the oven to 400°F.

Season the venison loins with salt and pepper.

Heat a cast iron skillet over high heat. Add the loins and sear until nicely browned all over, rolling them as they brown, about 10 minutes total cooking time. Transfer the pan to the oven and cook until the loins are cooked through, 5 to 7 minutes for medium-rare.

Remove the venison from the oven, and transfer to a cutting board, tent with foil, and let rest for 10 minutes before slicing into a total of 12 medallions.

Place 3 medallions on each of 4 plates, spoon a quenelle of quince puree and a spoonful of prune compote alongside, and drizzle with the sauce. Serve immediately.

## QUINCE PUREE

MAKES ABOUT 1 CUP

This puree may be served with a variety of meats and game. It's also delicious spread on toast with ricotta cheese, or as an accompaniment to a cheese course.

1 cup water
1 cup dry white wine
½ cup sugar
1 bay leaf, preferably fresh
2 quince, peeled, cored, and cut into small dice (about 1½ cups diced)
1 tablespoon unsalted butter

Heat a medium saucepan over medium-high heat and add the water, wine, sugar, and bay leaf. Bring the liquid to a boil, then add the quince. Boil until the quince pieces are tender to a knife tip, about 15 minutes. Remove the bay leaf and drain the quince in a colander. Transfer to a food processor and pulse to a puree. The puree can be refrigerated for up to 24 hours in an airtight container; serve at room temperature, or reheat gently over low heat.

## SWEET-AND-SOUR CIPOLLINI ONIONS

MAKES ENOUGH TO GARNISH 4 SERVINGS

These contemporary sweet-and-sour onions (see page 164 for the classic version) use white balsamic vinegar and verjus for their nuanced acidity, with rosemary emphasizing their rusticity. Because they are less assertively flavored than the traditional preparation, they can be served with just about any poultry or meat.

1 tablespoon olive oil
1 tablespoon unsalted butter
1 bay leaf, preferably fresh
1 rosemary sprig
8 ounces cipollini onions, peeled and trimmed
3 tablespoons sugar
Kosher salt
¼ cup white balsamic vinegar
¾ cup white verjus (see Sources, page 379)
¼ cup Chicken Stock (page 374), Vegetable Stock (page 371), or store-bought low-sodium chicken or vegetable broth

Heat a wide heavy sauté pan over medium-high heat. Add the olive oil and butter and heat until the butter is melted, tipping and tilting the pan to coat it. Add the bay leaf and rosemary and cook, stirring with a wooden spoon, for 2 minutes to infuse the butter and oil with the flavor of the herbs. Add the onions, sugar, and a pinch of salt and cook, stirring occasionally, until the onions are lightly caramelized all over, about 8 minutes.

Add the vinegar, stir, bring to a simmer, and simmer until reduced to a syrup, about 4 minutes. Add the verjus, stir, bring to a simmer, and simmer until reduced to a syrup again, about 6 minutes. Pour in the stock, bring to a simmer, partially cover, and simmer until the onions are tender to a knife tip, about 8 more minutes. Serve.

# DESSERTS

In modern American restaurants, desserts have evolved into a place for culinary showmanship to rival that of the savory courses that preceded them, and my restaurants are no exception. Our customers look to dessert not just for a sweet coda to their meals, but also as one last opportunity for their eyes and their palates to be dazzled.

The recipes in this chapter, based primarily on desserts served at Marea and Ai Fiori, offer you the opportunity to create complex, visually arresting desserts at home. Contrasted with the simplicity of classic Italian dolci, the compositions that follow are audacious. They gather multiple preparations on one plate, many more than you would ever encounter in an Italian home, or even in a traditional Italian restaurant. (Accordingly, it should also be noted that they are not for the beginner or causal cook.)

What's more, several of the components and combinations are quite unconventional, such as squash and rosemary sorbet, and the liberal use of savory ingredients such as basil. And yet, they all have an authentic Italian character, because they are based on Italian desserts and draw primarily on Italian flavors and associations. When you eat them, you may be surprised at how much they still have in common with the classics that inspired them.

# CHOCOLATE CAKE WITH CHOCOLATE MOUSSE AND CHOCOLATE SAUCE

SERVES 6

This chocolate lover's dream come true pairs devil's food cake with milk chocolate and dark chocolate mousses. Indulgent as that is, much of what makes this dessert truly special are the adornments, including candied cocoa nibs and the essential sweetness of maraschino cherries. Extra virgin olive oil and sea salt, two finishing touches that are ubiquitous in Italian savory dishes, prove just as much at home in pastry environs, the optional salt a natural foil for the chocolate and the olive oil an understated complement to the vanilla ice cream.

Note that you will need a cake frame to make this cake (see Sources, page 379).

FOR THE DEVIL'S FOOD CAKE

½ cup egg whites (from about 3 large eggs)
1 cup sugar
3 large egg yolks
¼ cup water
¼ cup vegetable oil
½ cup cake flour
3 tablespoons unsweetened cocoa powder (Dutch processed or natural)
3 tablespoons black cocoa powder (See Sources, page 379; 3 tablespoons regular cocoa power can be substituted)
½ teaspoon baking powder
¼ teaspoon baking soda

FOR THE DARK CHOCOLATE MOUSSE

1¼ cups whole milk
3¼ cups heavy cream
3 tablespoons sugar
½ vanilla, split in half lengthwise, seeds removed, seeds and pod reserved
3 egg yolks
¼ teaspoon powdered gelatin
8 ounces 70% dark chocolate, preferably Valrhona Guanaja (see Sources, page 379), coarsely chopped

FOR THE MILK CHOCOLATE MOUSSE

¼ teaspoon powdered gelatin
2¼ cups heavy cream
Finely grated zest of 1 lemon
8 ounces 40% milk chocolate, preferably Valrhona Jivara (see Sources, page 379), coarsely chopped

FOR THE CANDIED COCOA NIBS

1 cup sugar
1 tablespoon water
1 cup cocoa nibs, toasted (see page 367)
1 teaspoon kosher salt

FOR THE CHOCOLATE SAUCE

1½ cups sugar
2 cups water
3½ ounces 80% dark chocolate, preferably Valrhona Coeur de Guanaja (see Sources, page 379), coarsely chopped (about ¾ cup chopped)
About ½ cup fresh cherry juice (the juice from a jar of maraschino cherries can be substituted)

TO ASSEMBLE AND SERVE

½ cup freshly brewed espresso or coffee liqueur
18 Maraschino cherries
1 pint high-quality vanilla ice cream
About ¼ cup chocolate shavings, shaved with a Microplane or zester
Extra virgin olive oil
Flaky sea salt (optional)

To make the cake: Position a rack in the center of the oven and preheat the oven to 325°F. Line two 18 by 13-inch rimmed baking sheets with parchment paper and spray with nonstick spray. (Alternatively, grease the sheets with butter and lightly dust with flour.) (Note that you will not use all the cake when plating this dessert).

Put the egg whites in the bowl of a stand mixer fitted with the whisk attachment. Whisk on medium speed until foamy. Slowly add ¾ cup of the sugar, continuing to whisk on medium speed for 5 minutes, then raise the speed to high and whisk until the meringue is glossy and has tripled in volume, about 2 more minutes. Transfer the meringue to another bowl and wash and dry the mixer bowl and whisk.

Return the bowl to the mixer, add the egg yolks, water, vegetable oil, cake flour, the remaining ¼ cup sugar, the cocoa powder, black cocoa powder, baking powder, and baking soda, and whisk on high speed until the mixture has tripled in volume, 7 to 10 minutes.

Remove the bowl from the mixer stand and, using a large rubber spatula, fold the meringue into the yolk mixture until just combined. Spread the batter into the prepared baking sheet and bake until the cake is set (a toothpick inserted should come out clean), 7 to 10 minutes. Cool the cake completely on a cooling rack.

To make the dark chocolate mousse, first make a crème anglaise: Fill a large bowl halfway with ice and water. In a large heavy saucepan, combine the milk, heavy cream, sugar, and vanilla bean and seeds and cook, whisking, until the mixture reaches a temperature of 176°F. In a separate bowl, whisk the egg yolks and add a little of the cream mixture to temper the yolks. Whisk in the egg yolks, then strain the crème anglaise through a fine-mesh strainer into a heatproof bowl. Set the bowl over the ice water and let cool, stirring occasionally. Put the gelatin in a small bowl and cover with 1 teaspoon cold water. Set the gelatin aside to soften for 5 minutes. Meanwhile, pour the cream into a large bowl and, using a whisk or handheld mixer, whip until soft peaks form. Refrigerate until ready to make the mousse.

Put the crème anglaise in a medium saucepan and heat over medium heat, stirring occasionally, until hot to the touch. Add the gelatin and stir until the gelatin dissolves. Remove from the heat.

Set a heatproof bowl over a medium pot of simmering water and add the chocolate to the bowl, or add the chocolate to the top of a double boiler over simmering water. Melt the chocolate, whisking occasionally until smooth, then remove from the heat.

Pour the warm crème anglaise over the chocolate and stir until the mixture is emulsified. Let the mixture cool to below 104°F, then fold in about one quarter of the whipped cream to lighten the mixture, then fold in the remaining whipped cream. Cover and refrigerate the mixture.

To make the milk chocolate mousse: Put the gelatin in a small bowl and cover with 1 teaspoon cold water. Set the gelatin aside to soften for 5 minutes.

Meanwhile, pour 1¼ cups of the heavy cream into a large chilled bowl and whisk until soft peaks form. Cover and refrigerate.

Warm the remaining 1 cup heavy cream, along with the lemon zest, in a medium saucepan over medium heat. Add the gelatin and stir until it dissolves. Remove from the heat.

Melt the chocolate in a heatproof bowl over a medium pot of simmering water or in the top of a double boiler. Remove the bowl from the heat.

Pour the warm heavy cream over the chocolate and stir until emulsified. Fold in the whipped cream. Cover and refrigerate.

To make the cocoa nibs: Line a rimmed baking sheet with parchment paper or a silicone baking mat. Combine the sugar and water in a medium heavy saucepan and stir together briefly with a wooden spoon until it resembles wet sand. Cover and cook over medium heat (this will create condensation inside the pan, eliminating the need to brush the sides), checking every 5 minutes until it begins to attain a dark amber color. At this point you can stir in any crystallized bits to dissolve them. (Tip: To clean the pot, fill it with water, bring to a boil, and scrub clean.) Immediately mix in the cocoa nibs and salt, stirring to coat the nibs. Pour the mixture onto the prepared baking sheet and set aside to cool.

To make the chocolate sauce: Combine the sugar and water in a large heavy saucepan and heat until the sugar dissolves and the temperature reads 320°F on a digital or candy thermometer. Remove the pan from the heat and stir in the chocolate with a wooden spoon until the chocolate is completely melted and the sauce is smooth and emulsified. Stir in just enough cherry juice to thin the chocolate into a shiny, pourable sauce and set it aside to cool.

To assemble the cake: Cut 2 pieces of the devil's food cake to fit into an 18- by 12- by 3-inch (high) cake frame (see Sources, page 379). Place 1 cake layer upside down in the frame. Use a pastry brush to brush the cake with some of the espresso. Spread the dark chocolate mousse evenly over the layer and top with the second cake layer. Brush the layer with espresso and refrigerate for 30 minutes.

Remove the cake from the refrigerator and spread the milk chocolate mousse evenly over the top. Return the cake to the refrigerator and chill for at least 6 hours, or overnight.

To serve, unmold the cake and use a serrated knife to slice into 6- by 2-inch rectangles.

Center a piece of cake on each of 6 plates. Spoon some of the cherries over each one and arrange some nibs to one side. Set a scoop of ice cream over the nibs and garnish each plate with some chocolate shavings, a drizzle of extra virgin olive oil, and a pinch of sea salt, if using. Drizzle some chocolate sauce over and around the dessert on each plate.

**Variation** For a final flourish, garnish with gold leaf.

# PANNA COTTA WITH MEYER LEMON–BASIL SORBET AND ALMOND MILK FROTH

SERVES 6

This elaborate, contemporary take on a panna cotta (see page 175 for the original) is not for beginner cooks, but the result, both visually and from a flavor and textural standpoint, is spectacular.

This recipe uses Ultra-Tex, a modified cornstarch that thickens mixtures without needing to be heated as conventional cornstarch does.

Note that the sorbet base must be refrigerated overnight.

FOR THE MEYER LEMON–BASIL SORBET

½ cup water
½ cup sugar
½ teaspoon milk powder
1 cup freshly squeezed lemon juice
Finely grated zest of 1 Meyer lemon
Leaves from 1 bunch of basil, torn into pieces

FOR THE ALMOND MILK FROTH

1½ cups whole milk
½ cup heavy cream
1 cup blanched whole almonds, toasted (see page 367)
½ cup sugar
½ teaspoon lecithin (available at health food stores, or see Sources, page 379)
Pinch of kosher salt

FOR THE PANNA COTTA

5 teaspoons powdered gelatin
1½ cups heavy cream
1 cup whole milk
½ cup sugar
1 cup honey
4 vanilla beans, split lengthwise in half, seeds removed, seeds and pods reserved
Pinch of kosher salt
3 cups crème fraîche

FOR THE LEMON PEEL PUREE

1 cup (loosely packed) Meyer lemon peel (removed in strips with a peeler, any white pith removed)
6 whole star anise, toasted (see page 367)
15 whole black peppercorns, toasted (see page 367)
1 vanilla bean, split lengthwise in half, seeds removed, seeds and pod reserved
1 cup water
1 cup freshly squeezed lemon juice
¾ cup sugar

FOR THE FRUIT SOUP

4 cups freshly squeezed blood orange juice
¾ cup sugar
Zest of 1 orange, removed in strips with a vegetable peeler, white pith removed
1 tablespoon green cardamom pods
3 lemongrass stalks, cut into 1-inch pieces
⅔ cup freshly squeezed Meyer lemon juice
¼ cup 1.5–2% Ultra-Tex 3 (see Sources, page 379)

TO SERVE

1 cup chopped assorted seeded citrus segments, such as blood oranges, Cara Cara oranges, Meyer lemons, grapefruit, or Satsuma mandarins
¼ cup roasted Marcona almonds

To make the Meyer Lemon–Basil Sorbet: Combine the water, sugar, and milk powder in a medium pot and stir over medium heat just until the sugar dissolves. Transfer the simple syrup to a container, let cool to room temperature, then refrigerate until chilled.

Add the lemon juice, lemon zest, and basil to the chilled simple syrup, cover, and refrigerate overnight.

The next day, strain the lemon juice mixture through a fine-mesh sieve into a bowl, then pour into an ice cream machine and freeze according to the manufacturer's instructions. Transfer the sorbet to a covered container and store in the freezer until ready to use.

To make the almond milk froth: Combine the milk, heavy cream, almonds, sugar, lecithin, and salt in a large saucepan and bring to a boil over high heat, stirring to dissolve the sugar, then transfer to a container, let cool to room temperature, cover, and refrigerate overnight.

To make the panna cotta: Put the gelatin in a small bowl and cover with ⅝ cup cold water. Set the gelatin aside to soften for 5 minutes.

*(continued on page 358)*

Combine the heavy cream, milk, sugar, honey, vanilla pods and seeds, and salt in a medium pot and heat over medium heat until the mixture reaches 160°F on a digital or candy thermometer. Add the gelatin and stir until it and the sugar are dissolved. Whisk in the crème fraîche and strain the mixture through a fine-mesh sieve into a bowl. Ladle or pour the mixture into 6 wide shallow bowls or small parfait glasses. Refrigerate the panna cotta until set, at least 6 hours.

To make the lemon peel puree: Fill a medium saucepan with water, add the lemon peel, and bring to a boil over high heat, then drain the peel. Fill the saucepan with fresh water, add the lemon peel, and bring to a boil again. Drain and repeat the process once more.

Wrap the star anise, black peppercorns, and the vanilla pod in a cheesecloth bundle. Put the blanched peel, the water, lemon juice, sugar, herb sachet, and vanilla seeds in a small heavy pot, bring to a simmer over low heat, and cook until the lemon peel is translucent, 10 to 15 minutes. Remove from the heat and let cool to room temperature.

Remove and discard the sachet. Drain the lemon peel mixture and reserve the liquid. Add the peel to a blender with ½ cup to ¾ cup of the liquid (just enough for the blade to catch and create a smooth puree) and blend until pureed. Transfer to a small piping bag fitted with a fine tip, or into a squeeze bottle, and refrigerate until ready to use.

To make the fruit soup: Put 2 cups of the blood orange juice, the sugar, orange zest, cardamom, and lemongrass in a medium heavy pot and heat over medium heat. Cook, stirring, until the sugar dissolves, about 5 minutes. Meanwhile, fill a large bowl halfway with ice water. Remove the pot from the heat, transfer the mixture to a heatproof bowl, and cool over the ice water, stirring occasionally. Stir in the Meyer lemon juice and the rest of the blood orange juice. Cover the bowl with plastic wrap and chill overnight.

The next day, finish the fruit soup: Strain the mixture through a fine-mesh strainer into a stand blender. Add the Ultra-Tex and blend on high speed for 30 seconds.

To finish the almond froth: Transfer the almond mixture to a large saucepan and reheat over medium heat until warm. Use an immersion blender to lightly blend the mixture. Strain the mixture through a fine-mesh sieve into a bowl and cover to keep warm. Clean the blender to remove any almond debris and blend again, holding the bowl at a slight angle, to froth the mixture.

To serve, set a bowl of panna cotta on each of 6 plates, pipe some lemon puree on top, and spoon some citrus segments and soup alongside. Arrange a scoop of sorbet on the other side of each panna cotta and top with the citrus, almonds, and almond froth.

# OLIVE OIL CAKE WITH ROSEMARY ICE CREAM, PINE NUT PRALINE SABAYON, AND MERINGUE

MAKES ONE 10-INCH CAKE

Dense, moist, and exquisitely grainy, olive oil cake doesn't require much to render it complete, as evidenced by the classic recipe on page 177. On the other hand, because of those same qualities, the cake can get along with a variety of flavors and textures. Here it's matched with rosemary ice cream, a nut sabayon, and meringue, then finished with basil and balsamic vinegar.

Note that the ice cream base must be refrigerated overnight.

FOR THE ROSEMARY ICE CREAM

3 cups whole milk
¾ cup heavy cream
3 large rosemary sprigs
¾ cup sugar
1 tablespoon milk powder
1 cup plain Greek yogurt
Pinch of kosher salt

FOR THE OLIVE OIL CAKE

8 tablespoons (1 stick) unsalted butter, at room temperature
2 cups sugar
½ cup eggs (about 3 large eggs)
½ cup extra virgin olive oil
3 cups all-purpose flour
½ teaspoon baking powder
½ teaspoon kosher salt
1 cup whole milk

FOR THE OLIVE OIL SOAK

1 cup water
1 cup sugar
1 cup lemon marmalade
½ cup freshly squeezed lemon juice
½ cup extra virgin olive oil

FOR THE PINE NUT PRALINE SABAYON

1 envelope (about 2¼ teaspoons) powdered gelatin
4 cups heavy cream
¾ cup sugar
1 cup egg whites (about 6 large eggs)
½ cup pine nut praline paste (see Sources, page 379; roasted almond butter can be substituted)
1 vanilla bean, split lengthwise in half, seeds removed, seeds and pod reserved

FOR THE CANDIED PINE NUTS

1 cup sugar
¼ cup water
1 cup pine nuts, toasted (see page 369)
1 tablespoon honey
Pinch of kosher salt

FOR THE ITALIAN MERINGUE

½ cup egg whites (about 3 large whites)
1½ cups sugar

FOR THE CRÈME FRAÎCHE SABAYON

1 package (about 2¼ teaspoons) powdered gelatin
4 cups heavy cream
¾ cup sugar
1 cup egg whites (about 6 large eggs)
Finely grated zest of ½ lemon
1 vanilla bean, split lengthwise in half, seeds scraped out, seeds and beans reserved
1 cup crème fraîche
6 fresh basil leaves
3 tablespoons aged balsamic vinegar
½ cup shaved white chocolate

To make the rosemary ice cream: Combine the milk, heavy cream, and rosemary in a large heavy saucepan and bring to a boil over medium heat. Remove the pan from the heat, cover, and set aside to steep for 10 minutes.

Fill a large bowl halfway with ice water and set aside. Uncover the saucepan and return it to medium heat. Add the sugar and milk powder and whisk to incorporate. Cook, stirring occasionally with a wooden spoon, until the mixture reaches 183°F on a digital or candy thermometer. Remove from the heat.

Place a medium bowl over the ice bath and strain the milk mixture through a fine-mesh sieve into the bowl. Let cool, stirring occasionally, then whisk in the yogurt until incorporated. Cover with plastic wrap, placing the plastic wrap directly on top of the mixture. Refrigerate for at least 6 hours or, preferably, overnight.

Pour the ice cream base into an ice cream machine and freeze according to the manufacturer's instructions. Transfer the ice cream to a covered container and store in the freezer until ready to use.

To make the olive oil cake: Position a rack in the center of the oven and preheat the oven to 300°F. Butter and flour a 10-inch round cake pan.

Combine the butter and sugar in the bowl of a stand

*(continued)*

mixer fitted with the whisk attachment and whisk on medium-high speed until the mixture is light and fluffy. Add the eggs one at a time, mixing until incorporated. Slowly pour in the olive oil in a thin stream and mix until well incorporated.

Sift the flour, baking powder, and salt together into a medium bowl. Add one third of the flour mixture to the olive oil mixture and mix to incorporate. Pour in one third of the milk and mix to incorporate. Continue adding the remaining flour and milk one third at a time, mixing until fully incorporated.

Pour the batter into the prepared cake pan and bake until the sides of the cake pull away from the pan, 50 minutes to 1 hour.

To make the olive oil soak: Combine ½ cup of the water and the sugar in a medium pot and stir over medium heat just until the sugar dissolves. Transfer the simple syrup to a container, let cool to room temperature, then refrigerate until chilled. Put the simple syrup, marmalade, lemon juice, remaining ½ cup water, and olive oil in a blender and blend until smooth. If the marmalade contains pieces of fruit or peel, strain the mixture through a fine-mesh strainer and discard the solids.

Remove the cake from the oven, brush lightly with the soak, and set the pan on a rack to cool completely. Brush again with the soak.

To make the pine nut praline sabayon: Put the gelatin in a small bowl and cover with ¼ cup cold water. Set aside to soften for 5 minutes.

Fill a medium bowl halfway with ice water and set aside. Combine the heavy cream, sugar, egg whites, nut paste, and vanilla pod and seeds in a large heavy saucepan, stir together, and heat over medium heat until the mixture reaches 176°F on a digital or candy thermometer. Add the gelatin and stir until it is dissolved.

Place a medium bowl on top of the ice bath and strain the sabayon through a fine-mesh sieve into the bowl. Let cool, stirring occasionally, until the sabayon is completely chilled.

To make the candied pine nuts: Have all of the ingredients prepared and at hand to facilitate moving quickly as you prepare this recipe. Line a rimmed baking sheet with parchment paper or a silicone baking mat and set aside. Combine the sugar and water in a medium heavy saucepan and stir together briefly with a wooden spoon until it resembles wet sand. Cover and cook over medium heat (this will create condensation inside the pan, eliminating the need to brush the sides) until a dark amber caramel forms, checking every 5 minutes until it begins to attain a dark amber color. At this point you can stir in any crystallized bits to dissolve them. Add the pine nuts and honey and stir to combine, then immediately pour the mixture onto the prepared baking sheet and sprinkle with the salt. (Tip: To clean the pot, fill it with water, bring to a boil, and scrub clean.) Set aside to cool completely. Once cool, break the praline apart by hand, or coarsely chop with a knife. Transfer the pieces to an airtight container immediately; they take on moisture quickly.

To make the Italian meringue: Put the egg whites in the bowl of a stand mixer fitted with the whisk attachment and mix the whites on low to medium speed while you cook the sugar. Combine the sugar and just enough water to moisten the sugar thoroughly (the mixture should be the consistency of wet sand) in a medium heavy saucepan and heat over medium heat, stirring, until the sugar dissolves, then cook until the syrup reaches 250°F on a digital or candy thermometer. Immediately remove from the heat.

Turn the stand mixer to high speed and carefully stream in the hot syrup, being careful to avoid the spinning whisk. Then continue whipping until the meringue is shiny and has cooled to just a bit warmer than room temperature. Transfer to a pastry bag fitted with a medium plain tip or medium star tip and pipe the meringue onto the top of the cake.

To make the crème fraîche sabayon: Put the gelatin in a small bowl and cover with ¼ cup cold water. Set aside to soften for 5 minutes.

Fill a large bowl halfway with ice water and set aside. Add the heavy cream, sugar, egg whites, lemon zest, and vanilla pods and seeds to a large heavy saucepan and cook over medium heat until the mixture reaches 176°F on a digital or candy thermometer. Add the gelatin and crème fraîche and whisk until the gelatin dissolves and the mixture is smooth.

Place a medium bowl over the ice bath and strain the sabayon through a fine-mesh sieve into the bowl. Let cool, stirring occasionally, until the sabayon is completely chilled.

About 30 minutes prior to serving, use a whisk to gently whip the pine nut praline sabayon and the crème fraîche sabayon until soft-medium peaks form.

To serve, brush the cake lightly a third time with the soak, then cut the cake into slices. Put a slice on each plate, top with the two sabayons, drizzle with the olive oil soak and vinegar, and garnish with the candied pine nuts, basil, and white chocolate.

# APRICOT-CHOCOLATE BUDINO

SERVES 6

This is a go-for-broke contemporary riff on chocolate pudding, loaded with complementary flavors and textures—from a smooth and sweet apricot coulis to a cold, crunchy, amaretto granite. Note that the milk for the gelato must infuse overnight. The optional coffee sabayon may be replaced with whipped cream or coffee-flavored whipped cream made by infusing cream with coffee beans overnight, straining out the beans, and whipping the cream.

FOR THE MACADAMIA GELATO

- 1 ½ cups whole milk
- ½ cup (2 ounces) macadamia nuts, toasted (see page 367) and lightly crushed (under the bottom of a heavy skillet)
- 1 cup heavy cream
- ½ cup granulated sugar
- ¼ cup milk powder
- ½ cup egg yolks (about 6 large yolks)

FOR THE APRICOT-CHOCOLATE BUDINO

- 1 envelope (about 2 ¼ teaspoons) powdered gelatin
- 6.5 ounces 40% milk chocolate, preferably Valrhona Jivara (see Sources, page 379), finely chopped (about 2 ½ cups chopped)
- 6.5 ounces 66% bittersweet chocolate, preferably Valrhona Caraibe (see Sources, page 379), finely chopped (about 2 ½ cups chopped)
- 4 cups half-and-half
- 1 cup granulated sugar
- 8 large egg yolks
- 1 vanilla bean, split in half lengthwise, seeds removed, seeds and pod reserved
- ¾ cup plus 2 tablespoons apricot puree (see Sources, page 379) or nectar, strained

FOR THE CANDIED MACADAMIA NUTS

- ¾ cup granulated sugar
- ¼ cup water
- 2 cups macadamia nuts, toasted (see page 367)
- Pinch of kosher salt

FOR THE APRICOT COULIS

- 1 ¼ cups apricot puree
- 1 cup water
- ½ cup granulated sugar
- ¼ cup freshly squeezed lemon juice
- 2 tablespoons Ultra-Tex 3 (See Sources, page 379)

FOR THE TUILES

- 12 tablespoons (1 ½ sticks) unsalted butter, at room temperature
- 1 cup confectioners' sugar
- 1 tablespoon apricot puree (1 large egg white can be substituted)
- 2 tablespoons all-purpose flour

FOR THE PEDRO XIMENEZ REDUCTION

- 1 cup Pedro Ximenez sherry
- ¼ cup dark muscovado sugar (dark brown sugar can be substituted)
- Peel of ¼ lemon, removed in strips with a vegetable peeler

FOR THE AMARETTO GRANITA

- 3 cups water
- ¼ cup granulated sugar
- ¼ cup (packed) muscovado sugar
- ¼ cup amaretto
- ¼ cup freshly squeezed lemon juice

FOR THE COFFEE SABAYON (OPTIONAL)

- 1 envelope (about 2 ¼ teaspoons) powdered gelatin
- 4 cups heavy cream
- ¾ cup granulated sugar
- 1 cup egg whites (about 6 large eggs)
- ¾ cup coffee beans

To make the macadamia gelato: Heat the milk in a large saucepan over medium heat until just warmed. Transfer the milk to a large plastic container, add the macadamia nuts, cover, and refrigerate overnight to infuse the milk.

The next day, pour the milk and nut mixture into a large pot and heat over medium heat until just warmed through. Transfer to a blender and blend just until the nuts are broken up; do not process to a smooth puree.

Fill a large bowl halfway with ice water and set it aside. Transfer the macadamia milk to a large pot. Add the cream, place the pot over medium heat, and heat until the mixture reaches 140°F on a digital or candy thermometer. Add the granulated sugar and milk powder and stir to incorporate, then remove from the heat.

Put the egg yolks in a medium bowl and whisk together lightly. Gradually pour in some of the hot milk mixture, whisking constantly, until the eggs are warmed, then return the mixture to the pot and cook over medium heat, stirring constantly with a wooden spoon, until it reaches 183°F on a

*(continued on page 364)*

digital or candy thermometer (the mixture should hold a line drawn on the back of the spoon).

Place a medium bowl on top of the ice bath and strain the custard through a fine-mesh sieve into the bowl. Let cool, stirring occasionally, then cover with plastic wrap, placing the plastic wrap directly on top of the custard. Refrigerate for at least 6 hours or, preferably, overnight.

Pour the custard into an ice cream machine and freeze according to the manufacturer's instructions. Transfer the ice cream to a covered container and store in the freezer until ready to use.

To make the apricot-chocolate budino: Put the gelatin in a small bowl and add ½ cup plus 1 tablespoon cold water. Set aside to soften for 5 minutes.

Put the two chocolates in a large heatproof bowl and set aside. Combine the half-and-half, granulated sugar, egg yolks, and vanilla pod and seeds in a medium pot, stir together, and cook over medium heat until the mixture reaches 183°F on a digital or candy thermometer. Add the gelatin and stir until it dissolves. Add the apricot puree and stir to combine.

Strain the hot custard through a fine-mesh sieve into the bowl with the chocolate. Blend with an immersion blender or handheld mixer until the liquid is fully incorporated. Ladle or pour the mixture into 6 serving cups and refrigerate for at least 4 hours, or overnight, to set.

To make the candied macadamia nuts: Line a rimmed baking sheet with parchment paper or a silicone baking mat and set aside. Combine the granulated sugar and water in a medium heavy saucepan and stir together briefly with a wooden spoon until it resembles wet sand. Cover and cook over medium heat (this will create condensation inside the pan, eliminating the need to brush the sides) until a dark amber caramel forms, checking every 5 minutes until it begins to attain a dark amber color. At this point you can stir in any crystallized bits to dissolve them. Add the macadamia nuts and stir until completely coated with caramel, then immediately pour the mixture onto the prepared baking sheet and sprinkle with the salt. Set aside to cool completely, then pulse in a food processor fitted with the steel blade to make a rough crumb.

To make the apricot coulis: Fill a large bowl halfway with ice water and set aside. Add the apricot puree, water, granulated sugar, lemon juice, and the Ultra-Tex 3 to a medium saucepan and heat over medium heat, stirring to dissolve the sugar, until the mixture reaches 160°F on a digital or candy thermometer.

Place a medium bowl on top of the ice bath and strain the coulis through a fine-mesh sieve into the bowl.

To make the tuiles: Preheat the oven to 350°F. Line a rimmed baking sheet with parchment paper or a silicone baking mat and set aside.

Combine the butter and confectioners' sugar in the bowl of a stand mixer fitted with the paddle attachment and beat until the mixture is light and fluffy, 2 to 3 minutes. Add the apricot puree and mix to combine. Add the flour and mix just to incorporate.

Use an offset spatula to spread the mixture ¼ inch thick onto the prepared baking sheet. Bake until the tuile is golden brown, about 10 minutes. Remove the pan from the oven and cool completely. Break the tuile into shards and set aside until ready to use. (The tuile will be buttery, which is normal. For extended storage, keep the shards on paper towels in an airtight container at room temperature.)

To make the Pedro Ximenez reduction: Combine the sherry, muscovado sugar, and lemon peel in a small heavy saucepan, bring to a boil, stirring to dissolve the sugar, and cook until the mixture is reduced to a syrupy consistency, 6 to 8 minutes. Set aside to cool.

To make the amaretto granita: Combine the water, granulated sugar, and the muscovado sugar in a large heavy saucepan and bring to a boil, stirring until the sugar is dissolved. Pour the mixture into a medium heatproof bowl.

Add the amaretto and lemon juice and stir to combine. Carefully place the bowl in the freezer and freeze for 30 minutes.

Stir the granita with a fork or metal spatula, breaking up the large ice crystals, and return to the freezer. Continue to stir every 30 minutes until the granita is flaky, 2 to 3 hours total. Cover and store in the freezer until ready to serve.

To make the coffee sabayon, if using: Add the gelatin to a small bowl and cover with ¼ cup cold water. Set aside to soften for 5 minutes.

Fill a large bowl halfway with ice water and set aside. Add the heavy cream, granulated sugar, egg whites, and coffee beans to a large heavy saucepan and cook until the mixture reaches 183°F on a digital or candy thermometer, about 10 minutes. Add the gelatin and whisk until it dissolves.

Place a medium bowl over the ice bath and strain the mixture through a fine-mesh sieve into the bowl. Let cool, stirring occasionally, until completely cooled, then cover with plastic wrap and refrigerate.

About 30 minutes before serving, use a whisk to gently whip the sabayon until soft peaks form, then set aside at room temperature until serving.

To serve, put some apricot coulis in the center of each of 6 plates. Top with some of the sherry reduction, then some macadamia crumble. Pipe 3 dots of sabayon around the coulis on each plate. Set the budino cups on the plates, and top each budino with a scoop of macadamia gelato and a scoop of amaretto granita. Decorate with the tuile shards.

# ROSEMARY YOGURT–BUTTERNUT SQUASH SEMIFREDDO WITH BLACKBERRY SAUCE AND PISTACHIOS

SERVES 6

Among the many inspired touches in this contemporary spin on semifreddo (see page 176 for a more traditional one) is replacing the whipped cream in the original with marshmallow and including butternut squash for its inherent sweetness. Although the semifreddo leans toward Northern Italy with its combination of squash and rosemary, the pistachio puree and ground pistachios add a distinctly Sicilian flourish.

FOR THE ROSEMARY YOGURT SQUASH SEMIFREDDO

3¾ cups whole milk
½ cup heavy cream
2 teaspoons milk powder
2 fresh rosemary sprigs
8 ounces butternut squash, peeled, seeds removed, and cut into ½-inch cubes
1 cup store-bought marshmallows
1 cup plain yogurt
1 cup pistachios, toasted (see page 369) and coarsely chopped
1 cup finely diced dried apricots

FOR THE BLACKBERRY SAUCE

1 cup whole blackberries
½ cup water
¼ cup sugar
2 teaspoons freshly squeezed lemon juice

FOR THE PISTACHIO PUREE

1 cup pistachios, preferably Sicilian
1½ cups water
½ cup sugar
Kosher salt

TO SERVE

1 tablespoon ground pistachios

To make the rosemary yogurt squash semifreddo: Put the milk, cream, milk powder, rosemary sprigs, and squash in a medium heavy pot, bring to a simmer over medium-high heat, and cook until the squash is tender, about 10 minutes. Use tongs to remove and discard the rosemary sprigs.

Transfer the mixture to a blender in batches, and blend until smooth (see Blender Safety, page 75). Return the mixture to the pot and place over medium heat. Add the marshmallows and cook, stirring, until the marshmallows are melted. Meanwhile, fill a medium bowl halfway with ice water. Place a medium heatproof bowl over the bowl of ice water and strain the marshmallow mixture through a fine-mesh strainer into the bowl, pressing down gently with the bottom of a ladle but not so hard as to push any particles through the strainer. Cool, stirring occasionally, until the mixture is thoroughly chilled, then fold in the yogurt.

Transfer the mixture to an ice cream machine and freeze according to the manufacturer's instructions. While the ice cream is still churning but is almost finished, add the pistachios and apricots. Set 6 ring molds (2-inch diameter, 3 inches high) on a parchment-lined baking tray. Pour the frozen mixture into the ring molds, and freeze until ready to serve.

To make the blackberry sauce: Fill a medium bowl with ice water. Add the blackberries, water, sugar, and lemon juice to a medium saucepan and bring the mixture to a boil, stirring occasionally. Place a medium heatproof bowl over the ice water and strain the sauce through a fine-mesh sieve into the bowl. Cool, stirring occasionally, until the sauce is chilled, then refrigerate until ready to serve. Set the bowl of ice water aside.

To make the pistachio puree: Put the pistachios, water, sugar, and a pinch of salt in a medium saucepan. Bring to a boil over medium heat, stirring occasionally to dissolve the sugar, and cook for 5 minutes. Transfer the mixture to a blender and blend until smooth (see Blender Safety, page 75).

Place a medium heatproof bowl over the bowl of ice water and strain the pistachio puree through a fine-mesh strainer into the bowl. Cool, stirring occasionally, until the puree is chilled.

To serve, unmold one semifreddo into the center of each of the 6 chilled molds. Spoon some pistachio puree over each one, then top with some blackberry sauce. Sprinkle with the ground pistachios.

# BASIC TECHNIQUES AND RECIPES

# BASIC TECHNIQUES

Here are some useful techniques that are called for repeatedly throughout the book.

## BLANCHING AND SHOCKING VEGETABLES, GREENS, AND HERBS

To blanch vegetables, greens, or herbs, fill a medium pot halfway with water, salt it, and bring to a boil over high heat. Fill a large bowl halfway with ice water.

If using vegetables, add to the boiling water and blanch until al dente, 2 to 3 minutes; if using leafy greens or herbs, blanch until wilted and bright green, about 1 minute. Drain in a colander and immediately transfer to the ice water to stop the cooking (shock) and set the color. Drain again.

If you own a salad spinner, spin shocked greens in it to dry them and sharpen their flavor.

## PEELING AND SEEDING TOMATOES

To peel tomatoes, fill a medium pot halfway with water and bring to a boil over high heat. Fill a large bowl half-way with ice water.

Use a paring knife to remove the core from the top of each tomato. Score the bottoms of the tomatoes with a shallow X. Submerge them in the boiling water just until the skin begins to pull away from the flesh at the X, 10 to 15 seconds. Use tongs or a slotted spoon to transfer the tomatoes to the ice water to stop the cooking. Once they are cool enough to handle, remove the skins, which should come off easily, with the aid of the paring knife if necessary.

To seed tomatoes, cut them in half and gently squeeze out the seeds.

## ROASTING GARLIC

To roast garlic, position a rack in the center of the oven and preheat the oven to 350°F.

Cut the very top off a head of garlic and set it in a small ramekin or other small ovenproof vessel. Drizzle 1 tablespoon olive oil and 1 tablespoon water over the garlic and season with salt and pepper. Roast until the cloves have softened (a knife tip should slide easily in and out), 35 to 40 minutes. Let cool until cool enough to handle, then pop the cloves out of their jackets.

## TOASTING AND GRINDING NUTS AND SPICES

To toast nuts and spices, put them in a wide heavy sauté pan and toast over medium heat, shaking the pan to prevent them from scorching, until lightly toasted and fragrant, about 2 minutes for spices, 5 minutes for nuts. Remove the pan from the heat and let cool.

To grind spices and nuts, use a dedicated grinder. You can also use a coffee grinder; just be sure to wipe it out well before and after using it.

## FRYING CAPERS

To fry capers, heat an inch or so of canola oil to 350°F in a deep saucepan. Pat the capers dry with a paper towel and fry until lightly golden and crispy, about 1 minute. Use a slotted spoon to transfer them to paper towels to drain. They are already salty, but they may be seasoned with a pinch of sea salt just after frying, if desired.

Add fried capers to vegetable side dishes and salads, or use as a garnish for seafood soups.

## TO OBTAIN BONE MARROW

To obtain bone marrow, have your butcher halve veal femur bones lengthwise to expose the marrow; 2 pounds bones will yield approximately 8 ounces marrow. Soak them in salted ice water for 3 to 6 hours, changing the water if it becomes bright red. As it chills and constricts, the marrow will come right out of the bones.

## SHUCKING OYSTERS

To shuck an oyster, using a towel to protect your hand, grasp the oyster and, using your other hand, force an oyster knife or other small sturdy knife into the oyster and move it around, taking care not to cut into the oyster, until the shell "pops" open. To separate the oyster from the shell, cut through the muscle where it meets the shell. Store the oysters in their liquid in an airtight container.

# BASIC RECIPES

## BASIL PESTO

MAKES ABOUT 1½ CUPS

This well-known Ligurian condiment has a multitude of uses, from tossing it with hot pasta to stirring it into soups to spreading it on sandwiches to spooning it over white-fleshed fish, chicken, or other meats and poultry.

2 cups (loosely packed) fresh basil leaves
1/3 cup (loosely packed) fresh flat-leaf parsley leaves
2 tablespoons pine nuts
2 tablespoons coarsely chopped walnuts
1 large garlic clove, smashed with the side of a chef's knife and peeled
¼ cup extra virgin olive oil, plus more if storing the pesto
¼ cup finely grated Parmigiano-Reggiano
¼ cup finely grated Pecorino Romano
Kosher salt
Freshly ground black pepper

Put the basil, parsley, pine nuts, walnuts, and garlic in the bowl of a food processor and pulse until a coarse mixture forms, then add the olive oil and pulse a few times to incorporate it. Using a rubber spatula, scrape the pesto into a bowl, then fold in the Parmigiano and Pecorino. Season with salt and pepper.

The pesto can be refrigerated in an airtight container for up to 2 weeks, covered with a thin film of olive oil to keep it from discoloring. Let come to room temperature before using.

## TOMATO CONFIT

MAKES ABOUT 1 CUP

These oven-dried tomatoes are packed with flavor; the recipe is especially useful for coaxing flavor out of wan off-season tomatoes.

4 plum tomatoes, peeled (see page 367), quartered, seeded, and ribs removed
2 tablespoons extra virgin olive oil, plus more if storing the confit
1 garlic clove, minced
1 teaspoon fresh thyme leaves
Kosher salt
Freshly ground black pepper

Position a rack in the center of the oven and preheat the oven to 200°F.

Put the tomatoes in a bowl and add the olive oil, garlic, and thyme. Season with salt and pepper and toss well. Spread the tomatoes out on a rimmed baking sheet and roast until shriveled but still moist, about 1½ hours.

The tomatoes can be used right away or refrigerated in an airtight container, covered with olive oil, for up to 2 days.

# GARLIC CONFIT

MAKES ABOUT ½ CUP

Slow-cooking garlic in olive oil results in a luscious texture and mellow flavor. Add the garlic cloves to fish and meat dishes, or mash and spread them on toast for a snack or as an accompaniment to salads.

8 large garlic cloves, peeled
1 cup extra virgin olive oil

Put the garlic and olive oil in a small heavy saucepan and bring to a simmer over medium heat, then remove the pot from the heat and set aside until the garlic is soft, about 30 minutes.

The garlic confit can be refrigerated in an airtight container in its oil for up to 2 days.

# RED WINE SAUCE

MAKES ABOUT ¾ CUP

4 tablespoons unsalted butter
4 large shallots, thinly sliced
1 large garlic clove, minced
1 thyme sprig
1 bay leaf, preferably fresh
1 cup coarsely chopped whole button mushrooms (optional)
2 cups dry red wine
2 cups Veal Stock (page 375) or Dark Chicken Stock (page 374)
Kosher salt
Freshly ground black pepper

Heat a medium heavy saucepan over medium heat. Add 2 tablespoons of the butter and tip and tilt the pan to coat it. Once the butter is melted and foaming, add the shallots and garlic and cook, stirring with a wooden spoon, until tender, 3 to 4 minutes. Add the thyme, bay leaf, and mushrooms, if using, and cook, stirring occasionally, until the shallots are lightly browned and the mushrooms are tender.

Pour in the wine and use the wooden spoon to loosen any flavorful bits cooked onto the bottom of the pan, then cook until the liquid has almost completely evaporated, about 12 minutes. Pour in the stock, bring to a simmer, and simmer until reduced by half, about 8 minutes.

Strain the sauce through a fine-mesh strainer into a medium bowl, pressing on the solids with a wooden spoon or a ladle to release as much flavorful liquid as possible; discard the solids. Return the sauce to the pan and bring to a simmer. Whisk in the remaining 2 tablespoons butter and continue to whisk until fully incorporated. Season with salt and pepper and remove from the heat.

The sauce can be refrigerated in an airtight container for up to 2 days.

## VEGETABLE STOCK

MAKES ABOUT 2 QUARTS

While it can be advantageous to cook some stocks for longer than the recipe prescribes, here long cooking can produce a muddled flavor, so do not simmer for more than 45 minutes.

1 small onion, coarsely chopped
1 leek (white and light green parts only), well washed and coarsely chopped
1 celery stalk, trimmed and coarsely chopped
1 carrot, coarsely chopped
1 fennel bulb, trimmed and coarsely chopped
10 white button mushrooms, trimmed and halved
2 plum tomatoes, halved
3 fresh flat-leaf parsley sprigs
2 small bay leaves
2 garlic cloves, smashed with the side of a chef's knife and peeled
1 teaspoon whole black peppercorns
Kosher salt (optional)

Put the onions, leeks, celery, carrots, fennel, mushrooms, tomatoes, parsley, bay leaves, garlic, and peppercorns in a large pot and add enough cold water to cover them by 1 inch. Bring to a simmer over medium-high heat, then lower the heat and simmer gently for 45 minutes.

Season the stock with salt, if desired. Strain it through a fine-mesh strainer into a bowl and discard the solids. Set aside to cool.

Refrigerate the stock in an airtight container for up to 2 days, or freeze it, in small batches, for up to 2 months.

## MUSHROOM STOCK

MAKES ABOUT 4 CUPS

I use this stock to emphasize the mushroom flavor in dishes featuring them.

2 tablespoons canola oil
1 pound white button mushrooms, trimmed and coarsely chopped
1 Spanish onion, cut into large pieces
2 large carrots, cut into large pieces
2 celery stalks, trimmed and cut into large pieces
2 large garlic cloves, smashed with the side of a chef's knife and peeled
1 rosemary sprig
1 thyme sprig
1 bay leaf
¼ cup brandy
½ cup dry white wine
8 cups Chicken Stock (page 374) or water
Kosher salt
Freshly ground black pepper

Heat a large heavy pot over medium-high heat. Add the canola oil and heat it, tipping and tilting the pot to coat it with the oil. Add the mushrooms, onions, carrots, celery, garlic, rosemary, thyme, and bay leaf and cook, stirring occasionally, until the vegetables are tender, about 6 minutes. Pour in the brandy, bring to a simmer, and simmer until the brandy has almost completely evaporated, about 3 minutes. Pour in the wine, bring to a simmer, and simmer until the brandy has almost completely evaporated, about 6 minutes.

Add the stock and bring to a simmer, then lower the heat and simmer, uncovered, until the stock has a strong but not overwhelming mushroom flavor, 2 to 3 hours. Season with salt and pepper.

Strain the stock through a fine-mesh strainer into a bowl and discard the solids. Set aside to cool.

Refrigerate the stock in an airtight container for up to 3 days or freeze it, in small batches, for up to 2 months.

## SHRIMP STOCK

MAKES ABOUT 1½ QUARTS

Shrimp stock is a terrific all-purpose stock for adding an undercurrent of shellfish flavor to dishes. For a more complex stock in the same vein, see the Seafood Stock (recipe below).

2 tablespoons olive oil
5 cups shrimp shells (from about 2 pounds shrimp)
3 large garlic cloves, smashed with the side of a chef's knife and peeled
1 small Spanish onion, coarsely chopped
1 small carrot, coarsely chopped
1 celery stalk, trimmed and coarsely chopped
2 tablespoons tomato paste
1 cup dry white wine
½ cup brandy
1 small bunch of basil
4 fresh flat-leaf parsley stems

Heat a large heavy pot over medium-high heat. Add the olive oil and tip and tilt the pot to coat it, heating the oil until it is shimmering and almost smoking. Add the shrimp shells and cook, stirring vigorously with a wooden spoon, until they turn bright red, about 4 minutes. Add the garlic, onions, carrots, and celery and cook, stirring frequently, until softened but not browned, about 4 minutes. Add the tomato paste, stirring to coat the other ingredients with the paste, and cook until it turns a shade darker, about 2 minutes.

Pour in the wine and use the wooden spoon to loosen any flavorful bits cooked onto the bottom of the pot. Bring to a simmer and simmer until the wine has almost completely evaporated, about 4 minutes. Stir in the brandy, bring to a simmer, and simmer until the brandy has almost completely evaporated, about 2 minutes. Stir in the basil and parsley, pour in enough cold water to cover the solids by 1 inch, and bring to a simmer, then lower the heat and simmer for 1 hour.

Pass the stock through a food mill into a bowl, or transfer to a blender, in batches if necessary, and blend (see Blender Safety, page 75). Strain the stock through a fine-mesh strainer into a bowl, pressing down on the solids with a wooden spoon or a ladle to extract as much flavorful liquid as possible. Discard the solids. Let the stock cool.

Refrigerate the stock in an airtight container for up to 3 days or freeze it, in small batches, for up to 2 months.

## SEAFOOD STOCK

MAKES ABOUT 2½ QUARTS

Although expressly devised for the brodetto on page 114, this is a good seafood stock to have in your repertoire. It can also be used to make a quick soup with the addition of diced and sautéed zucchini or poached shrimp.

¼ cup olive oil
3 large garlic cloves, smashed with the side of a chef's knife and peeled
1 leek (white and light green parts only), well washed and thinly sliced
1 large Spanish onion, cut into small dice
1 celery stalk, trimmed and cut into small dice
1 large beefsteak tomato, cut into small dice, or 1 15-ounce can whole tomatoes, preferably Italian San Marzano or organic, crushed by hand, with their juice
2 to 3 pounds fish bones, shrimp shells, and/or lobster bodies
4 flat-leaf parsley stems
1 large basil sprig
2 bay leaves
Kosher salt
Freshly ground black pepper
1 cup dry white wine

Heat a medium heavy pot over medium heat. Add the olive oil and tip and tilt the pot to coat it, heating the oil until it is shimmering and almost smoking. Add the garlic, leeks, onions, and celery and cook, stirring periodically with a wooden spoon, until the vegetables are softened but not browned, about 4 minutes. Add the tomatoes, the bones, shells, and/or lobster bodies, the parsley stems, basil, and bay leaves and cook, stirring, just until the tomatoes begin to break down, about 5 minutes. Season with salt and pepper and pour in the wine. Cook, using the wooden spoon to loosen any flavorful bits cooked onto the bottom of the pan, until the liquid has almost completely evaporated, 6 to 7 minutes.

Pour in enough cold water to cover the solids by 1 inch. Bring to a simmer over medium-high heat, then lower the heat so the liquid is gently simmering and simmer for 45 minutes. Use a wooden spoon to break up the lobster pieces, if using, to release their flavors, then strain the stock first through a colander (discard the solids), pressing on the solids with the wooden spoon or a spatula to extract as much flavorful liquid as possible, and then through a fine-mesh strainer into a large bowl. Let the stock cool.

Refrigerate the stock in an airtight container for up to 2 days or freeze it, in small batches, for up to 2 months.

## FISH STOCK

MAKES ABOUT 2 QUARTS

This stock will punch up the natural flavor of fish dishes. Note that you may need to call ahead to ask your fishmonger for the bones and trimmings.

- 2 cups dry white wine
- 1/3 cup white wine vinegar
- 2 Spanish onions, halved through the root end, 1 clove stuck in each half
- 2 carrots, coarsely chopped
- 1 celery stalk, trimmed and coarsely chopped
- 3 flat-leaf parsley sprigs
- 1 thyme sprig
- 1 bay leaf
- Kosher salt
- 6 cups water
- Trimmings and bones from 2 or 3 lean white-fleshed, nonoily fish

Put the wine, vinegar, onions, carrots, celery, parsley, thyme, bay leaf, and 1½ teaspoons salt in a large heavy pot. Pour in the water and add the fish trimmings and bones. Bring to a boil over medium-high heat, then lower the heat so the liquid is simmering, cover, and simmer for 1 hour.

Strain the stock through a fine-mesh strainer into a large bowl, pressing down on the solids with a wooden spoon or a ladle to extract as much flavorful liquid as possible. Taste and season with salt if necessary. (If the stock seems thin, transfer to a pot and simmer for a few minutes to reduce it slightly and intensify its flavor.) Let cool.

Refrigerate the stock in an airtight container for up to 3 days, or freeze it, in small batches, for up to 2 months.

## CHICKEN STOCK

MAKES ABOUT 2 QUARTS

Chicken is the most called-on stock in most kitchens and well worth taking the time to make and keep on hand.

2 large carrots, cut into large dice
2 Spanish onions, cut into large dice
2 celery stalks, trimmed and cut into large dice
4 or 5 flat-leaf parsley stems
1 bay leaf
5 pounds chicken bones, preferably wings and backs, chopped into small pieces and rinsed
A Parmigiano-Reggiano rind (optional)
Kosher salt
Freshly ground black pepper

Put the carrots, onions, celery, parsley stems, and bay leaf in a large heavy pot. Add the chicken bones, Parmigiano rind, if using, and enough cold water to cover the bones. Bring to a simmer over medium-high heat, lower the heat, and simmer for 2½ to 3 hours. Season with salt and pepper.

Remove and discard the bones. Strain the stock through a fine-mesh strainer into a bowl and discard the solids. Set aside to cool.

Refrigerate the stock in an airtight container for up to 3 days, or freeze it, in small batches, for up to 2 months.

## DARK CHICKEN STOCK

MAKES ABOUT 2 QUARTS

Use this stock when a forceful chicken flavor is desired in sauces and other preparations.

3 tablespoons canola oil
3½ pounds chicken bones, preferably wings and backs, chopped into small pieces and rinsed
1 cup coarsely chopped shallots
1 cup Spanish onion, cut into large dice
1 large carrot, cut into large dice
2 celery stalks, trimmed and cut into large dice
4 large garlic cloves, smashed with the side of a chef's knife and peeled
1 cup dry white wine
2 rosemary sprigs
3 bay leaves
4 or 5 flat-leaf parsley stems (optional)
About 4 quarts Chicken Stock (recipe above) or water
Kosher salt
Freshly ground black pepper

Heat a large heavy pot over medium-high heat. Pour in 1½ tablespoons of the canola oil and tip and tilt the pot to coat it. Add the chicken bones and cook, using a pair of tongs to turn the bones occasionally, until browned on all sides, about 8 minutes. Remove the bones from the pot and transfer to a large plate.

Pour out the oil and add the remaining 1½ tablespoons canola oil, along with the shallots, onions, carrots, celery, and garlic, to the pot. Cook, stirring occasionally with a wooden spoon, until the vegetables are browned, about 6 minutes. Return the chicken bones to the pot and stir well. Pour in the wine and use the wooden spoon to loosen any flavorful bits cooked onto the bottom of the pot. Add the rosemary, bay leaves, and parsley stems, if using, bring to a simmer, and cook, stirring occasionally, until the wine is reduced by half, about 5 minutes.

Add the stock and bring to a simmer, then reduce the heat and simmer for 3 to 4 hours. Season with salt and pepper.

Remove and discard the bones. Strain the stock through

a fine-mesh strainer into a bowl and discard the solids. Set aside to cool.

Refrigerate the stock in an airtight container for up to 3 days, or freeze, in small batches, for up to 2 months.

## VEAL STOCK

MAKES 2 QUARTS

For rich, complex beefy flavor, there's nothing like a homemade veal stock. It requires more steps than other stock recipes, but it is well worth the time and effort.

Note that the stock needs to be refrigerated overnight to allow the fat to separate.

- 8 pounds veal bones, larger bones cracked (by your butcher), chopped (again by your butcher) into 2-inch pieces
- 2 large carrots, each cut into 2 or 3 large pieces
- 2 large Spanish onions, unpeeled, halved through the root end, 1 clove stuck in each half
- 1 leek (white and pale green parts only), halved lengthwise and well washed
- 1 celery stalk, trimmed and cut into 3 large pieces
- 8 quarts cold water, or as needed, plus 1 cup warm water
- 1 28-ounce can whole tomatoes, with their juice
- 3 flat-leaf parsley sprigs
- 2 thyme sprigs
- 4 large garlic cloves, smashed with the side of a chef's knife and peeled
- ¼ teaspoon whole black peppercorns
- ½ teaspoon kosher salt

Position a rack in the center of the oven and preheat the oven to 400°F.

Put the bones in a roasting pan and roast, shaking the pan occasionally to turn the bones and ensure even cooking, until nicely browned all over, about 1 hour.

Pour out and discard most of the fat from the pan, leaving just enough to coat it. Add the carrots, onions, leeks, and celery, return the pan to the oven, and roast until the vegetables begin to caramelize, about 15 minutes.

Use tongs or a slotted spoon to transfer the bones and vegetables to a large heavy pot, preferably a stockpot. Pour in the cold water and bring to a boil over medium-high heat. Lower the heat so the liquid is simmering and simmer, using a kitchen spoon or tablespoon to skim any scum that rises to the surface (it should stop rising after about 1 hour).

Meanwhile, add the 1 cup warm water to the roasting pan and stir with a wooden spoon to loosen any flavorful bits cooked onto the bottom of the pan. Add the liquid to the simmering stock, along with the tomatoes, parsley, thyme, garlic, peppercorns, and salt. Partially cover the pot and simmer for a total of 4 hours. During that time, check periodically to ensure that the solids are covered by at least 2 inches of liquid; if they are not, add more water.

After 4 hours, use tongs to remove and discard the bones, then strain the stock through a fine-mesh strainer into a bowl, pressing down on the solids with a wooden spoon or a ladle to extract as much flavorful liquid as possible. Return the stock to the pot, bring to a simmer over medium-high heat, and boil until reduced to 2 quarts, about 20 minutes. Remove from the heat and let the stock cool, then transfer to an airtight container and refrigerate overnight.

The next day, use a tablespoon to skim off and discard the fat that has solidified on the top of the stock. Refrigerate the stock in the airtight container for up to 3 days, or freeze, in small batches, for up to 2 months.

# ACKNOWLEDGMENTS

I would like to offer my heartfelt appreciation to the following people for their invaluable contribution to this project:

Andrew Friedman, my collaborator: Thanks for all the hard work, and for capturing my voice and ideas so well on the page. Little did I know when I met you at Table 26 at Marea and said, "Hey, let's do a book," that you would become such a good friend and confidant. In addition to the great meals we've shared together, I'll always fondly remember all the take-out sushi eaten across my desk over the last two years.

Evan Sung, our brilliant photographer, for envisioning and realizing two distinct yet complementary looks, one Classico and one Moderno, for your generosity of spirit, and for being a wonderful traveling companion.

Thomas Keller, for your humbling and flattering foreword, and for your late-night visits to Marea; it's always an honor to serve you.

Pamela Cannon, our brilliant editor, who has been enthusiastic and passionate about this project from the first time we met and who patiently nurtured it every step of the way. Your good humor, even during the crunch times, saved our sanity, and we couldn't have asked for a more insightful guardian angel. Andrew and I are proud to call you our friend.

Judith Sutton, our sage and eagle-eyed copy editor, for all the catches and smart suggestions.

David Black, our literary agent, for your role in shaping this project from its inception, and for your advice and belief in the book along the way.

Olivia Young, Altamarea Group's head of media and public relations, for helping to get the word out, and for contributing mightily behind the scenes, from wrangling and marshaling corporate resources to organizing photo shoots to providing a wide range of day-to-day support—we could not have done it without you!

To the entire Random House/Ballantine Books team, especially designer Liz Cosgrove, who created such a smart and handsome look for the book; production editor Penelope Haynes, for her superhuman patience, Mark Maguire for his amazing eye for detail, Paolo Pepe for his patience and insight with the cover; and the public relations and marketing teams, headed up by Susan Corcoran, Alison Masciovecchio, and Quinne Rogers.

The team of testers at Altamarea Group: Marianne Bondad, Pedro Cruz, Lauren Desteno, Tim Lu, Heather Pelletier, and a special thanks to Anthony Jackson who tested most of the Classico recipes and helped organize the entire testing team.

My team of talented chefs, many of whom helped out by generating recipe drafts and tasting and guiding the work of the testers: Amador Acosta, PJ Calapa, Bill Dorrler, Gordon Finn, Jared Gadbaw, Ben Lee, Asi Maman, and Altamarea Group's corporate pastry chef, Bob Truitt.

Prop stylist Kaitlyn DuRoss and assistants Greg

Morris and Erik Freeland for their invaluable work on the photo shoots, and Ai Fiori's Jeanna Bellizzi, for hosting us while we worked.

Rebekah Peppler, for her help editing the recipes.

For their help during our visit to Italy, thanks to:

Valentino Marcattilii, executive chef of San Domenico, for letting us make the restaurant our home base and for his help sourcing and preparing food for the photo shoots; Gianluigi Morini, founder of San Domenico, and Massimilano Mascia, San Domenico's chef di cucina, for their generous hospitality; Gianluca Landi, for the use of his spectacular home; Rocco Iannone of Pappacarbone Cava di Terieni, for allowing us to photograph on his incredible property; Mario Vicidomani and his family, for the look behind the scenes at their pasta factory, a memorable lunch, and for hosting us in Southern Italy; Maria Camaggi and her granddaughter Federica Bettini, for showing us their fresh pasta techniques in Imola; Pasquale Torrente, of Al Convento ristorante in Cetara, for the impromptu photo shoot; Italo and Giuseppe Pedroni, for the crash course in all things balsamico; the gang at Trattoria Fita, for a memorable evening; the Bonati family, for showing us their Parmigianio facility; and the team at IASA, for the tour of their cannery in Cetara.

I must also thank Ahmass Fakahany, my partner in the Altamarea Group: We started down the path of our professional "second acts" together with a shared passion for good food and hospitality. It's been a great adventure realizing our dreams together, and I'm looking forward to making many more come true.

And, finally, to the entire Altamarea team, the greatest group of collaborators a chef could ask for, and, of course, to our customers, who make it all possible—thank you all!

# SOURCES

**Amazon**
www.amazon.com
00 flour, apricot puree, cotechino, fregola sarda, hijiki seaweed, roasted almond butter, salt cod, specialty chocolates, truffle paste

**Anson Mills**
www.ansonmills.com; 803-467-4122
polenta

**Buon Italia**
www.buonitalia.com; 212-633-9090
pasta, cured and dried meats, olive oil, truffles, truffle butter, bottarga, and other Italian products

**Catalina Offshore Products**
www.catalinaop.com
sea urchin roe

**D'Artagnan**
www.dartagnan; 800-327-8246
foie gras, pork and veal sausage, rabbit legs, truffles

**Di Bruno Bros.**
www.dibruno.com; 888-322-4337
cucumber vinegar

**Heritage Foods**
www.heritagefoodsusa.com; 718-389-0985
caul fat

**Kalustyan's**
www.kalustyans.com; 800-352-3451
Espelette pepper, fennel pollen, piquillo peppers, canned snails, verjus

**King Arthur Flour**
www.kingarthurflour.com; 800-827-6836
flours, including bread flour and Italian-style flour; black cocoa powder

**La Quercia**
www.laquercia.com; 515-981-1625
lardo, pancetta, speck

**Modernist Pantry**
www.modernistpantry.com; 469-443-6634
lecithin (sold here as soy lecithin), Ultra-Tex 3

**Murray's Cheese**
www.murrayscheese.com; 888-692-4339
a wide range of Italian cheeses

**Petrossian**
www.petrossian.com; 800-828-9241
caviar

**Valrhona**
www.valrhona-chocolate.com; 888-682-5746
specialty chocolates

**Zingerman's**
www.zingermans.com; 888-636-8162
colatura, lemon oil

# INDEX

# A

# B

# C

# D



# E

# F

# G



# H

# I



# J



# K



# L

# M

# O



# P

# Q



# R

# S

# T

# V

# W

# Z

## ABOUT THE AUTHORS

A Wisconsin native, MICHAEL WHITE began his award-winning culinary career at Chicago's renowned Spiaggia and Ristorante San Domenico in Imola, Italy. After eight years in Italy, he returned to New York City and partnered with Ahmass Fakahany to form the Altamarea Group, which currently owns seven restaurants, including Marea (which holds two Michelin stars and won the 2009 James Beard Award for Best New Restaurant and membership in Relais & Châteaux) in New York City and Al Molo in Hong Kong. Additional locations include the Michelin one-starred Ai Fiori, Osteria Morini in SoHo and Washington, D.C., Due Mari and Osteria Morini in New Jersey, and Nicoletta Pizzeria. The group will be opening three additional New York City locations in 2013. Michael White lives in New York City with his wife and daughter.

ANDREW FRIEDMAN has collaborated on more than twenty cookbooks and other projects with some of America's finest and most well-known chefs, including Alfred Portale, Michelle Bernstein, Laurent Tourondel, and former White House chef Walter Scheib, and he co-authored (with American tennis player James Blake) the *New York Times* bestselling memoir *Breaking Back*. Friedman is a two-time winner of the IACP Award for Best Chef or Restaurant Cookbook and co-editor of the popular anthology *Don't Try This at Home*, which features stories from chefs such as Mario Batali, Daniel Boulud, and Marcus Samuelsson. In 2009, he published his first nonfiction book, *Knives at Dawn*, about the Bocuse d'Or culinary competition. He is also the founder and chief contributor to the chef-focused website Toqueland.com. He lives in Brooklyn, New York, with his family.

## ABOUT THE TYPE

The text of this book was set in Filosofia, a typeface designed in 1996 by Zuzana Licko, who created it for digital typesetting as an interpretation of the eighteenth-century typeface Bodoni, designed by Giambattista Bodoni (1740–1813). Filosofia, an example of Licko's unusual font designs, has classical proportions with a strong vertical feeling, softened by rounded droplike serifs. She has designed many typefaces and is the cofounder of *Emigre* magazine, where many of them first appeared. Born in Bratislava, Czechoslovakia, in 1961, Licko came to the United States in 1968. She studied graphic communications at the University of California, Berkeley, graduating in 1984.